THE
LEGACY
OF
HISTORY
IN
RUSSIA
AND THE
NEW STATES
OF EURASIA

THE INTERNATIONAL POLITICS OF EURASIA

Editors:
Karen Dawisha and Bruce Parrot

This ambitious ten-volume series develops a comprehensive analysis of the evolving world role of the post-Soviet successor states. Each volume considers a different factor influencing the relationship between internal politics and international relations in Russia and in the western and southern tiers of newly independent states. The contributors were chosen not only for their recognized expertise but also to ensure a stimulating diversity of perspectives and a dynamic mix of approaches.

Volume 1
The Legacy of History in Russia and the New States of Eurasia
Edited by S. Frederick Starr

Volume 2
National Identity and Ethnicity in Russia and the New States of Eurasia
Edited by Roman Szporluk

Volume 3
The Politics of Religion in Russia and the New States of Eurasia
Edited by Michael Bourdeaux

THE INTERNATIONAL POLITICS OF EURASIA

Volume 1

THE
LEGACY
OF
HISTORY
IN
RUSSIA
AND THE
NEW STATES
OF EURASIA

Editor:
S. Frederick Starr

M.E. Sharpe

Armonk, New York
London, England

Library of Congress Cataloging-in-Publication Data

The Legacy of History in Russia and the new states
of Eurasia / S. Frederick Starr, editor
p.   cm.—(International politics of Eurasia: v. 1)
Includes bibliographical references and index.
ISBN 1-56324-352-0 (c)   ISBN 1-56324-353-9 (p)
1. Former Soviet republics—foreign relations.
2. Former Soviet republics—Ethnic relations.
3. Nationalism—Former Soviet republics.
4. Former Soviet republics—Politics and government.
I. Starr, S. Frederick. II. Series.
DK293.L44   1994
947.08—dc20   94-17293
CIP

Printed in the United States of America

The paper used in this publication meets the minimum requirements of
American National Standard for Information Sciences—
Permanence of Paper for Printed Library Materials,
ANSI Z 39.48-1984.

BM (c)   10   9   8   7   6   5   4   3   2   1
BM (p)   10   9   8   7   6   5   4   3   2   1

Contents

About the Editors and Contributors

S. Frederick Starr is a historian and jazz musician. Educated at Yale, Cambridge University, and Princeton, he was the founding secretary of the Kennan Institute for Advanced Russian Studies at The Wilson Center in Washington and served for eleven years as president of Oberlin College in Ohio. In addition to his writings on Soviet and Russian affairs, he has taken an active role in Russian-American relations and served in various advisory capacities to the United States government. Most recently, he is the author of a major biography of the American composer Louis Moreau Gottschalk.

Karen Dawisha has been a professor in the Department of Government and Politics at the University of Maryland at College Park since 1985. She received her Ph.D. from the London School of Economics in 1975. Her publications include *Russia and the New States of Eurasia: The Politics of Upheaval* (coauthored with Bruce Parrott, 1994), *Eastern Europe, Gorbachev, and Reform: The Great Challenge* (2nd ed. 1990), *The Kremlin and the Prague Spring* (1984), and *Soviet Policy Toward Egypt* (1979).

Bruce Parrott is Professor and Director of Russian Area and East European Studies at the Johns Hopkins University School of Advanced International Studies where he has taught for twenty years. He received his B.A. in religious studies from Pomona College in 1966, and his Ph.D. in Political Science in 1976 from Columbia University where he was assistant director of the Russian Insititute. His publications include *Russia and the New States of Eurasia: The Politics of Upheaval* (coauthored with Karen Dawisha, 1994), *The Dynamics of Soviet Defense Policy* (1990), *The Soviet Union and Ballistic Missile Defense* (1987), *Trade Technology and Soviet-American Relations* (1985), and *Politics and Technology in the Soviet Union* (1983).

Kadir Z. Alimov is director of the Legal and Political Problems Program at the University of World Economy and Diplomacy in Tashkent and president of the Association of Political Science of Uzbekistan. He is the author of a number of books and articles, including "The Disintegration of the USSR and the New World" (1993), *Nationality Issues in the USSR in the Context of Gorbachev's Reforms* (1990), *American Foreign Policy in Iran* (1989), and *Political Reforms in the Central Asian Republics* (1989).

Yaroslav Bilinsky is professor of Political Science and International Relations at the University of Delaware. He was born in Ukraine and was educated in Poland, Germany, and the United States. He is the author of *The Second Soviet Republic: The Ukraine After World War II* and numerous articles, and is now writing *Ukraine: From Nationality to Nation*.

Richard G. Hovannisian is professor of Armenian, Caucasian, and Near Eastern History, holder of the Endowed Chair in Modern Armenian History, and associate director of the G.E. von Grunebaum Center for Near Eastern Studies at the University of California, Los Angeles. A John Simon Guggenheim Fellow, he is the author of a multivolume history of the first Republic of Armenia (1918–1920) and has published extensively on the modern history of Armenia and the Caucasus.

Firuz Kazemzadeh is professor emeritus at Yale University, where he has taught since 1955. He is the author of numerous books and articles, including "Iranian Relations with Russia and the Soviet Union to 1921" (1992), "Afghanistan: The Imperial Dream" (1980), "Soviet-Iranian Relations: A Quarter Century of Freeze and Thaw" (1974), *Russia and Britain in Persia, 1864–1914: A Study in Imperialism* (1968), and *The Struggle for Transcaucasia, 1917–1921* (1952).

Edward L. Keenan is Andrew W. Mellon Professor of Humanities at Harvard University. He is currently the president of the American Association for the Advancement of Slavic Studies. He is the author of *The Kurbskii-Groznyi Apocrypha: The Seventeenth-Century Genesis of the "Correspondence" Attributed to Prince Andrew Kurbskii and Tsar Ivan IV* (1971) and "Muscovite Perceptions of Other East Slavs Before 1654" (1992), among other works.

Zenon E. Kohut is acting director of the Canadian Institute of Ukrainian Studies at the University of Alberta. He taught at the University of Pennsylvania and Michigan State University and was a Soviet analyst at the Library of Congress. He is the author of *Russian Centralism and Ukrainian Autonomy: Imperial Absorption of the Hetmanate 1760s–1830s.*

Romuald J. Misiunas is senior associate with Trumbull Associates, Ltd., in New York and associate scholar at the Harriman Institute at Columbia University. He is co-author of *The Baltic States: Years of Dependence: 1940–1990* (2nd edition, 1993) and has published extensively on the Baltic region. In 1991–92 he served as a consultant to the government of Lithuania.

Serhii M. Plokhy is a research associate of the Institute of Ukrainian Archeography (Kiev) and the Canadian Institute of Ukrainian Studies at the University of Alberta. He was chair of the General History Department at the University of Dnipropetrovs′k and is the author of *Papacy and Ukraine: Vatican Policy in Ukrainian Lands (Sixteenth–Seventeenth Centuries)* (in Russian).

Alfred J. Rieber is professor of history at the University of Pennsylvania. Among his published works are *Merchants and Entrepreneurs in Imperial Russia* (1982) and *The Politics of Autocracy: Letters of Alexander II to Prince A.I. Bariatinskii, 1857–1864* (1966).

Sergei A. Romanenko is a research fellow at the Institute of Slavonic and Balkan Studies of the Russian Academy of Sciences, Moscow. He is the author of numerous articles, including "Nationalism and Empire: The Habsburg Monarchy and the Soviet Union" (1992), "National Autonomy in Russia and Austria-Hungary: A Comparative Analysis of Finland and Croatia-Slavonia" (1992), and "Yugoslav Politicians and Neoslavism" (1989).

Tadeusz Swietochowski is professor of Middle Eastern and Soviet Nationalities History at Monmouth College, New Jersey. He is the author of *Russian Azerbaijan 1905–1920: The Shaping of National Identity in a Muslim Country* and *Russia and Divided Azerbaijan: Foreign Conquest and Divergent Historical Development* (forthcoming).

Preface

This book is the first in a projected series of ten volumes produced by the Russian Littoral Project, sponsored jointly by the University of Maryland at College Park and the Paul H. Nitze School of Advanced International Studies of the Johns Hopkins University. As directors of the project, we share the conviction that the transformation of the former Soviet republics into independent states demands systematic analysis of the determinants of domestic and foreign policies of the new countries. The series of volumes is intended to provide a basis for comprehensive scholarly study of these issues.

This volume analyzes the legacy of history and its impact on the foreign relations and political identity of the new states. The nearly seventy-five years of Soviet rule, while a long time, did not erase the historical memories of the Russians or of the Soviet empire's other peoples. As the newly independent nations search for their place in the world, they are guided in part by their memories, some clearer than others, of a past without Soviet or Russian domination. The volume examines the new states' perceptions of history and how they have manipulated the images of the past in formulating contemporary policy. It also examines past relations among the post-Soviet nations and other peoples. Where do the sympathies of the new states rest, and to what extent are old "alliances" and "hatreds" being revived?

We would like to thank the contributors to this volume for their help in making the first phase of the Russian Littoral Project a success and for revising their papers in a timely fashion. We are especially grateful to S. Frederick Starr for agreeing to be the editor of this first volume "sight unseen," and for his enthusiastic support of the project and the series of volumes from the very beginning.

Russian Littoral Project

The objective of the Russian Littoral Project is to foster an exchange of research and information in fields of study pertaining to the international politics of Eurasia. The interaction between the internal affairs and foreign policies of the new states is studied in a series of workshops taking place in Washington, D.C.; London; Central Asia; and other locations between 1993 and 1995. Scholars are invited from the new states, North America, and Europe to present papers at the workshops.

Focusing on the interaction between the internal affairs and the foreign relations of the new states, the project workshops examine the impact of the following factors: history, ethnicity and national identity, religion, political culture and civil society, economics, foreign policy priorities and decision-making, military issues, and the nuclear question. Each of these topics is examined in a set of three workshops, first with respect to Russia, then with respect to the western belt of new states extending from Estonia to Ukraine, and finally with respect to the southern tier of new states extending from Georgia to Kyrgyzstan.

The Russian Littoral Project could not have been launched without the generous and timely contributions of the project's Coordinating Committee. We wish to thank the committee members for providing invaluable advice and expertise concerning the organization and intellectual substance of the project. The members of the Coordinating Committee are: Dr. Adeed Dawisha (George Mason University); Dr. Bartek Kaminski (University of Maryland and The World Bank); Dr. Catherine Kelleher (The Brookings Institution); Ms. Judith Kipper (The Brookings Institution); Dr. Nancy Lubin (Carnegie Mellon University); Dr. Michael Mandelbaum (The School of Advanced International Studies); Dr. James Millar (The George Washington University); Dr. Peter Murrell (University of Maryland); Dr. Martha Brill Olcott (Colgate University); Dr. Ilya Prizel (The School of Advanced International Studies); Dr. George Quester (University of Maryland); Dr. Alvin Z. Rubinstein (University of Pennsylvania); Dr. Blair Ruble (The Kennan Institute); Dr. S. Frederick Starr (Oberlin College); Dr. Roman Szporluk (Harvard University); and Dr. Vladimir Tismaneanu (University of Maryland).

We are grateful to the John D. and Catherine T. MacArthur Foundation for funding the workshops from which this book is derived; we are especially grateful to Kennette Benedict for her firm support of the whole project from its inception. For funding the workshops on which several future volumes will be based, we express our thanks to the MacArthur Foundation, the Friedrich Ebert Stiftung (in particular, Dieter Dettke), the Pew Charitable Trusts (particularly Kevin Quigley and Peter Benda), and the National Endowment for the Humanities.

We also wish to thank President William Kirwan of the University of Maryland at College Park and President William C. Richardson of The Johns Hopkins University, who have given indispensable support to the project. Thanks are also due to Dean Irwin Goldstein, Associate Dean Stewart Edelstein, Director of the Office of International Affairs Marcus Franda, and Department of Government and Politics Chair Jonathan Wilkenfeld at the University of Maryland at College Park; to Provost Joseph Cooper and Vice-Provost for Academic Planning and Budget Stephen M. McClain at The Johns Hopkins University; to Professor George Packard, who helped launch the project during his final year as dean of the School of Advanced International Studies, and to SAIS Associate Dean Stephen Szabo.

Finally, we are grateful for the guidance and encouragement given by Patricia Kolb at M. E. Sharpe, Inc. Her confidence in the success of the project and the volumes is deeply appreciated.

Karen Dawisha
University of Maryland
at College Park

Bruce Parrott
The Johns Hopkins University
School of Advanced International Studies

THE
LEGACY
OF
HISTORY
IN
RUSSIA
AND THE
NEW STATES
OF EURASIA

1

Introduction

The Legacy of History in Russia and the New States of Eurasia

S. Frederick Starr

On the eve of Latvia's independence from the Soviet Union, its succession-minded government decided to fly the country's interwar flag from Riga Castle. In a telling gesture, the leaders enlisted as flag-raiser an old man of nearly one hundred years who had been a popular actor and public figure during the brief flowering of Latvian independence between World War I and World War II. Soon after this, leaders of the Soviet Republic of Georgia resolved to make the same symbolic gesture. The situation there was far more complex, however. It had been nearly three-quarters of a century since Georgia had last enjoyed independence, and that period had been very brief. Worse, Georgians inherited several different flags from their past, and each carried a different meaning for the present. Nonetheless, the Georgian government found a few living links with the days of Georgia's brief independence and enlisted these people for the task of raising the old colors.

Theatrics aside, why should anyone expect that history should influence the policies of the post-Soviet states to any significant degree, and why should such influence extend in particular to foreign policy? Clearly, the immediate demands of the present moment overwhelm all other influences acting on these new countries. Besides, only the three Baltic states and Russia enjoyed anything near a sustained independent political existence within the past century and three-quarters. Leaving aside the sham "foreign ministries" that Stalin established in various republics, none of the other new states can claim in their modern history to have possessed even the most basic institutions necessary for formulating and executing foreign policy. As former colonies and dependencies, their ties with other peoples were suppressed in favor of links with Moscow, which dominated their attention. Under such circumstances, the immediately usable past is surely limited, especially in the area of foreign policy.

Viewed in broader perspective, however, history assumes greater importance in the foreign policy of the new states. Whatever their aspirations for the future, the leaders of these countries have been formed by their personal, communal, and national pasts, and are applying on the job whatever truths they have derived from that historical experience. History, then, is the dowry borne by leaders and citizens of these new states as they leave the Soviet family and set up housekeeping on their own. In this broader sense, history, as perceived by present actors, can be a powerful determinant of action.

Yet history is not a unitary thing. Bernard Lewis, the noted specialist on Turkish history, distinguishes between history that is remembered, history that has been recovered, and history that is invented. In the newly independent states history is important in each of these three senses.

Nowhere does the living memory of the past more directly influence the present than in Latvia, Lithuania, and Estonia. In these countries a simple and near-universal conclusion being drawn from historical experience is that they should look not to Russia but to the West. A recent exhibition of technologically sophisticated Latvian export products from the 1930s has inspired a new generation of Latvians to raise the standards of their manufactured goods and to look westward for markets. The current president of Estonia, Lennart Meri, a film maker, once filmed interviews with Estonians who had been exiled to Siberia when the Soviet Union took control of their country in 1939. Invoking living memory, he presents these members of Estonia's old intelligentsia as models of Western culture and victims of Russian rule.

Remembered history prompts other peoples who are still part of Russia to rebel against Russian rule. Thus, communal memory among the Chechen people of the North Caucasus recalls their forty-year war against tsarist Russia in the nineteenth century and their deportation to Central Asia by the Soviets. They remain unassimilated in the new Russia and have in fact declared their independence from it. Tatarstan, meanwhile, although it has been ruled by Russia since the sixteenth century, maintains a living memory of the golden age in its past and on that basis claims the right to conduct its own foreign policy as a confederated sovereignty within Russia. In sharp contrast, Armenia's living memory depicts that country's relationship with Russia in a very positive light. Every Armenian knows that the only region of their ancient land to retain its political identity in the twentieth century was the part that remained under Russian control. Yet if this would appear to provide a clear orientation for the new Armenia, Armenians also remember with gratitude that their many conationals living in Iran have for the most part been left in peace by the various governments in Tehran. As Richard G. Hovannisian points out, this leaves Armenians today more open to the idea of an Iranian role in resolving their troubles with neighboring Azerbaijan than either Russia or the West would prefer.

Issues that the rest of the world has forgotten remain part of living memory throughout the region. The memory of Georgia's failed blitzkrieg war against Abkhazia in 1920 may have died elsewhere, but it lives on within Abkhazia itself, as does the memory of the Russian-brokered treaty between Abkhazia and the Georgian Republic that was in force briefly between 1925 and 1931. In this case, direct memory has inspired and justified a bloody and successful war of independence on the part of the small Abkhazian population along the Black Sea littoral. Georgians, too, recall the earlier events but, needless to say, draw diametrically different conclusions from them.

Living memory also provokes current leaders to action in Russia. Average Russians may have little knowledge of the impact that Soviet rule had on the non-Russian peoples, but they know full well the toll it took on their own families and country and are able now to talk about it. Recalling their own sufferings and also the sacrifices they made in order to develop the other republics, they arrive at a surprising conclusion, namely, that Russia was less the perpetrator of Communist oppression, as people in virtually every one of the non-Russian republics believe, than its chief victim. Such thinking leads many Russians to justify and defend the various forms of pressure their government is imposing on its neighbors.

Modern history presents few, if any, instances of so much historical experience being recovered from oblivion as in the post-Soviet states today. As Zenon E. Kohut shows, the suppressed history of Ukrainian

cultural and political identity is being recovered through the republica-
tion of works by the early twentieth-century Ukrainian historian
Mykhailo Hrushevs'kyi. These works present a picture of a vital and
culturally developed country interacting fully with countries abroad
over many centuries. Historians in Belarus are also busy exhuming the
lost or suppressed history of their people and, especially, its links with
the West. In the five new countries of Central Asia, the rediscovery of
the many international links once maintained by their peoples is even
more important, for, as Firuz Kazemzadeh argues, this crucial region
has been isolated from the larger world since the early sixteenth century. As Uzbeks and Tajiks rediscover their national glories, they reaf-
firm the cosmopolitanism of their culture and seek to reclaim it. To be
sure, their first steps abroad as independent states have been tentative,
and they remain heavily beholden to Russia, thanks to the fact that
their old-guard rulers were educated in the Soviet mode and still look
to Moscow. But the reorientation toward the East, West, and South is
bound to develop when younger leaders eventually come to power.

The recovery of suppressed history can take contradictory forms.
Thus, the world is aware that Russia itself seceded from the Communist empire, but it has paid less attention to the fact that as Russians
today rediscover their tsarist past, they come face-to-face with an older
and deeper national tradition of imperial rule over their neighbors.
Thus, just as Ukrainians or Uzbeks are rummaging through their history to reclaim anti-imperial traditions that can help free them from
Russian tutelage, Russians are rediscovering the imperial tradition of
the tsarist countries that subjugated these peoples in the first place. For
Russians to reject this heritage entirely would be to jettison one of the
few psychological rafts that Russians can cling to after the sinking of
the Soviet ship of state.

By no means all of the history now being rediscovered fits comfort-
ably with ideas of liberal democracy. Kadir Z. Alimov argues that
Uzbekistan's political culture has traditionally been authoritarian and
that liberals abroad (including those in Moscow and Washington)
should not seek to impose their views when they so squarely contradict
the historical essence of the Uzbek people. One might ask whether a
French observer writing in 1750 might not have drawn similar conclusions about his own country, and thereby ruled out the development of
democratic institutions in France that began only a few decades later.
Russians use similar historical arguments to deny the validity of Ukrai-

nian independence and to defend their country's claims to a kind of Monroe Doctrine extending across the region. The point at issue in all these cases is not the history itself but the manner in which its supposed truths are applied to the present. In nearly every instance, invocations of the past in Russia are used to buttress the case against change in the future, while in the newly independent states history serves as an agent of change.

By no means all relevant history is being recovered in the midst of this wave of rediscovery. Russian intellectual history, for example, contains a powerful subcurrent of anti-imperialist thinking, epitomized by Alexander Herzen in the nineteenth century, just as it also includes a strong tradition of federalist and constitutional thinking in the realm of domestic affairs. Assimilative currents in Ukrainian culture are similarly being ignored, as is the powerful Pan-Islamic strain in the early history of the Uzbeks and Tajiks. Both of the latter, presumably, will be exhumed when and if pro-Islamic leaders come to power in Uzbekistan and Tajikistan.

Historical consciousness is less the product of dispassionate analysis of the past than of acts of national passion and will. Far from being defined or constrained by facts, historical consciousness is a creative process that can handily ignore or dismiss historical reality when it is at odds with the purposes at hand. Down to the time Yeltsin closed the parliament in September 1993, there were many in that body who favored the Serbian cause in Bosnia, in opposition to Yeltsin's policy. They based their case on what they wrongly believed was a tradition of pro-Serbian activism in Russia. Sergei A. Romanenko's careful historical research demonstrates how sympathy for Serbia was not widespread among members of the educated Russian public in the early twentieth century, even though the tsarist state had directly championed Serbian independence and official spokesmen sought to rally Russian sympathies for their fellow Slavs and Orthodox Christians in the Balkans. Interestingly, the myth of Russian support for Serbia in the nineteenth century proved incapable of arousing today's public to the same cause.

In his chapter, Alfred J. Rieber argues that tsarist Russia was not impelled by a drive for limitless expansion, as many have claimed, and that during their final century of rule the tsars and their ministers failed to build any coherent and sustained imperial policy at all. Granted that this thesis is highly controversial, it is nonetheless based on a serious reading of Russian history and therefore requires a response in the same vein. Under the current climate of thought in most of the fourteen non-Russian states, however, it is unlikely that such a sober response will be forthcoming. For as each country seeks to assert its new sovereignty, it responds less to historical facts than to a visceral psychological urge to debunk the one-sided historical mythologies of the Soviet state that were used to repress their sovereignty for so many decades. Thanks to this understandable but irrational urge, mythology is often met with mythology.

In his interesting chapter, Serhii M. Plokhy demonstrates how the history of the Cossacks in southern Russia and the Black Sea region has been recast by publicists and historians in present-day Ukraine in order to undergird that country's independence. At first blush such an effort would seem preposterous, given the extent to which Cossack units in the tsarist army came to epitomize and symbolize the imperial Russian state as a whole. But Plokhy details the intriguing process by which myth has been replaced with countermyth. He identifies the particular importance played in recent years by writers in the far western reaches of Ukraine—the one region in which Cossacks played no historical role at all. Elaborated and preserved in western Ukraine and Galicia, the Cossack myth spread quickly to the rest of the country during the period immediately preceding and following independence. The notion of a Cossack Ukraine has achieved the ultimate prize of historical mythmaking by having been enshrined in the new Ukrainian national anthem.

Zenon E. Kohut treats the same theme but from the perspective of Russians' efforts over many centuries to assert the unity of their state. He presents a broad-brush overview of the so-called state school of Russian historiography founded by Nikolai Karamzin and Sergei Solov'ev in the nineteenth century. Reviving a critique first elaborated by nineteenth-century Russian regionalist historians (*oblastniki*), Kohut argues that the state school's conception of Russian history owed more to the aspirations of the centralizing Tsar Nicholas I than to any study of the historical evidence. In a conclusion that should unsettle Western students of Russia, he goes on to argue that the state school's conception of Russian unity was uncritically absorbed by European and American scholars and is reflected in their writings down to the present, to the detriment of a more accurate understanding of the roots of Ukrainian independence.

An even more devastating attack on the conceptions underlying the state school of Russian historiography comes not from one of the newly independent states but from an American scholar, Edward L. Keenan. The political context of Keenan's argument is worth noting. During 1992–93 many nationalists in Moscow put forward the thesis that Russia could not be whole without controlling Ukraine. Academician Dmitrii Likhachev had long maintained this, but the argument gained an entirely new valence after Ukraine became independent. Now it was taken up by the Afghan war hero Aleksandr Rutskoi, who made it the capstone of his attack on Ukrainian sovereignty. Rutskoi, an ethnic Russian who was raised on a Red Army base in Ukraine, convinced himself that the very national identity of Russia arose first on the territory of present-day Ukraine and that a new Russia that did not include Ukraine would be a mere banana republic.

The core of the argument offered by Likhachev and other apostles of a unitary Russia is that the genealogy of the Russian state traces directly to Kievan Rus' of the tenth through thirteenth centuries. Because they considered themselves the legitimate heirs to this Kievan heritage, the early tsars of Muscovy believed they had the full right to assert their hegemony over the entire East Slavic region and to see themselves as the inheritors of the Byzantine heritage that Kiev had received directly from Constantinople.

In a stunning stroke of revisionism, Keenan argues that this entire conception of history was alien to the early tsars of Muscovy and was in fact concocted by Kremlin ideologues only in the seventeenth century, after Moscow had conquered Kiev and most of Ukraine. The historical debate will not be resolved quickly, if at all, but Keenan's thesis demonstrates how deeply historical mythology can penetrate even scholarly discourse, and how profoundly important is the task of reexamining the cornerstone of historical consciousness today.

The central foreign policy issue for all of the newly independent states is their relationship with Russia. Conversely, the most urgent foreign policy issue for Russia is its relations with its former colonial dependencies. These relationships, moreover, have more potential to alter strategic balances throughout Eurasia than has any other single issue, and contain the seeds of potential instability and conflict. Historical examples are instructive. In 1863 Poland rebelled against Russian control. When Tsar Alexander II attempted to reassert Russian rule over Poland through force of arms, he destroyed the reform movement within Russia and ushered in a generation of strife in his realm.

Can Russia accept the sovereignty of its neighbors? As of the time of this writing, the Yeltsin government has tried to assert a kind of Russian Monroe Doctrine in the region. Moreover, it has moved rapidly to strengthen the Commonwealth of Independent States by integrating currencies and monetary policy, reestablishing common security arrangements, and using energy pricing and other means to force into the fold nonparticipating countries, notably Georgia and Ukraine.

Rieber denies that there was a popular base for tsarist imperialism but affirms nonetheless that Russia's imperial identity arose before it became a modern state. As if reflecting this historical reality, *Moscow News* reports that 24 percent of Russians believe their country cannot be whole without Ukraine, while only 20 percent hold that Russia has no need to acquire additional territory. Rieber also notes that Peter the Great actively cultivated the "Russian party" in neighboring states and among steppe nomads in order to expand Russia's hegemony in the region. One must ask to what extent these remote historical antecedents are still pertinent today.

The chapters in this volume suggest that the pre-Soviet experience, for all its importance, pales in significance by comparison with the experience of the Soviet era. Indeed, all parties concerned seem to act on the assumption that it is above all the history of the Soviet period that influences today's policies, both positively and negatively. Some scholars have pointed out the continuity from the Soviet era that exists in the foreign policy establishment in Moscow. By contrast, the Baltic states, as described by Romuald J. Misiunas, present a picture of such stark contrast with the immediate past as to suggest the possibility that current policies there are the mirror image of Soviet policies, and hence still defined by them. Either way, the relevant past is quite recent.

The fate of republican borders established by Stalin attests to this truth. Kadir Alimov rightly notes that Stalin's government drew borders within Central Asia in such a way as to divide peoples who share common ethnic, linguistic, and historical identities. Nonetheless, Firuz Kazemzadeh stresses that these Soviet-era borders, for all their initial artificiality, have now gained a reality of their own, and true nation building has begun to take place within them. This, along with the continuing cultural impact of Russia, assures that the Soviet legacy in Central Asia might endure for centuries longer.

Yaroslav Bilinsky advances an even more striking point regarding Ukraine. Every schoolchild in that country is now aware of the gruesome man-made famine of 1931–33 that claimed millions of Ukrainian lives as Stalin stood by passively. Yet it was also Stalin who consolidated the territory of Ukraine as we know it today, thanks to the acquisitions he made at the end of World War II. And it was Stalin, too, who oversaw the exchange of populations with Poland that successfully transformed the heavily Polish city of Lwów into the Ukrainian city of L'viv. As we have seen, it was precisely in these newly acquired districts of western Ukraine that a new Ukrainian consciousness arose in the 1980s and spread eastward.

Stalin attempted a similar process of consolidation when he briefly seized a region of northern Iran inhabited by Azeris and attempted to unite it with Soviet Azerbaijan. In the end he was thwarted in this by the Allies, but an echo of his old policy can be found among those many Azeri leaders today who still champion the dream of Pan-Azeri unity, as Tadeusz Swietochowski points out.

Moldova owes its very existence to Stalin, who, having extracted the region from Romania as a result of the Hitler-Stalin pact, constituted it as a republic of the USSR. Following its recent independence, Moldova was faced with the choice of developing itself as a separate state or reuniting with Romania. Had the claims of deep history prevailed, Moldova would have followed the latter course. Under President Mircea Snegur, however, it has chosen instead to pursue an independent course within roughly the borders established by Stalin, and to postpone reunion with Romania to some indefinite future.

During the Soviet era it was popular in the West to dismiss as fraudulent Stalin's penchant for assigning the symbols and trappings of statehood to what were in fact administrative districts fully subordinate to Moscow. The fact that the United Nations recognized a country called Belorussia, which boasted a minuscule foreign ministry and maintained an ambassador in New York, epitomized this cynical process. Yet in the long run such seemingly hollow symbols were to gain content, first psychological and then political. Again, the history that counts is that of the Soviet era rather than the more antique past.

Eventually, historians in the new Belarus were to reexamine the entire history of their country, going so far as to claim that the great medieval Kingdom of Lithuania was in fact the forebear of Belarus. More plausibly, they also argued that it was thanks to Belarus that printing and hence Western culture generally was first introduced into Muscovy. These historical claims, which so clearly remove Belarus from Moscow's orbit and link it with Central Europe, again trace to debates of the Soviet era, rather than to earlier times.

By no means all Soviet nation building was merely symbolic. It is true that modern Uzbekistan includes many non-Uzbeks, and that the Soviet government drew the border of Uzbekistan in such a way as to leave millions of Uzbeks in Kazakhstan, Kyrgyzstan, and Tajikistan. Nonetheless, the Stalinist leaders of Uzbekistan enjoyed special favors under the Soviet system, which in fact confirmed the Uzbeks' leading role among the Turkic peoples of Central Asia. Thanks to this fact, Communist rule had the paradoxical effect of positioning the Uzbeks for the ambitious regional role they now aspire to play as an independent state.

These various examples all suggest that the history most likely to exert influence on present foreign policies is that which is fairly recent. In the non-Russian states it is defined overwhelmingly by their specific experience with Russian dominion during the Soviet period. Their deeper history is relevant, of course, but its direct influence pales by comparison with the pervasive drive to rectify distortions in their relation to Russia that were introduced during the Soviet period.

The international behavior of the post-Soviet states can best be understood within the broader context of new countries emerging from imperial systems. Yet this does not mean that more remote historical experience is irrelevant. On the contrary, it exerts a deep and pervasive influence, although as a very generalized force rather than as the memory of specific moments of past heroism that must be recaptured or ancient humiliations that cry for redress. In this broader sense, the earlier history that counts most is that which involves the relation of each newly independent state with cultures and peoples beyond its borders.

Centralized empires reorient national communications, cultural contacts, and trade of their subject peoples in the direction of the metropolis. This weakens preexistent foreign ties built up over hundreds and even thousands of years. A striking feature of the tsarist empire is the way it expanded into political vacuums created by the collapse of states on its periphery. Many of these had attained higher cultural levels than Muscovy and were important elements in cultural networks that focused in directions other than toward Moscow. The same can be said of expansion that occurred during the Soviet era. Now, as Moscow's control wanes, these old relationships are reasserting themselves. As this happens, an earlier cultural geography is reemerging, much the way ancient field boundaries and roads reappear when a dam that has long flooded a valley suddenly breaks. This reemerging cultural map of the Russian littoral will help define the new political geography of the region, and hence the foreign policies of the new states. Many examples of this process are already discernible. Typical is the manner in which the three Baltic states have reoriented themselves toward Northern Europe and Scandinavia. Estonian ties with Finland, Latvian links with Sweden, and Lithuanian affinities with Poland have quickly reasserted themselves. At issue in each of these reorientations are geographical proximity, ethnic or linguistic ties, shared religious confessions, commercial links, and even family connections. With the exceptions of Moldova (with Romania) and Tajikistan (with Afghanistan and Iran), no post-Soviet state is linked to a neighboring region by all these ties. However, the Baltic countries possess several of them, which help reorient their foreign policy northward and westward.

The reassertion of old transborder affinities takes many forms. In Moldova, for example, it was symbolized by the readoption of the Latin alphabet, a particularly important move given Romanians' self-image as descendants of the ancient Roman colonists of Dacia. The choice of alphabets in the newly independent states has an obvious foreign policy dimension. Thus, Azerbaijan has had to choose among three alphabets: the Cyrillic, imposed from Moscow; the Arabic-Iranian, as used by the large Azeri population of northern Iran; and the Latin alphabet, which for most of the twentieth century has symbolized Turkey's reorientation toward the West.

As these old affinities with neighboring peoples surface, they become the subject of spirited debates within each new country. The outcome of these debates will influence significantly the foreign policy of each state. Central Asia is a laboratory for this process. There was no more prominent feature of Soviet rule in Central Asia than the persistent effort to suppress Pan-Turkic and Pan-Islamic consciousness in the region. No sooner was Soviet control broken than both emerged as highly charged issues in the new states. Uzbekistan is still led by leaders from the Soviet era. Inevitably, these men approached Islamic internationalism with great caution, yet in 1992 they found it convenient to stress their Turkic identity when Turkish investors seemed to be looking favorably toward their country.

Ukraine offers instructive examples of how old cultural affinities can be reworked to fit the needs of the new order. In the first years after independence, the long-suppressed Uniate Church showed remarkable vitality as it achieved legal status and regained control over many of its old places of worship. More recently, however, it has shown signs of having reached its outer limit of expansion. One might infer that the new Ukraine, while oriented toward the West, is unlikely to become fully *of* the West. Nor, however, will it maintain its former ties with Russia, as is suggested by the fact that the Russian Orthodox Church in Ukraine has already split into a large Ukrainian Orthodox Church ruled from Kiev and a smaller remnant of the old Moscow-ruled structure, focused mainly in the eastern part of the country. Together, these incidents from Ukraine's religious life reflect the continuing influence of deeper historical and cultural forces that are bound to shape and inform international relations as well.

The ambiguous and mutually contradictory nature of both historical and cultural forces in Ukraine have parallels in the other newly independent states. Latvia's history may be westward looking, yet the ice-free port of Riga was always a major entrepôt for Russian produce, and numerous Latvians filled prominent positions in the Soviet system. Kyrgyzstan may take as its model the nonaligned state of Switzerland, yet that dream is itself the fruit of the long years the Kyrgyz president, Askar Akaev, spent in the worldly corridors of the Academy of Sciences of the USSR in Moscow. Kyrgyzstan, Turkmenistan, Azerbaijan, and Moldova may all cite their history to justify an independent position in the geopolitical firmament, yet it is due to Russian rule that they were elevated to the status of republics in the first place.

The ambiguous and self-contradictory character of historical experience is nowhere clearer than in Russia itself. Debates in the 1840s among a few young people calling themselves either Slavophiles or Westernizers have provided a convenient framework for analyzing broader trends within Russia's historical legacy. This old polarity also found expression within the institutional structures of foreign policy, beginning in the nineteenth century and extending down to the present; rivalries in the Ministry of Foreign Affairs between those oriented toward the Middle East and those oriented toward Europe existed in both the 1890s and the 1990s. In neither era, however, did history dictate the choice between these two forces. It can paint in the background against which current policy choices will be made, but it provides no clear and unequivocal policy advice. History, in short, is better at defining choices than making them.

Even this may overstate the importance of history for the foreign policies of the newly independent states. On a day-to-day basis, it is surely overshadowed by urgent issues of the moment. Pressing economic issues, like the need for economic reform, stable currencies, and access to international credit markets, provide more immediate stimuli to foreign and domestic policies than does the legacy of the past. Particularly notable is the way energy policy is capable of shaping foreign policies. Nor is this surprising, since the very sovereignty of new states can be jeopardized by failure to gain access to reliable sources of oil and gas.

Beyond this, global development, communications, and organizations are transforming the broader environment in which the foreign policies of the newly independent states are set. A strong cultural heritage may help a new state to get abreast of these changes and find a meaningful niche for itself on the global stage. However, unresolved international and domestic tensions inherited from the past are just as likely to derail a new state's effort to cope with these forces of modernity. It is significant that Armenia and Azerbaijan both possess assets crucial to success in the modern world. Yet for the entire period since independence both have been willing to permit their energies to be dissipated by an ancient conflict, which, if it continues, could destroy the possibility of either state taking its place among nations.

Yet history is not a nemesis. It shapes some questions that nations ask, but not all; still less does it determine the answers. In the end, the irrelevance of history to the foreign policies of the newly independent states can be summarized with the old truism that "one cannot step into the same river twice." The passage of time transforms everything, and even ancient proclivities surviving in the present have been altered, thanks to constant social and cultural change. However much the Russian Republic may wish to wrap itself in the trappings of the past, it is fundamentally new, as are the fourteen former Russian dependencies that are also now independent. Some will be fortunate to have leaders who are wise enough to use history as a means of broadening or deepening their people's understanding of the present world and their potential place within it. These countries will thrive. Others, not so fortunate, will turn for leadership to those for whom history is a source of unresolved conflict and neurosis. Any foreign policies deriving from the latter motives are bound to be a misfortune both for their own people and for their neighbors.

I

Russia

18

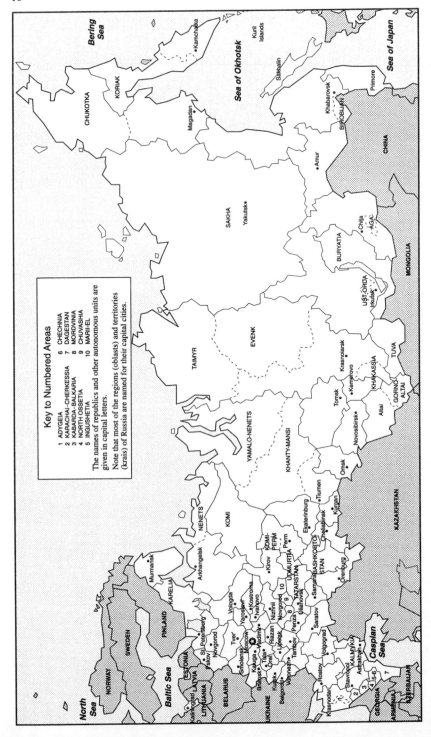

Key to Numbered Areas

1 ADYGEIA	6 CHECHNIA
2 KARACHAI-CHERKESSIA	7 DAGESTAN
3 KABARDA-BALKARIA	8 MORDVINIA
4 NORTH OSSETIA	9 CHUVASHIA
5 INGUSHETIA	10 MARII-EL

The names of republics and other autonomous units are given in capital letters.

Note that most of the regions (oblasts) and territories (krais) of Russia are named for their capital cities.

2

On Certain Mythical Beliefs and Russian Behaviors

Edward L. Keenan

The reexamination of a characteristic cluster of Russian national myths, most of which have become international scholarly myths, is no idle pursuit. Our findings as to how Russians and others have come to believe these myths are directly relevant to how we can expect Russians to behave as international actors now that they are no longer members of an imperial ruling nation, nor restrained by the doctrinal internationalism of Marxism-Leninism.

Particularly closely linked with Russians' perceptions of their national myths are their attitudes concerning relations with the United States and the West more generally, and with the new borderlands, where postcommunist internationalism will face severe tests.

Even a medievalist cannot remain unaware that the present political situation is so fluid that there is no predicting how Russians might behave in the near term, even were they to unanimously embrace my revision of their history. There is no telling, at this stage, which of the various available histories of their international behavior will be the one they prefer to refer to in making and justifying crucial decisions in the near term.

What I intend to do, having declared these warnings, is to discuss a series of commonly held views about the history of Russian official ideology (which I shall enumerate in a moment), to indicate the extent to which they represent any historical reality, and then, since they do not, to provide some speculation as to how they could have arisen and persisted.

I should point out, finally, that the myths I shall be most concerned with are not fantastic on their face, like the legend of Romulus and Remus, but narratives that have become what we might call standard received views. They took the forms we know and love, for the most part, in the nineteenth century or only slightly earlier, and they were not essentially modified by the historiography of the communist era (1917–91), despite some shifting of emphasis (for which, I might add, decent historians paid heavy prices). They became widespread in the West, and in particular in the United States, through the paradoxically combined influence of the older generation of émigré scholars, who were mostly cosmopolitan moderate liberals, and Soviet historiography, which was predominantly restrained, nationalist, and conservative. Now that the restraints have fallen away, national radical accents are to be heard as well.

Oddly enough, despite the lamentable degree to which some aspects of the historiography of Russia have become politicized in this country, left and right, alleged "Russophobes" and "Russophiles" happily agree about most of these myths, although some of them may accept them out of consideration for the feelings of Russians, while others repeat them to justify denigration of Russian behaviors. In any case, almost no one, to my knowledge, has taken the trouble to reexamine them at base.[1]

Thus what I have to say is part of a dialogue with Americans who accept the traditional view, and with Russians who are rediscovering it or restating it.

Let me, finally, turn to the partial list of national myths that I propose to revise. It runs roughly like this:

• The Muscovite state, the core and template for the later Russian and Soviet empires, arose around Moscow in the fourteenth century as the chief and direct heir to the political and national legacy of the Kievan state.
• It was an awareness of this Kievan inheritance, and the motive of reconstituting the erstwhile Kievan unity, that prompted the first Muscovite expansions, into neighboring Russian principalities, commonly known as the "gathering of the Russian lands."
• The princes of Moscow emerged as leaders of the whole Russian nation (which for most Russians is tacitly understood to include Ukrainians and Belarusians unless otherwise specified) in large measure as a

consequence of their leadership role in the national struggle against Tatar overlordship, conventionally called the "Tatar yoke" (a phrase that, perhaps because of some subliminal conflation with the "yellow peril," causes some orthographical confusion among American undergraduates).

• In this and later struggles, the princes of Muscovy drew political benefit from the close collaboration of the leadership of the national Orthodox Church, which was unfailingly the bearer and custodian of Byzantine cultural traditions, both ecclesiastical and political.

• In particular, it was the Church that propounded the theory of Russia as the Third Rome, according to which, Rome and Constantinople having fallen, Moscow had inherited the world-historical responsibilities of the Christian empire.

• It was a combination of anti-Tatar crusade and a sense of Christian manifest destiny that informed the first major Muscovite conquests of non-Russian territory, the taking of Kazan and Astrakhan in the middle of the sixteenth century.

• Later, the conquest of Belarus and the annexation of Ukraine were an expression of the yearning to reconstitute the lost Kievan unity, but this expansion was informed as well by religious concerns for the fate of Orthodox populations in those territories.

It will be clear to those familiar with the relevant scholarly literature that I have done scant justice to the views of those who have so characterized the evolution of Russia's self-image and ideology, but this summary of the received views must serve for the moment—especially in view of the fact that I shall now propose that none of these axioms can withstand modern analytical scrutiny and confrontation with the sources.

We can begin with the question of Moscow's putative self-conception as successor to the role of ancient Kiev. Did the Muscovites who surrounded Ivan III (1462–1505), the true founder of the Muscovite state, his son Vasilii III, and his grandson Ivan IV, as they transformed their rustic principality into a lumbering empire, believe that they were restoring or imitating the glory of Kiev? I think the answer is clearly that they did not—or if they did, they kept their views to themselves.

Indeed, it is astonishing that modern scholars should have believed that Muscovites of the ruling warrior caste in the time of Ivan III and Ivan the Terrible, for example, conceived of themselves as successors to the mantle of the Kiev of, say, Yaroslav the Wise. There is simply no evidence that they did.[2]

I may know better than most how careful one must be with arguments from silence in the Muscovite case: our evidence is often exiguous and unrepresentative, but it must suffice. There are numerous indirect indications, however, that Muscovite political elites in Ivan III's time—and much later—were only dimly aware of the history of the Kievan period, and even less interested in claiming it as their inheritance. Here I can mention only two of these indications, chosen because their implications seem so obvious and because they have never, to my knowledge, been pointed out in this connection.

Roughly a decade after the accession of Ivan III, and a generation after his father's victory in the civil war that had nearly destroyed Russia, the Grand Prince's handlers, like those who had surrounded Charlemagne around 800, realized that a major new power had taken shape around the court and army of their sovereign. And like the Carolingians, they set about the creation of an appropriately imperial style. They called in architects, a mintmaster, and what we might call style consultants from Renaissance Italy. These craftsmen transformed the provincial town of Moscow into a proud ducal residence: they built a fortified enclosure such as Russia had never seen, the first major palace, three monumental churches, and a "signature" campanile to give approaching travelers the first visual impression of the new crown city. Even today, it is these structures (heavily modified) that form the core of the Kremlin as tourists see it, and there can be little doubt that they were intended as a carefully considered statement of the self-conception of the emergent dynasty. Together they comprised the most important architectural statement that had ever been made in Muscovy.

In all of this—in sacred and secular buildings, in the naming and dedication of the churches, in the inscriptions and the chronicle account of the construction—there is not so much as a hint or allusion to the Kievan legacy. The churches, notwithstanding telltale Italian Renaissance details, are modeled on those of Russian Upper Volga towns, like Vladimir and Suzdal', not on those of Kiev. There is no Tithe Church, no Church of SS. Boris and Gleb, not even a St. Sofiia (as there were in Novgorod and Polotsk)—despite the fact that Ivan's second wife, who clearly had much to do with this redecorating project, was herself named Sofiia (Zoe). And not only are the gates in the Kremlin wall not named for the famous Kievan gates (especially the Golden Gate), but the main one had a Latin, rather than a Cyrillic, inscription![3] Fifty years later, in the obviously emblematic national church of the mid-sixteenth century, the so-called Vasilii Blazhennyi (actually the main altar in that complex of chapels is dedicated to the Intercession of the Virgin), one notes the equally astonishing and total absence of any reference to Kievan symbolism or nomenclature. And here, as university fundraisers might put it, there were many naming opportunities, but the various chapels are named for North Russian saints or for the days of important battles in the Kazan campaign of 1552.[4]

Even one hundred years later, when Boris Godunov rebuilt parts of the Kremlin and enlarged the bell tower as part of a major plan to renew the capital, one is struck by the absence of reminiscences of Kiev. These people were not even thinking of Kiev.

Another striking and unnoticed manifestation of this discontinuity or historical amnesia is to be found in the naming practices of Muscovite courtiers. There is no need to point out the importance attached to this act in all cultures, its symbolic significance, cultural determinedness, and responsiveness to vogues. For the time of Ivan the Terrible, the historical record has preserved the names of thousands of upper-class Muscovite males; they behave, in terms of frequencies, like names in other societies. The ten most popular cover 70 percent of individuals, the rest are scattered. The most popular are Muscovite dynastic names like Ivan, which accounts for 20 percent, and Vasilii, which accounts for another 10 percent. Thus far no surprises.

But what is astonishing, against the background of received wisdom about this culture, is the almost total absence of specifically Kievan names. Among just under three thousand names in Ivan's court rolls there is no Igor', no Sviatoslav, no Mstyslav, fewer than 1 percent of Vladimirs, three Glebs. A Muscovite courtier of Ivan's time was more likely to be called Temir or Bulgak than Vladimir or Gleb or Vsevolod.[5]

Note that I am speaking here of mature Muscovite culture, and not of the earlier historical "facts," of which Muscovites with rare exceptions were unaware. On the facts, one might say that the Muscovite state, like roughly a dozen other political formations from Moldova to Lithuania, inherited a number of important cultural innovations from the Kievan state: a belief in the charisma of descendants of the Kievan dynasty of warrior princes; the East Slavic version of Orthodoxy; a common legal or chancery language. But the inheritance was indirect and attenuated: in Kievan times, there were precious few Slavs in what became the Muscovite space; the settlers who migrated there, primarily from Novgorodian and Belarusian areas, did not form a distinctive demographic concentration until perhaps 1350, long after the eclipse of Kiev. It is true, of course, that Ivan III was a direct descendant of St. Vladimir in the male line—but so were many of his enemies and hundreds of princes in Muscovy, in other Russian principalities, in the Grand Duchy of Lithuania, and in Poland. And my point is that Ivan made little—almost nothing—of his Kievan ancestry.

One could go on at much greater length about the evidence that Muscovites barely remembered the Kievan experience; the point for our present purposes is that it is highly unlikely that Ivan III or his handlers were motivated by any deeply felt irredentism when they began to expand into Belarusian or Ukrainian—or, for that matter, Novgorodian—territory in the late fifteenth century.[6]

In diplomatic correspondence with the Polish-Lithuanian state, to be sure—this is the *locus classicus*—Ivan III's diplomats spoke of border territories as his patrimony, or *votchina*. But the reference is vaguely to his ancestors, and to the grand princes of Muscovy in the first instance, not to the Kievan period. The same language was used as well to justify claims to Baltic and Finno-Ugric territories that were never a part of the Kievan inheritance. What it meant, really, was "these lands once were claimed by an unspecified ancestor of mine and I now claim them."[7]

Some might object, for example, that it was in the time of Ivan that the historic crown of the Muscovite tsars, the so-called Cap of Monomakh, is first mentioned, and that this is a reference to the Kievan Vladimir Monomakh. Alas, this commonly held view is doubly erroneous: the crown itself was made for a Tatar khan, probably Uzbek, in the 1330s; when it was renamed (or rebaptized) and altered through the addition of a cross in the late fifteenth century, it was given a new passport in the form of a garbled legend connecting it with Constantine Monomachus of Byzantium, but this is clearly primarily a Greek, not a Kievan reference, chosen by the Greco-Italian consultants who came from Italy with Ivan's second wife, Sofiia, in 1472.[8] But more on Byzantinism in a moment.

To sum up these few remarks on the "Kievan heritage" myth: Muscovy clearly expanded into old Kievan territory in the time of Ivan

III and Vasilii III, but I for one see no reason to believe that they were driven by, or for that matter were even aware of, any theoretical or ideological program that admonished them to reunite East Slavs under the banner of a restored Kievan heritage. The reason the persistence of such a view does not astonish me is that I believe modern scholars have been misled by seventeenth-century evidence, in which much is made of the Kievan past. But the seventeenth-century texts appeared during or shortly after Muscovy's expansion into Kievan territory and, moreover, were produced largely by émigré Ukrainian or Belarusian Orthodox scholars or their imitators. I shall return to this important influence shortly.

For the moment, I should like to return to our list of national myths and say a few words about the "Tatar yoke" myth. However little Muscovite politicians were moved by nostalgia for Golden Kiev, it is even less likely, in view of the excellent documentary evidence we have of relations between Muscovy and its Tatar allies and adversaries, that they construed their expansion into the steppe as the realization of a centuries-old national and religious struggle against Muslim Tatar overlordship. In fact, as I have often pointed out elsewhere, the close reading of the diplomatic correspondence—and even the occasionally jingoistic Muscovite court chronicles—provides astonishing evidence of how pragmatic and close were the relations between Muscovite and Tatar politicians.

It seems hard to imagine how they could have been otherwise, for it was a close and durable alliance between Muscovite and Tatar political organizations (those of Ivan's father, Vasilii II, and Khan Ulu Magmet) that in large measure determined the final Muscovite victory in the fifteenth-century civil war against Vasilii's Russian Orthodox cousins.

In the next generation, the most successful khan of the Crimea, Mengli-Girei, was Ivan III's closest foreign ally, with whom he maintained the firm and mutually profitable alliance that made possible, *inter alia*, the conquest of Novgorod and Pskov; Ivan IV's conquests of Kazan and Astrakhan could not have been undertaken without the close collaboration of his perennial Tatar allies, the Nogais. With both of these Muslim Tatar entities Muscovites exchanged innumerable peaceful embassies and untold amounts of goods and symbolic gifts, including, for example, horses that had made, or were intended to make, the hajj to Mecca—and, probably, the Cap of Uzbek, a.k.a. Monomakh. Muscovite politicians, however they may have constructed their private devotional lives, were refreshingly relaxed about dealing with Muslim allies—they sold Christian slaves to them, intermarried with their ruling houses, and unhesitatingly recruited their court mullahs as spies. Thus the "Tatar yoke" myth.[9]

It will not, by this time, come as a surprise that the so-called Third Rome Theory is little more than a scholarly misunderstanding. The notion of *translatio imperii*, or the transfer of the imperial heritage from Rome to Byzantium or Carolingian France or other sites, is of course potentially available to any European Christian dynasty after the fall of Rome. (Our own founding fathers, indeed, availed themselves of one—the republican—version: the Empire was the First Rome, the Republic the Second, Washington, the Second Republic, the Third. . . .) Several echoes of this body of lore reached Russia by different channels over the centuries. But most specifically the scholarly and later popular idea of Muscovy as the Third Rome seems to derive from a single phrase in an otherwise unexceptional epistle, still poorly understood, allegedly sent by the monk Filofei to either Ivan III, Vasilii III, or Ivan IV. Since so much here has been made of so little it is worth our while to pause over this matter for a moment.

Although it is not entirely clear when the letter was written, it is most likely that it was written to Vasilii III in connection with the annexation of Pskov in 1510. The thrust of the letter, which deals primarily with religious matters, is that the Muscovite grand prince should not confiscate the property of the Church in the Pskov lands, as had been done a generation earlier in the enormous territories of Pskov's sister city, Novgorod. Were the grand prince to do such a thing, Filofei writes, he would hardly be a Christian monarch. And since two Romes have fallen, Moscow, the last remaining truly Christian—i.e., Orthodox—kingdom, remains, and if its tsar is not Christian there is to be no fourth Rome.

That is, Filofei's words, which had a narrowly religious context in any case, were a warning and not a call to greatness. They had nothing to do with foreign policy or Muscovite manifest destiny.[10]

There will be those who find my reading of Filofei's letter somewhat idiosyncratic. But even if some other interpretation is more convincing, the problem with the larger matter of the later tradition is that there is simply no evidence that Muscovite policy or politicians were in any way influenced either by this text or in general by the scribblings of bookish churchmen until the threshold of modern times—

roughly the end of the seventeenth century—at which time new, Western notions began most seriously to influence Russian thinking about matters of state and nation.

But before we deal with how Russians came to have the views they have in modern times, we must dispense with two variants of a final misconception: that of the deep and abiding influence of Byzantine religious and political thought on Muscovy.

I must say that the more I study this particular problem, the more convinced I become that it is one of the great mystifications of all of European cultural history. The fact of the matter is that, aside from the obvious and fundamentally important fact of the conversion of the Kievan East Slavs by Byzantine South Slavs, and the later episodic evangelical, political, and pastoral activities of itinerant Greeks and South Slavs in Muscovite territory, there is remarkably little evidence of any vital and continuing Byzantine-Muscovite cultural tradition. As Francis Thompson has demonstrated with crushing thoroughness,[11] almost nothing was translated from Greek in East Slavic territory in Kievan times; he is in the process of showing analogous results for Muscovy. And as Kapterev and others knew long ago, real Russo-Greek relations were characterized by long-standing mutual suspicion and hostility.[12]

It is difficult to identify a single native Muscovite who knew any significant amount of Greek before the second half of the seventeenth century.[13] It is probable that more students in the very provincial Harvard College of that era than in the contemporary Muscovy could construct a passage of the Greek New Testament. And two centuries earlier Muscovites, like their forgotten Kievan predecessors, knew almost no Greek, had almost no Greek texts, and translated almost nothing from Greek into Slavonic. In that crucial defining era of the building of the Kremlin and the establishment of the royal style in Moscow, any one of a dozen centers in the Catholic West could boast of more Greek learning, scholars, manuscripts, and general awareness of the Byzantine tradition than could be found in the whole of Russian territory. It was, indeed, from one of those Italian cities that came the famous Maximos, brought to Moscow in 1518 to revise the old translations of the Psalter and a few years later cast into the monastic prison where he spent the rest of his life. (One should, by the way, point out that Maximos, whose activities in Muscovy remain remarkably obscure, was not nearly as accomplished a Greek New Testament scholar as, for example, his Western contemporary Erasmus.)

There is more to be said about the specifically Greek aspect of the "Muscovite Byzantinism" myth, but the need for brevity constrains us to turn, finally, to the closely linked "Orthodox Muscovy" myth. Here we encounter a complex matter of some delicacy.

The delicacy arises on grounds of plain civility. It is graceless to express skepticism about another person's religious beliefs. And it is futile *and* offensive for a nonbeliever to challenge another's belief in, say, the Trinity. But no one need refrain, on such grounds, from expressing an opinion as to whether, for example, Erasmus was right to claim that the crucial Greek New Testament proof-text (the *comma Johanneum*) was an interpolation.

Similarly, when a Russian declares himself to be a believer it is not for the outsider to test his knowledge of the Creed—but if that same Russian declares that to be Russian is to be an Orthodox believer, while opinion surveys find that more Russians believe in horoscopes than in the Trinity, the outsider may draw his own conclusions without offense.

This rule of intellectual good manners applies to earlier times as well, where it is complicated by the sparseness of our information. We simply do not know what the majority of Muscovites thought about such matters, primarily because the vast majority—including most of the political elite and even the rank-and-file clergy—were very modestly lettered until the seventeenth century, and as a consequence left us no credible record of what they thought.

We do have evidence, however, that supports the view that the picture of the Muscovite political system as closely allied to the Orthodox hierarchy in a national alliance, or motivated by overpowering religious conviction, is an artifact of a later time. The Muscovite political system of Ivan III and his successors was forged in a generation of civil war among Orthodox princes who repeatedly violated sworn oaths taken on the cross, often in collusion with perfidious bishops. Once established, the Muscovite court spent the first century or so of its existence defeating the courts of nearby Slavic and Orthodox princes, frequently with the aid of Muslim allies. In a word, the behavior—shall we call it pragmatic?—of the Muscovite political system comports well with that of other European states before, say, the Reformation.

There are two respects in which Muscovy was starkly different, however, and both speak against the notion of a strong alliance of church and state in "Orthodox Muscovy." First, the Church as an institution was, in Muscovy, incomparably poorer, weaker, and less well organized than its Western equivalent or the secular power. Grand princes had their way with the Church, almost without exception, long before Peter finally made the Church a branch of government. Second, there was strikingly less interpenetration of secular and religious elites in Muscovy than in the Western societies with which it is usually compared. There appear to be structural reasons for this isolation in the logic of the Muscovite clan system, the heredity patterns of the married parish clergy, and the monastic monopoly on episcopal power. However the difference is to be explained, it is clear that secular and religious elites never formed the establishment phalanx one finds elsewhere in Christendom.

For these and a host of other reasons, I find it odd that scholars should think that confessional politics played an important role in the thinking of Muscovite practical politicians during the formative centuries of the empire, and that the "Orthodox Muscovy" myth could have such durability.

But if the Muscovite Empire expanded without being motivated by any real recollection of the so-called Kievan legacy, and not as a Christian crusader against the Tatars, and not because of any operative beliefs derived from the nonexistent Third Rome Theory, and was in general ignorant of Byzantine caesaropapism and history generally, and was quite unmoved by the teachings of a Church that it systematically dominated, two questions arise: (1) What, then, *were* the motivating forces? and (2) Where do all these wrong ideas come from?

The knottier and more important conundrum is the first, because it appears to arise from a paradox: if none of the notions that have traditionally been perceived as driving the Muscovite imperial expansion was in fact a major part of the worldview of Muscovites themselves, then why did they expand so dramatically and dynamically?

Having recently reviewed most stages of that expansion in some detail, I think that we may say, simplifying somewhat, that Moscow expanded for three main reasons: because Muscovites were a demographically dynamic ethnic mass surrounded by very sparsely populated areas; because the Muscovite court had made itself a highly efficient, centralized, and monolithic militarized political organization; and because neighboring political-military organizations, over the period of Moscow's greatest expansion, were for various reasons weakened by

internal division, resource depletion, or third-party threat. Of course
these reasons interact: the essentially peaceful expansion into Siberia
provides resources for the military machine that marches into
Smolensk or Kiev; the internal divisions in Lithuania or the Caucasus
are influenced by Muscovite initiatives; the highly centralized political
system is particularly adept at mustering resources and absorbing local
elites, and so forth.

By contrast, where or when these conditions were insufficiently represented, expansion tended to stop: Russian colonists do not displace other
relatively dense populations in Ukraine, Belarus, or even the Middle
Volga; in periods when the central political system loses its monolithic
cohesion the expansion ceases or, as in 1605, the empire dissolves; when
neighbors are in a position to mount military counterforce, as was Sweden
or China or the Ottoman Empire, expansion stops.

I would argue, consequently, that this was a state that expanded
mightily, but was not necessarily "expansionist." That is, Muscovite
and later Russian political actors were not motivated by a transcendent
belief that they must expand or fail, that they were fated to expand, that
they could ignore mundane pragmatic considerations and the risks and
costs of expansion because they were unlike other mortals or their
expansion was unlike other practical matters. Muscovites typically be-
haved as pragmatic opportunists; they were characteristically risk-
averse and quite willing to give up any objective when resisted or
when the goal became too costly. These were not Crusaders. (I leave to
another day the question of whether Crusaders were Crusaders.)

If such, however, was the case—if the Russian Empire was in fact
the product of a long concatenation of cautious, opportunistic, and ad
hoc adaptations to favoring circumstances—whence the famous ver-
biage about the Kievan inheritance, the Third Rome, Muscovite Byzantinism, and the like?

I am afraid I would have to argue that these un-Russian notions and
nonoperative abstractions came from the same sources as almost all
other modern intellectual and ideational currents, including the bulk of
what is today Russian Orthodox thought and practice, Marxism, and
Reaganite-Thatcherite-Pinochetian free-marketism—from the post-Re-
naissance West.

These ideas penetrated into Russian thought in diverse ways and
from many sources, far too numerous and complex even for enumera-
tion here. But the notions we are most concerned with have some

unexpected features in common: they originate in major European intellectual movements and preoccupations, and their importation typically served the interests of someone other than Russians. We can begin our story with the same Ivan III whom I mentioned above as the founder of the Muscovite state. Now it is true, as all remember, that his second wife, Zoe/Sofiia, was the niece of the last Byzantine emperor. It is also true that the wedding was arranged in the Vatican by the famous Greco-Italian Platonist Cardinal Bessarion (d. 1472), and was part of a Greco-Papal design to recruit the Muscovites and their Tatar allies in a major anti-Ottoman military alliance. In the end, characteristically, Ivan joined no such enterprise; his pragmatic Tatar policy and his Oriental trade were far more important to him than any Western alliances. Nonetheless his new wife, and many of the large number of Greco-Italians who came with her, became very important in the shaping of the practices of the Muscovite court in almost every domain: Italian architects built that new Kremlin fortress in the style of Milan; that faceted royal palace almost identical to the one in Ferrara; those three cathedrals in imitation of Russian styles but with lots of Italian Renaissance details and orange tile roofs.[14] But—and here is the point—these profoundly deracinated Uniate Greeks, as they Italianized Russian court life, did apparently intimate to their Muscovite clients that it was the traditions of the Paleologues and of Byzantine greatness that they represented. But, like the rest of the new Muscovite imperial style, this was a very Western, essentially Italian, form of Byzantinism—indeed, Sofiia's patron, the Uniate Cardinal Bessarion, spent his life convincing Italians that the mantle of Byzantium (the *translatio imperii* again) had passed to—Rome![15]

Another theme that comes from the West—probably from Bessarion—at roughly this time is the anti-Muslim bias that begins to be found in Muscovite literary and chronicle texts. Although Bessarion seems not to have sent Ivan III a copy of his "Orations and Letters to Christian Princes against the Turks,"[16] the Greeks never lost hope that they could turn the Russians—and others—against the Ottomans. These efforts, for the most part, seem to have taken the form of constant reminders to the pragmatic Russians of the defining importance of their Byzantine and Orthodox heritage.

After the Counter-Reformation had turned the Polish-Lithuanian Commonwealth, for the first time, into a Catholic kingdom, émigré Ukrainian and Belarusian Orthodox clerics added their voices to those of the Greeks in urging Muscovy to stand up for Orthodoxy. It was these eloquent and politically experienced visitors, joined later by representatives of the Cossack elite recruited into the imperial establishment, who firmly established—in their own interests—the "Kievan heritage" myth for Muscovites, in the late seventeenth and eighteenth centuries.[17]

It is true, of course, that copies of the Primary Chronicle had long been known to some clerical bookmen in Muscovy. But these were not widely read by Muscovite laypeople, and even many of those chroniclers who read them did not, apparently, make the connection between Kievan history, which they considered a kind of classical antiquity, and Muscovite history. Laypeople did, by contrast, increasingly read *Sinopsis* and Prokopovich, largely because these were available in print. (The former, in particular, went through numerous editions and printings between 1674 and 1836.)

It was, apparently, the 1680 edition that Tatishchev used for his great work of integration, in which the notion of Muscovy's reception of the Kievan inheritance is fully developed. But even Tatishchev's sense of continuity was not specifically East Slavic: he began with Gog and Magog; Kiev plays a limited role in his construction, much of which he got not from Russian, but from Western sources.[18]

Nikolai Karamzin had doubts that Tatishchev got some of his notions from any sources at all, but he seems not to have questioned his predecessor's assumption that all history after Vladimir was Russian history. Karamzin, whose still remarkable *Istoriia gosudarstva rossiiskogo* set conceptual foundation stones that have remained unmoved and largely unexamined for nearly two centuries, advanced the notion of a unitary "*Rossiia*," populated by "*rossiiane*" from the ninth century onward, embracing all East Slavs, and almost all European parts of the Russian Empire (as of ca. 1801). Justly remembered as a master of Russian prose style, Karamzin chose his words carefully: "*Rossiia*" and its derivatives, he must have known, were imported into Russian from scholarly Polish, itself influenced by Greco-Latin conventions; they established themselves as standard nomenclature only in the seventeenth century. But although Karamzin, like Tatishchev, simply subsumed Kievan and all East Slavic history under "*Rossiia-n*," he said very little about it: in his famous programmatic *Memoir on Ancient and Modern Russia* there is no mention of either Kiev or Ukraine (which he would have called "*Malorossiia*").[19]

Most of the rest of the story is well known: when the European currents of romanticism and early nationalism come to Russia and take the domesticated forms of Slavophilism and Pan-Slavism, their adherents turn for their "text" to what they take to be the historical record but what in fact is a variegated body of texts produced or inspired by outsiders for their own purposes and quite alien to the modes of thought of practicing politicians of the Muscovite past, which is mistakenly perceived as the last age of national authenticity. We are only now beginning to realize what a mess these dilettantes made of things—but we may be too late.[20]

There is, of course, much more that could be said on all of these topics; I am reminded that Lavrenti Beria once lectured for two whole days, in a language not his own, on the exiguous subject of the history of the prerevolutionary Bolshevik Party in the Transcaucasus—a performance that, taking both quality and quantity into account, may stand forever as the nadir of historical popularization. (It is true that the expectations of his audience may have been lowered by other preoccupations.) What I should like to do next is to indicate how, as it seems to me, what I have declared thus far relates to present-day concerns about Russian popular attitudes in the foreign policy arena.

The discussion has three aspects: to what extent are any of these myths believed by the politically active segments of Russian society today; how might such beliefs affect the formulation and conduct of policy; and in which specific areas will such beliefs have the greatest significance?

It is clear from the reading of current publications, both mainstream and marginal, that the great bulk of mythic lore that I have tried to discredit above has, in one or another form, become almost universally embraced by those Russians who choose to consider historical forms of argument at all. Such an outcome appears to be the result of five main factors:

1. the inexorable standardization and degradation of historical thinking in a speech community whose mass media were for several generations centrally controlled and manipulated for political purposes;
2. the well-known expedient zigzags of propaganda and policy, from attacks on Great-Russian chauvinism to appeals to Russian patriotism, from Marxist internationalism to anticosmopolitism, etc.;

3. the resulting tendency of the public to assign preferential credence to suppressed or contrarian views—in the present instance, typically to semiofficial nineteenth-century or émigré nationalist positions;

4. the underlying tensions created by the implicit association of Russian national myths with the forbidden topic of intercommunal relations;

5. the isolation of nearly all Russians, in differing degrees, from Western social-science dialogue concerning such matters as national myths and imagined pasts.

Should current trends toward open discussion and international dialogue continue, one may hope that the effects of the first two factors will be diminished significantly, and those of the last to a lesser extent. But the hardship and national malaise that are to be expected in the near term, together with the near-collapse of academic institutions and the resurgence of nostalgic nationalism, will probably serve to counteract such amelioration of the general situation; most Russians will be more likely than they have been in recent decades officially to embrace the traditional myths we have been discussing and to consider them justifications for political positions and actions.

As to the extent to which these widely held mythical beliefs will affect the formulation and conduct of Russian foreign policy—including relations with the "near abroad"—the prospect seems to me dependent on the near-term evolution of political structures. For the moment, the old policy elites, whose pragmatism and greater access to alternative sources of information tend to make them skeptical about national myths or relegate them to an inferior status in their belief system, have both retained sufficient group cohesion and distributed themselves among the main factions in such a way that it seems unlikely—but not impossible—that they will formulate or carry out policies based on national-mythic convictions.

It also appears to be the case that many of the most outspoken purveyors of traditional views, of whom Aleksandr Solzhenitsyn might be taken as an example (but only as an example, as his claims to speak for all Russians are questionable), are so preoccupied with the internal spiritual and material travails of the Russian nation that, aside from a general antagonism toward post-Enlightenment Western materialism and Cartesianism, they are unlikely to come forth with a coherent program for the conduct of Russia's affairs in the modern community of nations. In addition, Solzhenitsyn and others have expressed a somewhat surprising readiness to abandon portions of the imperial territory, and to view with equanimity the dismemberment of the Old Union. There are, however, three areas where the persistence of the old myths can combine with current political realities to affect policy outcomes in tragically harmful ways.

The first and most dangerous is Russo-Ukrainian relations. It should be said at the outset that there are national myths at work on both sides here; one could, in a paper similar to this one, conduct an equally skeptical review of the historical justification for many of the most dearly held Ukrainian national myths. What should be said here is that one of the modern Russian refractions of the "Kievan heritage" myth (a myth, as may be remembered, that was in some periods reinforced by certain Ukrainians for their own purposes) is a startling incapacity—in many cases quite ingenuous, I believe—to acknowledge the authenticity of Ukrainian claims to their national identity, not to mention what they take to be their national territory. Here again I shall refer to Solzhenitsyn (who, I repeat, has no mandate to speak for Russians): in his "Letter to the Leaders of the USSR," to which I have referred above, his willingness to cast off the shameful burden of empire with regard to, say, Tajikistan, does not extend to Ukraine, which, as a believer in the Kievan heritage myth, he considers a part of the larger Russia. He "just doesn't get it," and he is not alone.

The matter, to be sure, is not a simple one. The cartographer's Ukraine is a territorial-notional legal entity that was formed as the cumulative consequence of a series of acts of Russian and Soviet government bodies between 1654 and 1954. Some of these acts might be likened to the Louisiana Purchase, others to the French and Indian or Spanish-American War. When originally acquired by the Russian Empire, most of the territory was very sparsely inhabited, as fully half of it remained until roughly the time of Mozart. The settled areas, to the northwest, were occupied (outside the cities) primarily by Ukrainians, but subsequently its rich prairies were settled by Ukrainian, Russian, Belarusian, Jewish, Bulgarian, Serbian, German, and Tatar communities.

But Ukraine is not the only state to have a variegated history; the crucial point is that the current entity is an object of international law, and its status and borders have repeatedly been acknowledged by the UN Charter, the Helsinki Agreement, the Soviet Constitution of 1977, and other treaties from the Soviet and post-Soviet periods, currently in force. It is fortunate that the governments of Leonid Kravchuk and Boris Yeltsin are very pragmatically viewing the new republic primarily as a jurisdiction, rather than as a homeland. And Russians resident in Ukraine, for the most part, seem no less satisfied with current political arrangements than they do in the Russian Federation. Should, however, either government find itself motivated to "act out" any of the relevant national myths—including the "national unity" myth—unimaginable chaos could result.

A second area in which old national myths might well affect foreign policy is Russian reaction to the agony of Yugoslavia. The myth in question here is the "Orthodoxy" myth, which, since it was cynically invoked in the late nineteenth century to justify imperial Russian foreign policy vis-à-vis the other Powers, has acquired a secondary mythic veneer. But the notion that broad sectors of the politically relevant Russian population have a deep and intrinsic emotional attachment to the cause of the Serbs is nonsense; those who invoke it are, in my view, criminally cynical; those who accept it without challenge are culpably unknowing. Anyone who has reviewed Russian-Serbian interactions over the last century can only treat this double myth skeptically, because it makes no sense: Russians are alleged to have "feelings" for their "brother Slavs"—are these more or less strong than their "feelings" for Ukrainians, Belarusians, or Poles? Is their support for their "fellow Orthodox" more or less firm than that for Ukrainians and Romanians? This ploy, for the current Russian government, can be little more than a scandalously cynical, low-risk, low-cost sop to a tiny minority that fears or resents Western or American hegemony or Russian humiliation in the ongoing collapse of the Soviet system.

There is a third area in which a potential problem may arise from the "national unity" or "narod" myth, although it is possible that quite pragmatic, non-notional difficulties of intercommunal competition will determine the course of events. I have in mind, of course, the circumstance of the millions of Russians who find themselves, like the Algerian *pieds noirs*, stranded on the wrong side of receding imperial borders. This is a very significant number of people—equal, roughly, to half of the total number of Russians on the planet in 1900.

Here, too, there is more than one set of national myths at work—I cannot begin to deal with the Kazakh, Estonian, Chechen, or other cultural artifacts involved. But for the sake of all concerned it seems absolutely crucial that the lure of easy national-traditional sloganeering be avoided to the extent possible by the principals and not countenanced by third parties. This refusal to entertain arguments traditionally allowed will not be easy; many Russian communities are already in flight, and others are being made to feel unwanted; in a time of general economic hardship there will simply not be enough of some goods—especially housing—to go around. Moreover, the complexity and diversity of circumstances is extraordinary: some Russians will eventually wish to go home, others to remain. For the moment, the potentially most dangerous case, that of Kazakhstan, seems to be working out better than expected in large measure because President Nazarbaev, like President Kravchuk, is treating his republic as a political jurisdiction rather than a nation-state, and is holding his own nationalists at bay. We must wish him well.

To sum up: The Russian political culture, which first took recognizable form in the late fifteenth century and has a continuous evolutionary development into modern times, is not at base expansionist. The Muscovite and later Russian state, however, has had a remarkable record of expansion. In modern times, myths about its origins and nature have been generated and generally accepted by scholars and the educated public; some have even been interpreted as causes of that expansion and reflections of an expansionist or messianic urge. Most of these myths, however, arose not spontaneously within Muscovite culture but under the influence of major trends in European cultural history and in the context of European politics. And they did not drive Muscovite expansion.

During the Soviet period, complex processes of popularization, including widespread resistance to the official internationalism, led to the general embrace of most of these national myths. Most, however, have little relevance to foreign policy options available to the Russian Federation, or to the most pressing concerns of most Russians.

But the burden of these concerns, transmuted by the widespread perception of Western condescension and self-serving into diversely articulated feelings of national humiliation, is taking its toll. Nationalism is again in the air. It is possible that Russians—and their politicians—will inhale it and express the pain of their current predicament in irrational forms. It will matter little whether these national myths have any basis in fact. Nor will they stop to ponder whether—a more interesting topic in some ways—this Russian nation, urban and industrialized, is arguably a different nation in fact, because they will believe that they are reconstructing the old mythical nation. For them to act on such delusional beliefs would be tragic—but all too much of history is tragic. It could well be this fact in part that prompts people everywhere to construct and believe in national myths.

Notes

1. For the received views as recently summarized by distinguished scholars, see N.V. Riasanovsky, *A History of Russia*, 4th ed. (New York: Oxford University Press, 1984), and Richard Pipes, *Russia Under the Old Regime* (New York: Collier Books, 1992). Although a number of recent works have dealt with important aspects of Russian historiography, I know of no adequately comprehensive treatment of the formation and development of the central ideas listed below. For some helpful treatments of specific matters, see Sergei Peshtich, *Russkaia istoriografiia XVIII veka* (Leningrad, 1961); P.N. Miliukov, *Glavnye techeniia russkoi istoricheskoi mysli* (Moscow, 1897); Anatol G. Mazour, *Modern Russian Historiography* (Princeton: Van Nostrand, 1958); N.L. Rubinshtein, *Russkaia istoriografiia* (Moscow: Ogiz, 1941). The posthumous *Russian Historiography: A History* by George Vernadsky (Belmont, MA: Nordland, 1978) is sadly obsolete.

2. A bold statement, to be sure. The crucial specification here is "ruling warrior caste," which I take to have comprised the military-political elite roughly described by the term *dvor* in documents of the time. These individuals appear to have been almost universally illiterate until roughly the end of the sixteenth century; their mentality was best, albeit only indirectly, reflected in the working documents of their chanceries. It might be argued that the existence of Muscovite copies of the Primary Chronicle (Horace Lunt is undoubtedly right to amend the traditional title, *Povest' vremen i let*) demonstrates Muscovites' awareness of the Kievan past—but there is little evidence that such texts were read by members of the secular leadership before the time indicated.

3. Noted by Antonio Possevino in 1582. See Hugh F. Graham, trans., *The Muscovia of Antonio Possevino, S.J.* (Pittsburgh: University Center for International Studies, 1977), p. 6.

4. Personal communication from my colleague Michael Flier, based on his forthcoming study of the symbolism and iconography of St. Basil's.

5. See the tabulations produced for another purpose in V.B. Kobrin, "Genealogiia i antroponimika," in *Istoriia i genealogiia* (Moscow: Nauka, 1977), pp. 80–155, esp. Table 3, pp. 89–90. Kobrin, who deals with the matter of *kalendarnye* and *nekalendarnye* names, does not discuss the matter of the absence of Kievan reminiscences.

6. I have attempted to deal with this matter from a slightly different perspective in "The Trouble with Muscovy: Some Observations upon Problems of the Comparative Study of Form and Genre in Historical Writing," *Mediaevalia et*

Humanistica: Studies in Medieval and Renaissance Culture, new series, no. 5 (1974), pp. 103–26.

7. The commonly cited passages are in the diplomatic correspondence with the Poles, e.g., *Pamiatniki diplomaticheskikh snoshenii Moskovskogo gosudarstva s Pol'sko-litovskim*, vol. 2; vol. 59 of *Sbornik russkogo istoricheskogo obshchestva* (St. Petersburg, 1887), passim. In the negotiations with the Poles at Iam Zapol'skii in 1581, Ivan IV's diplomats, for example, tried to insinuate that Livonia was a part of his "patrimony." See Graham, *Muscovia of Antonio Possevino*, p. 107.

8. A.A. Spitsyn, "K voprosu o Monomakhovoi shapke," *Zapiski otdeleniia russkoi i slavianskoi arkheologii russkogo arkheologicheskogo obshchestva*, vol. 8, pt. 1 (St. Petersburg, 1908).

9. I treat these matters in "Muscovy and Kazan: Some Introductory Remarks on the Patterns of Steppe Diplomacy," *Slavic Review*, vol. 26, no. 4 (December 1967), pp. 548–58. The sale and transportation of Christian slaves are discussed often, for example, Snosheniia s Nogaiskoi ordoi Rossiiskii gosudarstvennyi arkhiv drevnikh aktov (RGADA), fond 127, kn. 9. The recruitment of the mullah is demonstrated by the following instruction to a Russian emissary to the Nogai Horde in 1581: "Da pamiat' Ivanu: Poslano s nim gosudarevo zhalovanie Ian-Gardy Molne piat' rublev. I emu gosudarevo zhalovanie Ian-Gardy Molne otdati taino. A govoriti emu, chto gosudariu sluzhba ego vedoma, i on by gosudariu i vpered' sluzhil potomu zh, kak prezh togo sluzhil, i gosudarevo zhalovanie k nemu i vpered' budet bez oskudeniia," RGADA, fond 127, kn. 9, 1.54ob.–55.

10. A balanced summary of this massively confused historiography on this subject can be found in David M. Goldfrank, "Moscow, the Third Rome," *Modern Encyclopedia of Russian and Soviet History*, ed. Joseph Wieczynski (Gulf Breeze, FL: Academic International Press, 1981), vol. 23, pp. 118–21.

11. See his series of articles: "The Nature and Reception of Christian Byzantine Culture in Russia in the Tenth to Thirteenth Centuries and its Implications for Russian Culture," *Slavia Gandensia* (Ghent), vol. 5 (1978), pp. 107–39; "Quotations of Patristic and Byzantine Works by Early Russian Authors as an Indication of the Cultural Level of Kievan Russia," *Slavia Gandensia*, vol. 10 (1983), pp. 65–101; "The Implications of the Absence of Quotations from Untranslated Greek Works in Original Early Russian Literature Together with a Critique of a Distorted Picture of Early Bulgarian Culture" *Slavia Gandensia*, vol. 15 (1988), pp. 63–91; "The Bulgarian Contribution to the Reception of Byzantine Culture in Kievan Rus'," *Harvard Ukrainian Studies*, vols. 12/13 (1988/9), pp. 214–61. See also Ihor Sevcenko, "Remarks on the Diffusion of Byzantine Scientific and Pseudo-Scientific Literature among the Orthodox Slavs," *Slavonic and East European Review*, vol. 59, no. 3 (July 1981), pp. 321–45.

12. N.F. Kapterev, *Kharakter otnoshenii Rossii k pravoslavnomu vostoku v XVI i XVII stoletiiakh* (reprint, The Hague, 1968).

13. On the extent of Russians' knowledge of Greek, see B.L. Fonkich, *Grechesko-russkie kul'turnye sviazi v XV–XVII vv.: Grecheskie rukopisi v Rossii* (Moscow: Institut istorii, 1977).

14. On the early state of the Kremlin, see N.N. Voronin and M.G. Rabinovich, eds., *Drevnosti Moskovskogo Kremlia*, Materialy i issledovaniia po arkheologii SSSR, no. 167 (Moscow: Nauka, 1971).

15. On Bessarion and his activities, see James Hankins, *Plato in the Italian Renaissance*, 2 vols. (Leiden: E.J. Brill, 1990), esp. vol. 1, pp. 232f.

16. *Orationes et epistalae ad Christianos principes contra Turcos* (Paris: Gering, Crantz and Friberger, 1471). Cf. James Hankins, "The Popes and Humanism," in *Rome Reborn*, ed. Anthony Grafton, The Vatican Library and Renaissance Culture (Washington, DC: Library of Congress, 1993), pp. 63f.

17. The crucial texts, for Russians' appreciation of Kievan history as a part of their own past, are the famous *Sinopsis of Inokentii Gizel'* (Giesel), a German-Ukrainian historian, and the writings of Dymytro Tuptalo (St. Dmitrii Rostovskii) and Feofan Prokopovich, whose play *Vladimer*, written for Peter I, merits study not only as a foundation text of East Slavic historical unity, but for its invention of the first portrayals of East Slavic paganism.

18. A.I. Andreev, "Trudy V.N. Tatishcheva po istorii Rossii," in V.N. Tatishchev, *Istoriia Rossiiskaia v semi tomakh* (Moscow-Leningrad: Izdatel'stvo Akademiia nauk USSR, 1962), vol. 1, pp. 16–20. Tatishchev's library at his death contained not only the *Sinopsis* and a small collection of Russian chronicles and *khronografy*, but also a rather more comprehensive (in terms of the amount of data presented) library of Western works on Russian and East Slavic history: Henning's *Liflaendische-Curlaendische Chronica*, J. Bielski's and Gwagnin's Chronicles, an *Historie von Azow*, an *Einleitung zur Moscovitischer Historie* (probably Gottleib S. Treuer, Leipzig, 1720), a *Sammlung russischer Geschichte* (probably G.-F. Miuller [St. Petersburg: Mueller, 1732–]), etc. See "Katalog biblioteki V. N. Tatishcheva," in P.[P.] Pekarskii, *Novye izvestiia o V.N. Tatishcheve* (St. Petersburg, 1864), pp. 56–63 (also as *Prilozhenie no. 4* to vol. 4 of *Zapiski imp. Akademii nauk* [St. Petersburg, 1864]).

19. I rely here on the index in Richard Pipes, trans. and ed., *Karamzin's Memoir on Ancient and Modern Russia* (Cambridge, MA: Harvard University Press, 1959), there being to my knowledge no indexed Russian edition.

20. Bruce Parrott has reminded me of the useful survey of official/popular historiography to be found in Seymour Becker's articles, "The Muslim East in Nineteenth-Century Russian Popular Historiography," *Central Asian Survey*, vol. 5, nos. 3/4 (1986), pp. 25–47, and "Russia Between East and West: The Intelligentsia, Russian National Identity and the Asian Borderlands," *Central Asian Survey*, vol. 10, no. 4 (1991), pp. 47–64.

3

The Yugoslav Question in the Foreign Policy of Russia at the Beginning of the Twentieth Century

Sergei A. Romanenko

The twentieth century began, and is ending, with extremely vicious wars in the Balkans among "the brotherly South Slav peoples" for national and political self-determination—along ethnic lines—and for better economic and strategic conditions.

In the first two decades of the twentieth century, in events originating before World War I, contradictions and conflicts among the South Slavs resulted in one of the major interethnic conflicts of the twentieth century, the Balkan wars.

The First Balkan War (October 1912 to May 1913) involved the so-called Balkan alliances—Serbia, Greece, Montenegro, and Bulgaria—against the Ottoman Empire. The alliances defeated Turkey. The London peace treaty was signed, and the allies acquired new territories. But Bulgaria was not satisfied. This discontent caused the Second Balkan War (June–August 1913) between Bulgaria on the one hand and Serbia, Greece, Montenegro, Romania, and Turkey on the other. Bulgaria was defeated and lost part of its territory under the Bucharest treaty.

Because of the involvement of the great powers—separated into two military blocs with Great Britain, Russia, and France (the Triple Entente) opposed to Germany and Austria-Hungary—in the Balkan conflicts, those wars threatened to cause a world war. But in 1912–13 the great powers were desirous of safeguarding their strategic and political interests without risking war.[1] Russia played a major role in the Balkan situation that, in turn, had a significant impact on the general situation in Europe. One of the great powers whose interests were directly associated with the Balkans and the whole "Eastern question," Russia was at the same time a Slavic country that supported South Slavic and, even more important, Orthodox peoples.

Current events in the former Yugoslavia not only are reminiscent of events eight decades ago but also stem directly from them. An analysis of past and current events can explain much of what has happened and is happening.

First of all, such an analysis can help one understand the traditions of Russian diplomacy in the Balkans and Russia's rapport with Serbia, Montenegro, and the Croats, who up until 1918 had lived under the domination of Austria-Hungary; it can help one see how various political forces, including Russian right-wing nationalists (whose successors have considerable influence in Moscow today), have presented Russia's role in the Balkans and in the whole Slavic world. These political groups idealize prerevolutionary Russia and view themselves as inheritors of its policy. They construct superficial and—from the viewpoint of a professional historian—incorrect parallels between the Russian and Serbian nations. Such an analysis will go far in unveiling the influence of Pan-Slavic ideology and psychology on Russian foreign policy. By the same token, a comparison of Russia's role in the current situation and in the events of 1908–14 can contribute to one's understanding of the causes of the Serbian-Croatian-Muslim armed conflict.

But first one must examine some basic facts. What are the traditional, historically generated features of Russia's reaction to the situation in the Balkans? What are the recent features?

The historical elements include the following:

• The process of political self-determination in the South Slavic nations is not finished; the same holds true for the peoples of Eastern and Central Europe.

• The South Slav and Balkan situations are still strongly connected with European and world affairs: in the absence of solutions, regional interethnic conflicts threaten to provoke a new world war. The conflicts between the South Slavic peoples and states are completely unregulated.

• The great powers—Russia, the United States, Great Britain, France, and Germany—are involved in these conflicts; at the same time, Italy, Turkey, Bulgaria, Hungary, Greece, and Austria preserve their interests in the region.

• There are strong connections between Serbian and Russian nationalists (imperialists and communists).

• The main principles of Serbian and Croatian nationalism are unchanged.

• The Bosnian problem has not yet been resolved.

The new features are as follows:

• Multiethnic empires no longer exist.

• When the Russian borders changed dramatically and Russia no longer neighbored the Balkan Peninsula, the Russian position weakened in Central Southeastern Europe, as well as in the Slavic world as a whole.

• There are no longer any adversarial political-military blocs in the world. However, there are attempts to get Russia involved in the new polarization between East and West, totalitarianism and democracy.

• The Slavic idea failed completely both as a uniting principle of multiethnic states and as a principle of international relations.

• World diplomacy faces a new task: to mediate in the disintegration of the former communist multiethnic states.

Considering all of these features of the new environment in the Balkans, it is worth noting some distinctive traits in the evolution of the former Yugoslavia and the Soviet Union. Specifically, several crises that occurred simultaneously in both countries led to their disintegration:

• the crisis of the communist economic system;

• the crisis of the totalitarian political system;

• the crisis of both the federal and autonomous structures of multiethnic states that provided a mechanism of self-determination for their nations;

• the crisis of the Pan-Slavic idea as a means for solving the nationality question and preventing the outbreak of nationalism.

These crises and the disintegration of both Yugoslavia and the Soviet Union—countries that many Russians and Serbs considered their national states—gave rise to identical processes, awakening an ethnic consciousness in both Russian and Serbian societies. States in which Serbs and Russians had taken the leading role broke up, and in the newly emerged states Russians and Serbs constituted a minority—a minority that turned out to be unprepared to accept the new conditions psychologically, legally, and politically. The collapse of both countries brought a loss of prestige and standing in international politics and a loss of the support of former, traditionally allied states. New borders were humiliating to accept.

In this environment historical consciousness assumed great significance as a foundation for a new political conception of interethnic relations and a new foreign policy doctrine. Unfortunately, neither the Russian nor the Serbian democrats were able to define their domestic and foreign political doctrines. Among the conservative populace professing old values, politicians and scholars turned for inspiration to prerevolutionary Russia, which they strongly idealized and whose rebirth they considered a continuation of a historical process that was brutally stopped in 1917.

The most important tenets of Russian official politics and of a part of the Russian intellectual elite—orthodoxy, ideology, and the psychology of Slavic closeness—influence Russia's perception of the Serbian-Croatian-Muslim crisis. Events occurring in the former Soviet Union and Yugoslavia, in Russia and Serbia, display important similarities. The Russian nationalists speculate on these similarities, disregarding historical, cultural, and political differences between Russia and Serbia. They also disregard the differences between prerevolutionary Russia and royal Serbia and their current successors.

Historical Russian Perceptions of the South Slavs

How did the prewar Russian diplomats understand the South Slavic commonality? First of all, as the diplomatic correspondence and Sergei Sazonov's memoirs show, Serbs and Croats as well as Czechs and Slovaks were not regarded as separate nations (neither were Russians, Ukrainians, and Belarusians). There was an idea that Croats were nothing more than "Catholic Serbs"—Serbs oriented toward Vienna.[2] Writing about the relations between Serbia and Austria-Hungary in 1908–14, Sazonov mentions the Croats only in one case, when describing how the "Croat and Dalmatian brethren" of the Serbs populated the Adriatic coast and cut off Serbia from access to the sea. It is worth noting, however, that it was not only Russian diplomats who considered Serbs and Croats a single nation; the concept was a common error of the late nineteenth and early twentieth centuries. It suffices to say that persons such as Robert Seton-Watson, Otto Bauer, and V.I. Lenin thought of Serbs and Croats as one nation.[3]

In the beginning of the twentieth century two myths, Serbian and Croatian, emerged in Russian foreign policy, and they persist to the present. According to St. Petersburg's "Serbian image," Serbia was a loyal ally of Russia in the Balkans. This notion was based on Russia's geopolitical and strategic interests (rivalry with Austria-Hungary and Turkey); the linguistic, religious, and ethnic closeness of Serbs and Montenegrins with Russians also played a part.

In the Russian press of that period one can find a good deal of information on Serbia and Montenegro that doubtless propped up this feeling of closeness and affinity. Serbia was portrayed as a country with justified territorial claims on its neighbors, striving to create a motherland for all Serbs and to gain its due access to the Adriatic Sea. Serbia's interest in the fate of all South Slavs was described as a just interest in brotherly nations suffering under an alien yoke. Whether this was an idealization or a reality, a study of Serbian diplomatic correspondence and political documents of the early twentieth century can offer some illumination.

Using popular slogans such as "South Slavs, Unite," "The Balkans to the Balkan Peoples," and "Unification of All Serbs," the Serbian government of King Peter I (Karadjordjević) pursued its own interests. The centerpiece of Serbian foreign policy was the ethnic as well as political unity of all Serbs, Croats, and Slovenes. Serbian politician Jovan Cvijić, for example, argued for the necessity of merging Bosnia and Herzegovina with Serbia because these regions "were to Serbia what Moscow was to Russia, the center and core of the Yugoslavian unity."[4] The 1908 program of the Serbian organization Narodna Odbrana (National Defense) read: "Our nation must be told that Bosnia's freedom is a necessity not only on the grounds of Slavic solidarity with a brotherly people that is subject to suppression but also on the grounds of opening up Serbian access to the sea."[5]

In the course of World War I, the head of the Serbian government, Nikola Pašić, wrote on future plans to create a Yugoslav state: "Serbia and Montenegro are fighting for the liberation of their brothers. Once these countries are liberated, they will not be allowed to establish a confederation, because they will create a single state with Serbia or will join Serbia as areas with their autonomy. There is no other option."[6] King Nikola's government in Montenegro had in mind, first of all, Albania.[7]

The Serbian government expected Russia to support it in its effort—both in the struggle with Vienna and Istanbul and in the rivalry with Zagreb and Sofia. It did its utmost to inculcate in St. Petersburg a conviction that Serbia was Russia's only loyal ally, for whom Russia must do everything within its power, including supporting Serbia in its rivalry with the Croat nationalist movement for domination over the future of the South Slavs.

The plans of the Balkan governments were met with the enthusiastic support of a part of Russian public opinion that refused to see the aggressive and provocative basis of this policy and the possible harm that it could inflict on Russia itself, let alone the kind of "liberation" Serbian official policy had in mind, which did not mean the national liberation of the Serbs' Slavic "brothers," as it did not respect their freedom of choice and the right of national self-determination. Belgrade's "integrationist Yugoslavism" meant not only a rejection of that right, but also a denial of the very existence of Croats and Slovenes as separate peoples.

The Croat image in Russian diplomacy was different. The Croats were not considered as close to Russians as were the Serbs, and support for them, therefore, was difficult to forge. The reasons were as follows: Croat territories belonged to Austria-Hungary; Croats were a Catholic nation; and a good many Croats supported the annexation by Austria-Hungary of Bosnia and Herzegovina in 1908. Although the Croats were considered to be a part of a single South Slav nation, they also were perceived as constituting an obstacle to the realization of Serb unification plans.

Like the Serb national movement, the Croat national movement had its own ideas of national self-determination. But Croatia's situation was different: the political scene was split between two main camps—the national-liberal (Yugoslav idea) and the national-radical (Croatian idea). The former was started by supporters of the "new course" and spiritual disciples of J.J. Strossmayer and Father Franjo Racki, who founded a Serbo-Croatian coalition in 1905. The main ideas of this group were Yugoslavism—recognition of Serbs and Croats as one nation, with respect for their cultures and religions, an anti-German and anti-Austrian stance, cooperation with Budapest against Vienna, reform of the Dualist system in Austria-Hungary, and last but not least, the hope that Russia would support the group's struggle for self-determination.[8] The daily newspaper of the Serbo-Croatian coalition, *Pokret*, stated in 1908: "The only question is whether the name of the country will be Serb or Croat and also whether the common culture will have more imprints of Western Catholicism or Eastern Orthodoxy. The consideration whether the newly emerged state will bear the name of Great Croatia or Great Serbia is of secondary importance."[9] It is worth noting that even this kind of Yugoslavism implicitly rejected the rights of both peoples—Serbs and Croats. Furthermore, up until the Balkan wars, none of the political parties in Croatia considered leaving the Austro-Hungarian monarchy.[10]

The other group—national radicals and the Croat nationalists who descended directly from the ideas of Ante Starčević—refused outright to admit the presence of Serbs in Croatia as a distinct group with the right of self-determination. Their leaders, Josip Frank and Ivo Krsnjavi, directed their sights to Vienna in foreign policy. Having been disappointed in the nineteenth century by Russian and French policies with regard to the liberation of Croatia, they sought support in Berlin.[11] The nationalists believed that the way to achieve the right of self-determination was the creation of a three-state monarchy (Austria, Hungary, and Croatia) in which each state would enjoy equal rights under a single Habsburg scepter. This is the origin of the tragedy of the Croat national movement, which in the rest of Europe was viewed as closely connected with the ascendancy of Germany in Europe. When Germany and Austria-Hungary were defeated, the Croat national movement was defeated with them.

Croatia's support for the Austrian annexation of Bosnia and Herzegovina deprived it of the last chance to get Russia's backing for its national aspirations. For the liberal part of the Croat political leadership, the annexation promised to create a South Slav entity within Austria-Hungary; for the radicals it was a way to take Bosnia from Serbia and possibly to create a genuinely Croat entity in the Habsburg monarchy. Frano Supilo, one of the leaders of the Serbo-Croat coalition, who before the annexation suggested the possibility of Bosnia's joining Serbia, was subject to harsh criticism.[12]

Russian public opinion was naturally much better informed about the events in Serbia than in Croatia. This was due partially to Croatia's position as a part of a hostile Austria-Hungary, and partially to the estrangement that was a consequence of different religions and cultures. In the Russian press, news about Croatia was much less frequent than news about Serbia. Oddly enough, Russia, which presented itself as the sponsor of all Slavic nations, selectively supported some and alienated others. At the same time, in Croatian newspapers like *Hrvatska, Pokret, Novi Srbobran*, and others, it was possible to find news from Russia (especially in 1905–7), translations of Russian writers, and news about visits of Russian cultural and political celebrities (such as Pavel Miliukov, head of the Constitutional Democratic Party, and General M.V. Volodimirov). Unfortunately, however, many of these visitors did not understand the difference between the Croats and the Serbs. The Russian diplomats saw Croatian nationalism as an obstacle to the unification of the South Slavs under the leadership of their beloved Serbia. In September 1908 the Russian diplomat N.V. Charykov wrote to Russian Foreign Minister A.P. Izvol'skii about the possibility of Bosnia's joining Dalmatia:

> I have to admit that this option does not disconcert me. The merger of Bosnia-Herzegovina with Dalmatia will in the end give an impetus to the Slavic and Serbo-Orthodox element; it will destroy the legendary Croat-Catholic "kingdom of Zvonimir"; it will add another twenty Slavic and all the more orthodox votes in the Reichstag.[13]

If Austria-Hungary disintegrated, Russia would doubtless back the foundation of a new Yugoslav state, under the leadership of Belgrade, not Zagreb. Russia, in supporting the Serbian aspirations and considering the Croats and Serbs one nation, was therefore unable to play a mediating role between Serbs and Croats.

Thus, official Russia considered Serbs and Croats as well as Czechs and Slovaks as one nation in the same way it equated Russians, Belarusians, and Ukrainians in domestic politics. This attitude had negative consequences for Russian foreign policy, which as a result denied Slavic nations the right of self-determination. On the other hand, in the conditions of the early twentieth century, the Slavic idea partly coincided with the effort to liberate the Slavic nations from the yoke of foreign domination. As it turned out, however, these ideas were not and could not be the key to a solution to the ethnic conflicts in Southeastern, Eastern, and Central Europe.

Principles of Russian Foreign Policy in the Balkans

What were the principles of Russian foreign policy in the Balkans? What was the share that interethnic conflicts played in the outbreak of World War I? How did Russia try to prevent the conflicts between the South Slavic peoples and states? And what was the reaction to this effort?

A valuable source in this respect is Russian Foreign Minister Sergei Sazonov's memoirs. "The historical mission of Russia," Sazonov wrote, "to liberate brotherly Christian nations of the Balkan peninsula from under the Turkish yoke was by the beginning of the twentieth century fulfilled to the extent that its completion could be left to the liberated nations, which stepped onto the road of independent political existence and managed to prove their state viability."[14] Sazonov conceded, however, that the South Slavic nations could not defend their national goals when faced with pressure from mighty Germany.

Idealizing Russian foreign policy, Sazonov tried to argue that Russia never pursued selfish interests in its Balkan policy: "The only goal that Russia continuously aimed at was . . . for the Balkan peoples not to fall under the influence of the hostile nations and not to turn into an obedient weapon of their intrigues."[15] Russia's Balkan policy coincided with Serbian policy, which was stated as "The Balkan Peninsula to the Balkan Peoples." "Russia declared and defended the principle of independence of the Balkan states as a just principle in view of the undeniable right of the Balkan peoples for political self-determination."[16]

Nevertheless, Sazonov in fact admitted the "political selfishness" of Russia in trying to expand its space for development of economic potential and to assure its security in one of the most vulnerable regions. Russia was trying to pursue two specific goals—namely, to gain access to the Mediterranean and to facilitate the defense of the Black Sea.

What influenced Russia's policy in this conflict situation, which had originated both in the rivalry among the South Slavs themselves and in the drive for political self-determination during the Balkan wars? The main goal of Russia was "to assure the free development of the Balkan nations supported by Russia in the search for an independent existence."[17] There were, according to Sazonov, two main obstacles on the road to this goal: first, the interests of Germany and Austria-Hungary in the region and second, "mutual disagreements" among the South Slavs themselves, which revealed themselves fully in the Second Balkan War. Russia welcomed attempts at the peaceful synchronization of Serbia and Bulgaria, and made a major effort toward it, using its influence and capacity to give advice to, and exert pressure on, the governments in Belgrade and Sofia. "Every attempt at a rapprochement among the Balkan nations . . . must get sympathy and support from the Russian diplomacy," Sazonov wrote in explaining the beginnings of the Balkan alliances.[18]

The possibility of an interethnic conflict between the "South Slavic brothers," who in the First Balkan War felt brotherly enough to unite against Turkey, worried all of Russia. After the common victory and liberation in the First Balkan War, the scramble of special national interests to create their own states on the largest possible territory replaced the previous concord. Also, the Great Power rivalry had an impact on events in the Balkans.

The speaker of the Duma, M.V. Rodzianko, is an example of this consensus:

> The Balkan war with Turkey was raging. In the Duma the heroic struggle of the Slavs for freedom was closely followed. Sympathy for it was absolute. It grew with the indignation over the mistakes of our diplomacy, especially Minister of Foreign Affairs Sazonov, who according to the Duma made Russia play only a minor role in international events. The feeling of general indignation and national outrage was pronounced, besides the Duma, in the press of all orientations.[19]

Neither Rodzianko nor the press did full justice to Sazonov. Sazonov, although a Russian imperialist, was an adherent of Realpolitik and tried to implement a foreign policy that an internally enfeebled Russia could be capable of supporting. Only a reformed country could embark on a more active foreign policy, and the proponents of a more active foreign policy were opposed to any attempt at reforming Russia internally. Sazonov used all the means at his disposal:

The Balkan alliance benevolently supported by Russia met the hopes that were pinned on it. The ultimate goal from the Russian point of view, an eternal peace in the Balkans . . . and their preservation from outside influences, was, however, distant.[20]

In the arguments between the Duma and the Ministry of Foreign Affairs, a traditional, and still existent, aspect of Russian foreign policy making can be seen. There was a conflict between the executive and the representative body, a major part of which professed extreme Pan-Slavic, imperialist, and Russian nationalist positions. The struggle over foreign policy orientation became an extension of Russia's internal struggle.

Many adherents of a more active Russian foreign policy failed to see that a policy based on Pan-Slavic myths and illusions could bring Russia nothing but harm. Sazonov understood it fully:

Serbia's access to the Adriatic became for a considerable period of time a focal point of European politics, although it had, in fact, not more than a purely local meaning. The Serbian passion regarding this issue soon flooded Russia. Some St. Petersburg circles, which were close to the Imperial court, and all the nationalistic press in the capitol, hostile from the past towards Sazonov, started a vocal campaign against Russian foreign policy. This campaign found expression in street rallies and meetings, where patriotic speeches declaring the necessity of war to protect Slavic interests could be heard, and a series of newspaper articles accusing Russian diplomacy almost of high treason.[21]

Russia was faced with a choice, either to follow a chimera, satisfying its drives and indulging the Serbian and Montenegrin claims—thus alienating its allies France and Britain and entering isolated into a local conflict—or to use its influence on Belgrade and Cetinje in order to calm down the Serbian and Montenegrin politicians, explaining to them the impossibility of carrying out their goals. Sazonov, as he maintained, chose the latter, with the support of Nicholas II, and became a subject of harsh criticism not only in St. Petersburg but also in Belgrade. The tsar's opinion probably spared Russia from a war with Austria-Hungary and Turkey, with France, England, and Germany remaining aloof. That is what the policy of "admirers of intrigues and scandals from the group of our patented patriots could have brought about."[22] Further, Sazonov wrote:

> My task was complicated by the fact that in Serbia, which was the object of passionate and sincere support by the Russian government, I did not find the self-control and the sober opinion of the danger of the moment that was necessary to prevent a disaster.[23]

Friendly advice from Sazonov did not find particular success either with the Belgrade government or with the public, both of whom held ambitious plans for uniting all Serbian territories, including those where Serbs constituted a minority, and enlarging the Serbian state. Sazonov complained that Serbian politicians

> were unwilling to listen to the reasons . . . for waiting for the events to proceed further. I argued from the history of the Russian state over the last 150 years, in the course of which it had had to fight northward and southward to reach the seashore, which task has not been completed yet.[24]

Sazonov, at the end of the day, cabled to the Russian envoy to Belgrade, N.N. Gartvig, to inform the Belgrade government that Russia would not fight the Triple Alliance for the sake of Serbia's gaining a port on the Adriatic. Sazonov himself remembered how uneasy he felt playing the role of a moralistic elder brother, but he felt compelled to do it because the situation in Serbia had reached the verge of a national catastrophe, which had to be "prevented in the interest of Serbia itself." Besides, Sazonov wrote, "if there was in Europe any government that Serbia would accept advice from, it was the Russian government, the sincerity of which they have no reason to doubt."[25]

As to Russia's strategic and economic interests in the Balkans, Sazonov wrote that

> possession of the Croat and Dalmatian shore with the possibility of reaching the Aegean Sea could provide Serbia with a solution to its economic troubles, about which the Serbian people dreamt from the very first minute when the Great Serbian idea reached the ears of the Serbian politicians. By the time of the Balkan wars these ideas had not been realized."[26]

After World War I, Serbia achieved the political unification of ethnic territories and access to the sea through the creation of the Kingdom of Serbs, Croats, and Slovenes and later Yugoslavia.

In the meantime, the tension between the former members of the Balkan alliance rose with their ambitions, and as tensions rose, Europe split into hostile blocs. The Russian Ministry of Foreign Affairs worried about the Serbian-Bulgarian tension and the ambitions of Montenegro, and tried to exert all its influence to prevent conflict. In 1913, in regard to the Romanian claims, a conference in St. Petersburg was called to solve all of the issues in the Balkans. The conference was ineffective.

Russia undertook a major effort to reason King Nikola of Montenegro out of his claims to Shkodra. The crisis over Shkodra could turn a small local conflict into a major European conflagration. Russia made it clear that it could neither get involved in a war because of "a Balkan conflict of secondary importance to it" nor participate in "coercive measures" against Montenegro in order to force it to accept the will of the Great Powers.[27] The Russian government strove to give any possible military action an international character.

At the same time the tensions between Serbia and Bulgaria sharpened. Realizing that his efforts were not successful, Sazonov tried for the last time to turn to the tsar with a pledge to send to Belgrade and Sofia a mission calling on both governments to put aside their disputes and leave them to Russia's "honor arbitration." Tsar Nicholas authorized the mission, and as Sazonov maintained, the mission made a big impression on the entire world. Sofia and Belgrade acquiesced to the mediation of Russia. The Serbian King Peter replied that he trusted Russia's justice and sound judgment. Sazonov thought that both countries had agreed to Russian mediation.[28]

The Duma also started an effort to mediate. A visit to St. Petersburg, for example, by the hero of the First Balkan War, Radko Dmitriev, was used by Rodzianko to warn against the danger of the Serbian-Bulgarian conflict:

> The results of a war campaign . . . are assessed by the successful completion of the war—by a peace treaty. Therefore, let me give you advice on behalf of your ancient sister, Russia—preserve the peace among yourselves. We are your brothers and we dream of the war victories of the Slavs. We plead with you to prevent with all your power the conflict among you, which would threaten the successful end of the war.[29]

Thus, over eighty years ago, Russia and the world community had dealt with the problem of maintaining peace in the liberated Balkans against external influences and conflicts among themselves. On the one hand, these tensions were long rooted in history, and, on the other hand, they emerged as a consequence of the interactions of the Great Powers in the Balkans. Russia was confronted with a new role as the mediator between "brotherly" peoples and its "only" allies. Russia was aware that its allies were ready to involve it in conflict in order to satisfy their own claims. In this situation Pan-Slavic psychology and commonality played only a minor role. Russia saw that in spite of noisy rhetoric about the Serbian-Russian friendship and about the enormous amounts of money sent to Belgrade and Cetinje, the rulers of Serbia and Montenegro—blinded by territorial ambitions and theories about a single Yugoslav nation—were unwilling either to submit themselves to Russia or to listen to Russia's advice in terms of relations in the Balkans.

This reluctance was the cause of the failure of mediation in the Balkans prior to the Second Balkan War and of the inability to contain Belgrade's impatience to unite all Serbs and play a leading role in uniting all South Slavs, although in this sense, Serbia's policy was no different from the policies of other participants of the Second Balkan War and World War I. Doubtless, Serbia, counting on the support of Russia, developed an aggressive and—with regard to Austria-Hungary—irresponsible attitude based on the slogan "One nation—one territory—one state."

However, the South Slavic nationalities living in Austria-Hungary were unwilling to exchange the Habsburg scepter for that of the Serbian Karadjordjevč dynasty. Indeed, up to the Balkan wars and even later, all political parties in Croatia and Vojvodina, including local Serbs, supported the preservation of the Habsburg monarchy.

In the meantime, Russia pursued its own national interests, which had nothing in common with the liberation of the South Slavs. The Russian government was trying to use Serbia and Montenegro as its bastions in the Balkans, as its bases in the Mediterranean, and as its instruments in its rivalry with Austria-Hungary and Turkey. Already at that time, the ruling circles had found their "favorite" Orthodox Slavic nations, which were connected with Russian official Orthodoxy. The Serbian myth of Serbia as a victim was spread in Russia as well; the Russian government adapted the myth of Russia's role in the liberation of the South Slavs. Both sides indulged in mythological images of Pan-Slavic psychology and ideology. Such images have reemerged in Russia over the current conflict in the former Yugoslavia.

The efforts of the South Slavs to gain liberation were equated by the Russian intelligentsia with its own internal struggle against autocracy (*samoderzhavie*) in the nineteenth century. The Russian intelligentsia viewed both movements as symbols of the purity of faith, loyalty, and freedom. By the beginning of the twentieth century, however, the myth had gradually receded. As Fedor Stepun wrote about the period prior to World War I: "The Slavic Question did not exist for the left-wing radical intelligentsia as much as the question of Constantinople and the Dardanelles."[30] Interestingly enough, Lenin characterized Serbia's war against Austria-Hungary as the only just struggle in the conflicts of World War I.

At the same time, Lenin was very critical of the Slavic question and the monarchy. This was a legal evaluation, as he considered Yugoslavia one nation. Furthermore, he compared the process of forming a monoethnic state to states with ethnically close nationalities. Lenin, in accordance with the Marxist tradition, considered the nationality question subordinate to social relations based on class. Ethnic commonality was, according to him, an obstacle on the road to the dictatorship of the proletariat. Unlike the Austrian Marxists, he maintained that socialism gradually led to the evaporation of national differences. It is possible to say that the Slavic idea might have served as a starting point in his consideration, because abolishing ethnic differences between ethnically related nations would be easier than between nations with completely different languages and cultures. The idea of the equality and brotherhood of the working people harmoniously matches the idea of the Slavic brotherhood. Speaking of the national revolution of the South Slavs, Lenin considered the Yugoslav theory an imperial notion from the point of disintegration of the empire.

It is interesting to compare Lenin's evaluation of 1914 with that of the leader of the Russian Constitutional Democrats (*Kadety*), Pavel N. Miliukov, who was himself an expert on Slavic history and politics, and who was frequently blamed for Russian imperialism. In 1914, for example, he strove, according to Mikhail Karpovich, "to localize the Austro-Serbian conflict and was willing to leave Serbia to its fate in order to avoid a general European war."[31] The Kadet newspaper *Rech'* was shut down for expressing the same thoughts. (Rodzianko petitioned Archduke Nikolai Nikolaevich for the newspaper to be allowed to publish again. Rodzianko argued that Miliukov's behavior was foolish and resented. The newspaper was allowed to reappear and held to its new nationalist ideas during the war.)[32]

Lessons Learned and Myths Maintained

What are the lessons of the events of eighty years ago that are relevant to the present? How does historical consciousness influence foreign policy? Which traditions of the old Russian diplomacy can be of some use for today's democratic Russia, and which traditions should be rejected?

Russia has to deal with the task of formulating a new foreign policy doctrine. It would be unwise, however, to ignore the historical consciousness, the tradition of Russian statehood, and the historical psychology and memory of the Russian people. Historical arguments have always played a role, and they were a necessary element in practical diplomatic activity. It is, however, important to avoid oversimplified historical analogies of current events with prerevolutionary Russia— not only because of a different political system but also because of a different historical environment. The Russian historical consciousness not only has to overcome many of the traditions of the last seventy-five years, but also has to look into the traditions that emerged during the existence of Russian statehood.

It appears valid to draw a parallel between the current situation and the diplomatic period prior to World War I, namely, Russia's effort to find a middle way between its own interests and the interests of the "brotherly" Slavic nations. It was important for Russia to overcome a unilateral orientation toward the Orthodox South Slavs and not place itself in a contentious situation, thereby complicating the possibility of playing a mediating role. The foreign policy of Russia at the threshold of the twenty-first century cannot be built on the principles of the Slavic solidarity of the early twentieth century. Concessions to Pan-Slavic motives in foreign policy would mean a return of Russia to the old imperial policy and would mean, in the end, concessions to the conservative forces, either communists or nationalists. No wonder that in the course of the twentieth century Pan-Slavic ideas were often utilized by these forces.[33] Today the Slavic idea is an indispensable element of various programs that call for the re-creation of greater Russia or even of the USSR. Many in Russia agree with Rodzianko's position: "A unified, great, indivisible, powerful and independent Russia is necessary both for us and our brothers, with whom we are connected through the commonality of interests, although not all Slavic nations are clear and certain about that."[34]

While in the late nineteenth and the early twentieth centuries Slavic ideas coincided with the prevailing movements for national liberation and self-determination, the Slavic movement had a liberal character. From the beginning of the twentieth century these Slavic ideas were taken over by purely imperialist nationalistic forces which were conservative yet aggressive in their domestic politics. The Slavic idea can no longer function as the basis for a foundation of multiethnic states or for solving conflicts among the Slavs themselves. On the contrary, the idea contains the potential for instigating conflict, as it is essentially a form of nationalism that provides a psychological and political basis for imperialist policy.

The creation of national independent states after the disintegration and downfall of communist multinational states does not mean the creation of true democratic political systems. As in the aftermath of the disintegration of the Habsburg empire, new states are grappling with the problem of national self-determination and identification. The Russians in the republics and the Serbs in Yugoslavia are facing problems similar to those of the Magyars and Austrian-Germans in Austria-Hungary.

But it is impossible to use any kind of Pan-Slavic ideology (like any other kinds of pan-ideologies) to solve interethnic conflicts. Pan-ideology and pan-psychology by their very nature provoke conflict. They are a kind of refined nationalism and imperialism contradicted by the process of national self-determination.

Russia, Russian diplomacy, and Russian right-wing nationalists tried to use the Pan-Slavic ideology and psychology to stop the conflict between two South Slav peoples and states—the Serbs and the Bulgarians, Serbia and Bulgaria—before World War I. But the attempt failed. Pan-ideological theories and the goodwill of both the Russian government and the tsar could not stop the conflict.

In contrast to their modern followers, 1913 Russian right-wing nationalists did not try to unleash the war between the two South Slav peoples but tried to reconcile them. The right-wing nationalists of today have supported only Serbia.

The application of the Slavic idea that is now popular with some groups in Serbia and Russia could bring about dire consequences. It might be viewed as nothing more than an attempt of the "older brother" to preserve its former dominant position and pit the Slavic nations against one another (the Slavic idea is not popular either in Croatia or in Ukraine). It could lead to a further deterioration in relations between Slavic and other multiethnic states, and provoke negative relations with other European nations. Non-Slavic nations of Central and Southeastern Europe will doubtless see any attempt to reintroduce the Slavic idea in foreign policy as an attempt to embark on a policy of external expansion. To build international economic relations on the basis of ethnic closeness makes no more sense than to build them on the basis of the same social system.

The role of Russia in the current Serbian-Croatian-Muslim conflict should embrace certain principles. Russia learned in the beginning of the twentieth century that it should not encourage or get involved in the territorial claims of Serbia. Any military solution today is clearly impossible. It has to be made clear that a democratic Russia cannot be a protector of Slobodan Milošević's Serbia. A sharp line must be drawn between the Serb people, the Serb government, and President Milošević himself. The same should be done with regard to Croatia.

The democratic forces of Russia should establish contacts with, and clearly show their support for, the democratic forces of Serbia and Croatia. They should induce them to strengthen unity of action and establish contacts and consultations among themselves. The Russian government should also mediate between the Croats, Serbs, and Muslims by insisting on parleys between Belgrade and Zagreb.

In consideration of the Russo-Serbian connection and its important position in public opinion, Russia has to mediate between Serbia and the West. It should explain the complexity of the conflict, which is often oversimplified as a conflict of "aggressive, totalitarian, communist Serbia" and "peace-loving and democratic" Croatia.

Russia cannot use the Slavic idea, based on historical myths and ethnic stereotypes, in its foreign policy. But it can and must use the experience and traditions of Russian foreign policy to mediate between South Slavs in their conflicts.

The Slavic idea cannot be used as the basis for solving inter-Slavic conflicts, either in domestic or international affairs, although this type of psychology is currently a reality of modern Russian ethnic and state historical consciousness. The Russian government and Western governments must take this fact into account. All the programs of both legal and illegal parties and organizations that have as their goal the restoration of the Russian Empire or the Soviet Union, whether nationalist- or communist-based, rely on the Slavic idea in both domestic policy and international affairs.

On the other hand, both sides, Russian and Serbian nationalists, use the Slavic idea for their own political interest without regard for the true interests of the Russian and Serbian peoples. If these political forces come to power in Russia, a Russian-Serbian conflict—like that in 1948–56 in Soviet-Yugoslav relations—would be inevitable.

The conflict in Yugoslavia can be viewed on two levels. It is an interethnic conflict stemming from causes rooted in the remote past and the quest for national self-determination of the South Slavic nations, as well as a result of the politics of the European countries in the eighteenth through the twentieth centuries.

Historical experience illustrates that there is no military solution for interethnic conflicts in the Balkans. Foreign military intervention is not able to solve these problems. In addition to the Balkan wars, the European powers interfered in South Slav and Balkan relations in 1878 (Berlin treaty), 1908 (annexation of Bosnia), World War I, World War II, and postwar settlements. But neither foreign multinational empires (Ottoman, Habsburg) nor the "national" Yugoslav state could extinguish or solve the contradictions and conflicts between Serbs, Croats, Muslims, and Bulgars. Moreover, these conflicts were (and are) the result of the policies of European powers, including the Russian empire.

Notes

1. See J.G. Schurman, *The Balkan Wars, 1912–1913* (Princeton: Princeton University Press, 1974); Edward C. Thaden, *Russia and the Balkan Alliance of 1912* (University Park: Pennsylvania State University Press, 1965); E.C. Helmreich, *The Diplomacy of the Balkan Wars, 1912–1913* (Cambridge, MA: Harvard University Press, 1938).

2. Branko Pavicević, ed., *Rusija i aneksiona kriza, 1908–1909* (Titograd, 1984), p. 401.

3. See Robert Seton-Watson, *The Yugoslav Question and the Habsburg Monarchy* (London, 1913); Otto Bauer, *Die Nationalitätenfrage und die Sozialdemokratie* (Moscow, 1906); and numerous articles written by V.I. Lenin during the Balkan wars and World War I. See also Frantisek Silnitsky, "The Nationalities Policy of the CPSU: 1917–1922," *Problems of Eastern Europe* (1990), p. 86.

60 SERGEI A. ROMANENKO

4. S.I. Danchenko, Iu.A. Pisarev, and E.I. Chepyzheva, "Serbiia na puti ot avtokratii k konstitutsionalizmu, 1878–1917," in *Balkany v kontse XIX–nachale XX veka*, ed. Iu.A. Pisarev (Moscow: Nauka, 1991), p. 39.

5. Ibid., p. 42.

6. Ibid., p. 50.

7. Iu.A. Pisarev and N.I. Khitrova, "Problemy chernogorskoi gosudarstvennosti," in Pisarev, ed., *Balkany v kontse XIX*, pp. 58–90.

8. S.A. Romanenko, "Problema natsional'noi gosudarstvennosti v programmakh politicheskikh partii Khorvatii-Slavonii i Voevodiny v kontse 19– nachale 20 veka," in Pisarev, ed., *Balkany v kontse XIX*, pp. 128–34.

9. Pavicević, *Rusija i aneksiona kriza*, p. 236.

10. Romanenko, "Problema natsional'noi gosudarstvennosti," pp. 135–37; Z.S. Nenasheva and S.A. Romanenko, "Formirovanie kontseptsii natsional'noi gosudarstvennosti i problema sblizheniia slavianskikh narodov Avstro-Vengrii na rubezhe vekov," in Pisarev, ed., *Balkany v kontse XIX*, pp. 102, 105–8.

11. I. Krsnjavi, *Zapisci* (Zagreb, 1986), vol. 2, pp. 525, 582; Romanenko, "Problema natsional'noi gosudarstvennosti," pp. 139–44.

12. *Korespondencija Franja Supila 1881–1914,* vol. 6 of *Arhivski vijesnik* (Zagreb, 1963).

13. Pavicević, *Rusija i aneksiona kriza*, pp. 429–30.

14. S.D. Sazonov, *Vospominaniia* (Moscow: Mezhdunarodyne otnosheniia, 1991), pp. 56–57.

15. Ibid., pp. 57–58.

16. Ibid., p. 58.

17. Ibid., p. 61.

18. Ibid., p. 62.

19. M.V. Rodzianko, *Krushenie imperii* (Valley Cottage, NY: Multilingual Typesetting, 1986), pp. 80–81.

20. Sazonov, *Vospominaniia*, pp. 84–85.

21. Ibid., p. 87.

22. Ibid., p. 93.

23. Ibid., p. 94.

24. Ibid., p. 96.

25. Ibid., p. 98.

26. Ibid., p. 100.

27. Ibid., p. 106.

28. Ibid., pp. 113–14.

29. Rodzianko, *Krushenie imperii*, p. 82.

30. F. Stepun, *Byvshee i nebyvsheesia* (New York: Izd. Im. Chekhova, 1956), vol. 1, p. 334.

31. M. Karpovich, "Russkii imperializm ili kommunisticheskaia agressiia," *Novyi zhurnal* (New York), vol. 25 (1951), p. 262.

32. Rodzianko, *Krushenie imperii*, p. 104.

33. M. Agurskii, *Ideologiia natsional-bol'shevizma* (Paris: YMCA Press, 1980); A. Ianov, *Russkaia ideia i 2000 god* (New York: Liberty Pub., 1988); Silnitsky, "Nationalities Policy of the CPSU," p. 86.

34. Rodzianko, *Krushenie imperii*, p. 334.

4

Struggle Over the Borderlands

Alfred J. Rieber

The collapse of the Soviet Union has thrown into bold relief the major problem that confronts all multicultural societies: the interaction between the center and the periphery.[1] The center is defined in spatial and cultural terms. It occupies the geographical core of the empire inhabited by the dominant ethnic group, which at times may only be a plurality, as in the Russian Empire in 1914, rather than a majority of the population. Dominance is measured then in political and military terms, that is, as the coercive power of the state. Cultural and economic dominance may be less strong, more disputed, and consequently may become highly politicized. Such was frequently the case in the Russian Empire, where commercial and even industrial activity on the periphery was technically superior, and cultural life, at least in the eyes of the non-Russians, more highly developed than at the center.

Throughout its history Russia's relations with its periphery have been interactive rather than passive. As the empire expanded, whole regions of the periphery lost their geographic location on the periphery, but remained culturally peripheral to the Russian core. Moreover, acculturation was never a one-way process. In pre-Petrine times, at least, there were possibilities that the Russian Church would be Ukrainianized and the Russian nobility Polonized. Even after Peter the crosscurrents of cultural exchange never ceased to influence the core as well as the periphery.

In territorial terms the periphery was and continues to be in flux. There were decades when territories were acquired or reorganized at a breathtaking pace. Two of the longest periods of frontier stability were from 1880 (delimitation of the Afghan frontier) to 1917 and 1945 to 1991. But frontier maintenance is not the sole measurement of center–periphery relations. These two relatively stable periods in relation to the outer world were notable for their high levels of internal migration and colonization, which profoundly affected the relations between core and periphery. They were also characterized by constant struggles over questions of ethnic identity, focused mainly on education and language issues. Ironically, too, in both cases the relatively stable periods of frontier maintenance were followed by deep internal crises and the collapse of the multicultural state.

As a mode of analysis in the current crisis, the center–periphery dichotomy needs to be placed in a broad historic context. In particular two dimensions should be kept in mind. The first concerns the more general issue of identifying the key determinants of Russian foreign policy. The second deals more specifically with the expansion and consolidation of the Russian multicultural empire, that is to say, the process of Russian state building.

There are four key, interrelated determinants of Russian foreign policy that continue, in my view, to exercise a powerful influence on policy makers in the contemporary context. First, since the sixteenth century Russia has been a multicultural society. Second, its frontiers have not been anchored on "natural" geographical or clear-cut ethnic lines, and throughout much of Russia's history they have been "porous," that is, open to a variety of border crossings ranging from runaway serfs to migrations of peoples. Third, the country has suffered from relative economic and technological backwardness in relation to the most highly developed societies in the global context, which necessitated a heavy reliance on either foreign trade, foreign investment, or a form of technology transfer from abroad. Finally, the ruling elites—and in the modern period the mass of the population—have been engaged in a continuous search for cultural identity on two levels, the first external, that is, whether or not Russia was part of the European cultural zone and international system and the second internal, that is, whether individuals or groups identified themselves with a Russian national (*russkii*) or a supranational (*rossiiskii* or *sovetskii*) idea.[2] Although the personal styles of ruling have varied widely throughout the imperial and Soviet periods, each political leader and his or her advisors were forced to confront these issues when formulating policies that dealt with relations between the center and the periphery as well as between Russia and other powers in both Europe and Asia.

In the specific context of the relations between the center and periphery, the collapse of the Soviet Union and the emergence of successor states may be perceived as the central event in a more general crisis in the Eurasian borderlands that has been building since the early 1980s.[3] Although there were tremors in the mid-sixties and even mid-fifties in Eastern Europe, the deep fissures opened up with the explosion of civil war in Afghanistan, the post-Tito constitutional crisis in Yugoslavia, and the recurrent ethnic strife in Sinkiang Autonomous Region. Once the Soviet Union began to crumble, reverberations were strongly felt in other multicultural states: Czechoslovakia broke apart, Yugoslavia dissolved into warring states, Romanian-Hungarian ethnic strife racked Transylvania, Bulgaria expelled its Turkish population, and civil wars broke out in the successor states of the phantom Commonwealth of Independent States.

As far as the former Soviet Union is concerned, the process of dissolution has already passed through two phases and may be entering a third. The first stage, beginning in 1989, was introduced by the failure of a federative solution and led to the separation and declarations of independence of the constituent Soviet socialist republics. The second stage was the outbreak of ethnic strife and secondary separatist movements within the successor states that led to the outbreak of eight civil wars, at last count. We stand poised on the edge of a third stage, the complete breakdown of public order and widespread civil war that will involve the army on a large scale and envelop the entire region. By the time this chapter is read, the threshold may already have been crossed.

Thus far into the short term, however, the dissolution of the Soviet Union has exhibited some unusual, even unique characteristics that may herald an alternative option to the dreaded third stage. Acts of separation of the constituent republics took place without foreign intervention; they were accompanied by a minimum of violence on the part of the central authorities, limited to brief actions mostly in Georgia and the Baltic republics; they have not led to reprisals against the Russian minorities in the new states—there has been little talk of ethnic cleansing; and the central state has retained intact most of its military capability and remains a great power if not a superpower on the world stage. These and other characteristics of the current situation can be attributed to the historical evolution of the Russian Empire and the Soviet state.

It is the main purpose of this chapter to suggest some of the broad and persistent themes that have helped to shape the present relations among the ethnic groups within the former Soviet Union. My aim is to treat these problems during the second half of the imperial period, from the late eighteenth century to the revolution. Having accepted an already ambitious project, I hope I will be forgiven for having absorbed some of the imperialist spirit and reaching from time to time beyond the chronological limits in both directions, in order to illustrate the dangers of facile generalizations about the continuities of history.

To shift our sights to the long term, the dissolution of the Soviet Union may also be perceived as the most recent episode in a series of great upheavals that have convulsed its Asian and European borderlands over the past half-millennium. These upheavals have repeatedly redefined the relations between the Russian center and its periphery. From the late fifteenth through the sixteenth centuries, a fundamental shift took place in the political and economic relations between the nomadic people of the steppe and deserts of Eurasia and the sedentary agricultural population positioned along their northern and southern flanks. Arguably, the steppe had occupied the center stage of Eurasian politics during the previous millennium, and the sedentary agricultural lands had represented the periphery. With the rise of the great bureaucratic empires—Muscovite, Ottoman, Safavid, and Qing—and their penetration of the steppe and deserts, the relationship was gradually reversed. The agricultural lands became the new centers and the steppe-deserts the periphery.

The geopolitical transformation of the Eurasian borderlands was a prolonged process that proceeded at different tempos in various regions. The last of the "barbarian" invasions took place in Russia in the early seventeenth century, in China in 1644 (founding a new dynasty), and in Persia in 1722. But over time the technological and organizational superiority of the Russian, Ottoman, Persian, and Chinese empires prevailed over the horsemen of the steppe, whose economies and social structures were seriously weakened by the shifts in trade routes during the seventeenth century and by endemic internecine warfare that could no longer be suppressed, as in the past, by charismatic leaders like Genghis Khan or Tamerlane, who were able to transform transient tribal coalitions into great steppe empires. The last successful attempt to unify the region was made in the early sixteenth century by Shaybani Khan, whose hero was Alexander the Great. As the head of the newly forming Uzbek peoples, he helped to give a new ethno-religious definition to Central Asia in his campaigns against the Shi'i Persian Safavids. For a century and a half his dynasty resisted the pressures of three bureaucratic empires, the Persian, Chinese, and Russian, only to succumb finally to internecine warfare.[4]

The growth of property relations among the nomads and the emergence of more sharply defined class structures along feudal lines raised additional obstacles to political unity. Beginning in the seventeenth century the advance of the bureaucratic empires into the borderlands touched off a major international power struggle over the legacy of the declining steppe empires. There has been an unfortunate tendency among scholars and publicists alike to take a one-sided view, both literally and figuratively, of the Russian imperial advance that neglects the concurrent imperial advance of the Ottoman, Persian, and Chinese bureaucratic empires along the southern rim of the steppe-desert lands. The subjugation of the steppe peoples was the result of a multipower competition and not just of Russian expansion.

A similar contest was taking place on the western periphery of the Russian state. Linked geographically and historically to the Asian borderlands, Eastern Europe also underwent a series of traumatic political and socioeconomic changes in the early modern period. Internal crises coupled with foreign invasions destroyed its independent regional states and converted the area into a contested zone wedged between rival bureaucratic empires. What Friedrich Engels first called "the refeudalization" of Poland and Danubian Europe took place at a time when West European capitalism was undergoing a period of rapid expansion. The collapse of the East European medieval states in the face of Ottoman, German, and Russian expansion led to the incorporation of the entire region into new multicultural bureaucratic empires. The reemergence of small East European states on a modern national foundation was a prolonged, painful, and incomplete process that began with Greece and Serbia in the early nineteenth century and culminated in the postwar treaties of 1919. The successor states were never truly nation-states but merely reproduced on a smaller scale the multicultural character of the empires of which they had been a part.

In the East European borderlands the internal struggle for national liberation was accompanied by Great Power rivalries for influence over the successor states. When the Great Powers cooperated against the common danger of revolution, as in 1848–49, the smaller nations were unable to throw off the foreign yoke. But when the powers were split, as in 1877–78, 1913–14, and 1914–18, the possibility existed for small nation-states to gain their independence or expand their territories. But in the long run their existence depended on the tolerance of the Great Powers. Thus the relationship of Russia to its Asian and European periphery must be set against two major historical processes: first, the struggle of the peoples of the borderlands to resist incorporation into one or another of the bureaucratic empires closing in on them, and second, the rivalry of the Great Powers for domination over the contested zones between them. Whatever its peculiarities, the imperial Russian historical experience should be fitted into a larger picture of a struggle on two levels for hegemony over the borderlands that involved the forces of internal resistance by the peoples of the region themselves and the external imperial wars between the bureaucratic empires.

The present and future relationships between the new Russian center and its periphery continued to be shaped in large measure by five major factors that have characterized empire building throughout the tsarist and Soviet periods. The first of these is the means of acquiring new territories: outright conquest, annexation by international treaty, or voluntary association singly or in combination. In each case a different pattern of juridical and politico-psychological relationships emerged between Russians and the ethnic groups along the periphery that persisted for decades (even centuries) after incorporation.

The second factor is the level of culture that distinguished the Russians from each ethnic group added to the empire. Careful precautions must be taken in this politically sensitive area, and comparisons should be made along two scales of measurement: first, with respect to institutions, that is, rates of literacy, levels of urbanization and industrialization, and forms of social organization based on class and status rather than tribes or medieval corporations; second, with respect to perceptions, that is, the identification of local elites with what they regarded as "superior" culture areas like the West or the Islamic world.

The third factor is the varying methods and degrees of assimilation or acculturation imposed by the Russians on the ethnic groups. Neither the tsarist autocracy nor the Soviet Union maintained a consistent "nationality policy." Even when a single policy appeared to be in effect, it was often applied unevenly to different regions.

The fourth factor is the extent of internal migration and colonization, primarily by the Slavic population, Ukrainian and Russian, into
newly acquired regions. Social cohesion, levels of education and training, and the spatial location of the immigrants all contributed to defining their presence in the imperial territories.

The fifth factor is the international context of empire building, that
is, the political rivalries between Russia and the powers that competed
with it for control over the same territories and peoples of the Eurasian
borderlands. Their rivalries were generally settled by armed conflict.
The outcome virtually dictated that the delimitation of Russia's international frontiers would be an arbitrary process reflecting power relationships and not following natural geographic or ethnic boundary
lines. Thus the periphery of the Russian Empire constituted a series of
frontier zones inhabited by non-Russians separated from their ethnic
compatriots by what appeared to them to be artificial barriers to social,
economic, and cultural intercourse.[5] In nomadic areas there was a great
deal of boundary crossing; to the west until 1861 runaway serfs took
advantage of the ethnically porous frontiers; everywhere smuggling
was rife.[6]

In many regions—western Belarus, western Ukraine, the North
Caucasus, Central Asia—the frontier zones were inhabited by a highly
diverse ethnic mix that was often in a state of flux. The pattern of
settlement was kaleidoscopic, that is, dynamic, rather than mosaic or
fixed, as a result of centuries of nomadic migrations, defeat and
flight, and Russian colonization both spontaneous and state-sponsored. The extreme edges of the periphery were, to borrow a term
from cultural anthropologists, shatter zones, socially unstable and
politically insecure.

Unlike the seaborne imperialism of the maritime powers, Russia's
overland expansion profoundly influenced the central institutions of
the metropolitan core. The gradual accretion of new territories inhabited by peoples of widely divergent cultures and levels of economic
development required periodic reorganizations of the state's administrative apparatus and the introduction of new juridical and constitutional forms. It was not possible to govern Finland and Poland in the
same way the North Caucasus and Central Asia were governed.
Throughout the nineteenth century the government experimented with
different administrative solutions for different borderlands: viceroyal-
ties for Poland and the Caucasus, even though their powers were not

the same, governors-general for New Russia, Turkestan, and Siberia, with various lines of command extending from special committees and ministries at the center. Even during periods of centralization, high officials were sensitive to regional peculiarities. As General Chernyshev reported to Nicholas I, what was needed in the Caucasus was "an administration that corresponds to the real needs of the inhabitants and is adapted to the morals, spiritual outlook and customs of the people."[7]

Thus the Russian government was engaged in an almost constant process of state building from the sixteenth century to the eve of World War I. The addition of its separate parts never constituted a well-integrated whole. There was no common citizenship. At the end of the empire, for example, the introduction of electoral laws for the State Duma revealed striking differences in voting rights by region. At times it appeared that the leadership suffered from a kind of frontier anxiety fed by the stream of runaways during the long period of serfdom; rebellions linked to foreign wars as in the case of the three great Bashkir uprisings in the eighteenth century; separatist national independence movements, as in the Kingdom of Poland in 1830 and 1863; or the mere suspicion of treason, which led, for example, to the deportation of the Jewish population from the western provinces after the outbreak of war in 1914. In brief, the political loyalty of populations living in the frontier zones was often in doubt or else called into question by a government responding to a conditioned reflex of repression. Consequently, the existence of a contiguous band of non-Russian, ethno-territorial blocs encircling the core of the state produced a real or imagined state of permanent insecurity on the periphery.

During times of international crisis the state confronted the nightmare of dismemberment, for example, in the latter stages of the Crimean War, during the revolution of 1905, and again in 1917–19. Yet to the external world, the fragility of the state was masked by the apparent monolithic character of the autocratic power. Russia's relations with its littoral resembled a geocultural seesaw: tipped in one direction it provided the heartland with a defensive glacis or a springboard to further expansion; tipped in the opposite direction it opened the way to the penetration of unwelcome foreign ideas, cheap imports, or hostile armies into the Russian heartland. If the problems were persistent, the proposed solutions varied widely.

Government policies toward the periphery reflected to a large degree the divergent temperaments, training, and experiences of the auto-crat—in a word, his or her personal style of ruling. Decision making was further complicated by the constant necessity of reconciling do-mestic and foreign policy in dealing with the periphery, that is, balanc-ing shifting international norms against the practical demands of internal security. In addition, bureaucratic rivalries among the minis-tries and between the central administration and ambitious proconsuls (viceroys, governors-general, and military leaders), especially when they were favorites of the autocrat, also contributed to the difficulties of pursuing consistent policies on the periphery. The remainder of this chapter will be devoted to analyzing the shifts in state policy toward the four major issues that shaped Russia's relations with its imperial littoral: the strategy of empire building, the policies of assimilation and acculturation, the pattern of internal migration and colonization, and Russia's place within the international system.

As the first modern Russian empire builder, Peter I set the course of Russian expansion, which was in four significant ways unlike that of contemporary colonial powers in Western Europe. First, new territories were acquired with the assistance of a coalition of powers, in other words with international sanction; second, they were incorporated with support from elements within the local population in the form of a so-called Russian party; third, the indigenous elites were not destroyed, enslaved, or segregated, but instead were assimilated into the Russian nobility; fourth, there were only sporadic and unsystematic attempts to carry out a cultural assimilation of the frontier zones, with an uneven and uneasy balance being preserved between centralization and accep-tance of regional peculiarities.

The Great Northern War began, it should be remembered, with the formation of a coalition of states determined to deprive Sweden of its empire on the eastern and southern shores of the Baltic. At the outset, an important group of Baltic noblemen supported Peter's ambitions, in the expectation—which in the event proved correct—of retaining their special privileges, which had been threatened by the centralizing poli-cies of the Swedish kings. Throughout the imperial period the Baltic German nobility occupied a disproportionate number of very high po-sitions in the tsarist bureaucracy. That Russia stood alone at the end of the war was a result of the military weakness of allies like Poland, the achievement of war aims by Prussia, Denmark, and the lesser German states, and the general concern that the substitution of a powerful Russia for a declining Sweden in the eastern Baltic might not be in the interests of the other riparian states.

After Nystadt, Peter and his successors continued to cultivate a "Russian party" in neighboring states, not only in Europe (Sweden and the Polish-Lithuanian Commonwealth) but among the steppe nomads as well. In 1730 the Russian government accepted the invitation of Khan Abulkair to take the Kazakh Lesser Horde under its protection, probably saving them from destruction at the hands of another nomadic steppe people, the Dzungars. But the pro-Russian party among the Kazakhs was only a small group that could not deliver the Middle and Greater Horde to the Russians. It required another century of frontier warfare and Russian colonization before the rest of the Kazakhs were incorporated into the empire.[8]

Because of their unusual geopolitical position and long experience in dealing with the east, the Russians were able to incorporate elements of steppe politics and diplomacy into their relations with European states. The cultivation of pro-Russian elements across frontiers and the co-optation of elites were not innovations of Peter and his successors. Its historical precedents may be traced to the policies of the grand princes of Moscow when dealing with the Tatar khanates. Moscow sponsored and protected pretenders to the khanate of Kazan; and its nobility intermarried with the Tatar upper class, a practice that was continued to the point where, in the eighteenth century, according to a recent estimate, fully one-third of Russian aristocratic families bore Turkic names.[9]

But the pattern of interaction between Russia and the Muslim peoples to the east was not entirely uniform or positive. For two centuries after the conquest of Kazan and Astrakhan, Russian civil and ecclesiastical officials attempted, often brutally, to break the power of the Muslim elites by confiscating their lands and forcing conversions to Christianity.[10] And there were the religious wars between the Russians and the peoples of the North Caucasus in the nineteenth century. Still, ever since Peter, Russia has sought to avoid crusading wars that would have turned every conflict with the Ottoman Empire into a civil war in Russia's Muslim borderlands.

There remained, then, an inner tension in the process of Russia's empire building during post-conquest periods between peaceful assimilation and coercive integration. The oscillation from one to the other, or even at times their coexistence, persisted and intensified right down to 1917. The lack of a consistent and coordinated policy toward the periphery was a function of the growing fragmentation of the political culture as well as the wide variety of geographic and ethnic situations in the borderlands.

Catherine the Great departed from the Petrine tradition by introducing a new concept of empire in both ideological and administrative terms.[11] First, inspired by the views of the Cameralists and the Physiocrats, she calculated the value of newly acquired territories in terms of their contribution to the state's total human and material resources.[12] By acquiring most of the Black Sea littoral and the lioness's share of the Polish-Lithuanian Commonwealth, she added a larger population and more productive provinces to the empire than any of her predecessors or successors.

Second, she promoted the colonization and settlement of the relatively empty but potentially highly productive black earth belt of Ukraine. To this end she encouraged foreign immigration—the only ruler who systematically pursued this policy—of Germans from Moravia and Serbs and Croats from the Ottoman provinces to settle under advantageous conditions in fertile lands along the Volga and in New Russia. She further promoted settlement by granting huge tracts of land to favorites and permitted them to transfer large numbers of serfs to the south in order to cultivate the newly granted estates.[13]

Third, guided in a similar way by ideas of efficiency and rationality in administration, she took decisive action to end the autonomous status of the Hetmanate in Ukraine and many of the political privileges of the Baltic German elites that had been confirmed by Peter the Great. But she also spurred the integration of non-Russian elites, particularly Ukrainian *starshyna* and Polish *szlachta*, into the Russian nobility.[14] Her strategy of acculturation of elites was carried on by Paul and Alexander with respect to the Georgian, Armenian, and Bessarabian nobility. Her passion for centralization and uniformity within the empire also informed her policies in the newly acquired Polish lands.

Fourth, she skillfully promoted a policy of religious toleration, also grounded in Enlightenment principles, in order to strengthen state control over the steppe nomads. She reversed two centuries of discrimination against the Volga Tatars and enlisted their support to convert the restless Kazakhs to Islam and strengthen trade relations between the steppe and the center. In both cases she was able to consolidate the government's political authority in areas where Russification had little appeal. At the same time she granted religious toleration to sectarians and Old Believers, enabling the most enterprising elements to return from their semi-exile on the northern and western borderlands in order to play a more active role in the commercial life of the center. Her policy of organizing the newly acquired Jewish population into the Pale of Settlement was designed to restrict their activities to areas where they would not come into contact with the Russian peasantry.[15]

Finally, in an even more radical departure from the earlier tradition, Catherine adopted an expansionist strategy that consciously undermined neighboring governments whose territories she coveted. Peter had cultivated the growth of a "Russian party" in neighboring states, Sweden, Poland, and some of the smaller German states in order to influence their foreign policies. But Catherine used the Russian party as an instrument of internal subversion to weaken and divide the ruling elites of territories that she sought to conquer and absorb into the empire. She practiced this tactic with consummate skill in Poland, the Crimean khanate, and the Transcaucasus, particularly Georgia and Armenia, where the Orthodox Christian population provided powerful internal support for adhesion to the Russian monarchy.[16] But Catherine was also careful to draw the European powers, especially Prussia and the Habsburg monarchy, into her imperial schemes in order to obtain international legitimacy for Russian expansion. She coordinated internal subversion and external alliance with Prussia and Austria to destroy the "containment policy" of France based on the "barrier states"—Poland, the Ottoman Empire, and Sweden—and helped initiate the process of their dismemberment.

The partitions of Poland, the expulsion of the Ottomans from the northern shores of the Black Sea, and the weakening of Swedish control over Finland that enabled her grandson Alexander I to acquire that province in 1815 tipped the geopolitical seesaw in Eastern Europe decisively to Russia's advantage. But the acquisition of a new layer along the western periphery had serious implications for Russia's position in the international system. To ensure the security of the borderlands against both foreign invasion and internal rebellion, it was necessary to enter into a semipermanent alliance with the two German courts and to terminate for the better part of a century, with a few minor lapses, any hope of alliance with the maritime powers of Western Europe.

Under the reign of Alexander I, Russian policies in Europe and Asia were not well coordinated. Territories outside the purview of Europe were mismanaged by local officials. In Georgia, for example, Russian generals meted out rough treatment to both the indigenous nobility and, more surprisingly, the autocephalous Georgian Orthodox Church, until the abuses were corrected by the enlightened viceroy Mikhail Vorontsov in 1845. Until then the area was, despite its voluntary accession to the empire, a hotbed of rebellion and anti-government plots.

Alexander's policies toward the western periphery were by contrast influenced by his views on constitutional order and his involvement as a key player in the European coalitions against Napoleon. As part of a general European settlement at the Congress of Vienna he was able to legitimate Russian control over the Kingdom of Poland and add the Grand Duchy of Finland and Bessarabia (ceded by Turkey in 1812). In Poland, Finland, and Bessarabia, Alexander recognized the relatively high degree of political consciousness and elite identification with European culture by granting extensive autonomy outside the administrative structure of the Russian provinces. The concessions were most extensive in the Kingdom of Poland and Finland and included their own national military units, countrywide representative institutions, indigenous law codes, and tariff frontiers with the rest of the Russian Empire. His policies gained support from an influential, if not dominant, segment of the Polish, Finnish-Swedish, and Romanian elites.[17] This was the first occasion in Russian history that the autocrat experimented with the idea of using the periphery as a test case for introducing major institutional reforms into the metropolitan core of the empire. In this case the experiment proved unsuccessful, due in large part to the victory of the conservative elements in the Russian ruling circles over the reformers in the political struggle to win the approval of the tsar, who was himself deeply divided over the choice between what Marc Raeff calls the constitutional solution of a "well-ordered police state" and a mystical, universalist moral order. In the western borderlands by 1820 the geocultural seesaw had tipped away from Poland as a cultural conduit for Western influence toward a new defensive glacis. When Nicholas I tried, a decade later, to convert it into a springboard for Russian intervention against liberal uprisings in the west, the kingdom flared into open rebellion.

In the spirit of Catherine, Alexander pursued the colonization of the Black Sea steppe with the help of enlightened proconsuls like Langeron, the Duc de Richelieu, and Mikhail Vorontsov. As ambitious and loyal as Potemkin but free of the taint of corruption, they exercised their exceptional powers as governors-general to build the colony of New Russia. Under Richelieu's benevolent administration the population of New Russia increased by a million souls. Indifferent to the question of ethnic identity, he regarded the multinational character of his region as a source of strength. "Never, Sire," he wrote to Alexander I, "in any part of the world, have there been nations so different in manners, customs and dress living within so restricted a space. The Nogais occupy the left bank of the Molochna; families from Great Russia, the right bank; then higher up are the Mennonites, facing the Germans, who are half Lutheran, half Catholic; higher up again at Tolmak, the Little Russians (Ukrainians), members of the Greek religion; then a Russian sect, the Dukhobors."[18] The colonization of New Russia continued well into the nineteenth century, bringing more exotic peoples into the region, including a contingent of Polish exiles after the revolt of 1831 and political émigrés from the Ottoman Empire—Serbs, Greeks, Armenians, and above all Bulgarians, following the wars of 1828–29 and Crimea.[19] An ironic by-product of the emigration was the creation of small conspiratorial groups of Greeks, Romanians, and Bulgarians who used sanctuary in Russia to plot revolutionary national liberation movements against the Ottoman state that repeatedly involved the Russian government in embarrassing situations and occasionally international crises.

A marked shift from peaceful assimilation to coercive integration began late in Alexander I's reign, though elements of both policies contended with one another for decades. Vorontsov, whose enlightened administration of New Russia survived into the reign of Nicholas I, went so far as to defend the property and civil rights of Russian sectarians and Jewish colonists as well as the local Tatar population against the discriminatory policies of the central government. Enthusiastic promoters of regional economic development, Richelieu and Vorontsov lobbied the central government hard and successfully to declare Odessa a free port. Toward the same end Vorontsov subsequently secured transit trade privileges for the Caucasus. Up to the Polish revolt in 1831, liberal economic policies drew the western and southern littoral of the empire into closer commercial relations with the outer world than with the Russian center. At the same time, under very different leadership, the notorious Count A.A. Arakcheev, military colonies were introduced into New Russia. Concentrated in Sloboda

Ukraine, mainly between the Bug and Dnieper rivers, they represented an attempt to combine colonization with military settlements on the frontiers. Harsh discipline and resentment by Ukrainian settlers of expropriation of their land sparked an uprising in 1829. Although unsuccessful in the long run, this "early experiment in state sponsored social engineering," as John Keep calls it, left behind a substantial population of free settlers (*odnodvortsy*), which assured the Russians a dominant position in Kherson province.[20]

The mounting nationalist reaction to the French Revolution, Napoleon, and the liberal settlement of 1815 underwent a radical transformation under Nicholas I. The tsar and his closest advisers devised and implemented an official nationality policy that rejected the cosmopolitan spirit of the eighteenth century multicultural state ignited by Peter and nourished to maturity by Catherine. Haunted by the Decembrist rising and deeply shaken by the Polish revolt five years later, Nicholas launched a campaign against foreign influences that had a profound effect on Russia's relations with its periphery. Nicholas's selective nationalism, directed mainly against Jews and Poles, occasionally slipped out of his control. Emblematic of the official nationalist policy was the attempt to suppress or Russify the secondary schools and universities in the western borderlands; Vilnius was closed, Dorpat purged, and a new university, St. Vladimir in Kiev, was established, in the words of the Minister of Education Uvarov, "to suppress in Polish youth the thought of its own nationality, to bring it ever nearer to Russian notions and morals and to transfer to it the general spirit of the Russian people."[21]

In a sharp reversal of Catherine's policy, the Orthodox Church, not intrinsically a militantly proselytizing faith, was urged to step up conversions among the Baltic peoples and the Muslims of the Volga region. The official campaign struck a sympathetic chord among young Russian nationalists, like Mikhail Pogodin and Iurii Samarin, releasing a wave of chauvinistic and xenophobic publicistic writing that thrust into the public arena for the first time in Russian history the explosive issue of ethnic conflict within the empire between the dominant Russian core and the western borderlands.[22] Russian merchants in the core provinces gradually began to identify their interests with the grassroots nationalism. They took a dim view of any special commercial regime, whether in Poland, Finland, New Russia, or the Caucasus, because it discriminated against them. By mid-century they were beginning to organize themselves for the first time in order to promote a Russian nationalist economic system that would resist the flood of cheap goods from abroad.[23] Here, then, was another incidence of regional development sparking a nativist reaction; on this issue the seesaw remained tipped against the interests of the Russian merchants until the advent of Vyshnegradskii and Witte during the last quarter of the nineteenth century.

Meanwhile, the renewed Russian advance into the Caucasus revived the cultural clash between the Islamic and Orthodox Christian worlds at a time when Russian nationalist sentiment was on the rise. In the early decades of the nineteenth century the prolonged three-way power struggle between the Ottoman Empire, Iran, and Russia for control over the strategic Caucasian isthmus entered its decisive phase. Russian military victories over the Persians and the Turks brought new territories into the tsar's domain that proved just as troublesome for Russian administrators as the western borderlands. With the Treaty of Turkmanchai in 1827 the Russians acquired roughly half of the Armenian population, who were delighted to come under the control of a Christian power, and by the treaty of Gulistan in 1813 about the same number of Azerbaijanis who were just as unhappy to fall under the domination of the infidel. But the government's administrative reorganization of the newly acquired provinces followed the line of breaking up ethnic blocs in order to check the dangers of regionalism and ethnic separatism. The first of these, in 1828, placed Karabakh and other pockets of Armenians outside the Armenian Provincial Administration, leaving a time bomb with a very long fuse that ignited only a century and a half later. Additional reorganizations in 1840, 1844, 1849, 1862, 1868, 1875, and 1880 were similarly aimed at preventing any ethnic group from becoming "the preponderant majority in any major province."[24]

The roots of another contemporary ethnic clash in the region sprang from the Russian need to subdue the mountain fastness of Daghestan in order to guarantee the strategic security of their newly acquired possessions in the Transcaucasus. As part of its traditional policy of reinforcing frontier zones with mixed ethnic populations, the government of Nicholas promoted the settlement of Old Believers and Cossacks in the North Caucasus. But Nicholas, too, was not entirely consistent in his policy toward the borderlands. By appointing Vorontsov viceroy with plenipotentiary powers, he gave free reign to a grandee of the enlightened school of proconsul. Vorontsov cleaned up the corrupt and brutal Russian administration and set the stage for the reforming activities of his successor, Fieldmarshal A.I. Bariatinskii, and his chief of staff and future War Minister, D.A. Miliutin. The combination of Russian conquest and colonization, which involved the government's confiscation of the mountaineers' land, touched off the great ethno-religious wars of the Avars, Chechens, and other North Caucasian peoples against the Russians. Beginning in the late 1820s, the fighting flared and smoldered on and off for forty years along the exposed southern frontier.[25] Although finally subdued by Bariatinskii in the sixties, the Chechens retained their reputation for fierce independence of mind, and repeatedly demonstrated, at least to the dissatisfaction of their Russian overlords, an ambiguous political loyalty. During the Russian Civil War they fought their own war against Russian colonists, whether Red or White, and their terrible fate in 1945 is well known.

During the last six decades of the imperial period Russia's relations with its littoral were increasingly shaped by domestic politics at the center. The crosscurrents of reform, Russification, and revolutionary agitation rippled out from the metropolitan core to the periphery, where they combined in an explosive mixture. On the periphery, reform proved to be the weakest of these impulses. There the emancipation of the serfs, the reform of local government, and the introduction of a Western-style court system proceeded at a much slower pace. At times they occasioned greater violence as well. The *zemstvo* system was never introduced into the borderlands, for fear that local government would fall into the hands of the nationalists. After the first genuinely free empire-wide elections to the first and second Dumas returned strongly nationalist delegations from the borderlands, the government made certain in the coup of 7 June to substantially reduce representation from these areas in the new electoral law. But the most serious discrepancies in legislation between the core and the periphery came over the agrarian question.

Outside the Great Russian core, ethnic differences between landlords and peasants complicated emancipation and land reform. The government frequently found itself forced to balance the need to retain the loyalty of local elites against the pressures to alleviate the plight of the rebellious peasants. The Polish revolt in 1863 forced the government to accelerate the process of emancipation in the provinces of

Lithuania (Litva), Belarus, and Right-Bank Ukraine. In order to blunt the appeal of the radical wing of the Polish national movement, which called for immediate transfer to the peasants, without compensation, of all the land they cultivated, the autocracy drove a wedge between the Polish landowners and Russian peasants with promises of favorable redemption terms. They succeeded in nipping in the bud the large-scale peasant disturbance that threatened their entire position in the western provinces and deprived the Polish national movement of its mass base.[26]

In the Transcaucasus, emancipation came later and more slowly. The peasant reform commenced in Georgia in 1864–65 and in Armenia and present day Azerbaijan only in 1870. But compared with the Russian core provinces, the terms of the legislation were more conservative. In Georgia the local middling and lesser nobles disregarded their own aristocratic leaders, who had close ties to St. Petersburg, and staged a veritable *fronde* against the state. The government, its hands tied by a real revolution in the Kingdom of Poland, made concessions. The peasants received their personal freedom but not the land. There was no limit set on the temporary obligatory period, so that the landlords were able to keep the peasants in semi-servile status as long as they wished. Compulsory redemption for the Transcaucasus in general was not introduced until 1912, thirty years later than in Russia.[27] Harsh policies produced polarization: during the revolution of 1905 and in the elections to the first Duma, the Transcaucasus turned out to be one of the most radical regions in the entire empire.

A similar outcome retarded the development of peasant proprietors in the Baltic provinces. Freed without land under Alexander I, the Estonian and Latvian peasants lost an opportunity to acquire a farmstead when on the eve of the emancipation in Russia the Baltic nobles persuaded Alexander II to leave them in full possession of the land. The status quo remained in effect until 1917. Once again the autocracy opted to placate its allies among the regional nobility at the expense of the depressed agriculturalists.[28] And once again the government reaped the whirlwind in 1905 and 1917, when the peasantry, antagonized on both ethnic and economic grounds, took its revenge.

In the 1860s Russification was transformed into a popular cause by the conjuncture of three fortuitous events: the Polish rebellion, the rise of a mass press, and the relaxation of government censorship. In the hands of powerful press lords like M.N. Katkov, cultural policy, which had been a monopoly of the church and ministries, became a matter of public debate. Katkov was able to steady a shaky and uncertain government and rally opinion behind a strong nationalistic policy at a critical moment. The regime could hardly object. But when Katkov, Ivan Aksakov, and others attempted to apply Russification indiscriminately to all regions on the periphery, including the officially protected species of Baltic German nobles, then deep splits developed within the bureaucracy itself.[29]

Until the end of the reforming generation in 1881 there were still proconsuls like Bariatinskii in the Caucasus and K.P. von Kaufman in Turkestan who sought to compromise with the indigenous cultural institutions so long as they posed no threat to Russian rule. "We must introduce Russian Christian civilization into the Turkestan region," von Kaufman recommended in the early seventies, "but must not attempt to impose the Orthodox faith upon the native population. . . . Only public education can conquer a region morally; neither arms nor legislation can do this."[30] In the protectorates of Bukhara and Khiva, the last of the Central Asian khanates to fall under Russian control, the Russian government was even less inclined during the first decade of its rule to intervene directly in local affairs. But the pressure was mounting within the government and the educated public to move in a different direction.

Under Alexander III the Russifiers, led by the procurator of the Holy Synod, K.P. Pobedonostsev, and Prince V.P. Meshcherskii, gained ground in their struggle with conservative nobles and reformers over two crucial issues: colonization and cultural policy. For the first time they were able to take advantage of direct support from the tsar himself. But their empire-wide campaign also stimulated an ethnic backlash among the non-Russian populations of the littoral, many of which had not developed a strong sense of national identity under an imperial regime that at its worst had never been systematic in pursuing a policy of Russification. For the Finns, Baltic peoples, Armenians, Jews, and Tatar Muslims, it was the era of national awakening. Side by side with regionally based national movements, there appeared for the first time programs appealing to certain ethnic-religious groups scattered throughout the empire. Zionism and Jadidism were the two most prominent. It is hardly coincidental that the first Zionist declaration, Leon Pinsker's Auto-Emancipation, and the first program of reform Pan-Turkism, Ismail Bey Gaspirali's *The Muslims of Russia,* appeared within a year of one another and at the very time, 1881–82, when the new avatar of Russification, Alexander III, had come to the throne.[31]

In the meantime, the pace of Russian colonization increased rapidly after the end of temporary obligatory status and the abolition of the poll tax in the early 1880s removed the joint responsibility for taxes that had for so long bound the Russian peasants to the commune in the overpopulated core provinces. The trans-Siberian and Central Asian railroads, built mainly for strategic and economic purposes, became the conduits for the great surge of migration to the east. The government attempted to control and direct the flow in order to avoid conflict with the indigenous population and provide them with adequate water and grazing lands. But unauthorized colonization overwhelmed their best efforts. Again and again the government had to accept faits accomplis. In Kazakhstan, for example, in-migration had already begun in the sixties but gained momentum rapidly after the famine of 1891–92 drove desperate peasants into the steppe lands. Within a few years the Russian peasantry owned all the agricultural land of the region, although they constituted only 10 percent of the population.[32] Stolypin's colonization program exerted further pressure on the Kazakhs, who were gradually deprived of their best pastureland and driven back into the desert. In the years 1909–13 they suffered a net population loss of 9 percent. The great Kazakh rebellion of 1916, though sparked by a military labor draft, was not unconnected with this demographic disaster.[33]

In the Transcaucasus, Russian colonization assumed great importance in the eyes of the governor-general, Prince G.S. Golitsyn, as a means of preventing local Armenian capitalists from becoming the dominant landholders in the region. A determined Russifier, Golitsyn proposed the establishment of a Land Bank to attract settlers from the Russian core provinces. He was also the driving force behind the campaign to divert the education fund of the Armenian Gregorian Church in order to pay for Russian-language schools in the Caucasus educational district. When the Armenians responded by a public boycott of law courts and public administration, the government countered by encouraging Azeri Muslims to attack and despoil the Armenians. By early 1905 a guerrilla war had broken out between the two ethnic groups in the area of mixed villages.[34]

In the Baltic provinces, administrative and cultural Russification ran into difficulties both at home and abroad. The German government protested against arbitrary treatment of the Baltic nobility. Within the region the controversy over the language question in the schools broadened into a three-way struggle, which for the first time involved a nationally conscious Estonian and Latvian intelligentsia. The government, caught between two ethnic fires, was forced to temper its Russifying zeal. It had not been able to do what alone could have assured it victory in the struggle over the schools, namely, to attract Russian colonists into the region.[35] By the end of the imperial period none of the three contending parties for cultural hegemony in the Baltic provinces was satisfied with the results of half a century of conflict.

Russification not only engendered its opposite, nationalism, but also helped to foster revolutionary agitation within the imperial borderlands. A wholly unexpected consequence of assimilationist policies was to expose the non-Russian educated elites to the subversive doctrines of the Russian intelligentsia, mainly through the medium of Russian universities. As the most striking example, the leading exponents of both populism and Marxism among the Finnish, Jewish, Baltic, and Transcaucasian intelligentsia were to be found among the most Russified elements of the population. In Armenia the three founders of the Armenian Revolutionary Federation (Dashnaktsutiun) were graduates of Russian universities. Their party absorbed the teachings of the Narodnaia volia and subsequently associated itself with the Russian Socialist Revolutionaries. The leader of the early Transcaucasian social democrats, Noa Zhordaniia, received his political education from Herzen in London. The radicalization of the Jewish intelligentsia was also closely related to the process of assimilation, in particular to opportunities for Jewish youth to study in Russian universities.[36] In 1905 the tsarist autocracy reaped the whirlwind of its errant cultural sowing.

The intensity and violence of the revolution of 1905 on the periphery of European Russia was first remarked upon by Martov and Lenin, but there has been no satisfactory answer to explain why this should have been so. To be sure, the combination of ethnic and class conflict was highly volatile, especially in industrial pockets of Latvia (Riga), the Polish provinces (Łódz and Warsaw), and Ukraine (Donbass). But in Georgia the uprising was overwhelmingly peasant, reflecting the long delay in the implementation of agrarian reform.[37] To add complexity to the picture, counterrevolutionary outbreaks took the form of workers' pogroms in the Donbass and clashes between Armenians and Azeris in Baku, both industrial centers with mixed ethnic populations.[38] The variety of regional responses to the crisis within the autocracy reveals the uneven, confused, and contradictory nature of the government's policies toward the periphery. The irony lies in the fact that Russian policies toward the borderlands were often inspired by the most benevolent intentions—Catherine's colonization projects and religious toleration, Alexander I's "constitutional projects," Alexander II's reforms, not to speak of individual proconsuls like Richelieu, Vorontsov, von Kaufman, and others. Yet even when led by a strong personality, the political structures of the autocracy were not well suited to coordinate interlocking problems such as industrialization, colonization, and cultural assimilation in the borderlands.

As we have seen, none of the rulers after Catherine conducted a consistent policy toward the periphery. In the absence of a decisive and activist figure on the throne, as occurred in the last decades of the monarchy, the crosscurrents of reform, Russification, and revolutionary agitation became too strong for the ship of state to navigate. To develop its military and industrial strength the government permitted or encouraged large manufacturing enterprises to be established in the borderlands, where there was already a history of political instability. But the advantages of drawing on a skilled workforce and local natural resources overcame political misgivings. Similarly, the disruptive effects of railroad construction on patterns of settlement were never given proper consideration. Attempts at cultural assimilation proved counterproductive, first when the ruling elites were co-opted, Russified, and lost to the government as effective instruments of its rule in the borderlands, second when the intellectual elites of the borderlands were educated in Russian universities and exposed to the subversive doctrines of populism and Marxism, and finally when, in the pre-1905 decades, harsh Russification was discontinued before it fulfilled its aims but not before it deeply antagonized local elites, unleashing a powerful backlash that spawned conspiracies wherever national feelings were highly developed, and arousing national feelings where none had existed previously.

In addition to Russia's institutional poverty, there was no well-articulated or fully conceived theory of the state (*gosudarstvennost'*). Various attempts to provide something like a moral or constitutional order, from Catherine's *Nakaz* and a Legislative Assembly through Speranskii's abortive reforms of the Fundamental Laws of 1906, failed to provide the autocracy with any raison d'être aside from the fact of its own existence.

There was no positive Russian theory of imperialism, not even the equivalent of a White Man's Burden, and only the faintest scent of a "civilizing mission." At times the autocracy appeared to certain ethnic groups on the periphery as a repressive force; at other times it appeared to different groups to represent a liberator or at least a protector. But by the end it had lost whatever elements of the latter it had possessed and had become a "prison of peoples," intellectually bankrupt and lacking any form of political legitimacy over a periphery largely held in place by force.

In foreign relations the crisis of 1905 ushered in a new phase in Russia's relations with its borderlands. Up to the end of the eighteenth and beginning of the nineteenth century, Russia's main rivals for control of the contested zone of the Eurasian steppe-deserts were the early modern bureaucratic empires—Ottoman, Safavid, Qing. Throughout most of the nineteenth century Great Britain attempted to check a further Russian advance into this zone by attempting to prop up the sagging bureaucratic empires or, failing that, to encourage the resistance of the indigenous peoples to Russian conquest. A third phase began in the late nineteenth and early twentieth centuries with the rise of two new powers on the flanks of Eurasia: Germany and Japan. Both had undergone late national awakening and internal unification and were seeking a prominent place in the international system; both were late industrializers seeking markets and opportunities for colonization. The Germans steadily penetrated the old British and French markets in Eastern Europe, the Balkans, and the Middle East. The Japanese expanded their economic penetration of Korea, Manchuria, and North China. By the eve of World War I, small but influential elements in the German ruling elites envisaged territorial expansion to the east in the event of a war with Russia. Once the war broke out, the Pan-Germans, in league with military leaders, developed a program of detaching Russia's western borderlands, creating an immense Mitteleuropa economic zone and thrusting Russia back to its pre-Petrine boundaries.[39] The Japanese had already challenged Russia for control over Korea and southern Manchuria in 1904–5. Although the Japanese were then willing to divide northwestern Asia into spheres of influence, they took the opportunity of Russia's defeat and the 1917 revolution to develop a program similar to that of the Germans for the detachment of the far-eastern borderlands that, if successful, would have lost Russia all of Transbaikal.[40] After a short hiatus and a change of regimes, the great three-way contest over the periphery resumed in the 1930s with the Japanese seizure of Manchuria and the German advance into Eastern Europe. World War II was the last episode in the third phase of struggle over the borderlands.

Throughout this period, 1904–45, Russia's relations with Germany and Japan alternated between negotiations for a peaceful resolution of the contest over the borderlands through establishing mutually acceptable spheres of influence and armed struggle. Leadership was the deciding factor in choosing one course over the other.

What is the historical legacy of Russia's struggle to dominate its periphery? It seems to me that it is possible to draw some tentative conclusions, but as we all know, history teaches many lessons and leaves open different options. Having observed one historically determined outcome suddenly be thoroughly discredited, one should hesitate to erect another in its place. Much has been written about the divisive and destructive features of national and ethnic rivalries in the contemporary world. There is no good purpose to be served in attempting to deny or discount the force of these sentiments in the states of the former Soviet Union. The purpose of these concluding remarks is to point out a number of mitigating factors that suggest the possibility of an alternative scenario to the outbreak of civil war and anarchy along the new periphery of the Russian state.

1. The myth of unlimited Russian expansionism deserves a final interment. There is no foundation for a belief in Russian messianism. There was no imperial plan either for expanding or administering the empire. The struggle over the borderlands was, in all three phases, a multistate competition among the flank powers over the legacy of the declining steppe empires. The absence of this great power rivalry in the contemporary setting is reassuring.

2. Imperial Russia's security interests in the borderlands involved a complex interaction between domestic and foreign policy. Because of the existence of arbitrary linear boundary lines drawn through ethnically mixed frontier zones, there was always the danger that internal rebellion would invite foreign intervention or, conversely, that foreign invasion would spark internal rebellions. This situation has undergone a radical transformation. Russia still shares ethnically mixed frontier zones with most of the successors states, which now constitute the outer borderlands, but the situation is quite the reverse of the imperial

period. Now it is the Russian minorities who live across the frontier from their countrymen.

3. Colonization of the borderlands by the center, whether government sponsored or spontaneous, did not involve only Russians, and many of the Russian speakers were culturally distinctive, like the Cossacks, or even socially deviant, like the sectarians and Old Believers. Consequently, the colonists never developed a settler mentality like that of the *pieds noirs* in Algeria or the Boers in South Africa. With the exception of the Cossacks, who were state servitors, they lacked their own organizations or even a sense of distinctive cultural identity. This has slowed, if not prevented, the emergence of a cohesive Russian political opposition to the governments of the successor states.

4. In tsarist Russia there was no popular base for imperialism. Relations with the periphery were largely the preserve of a small number of officials. Only rarely did the issue of Russification become popular, and then only in response to privileged groups, like the Baltic German nobility, or openly disloyal elements, like the Poles. The concept of empire meant little to the mass of the population. When given an opportunity to express their views in the most direct political fashion, as in 1905–6 and again in 1917, the bulk of the population assumed an anti-imperialist stance. The idea of empire does not seem to have sunk deep roots since that time. The absence of such a tradition is another source of optimism in considering the future of Russia's relations with the borderlands.

5. The pattern of ethnic conflict between Russians and non-Russians in the imperial period is more complex, although here too the historical record has a bright side to it. There was a long tradition of resistance to conquest and rebellion against Russian domination by the peoples of the borderlands. But with remarkably few exceptions, mainly taking place during periods of collapse of central authority as in 1917–19, there was little evidence of communal warfare between non-Russians and Russians.

With the exception of the extreme right-wing parties, after 1905 the overwhelming majority of Russian political organizations were multiethnic in composition. (The Black Hundreds were, despite their notoriety, never more than a small and ultimately ineffectual movement.) This tradition also survived into the Soviet period. Although there were cases in which the tradition was brutally violated, it was never repudiated in principle or altogether abandoned in fact. Taken together, these conclusions suggest that historically speaking there are grounds for an alternative outcome that avoids widespread, endemic civil war throughout the borderlands. Perhaps the best that can be expected is that the experience of the past will contribute to an understanding on the part of both the center and the periphery that the level of violence that already exists must be held down to the point where there is space and time for Russians and non-Russians of the borderlands to negotiate the establishment of a new political order in Eurasia.

Notes

1. The center–periphery dichotomy, which has a dynamic implication, seems to me preferable to the more static and unidimensional concept of littoral, which has the further disadvantage of suggesting its traditional meaning of a shore, most often of a sea.

2. For a more detailed explanation of these factors, see Alfred J. Rieber, "Persistent Factors in Russian Foreign Policy," in *Imperial Russian Foreign Policy*, ed. Hugh Ragsdale (New York: Cambridge University Press, 1993).

3. I use the term "borderlands" in two ways: first, to define the contested area between the great bureaucratic empires of the early modern and modern period; second, to define the territories within this region that were incorporated into the Russian, Habsburg, Ottoman, Persian, and Chinese empires and became part of their periphery. They can be distinguished by the modifiers "outer" and "inner," but for the most part I have simply used "borderlands" to indicate both varieties.

4. Edward A. Allworth, *The Modern Uzbeks* (Stanford: Hoover Institution Press, 1990), p. 59.

5. My understanding of frontier zones owes much to Owen Lattimore, *Studies in Frontier History: Collected Papers, 1928–1958* (London: Oxford University Press, 1962).

6. Robert E. Jones, "Runaway Peasants and Russian Motives for the Partitions of Poland," in Ragsdale, ed., *Imperial Russian Foreign Policy*, pp. 204–31.

7. Anthony L.H. Rhinelander, *Prince Michael Vorontsov: Viceroy to the Tsar* (Montreal: McGill-Queen's University Press, 1990), p. 135.

8. S.E. Tolybekov, *Kochevoe obshchestvo kazakhov v XVII–nachale XX veka: Politiko-ekonomicheskii analiz* (Alma-Ata, 1971), pp. 262–67. Although polemical in tone, this work provides useful summaries of the historiographical controversies over the absorption of the Kazakhs into the empire.

9. Chantal Lemercier-Quelquejay, "Cooptation of Elites of Kabarda and Daghestan in the Sixteenth Century," in *The North Caucasus Barrier: The Russian Advance Towards the Muslim World*, ed. Marie Bennigsen Broxup (New York: St. Martin's, 1992), p. 38.

10. Alexandre Bennigsen, "The Muslims of European Russia and the Caucasus," in *Russia in Asia: Essays on the Influence of Russia on the Asian*

Peoples, ed. Wayne S. Vucinich (Stanford: Hoover Institution Press, 1972), pp. 139–40.

11. Isabel de Madariaga, *Russia in the Age of Catherine the Great* (London: Weidenfeld and Nicolson, 1981) is the standard treatment now in English. But for the early period of Catherine's reign, N.D. Chechulin, *Vneshniaia politika Rossii v nachale tsarstvovaniia Ekateriny, 1762–1774* (St. Petersburg, 1896) remains unsurpassed.

12. Marc Raeff, *The Well-Ordered Police State: Social and Institutional Change Through Law: The Germanies and Russia, 1600–1800* (New Haven: Yale University Press, 1983); and *idem*,"The Well-Ordered Police State and the Development of Modernity in Seventeenth and Eighteenth-Century Europe," *American Historical Review*, vol. 80 (1975), pp. 1221–45. Cf. Isabel de Madariaga, "Sisters under the Skin," *Slavic Review*, vol. 41, no. 4 (winter 1982), pp. 26–28, who places greater emphasis on the French Lumières.

13. For a brilliant analysis of Catherine's policy in southern Russia, see Marc Raeff, "The Style of Russia's Imperial Policy and Prince G.A. Potemkin," in *Statesmen and Statecraft of the Modern West: Essays in Honor of Dwight E. Lee and H. Donaldson Jordan*, ed. Gerald Grob (Barre, MA: Barre Publishers, 1967), pp. 1–51.

14. Zenon Kohut, *Russian Centralism and Ukrainian Autonomy: Imperial Absorption of the Hetmanate, 1760s–1830s* (Cambridge: Harvard University Press, 1988).

15. John Klier, *Russia Gathers Her Jews: The Origins of the "Jewish Question" in Russia, 1772–1825* (De Kalb: University of Northern Illinois Press, 1986). This policy was consistently pursued by her successors: see Hans Rogger, *Jewish Policies and Right-wing Politics in Imperial Russia* (Berkeley: University of California Press, 1986).

16. Alan W. Fisher, *The Russian Annexation of the Crimea, 1772–1783* (Cambridge: Cambridge University Press, 1970); David M. Lang, *The Last Years of the Georgian Monarchy, 1658–1832* (New York: Columbia University Press, 1957).

17. For the Congress Kingdom, the best summary remains Szymon Ashkenzy, "Poland and the Polish Revolution," *Cambridge Modern History* (1907), vol. 10, pp. 445–74 (its vintage is itself a commentary on the state of the literature dealing with the periphery); for Finland, see John Wuorinen, *A History of Finland* (New York: Columbia University Press, 1965), chap. 4; for Bessarabia, see George F. Jewsbury, *The Russian Annexation of Bessarabia, 1774–1828* (Boulder: *East European Quarterly*, 1976), especially pp. 37–40 and 107–18.

18. Patricia Herlihy, *Odessa: A History, 1794–1914* (Cambridge: Harvard University Press, 1986), p. 34. See also E.I. Druzhinina, *Iuzhnaia Ukraina v 1800–1825 gg.* (Moscow: Nauka, 1970).

19. Druzhinina, E.I., *Iuzhnaia Ukraina v period krizisa feodalizma, 1825–1860 gg.* (Moscow: Nauka, 1981), pp. 35–36.

20. John L.H. Keep, *Soldiers of the Tsar: Army and Society in Russia, 1462–1874* (Oxford: Clarendon Press, 1985), pp. 276, 282–95; A.D. Ferguson, "The Russian Military Settlements, 1825–1866," in *Essays in Russian History: A Collection Dedicated to G. Vernadsky*, ed. A.D. Ferguson and A. Levin (Hamden, CT: Archon Books, 1964), pp. 109–28.

21. S.S. Uvarov, *Desiatiletie Ministerstva narodnogo prosveshcheniia, 1833–1843* (St. Petersburg, 1864), p. 39.

22. Edward C. Thaden, *Conservative Nationalism in 19th Century Russia* (Seattle: University of Washington Press, 1964).

23. Alfred J. Rieber, *Merchants and Entrepreneurs in Imperial Russia* (Chapel Hill: University of North Carolina Press, 1982).

24. Vartan Gregorian, "The Armenians and Russia," in Vucinich, ed., *Russia in Asia*, p. 180.

25. A.L. Zisserman, *Fel'dmarshal Kniaz' Aleksandr Ivanovich Bariatinskii, 1815–1879* (Moscow, 1890) contains much valuable material on the conquest and administration of the Caucasus. See also A.J. Rieber, *The Politics of Autocracy: The Letters of Alexander II to Fieldmarshal Prince A.I. Bariatinskii, 1857–1864* (Paris: Mouton, 1966).

26. P.A. Zaionchkovskii, *Provedenie v zhizn' krest'ianskoi reformy 1861 g.* (Moscow, 1958), pp. 365–72.

27. Ronald G. Suny, *The Making of the Georgian Nation* (Bloomington: Indiana University Press in association with Hoover Institution Press, 1988), p. 107. The standard Russian work on the agrarian question is S.L. Avaliani, *Krest'ianskii vopros v Zakavkaz'e*, 2 vols. (Odessa, 1912–14).

28. Edward C. Thaden, "The Russian Government," in *Russification in the Baltic Provinces and Finland, 1855–1914*, ed. Edward C. Thaden (Princeton: Princeton University Press, 1981), pp. 37–38.

29. For Katkov see V.A. Tvardovskaia, *Ideologiia poreformennogo samoderzhaviia: M.N. Katkov i ego izdaniia* (Moscow: Nauka, 1978).

30. David MacKenzie, "Kaufman of Turkestan: An Assessment of His Administration, 1867–1881," *Slavic Review*, vol. 26, no. 2 (June 1967), p. 281.

31. Alan W. Fisher, "Ismail Gaspirali, Model Leader for Asia," in *Tatars of the Crimea: Their Struggle for Survival*, ed. Edward Allworth (Durham: Duke University Press, 1988), p. 17.

32. Manuel Sarisyanz, "Russian Conquest in Central Asia: Transformation and Acculturation," in Vucinich, ed., *Russia in Asia*, p. 251; Richard Pierce, *Russian Central Asia, 1867–1917: A Century of Colonial Rule* (Berkeley: University of California Press, 1960), pp. 118–21, 125–27. In Turkestan, by contrast, the irrigated lands were heavily populated by Uzbeks and other peoples, providing a natural check on colonization. Russian plans to expand the irrigated areas in order to open new lands were forestalled by World War I and only completed under the Soviet regime. Ibid., pp. 135–36.

33. Allworth, *Modern Uzbeks*, p. 160.

34. Gregorian, "Armenians and Russia," pp. 184, 215.

35. Michael H. Haltzel, "The Baltic Germans," in Thaden, ed., *Russification in the Baltic*, pp. 150–83.

36. Gregorian, "Armenians and Russia," pp. 212–13; Noah Zhordanija, *My Life* (Stanford: Hoover Institution, 1968), chap. 2; Robert J. Brym, *The Jewish Intelligentsia and Russian Marxism* (New York: Schocken Books, 1978), pp. 54–55.

37. Iulii Martov et al., *Obshchestvennoe dvizhenie v Rossii v nachale II veka* (St. Petersburg, 1909–1912), vol. 2, pt. 1, pp. 117–18; Teodor Shanin, *Russia 1905–1907: Revolution as a Moment of Truth* (New Haven: Yale University Press, 1986), vol. 2, pp. 66–70; Abraham Ascher, *The Revolution of 1905* (Stanford: Stanford University Press, 1988), vol. 1, pp. 152–60.

38. Charters Wynn, *Workers, Strikes and Pogroms: The Donbass-Dnepr Bend in Late Imperial Russia, 1870–1905* (Princeton: Princeton University Press, 1992), chap. 7; Tadeusz Swietochowski, *Russian Azerbaijan, 1905–1920: The Shaping of National Identity in a Muslim Community* (Cambridge: Cambridge University Press, 1985), pp. 38–46.

39. Immanuel Geis, *Der Polonische Grenzstreifen, 1914–1918* (Hamburg and Lubeck: Matthiesen, 1960); Fritz Fischer, *War of Illusions: German Policies from 1911–1914* (London: Chatto and Windus, 1975); and *idem, Germany's Aims in the First World War* (New York: W.W. Norton, 1967).

40. The most recent treatment based on fresh archival material is David MacLaren McDonald, *United Government and Foreign Policy in Russia, 1900–1914* (Cambridge: Harvard University Press, 1992); see also W.G. Beasley, *Japanese Imperialism, 1894–1945* (Oxford: Clarendon Press, 1987); and Hosoya Chihiro, "Japan's Policies Toward Russia," in *Japan's Foreign Policy, 1868–1941*, ed. James William Morley (New York: Columbia University Press, 1974).

II

The Western
Newly Independent States

5

National Identity and Foreign Policy in the Baltic States

Romuald J. Misiunas

Historical Interaction with and Perceptions of Neighbors

Throughout their half-century existence as Soviet republics, the three Baltic states formed a distinct region in the USSR. In spite of—or perhaps even because of—official propaganda, indigenous self-perceptions focused on their differences from rather than on their similarities to the rest of the Soviet Union. Historically, they had always been a part of the West European cultural realm. They constituted the only region of the erstwhile empire to have experienced a period of genuine independence in modern times, existing throughout the interwar period as internationally recognized states. The circumstances of their occupation and absorption into the USSR in 1940 continued throughout the postwar period to bedevil Soviet efforts at securing genuine allegiance by the Baltic peoples and international recognition of their status as component entities of the USSR.

Their Soviet experience unmistakably colors the contemporary national identities of the three Baltic peoples and affects the formulation of their internal as well as external policies. One of the many ironies of Soviet development is that in practice it frequently served to foster precisely those aspects of human social life that communist ideology classified among the negative remnants of the past. One such area is national identity. In many respects, the period of Soviet occupation strengthened nationalism among the Baltic peoples to a degree it never would have attained under independent political existence. It has become difficult for modern Westerners to fathom the intensity of Baltic nationalism as a fountainhead for policies that to many outsiders appear rigid and unrealistic in a world where a pragmatic approach and compromise are considered hallmarks of modernity, and where abstract principle and right are not infrequently equated with unconstructive stubbornness. Yet such strong nationalism is unquestionably a product of their Soviet experience.

The Balts overwhelmingly evaluate the Soviet period in their histories in a negative light, as an anomaly rather than as a natural development. While some positive facets do have to be admitted, such become, as a rule, interpreted as having been achieved under hard conditions of occupation rather than as beneficial results of Soviet rule. Until the very end, the official canon maintained that in spite of some unfortunate mistakes and deviations in Stalin's time, the standard of living in all three Baltic republics had risen as a result of their membership in the Soviet family of nations. Such claims failed to secure internal resonance. Measured against the rest of the inner empire, their condition was indeed the best. However, the average Balt was considerably more inclined to measure his lot against that of Western Europe and considerably better able than most other Soviet citizens to do so. And here, any comparison proved detrimental to Soviet efforts. For instance, in 1939, the standard of living in Estonia had been at par with, or perhaps even slightly higher than, that of Finland. An effort by a Soviet propagandist Vladimir Petrov, *Dva berega—dva obraza zhizni* (Two Shores—Two Ways of Life) (Tallinn, 1984), provides a rather pitiful example of an official attempt to demonstrate why life a mere decade ago was so much better in Estonia than in Finland. And that was being done under circumstances where Finnish television broadcasts reached the greater part of Estonia, providing graphic comparisons to the contrary. The pervasiveness of negative evaluations of Soviet power has contributed significantly to popular self-perception that tends to accentuate the underlying differences between the Baltic peoples and the remainder of the former Soviet Union, especially Russia.

The process of state building—the establishment of the political, social, and cultural structures of the Baltic states—is unequivocally predicated on two general assumptions. The first is that the Baltic states are merely reestablishing their sovereign national existence after a long period of occupation. They tend to view themselves less as having been the vanguard of the dissolution of the Soviet state; rather, they seek to stress the fact that they had never de jure formed a part of the USSR in the first place. Such status as occupied countries continued to be recognized by most Western countries throughout the postwar period. It even came to be accepted by a moribund USSR in September 1991, a few months before its extinction. A clear resentment continues to be expressed by Baltic leaders at any Russian reference to the "new Baltic states."

The second general assumption by most Balts is a near-universal identification of all matters Soviet with Russia and Russians. The entire gamut of negative association with the Soviet past has automatically been transposed onto Russia as well. Fear of Russia and of Russians clearly continues to constitute the dominant leitmotif in the foreign and internal policies of all three Baltic nations. It is perhaps somewhat more acute in Estonia, where the indigenous ethnic portion of the population has shrunk to around 60 percent from a prewar figure of around 90 percent, and in Latvia, which is barely half Latvian. However, even in Lithuania, which remains 79 percent Lithuanian, fear and mistrust of Russia continue to color attitudes among a significant portion of the local population.

Negative perceptions of Russia and Russians have historical roots. Russian expansion into the region dates from the sixteenth century, almost from the very beginning of the appearance of a centralized Russian political entity. Estonia and most of Latvia fell under Russian control in the beginning of the eighteenth century. Eastern Latvia and most of Lithuania were incorporated into the Russian Empire in 1795.

In general the three Baltic peoples do not tend to view their historical experience within the Russian Empire in a favorable light. In Estonia and Latvia, the first century of Russian rule was a period of significant strengthening of the institution of serfdom. As a result, the Estonians and Latvians generally consider the preceding Swedish period during the seventeenth century a sort of golden age. For Lithuanians, incorporation into the Russian Empire signified the demise of their historic state.

To a large degree, however, Russian cultural pressure in the region did not become pronounced until the second half of the nineteenth century. At that time it coincided with the development of modern national self-identity among the three Baltic peoples. The Estonians, Latvians, and Lithuanians are ancient peoples, but their modern national identities are relatively young. Estonians and Latvians, overrun by crusading German knights in medieval times, never developed political entities prior to the twentieth century. The Lithuanians can look back to a medieval empire that included all of present-day Belarus and a good portion of Ukraine. However, while such past grandeur can and does in many ways serve as an inspiration for Lithuanian national self-identity, the direct link between the old state and the modern Lithuanian nation has been severed in two important respects. The old political entity ceased to exist at the end of the eighteenth century. By that time, the cultural elite of the Lithuanian state had become overwhelmingly Polonized. The old noble families invariably came to consider themselves Poles. Like its Estonian and Latvian counterparts, modern Lithuanian national identity, also appearing among an upwardly mobile educated elite with peasant roots, dates from the nineteenth century. However, the consciousness of past grandeur did and continues to fuel national identity to a significant degree. Lithuanians tended to view the interwar republic as a restoration of their old state. For a long period Lithuania had been the principal rival of Muscovy for hegemony over the East Slav lands. Soviet conditions rendered historiography on the old Lithuanian state a sensitive and problematic undertaking. It was virtually impossible to reconcile Lithuanian perceptions of their national past with official tenets in which Muscovy figured as a glorious precursor of a grand Soviet present. Changed circumstances during the late 1980s allowed an efflorescence of publication on historic topics, much of it reprints of prewar works.

In their initial stages, the Baltic national renaissances had not been directed primarily against Russian cultural influence. In Estonia and Latvia the German nobility, and to a lesser extent the Lutheran Church, provided the primary social and cultural obstacle to a rising native middle class. In Lithuania, the analogous process was directed against an indigenous Polonized nobility supported, at least initially, by a Catholic Church establishment. In both cases the tsarist government, seeking to further integrate the Baltic region into a centralized imperial structure, became a de facto ally of the emerging Baltic native elites. Most practical measures sought to decrease the position of the old German and Polonized nobilities of the area. Such development was particularly marked in Lithuania, where the tsarist administration considered the Polonized gentry the primary obstacle to its designs. As a result, in the aftermath of the abolition of serfdom in 1861, the tsarist government actively promoted the development of a class of independent farmers. The expectation was that these would form a loyal rural bulwark for the regime. Instead, this class provided the social base for the development of a nationally conscious Lithuanian intelligentsia. By the 1880s, however, the Russification policies of the tsarist government, which accompanied its efforts at transformation of the empire into a modern Russian nation-state, aroused significant anti-Russian feeling as well. Cultural Russification was most pronounced in Lithuania, where during the period between 1864 and 1904, the tsarist government, in an extremely ill-conceived effort, proscribed the publication of works in the Lithuanian language printed in the Latin alphabet.

The simultaneous collapse of the Russian and German empires during World War I enabled the emergence of the three modern Baltic nation states. Although independence was secured from Russian rule, on the whole, anti-Russian sentiment among the Baltic peoples remained relatively circumscribed throughout the interwar period of independence. The primary problem in Estonia and Latvia was posed by the residue of wealth and influence among the German nobility. An abortive Communist coup in Estonia in 1924 adumbrated what would transpire sixteen years later. The fear of Soviet Russia never abated entirely. However, the mutual benefit for the USSR on the one hand and for Estonia and Latvia on the other, of transit trade through Baltic ports took precedence over political considerations. In Lithuania, the principal threat to national existence was perceived as coming from Poland rather than from the USSR. Indeed, the Soviet Union consistently tended, for its own reasons, to support Lithuania in its quest for its historic capital, Vilnius, which had been seized by Poland in 1920. In general, all three Baltic states enjoyed reasonably good relations with the USSR until the outbreak of World War II.

The building of nation-states after World War I went relatively smoothly, though not without difficulty. Estonia and Latvia enacted extensive land reform that created a body of free farmers, who formed the backbone of society. There was less need for land reform in Lithuania, as that had already to a large extent been achieved under tsarist rule. Lithuania, considerably more so than its two northern neighbors, was a peasant society of free farmers. Economic and social difficulties led to the emergence of national authoritarian regimes in all three countries. But these were rather mild dictatorships of a conservative nature, differing significantly from some of the more radical mass-movement regimes that emerged in major countries such as Germany and Italy.

The experience of the first year of Soviet occupation in 1940–41, especially the mass deportations on the eve of the war, clearly changed the perceptions of the Baltic peoples. Soviet internationalism, the policy of repression of Baltic national identity pursued by the Soviet government, came clearly to be identified with Russification in the minds of the Baltic populations. As a result the Germans, who especially in Estonia and Latvia had been the traditional enemy, came to be welcomed as liberators in all three countries in 1941. The reality of German occupation practices dampened such attitudes somewhat. Nevertheless, apart from the Jews and certain other minorities who were targeted for extermination, the bulk of the indigenous populations considered the Germans the lesser of two evils. The postwar Soviet repression that accompanied collectivization, and even more extensive deportations in 1948–49, ingrained such attitudes even further. These occurred in the period of high Stalinism and were imbued with a highly visible Russianizing content.

The policies of the Soviet government throughout the postwar period reinforced the perception of a threat to the very national existence of the three peoples. Rightly or wrongly, development of large-scale industrial projects came to be considered, especially in Estonia and Latvia, a conscious effort on the part of the Russians to dilute and even perhaps extinguish altogether the indigenous national identities through the rapid introduction of unassimilable immigrant laborers, for the most part Russians, who were viewed mostly as boorish louts. Baltic attitudes can be said to be analogous to contemporary German views of Turkish *gastarbeiter*, French views of North African immigrants, or British views of Pakistanis. The situation was aggravated by the fact that the immigrants represented the ruling nation.

The overt Russifying element accompanying Soviet cultural management reinforced such attitudes. Fifty years of Soviet social engineering have successfully inculcated a deep sense of resentment of Russia and all things Russian among the indigenous Baltic ethnic groups. Throughout the postwar period it served to provoke all sorts of reactions. The pervasiveness of indiscriminate hatred of Russians is not hard to discern in all three countries. It appears perhaps most overtly in Estonia, where the two communities live largely apart. The situation resembles Belfast or Beirut. Narva and the northeast have become overwhelmingly Russian in settlement. Estonians have acquired a reputation of frequent refusal to speak Russian. Matters appear somewhat better in Latvia, where there is considerably more intermingling. Immigrant Russians in Lithuania, who are not nearly as numerous, are largely concentrated in three areas: Vilnius, Klaipeda, and Ignalina. Soviet reality created a vicious circle. Local resistance, overt or implicit, served merely to engender increased efforts at Russification.

A fundamental anti-Russian sentiment among the indigenous Baltic populations provides a key component in the formulation of policies of these newly independent states. It is complemented by a basic pervasive mistrust of all Russians and Russian intentions. Such evaluations are not limited to Russians on the scene but are imputed to Russians in Russia itself. And it has become extremely difficult for many not to ascribe underlying imperialist designs in virtually any and all Russian moves. Even positive Russian figures are frequently perceived as closet imperialists who are only acting the way they do because of dire circumstances in Russia itself. Yeltsin, for instance, is generally viewed by Balts in a favorable light. Resolutions of support for him have even been passed in Baltic parliaments. However, he appears either as an exception or as someone guided by practical political considerations that happen to coincide with Baltic interests.

Such attitudes are not infrequently accompanied by feelings of insecurity and impotence. Baltic independence is sometimes considered as much a product of Russian decline as of national resolve. And its preservation depends on international recognition. The realization among the thinking element that it is impossible to maintain independence single-handedly without broad foreign support, and that the region is basically economically dependent on Russia and the rest of the Commonwealth of Independent States (CIS), frequently only aggravates the desire to maximize distance and to minimize contact.

The generalizations about Russia and Russians are somewhat, though not entirely, transposed to Belarus, the other CIS member bordering two of the Baltic countries. Perhaps unjustly so, Belarus has frequently come to be identified by Balts as little more than an appendage of Russia. Until very recently, Lithuania, whose longest land border with any neighbor is with Belarus, did not maintain any formal representation in Minsk, which geographically is the closest foreign capital to Vilnius. Such a state of affairs varies significantly from Lithuanian historic tradition. Belarus formed part of the old Lithuanian state and shares the white horseman on its coat of arms. As now appears likely, however, if Belarus does indeed emerge with a clearly distinctive non-Russian identity, relations are bound to become closer, especially as Belarus will most probably become a significant trading partner. Recently the Belarus government expressed an interest in routing its international telephone communications through the new transmission facility in Kaunas, Lithuania.

The only land border that the Baltic states have with a non-CIS state is the approximately 100-kilometer Lithuanian border with Poland. Lithuanian-Polish relations have been somewhat problematic. For four centuries the Lithuanian state was linked with Poland, first dynastically through common sovereigns and subsequently in a commonwealth analogous to Scotland in the United Kingdom. After World War I, Polish-Lithuanian relations were largely inimical. The dispute was over the historical capital of Lithuania and its surrounding region, which had been seized by the Poles in 1920. Culturally, modern Lithuanian nationalism consisted of an effort at divorce from Polish influence. Popular Lithuanian perceptions of Poles resemble those by the Irish for the English. Although to a large extent historical, residues of negative feelings for Poles and a fear of Polish influence remain among many Lithuanians. The problems with the Polish minority in the southeast (not contiguous to the Polish frontier), although largely exaggerated and probably of KGB provenance (analogous to that in Trans-Dniestria) have tended to reinforce such attitudes. Polish interest, for the most part private, in supporting the Polish minority is generally viewed suspiciously by many Lithuanians.

Overall, the Polish government cannot be faulted for any anti-Lithuanian moves. The border crossings between the two countries, however, have presented nightmares. Pictures of long lines, several days' wait, and requisite bribery of officials on both sides abound. Poland claims not to be able to afford expanding the border points and is moreover genuinely afraid of swarms of immigrants from the east who can at present also pass rather easily through Lithuania. Moreover, the road systems on both sides of the border are not sufficiently developed for the amount of traffic currently passing through. Recently agreement has been reached over several new border crossing points, and a rail connection is already operating.

It can be expected that relations between the two countries will improve considerably in the relatively near future. Efforts in that direction have been made by both sides. Poland will in all likelihood become an important trade partner for Lithuania, though less so for the two other Baltic states.

Finland has become a country with a very special relationship to Estonia. The kinship of language and the close geographic proximity made Finland Estonia's primary route to the outside world in many respects, cultural as well as economic, when the ferry connection between Tallinn and Helsinki was reestablished three decades ago. The Finnish connection has allowed Estonia to lead the other two Baltic states in communications and economic reorientation away from the CIS, and it can be expected that Finland will continue to play such a role in the future.

Scandinavian interest in the Baltic states is also natural in view of their historic links. Estonia and most of what is today Latvia were Swedish possessions in the seventeenth century. Estonia even had a Swedish minority until World War II. There are significant communities of Estonian and Latvian émigrés in Sweden, who had arrived at the end of World War II as refugees. The links to the Baltic are natural. The Scandinavian countries were particularly supportive of Baltic strivings for independence during the period preceding the August 1991 coup. Iceland was the first country to recognize Lithuania's independence and did so even before the coup in Moscow. Sweden was the first to open information offices, quasi-embassies, in each of the Baltic capitals. Both Denmark and Sweden supported analogous Baltic offices in their capitals. It can be expected that ties between the Baltics and these two countries will continue to expand, even with Lithuania, where the historic and cultural links are weaker. Denmark is one of the few countries in the West to allow Baltic citizens visa-free entry.

Another significant neighbor is Germany. German political, cultural, and commercial ties with the Baltic lands resemble those of Sweden in Estonia and Latvia. And one small portion of Lithuania, the Klaipeda area, was part of the Reich until the mid-twenties (and again in 1939–45). Indeed, one can already discern considerable competition between Germany and the Scandinavian countries for influence in all three Baltic countries. The two foreign hotels in Riga, the German-run Hotel de Rome and the Swedish-run Eurolink, can be presented as a microcosm of that rivalry. Likewise, Lufthansa and SAS are the only two major foreign airlines to fly into all three Baltic capitals. Like the Scandinavian countries, Germany was among the first to extend diplomatic recognition. Its missions in the three capital cities are among the largest. The lines of Balts outside the German consulates applying for visas certainly are. German tourists form the largest contingents of foreign visitors. The German commercial presence is clearly visible in all three countries, and it can be reasonably expected that, in time, the German economic presence will become preeminent. Culturally, the Scandinavian countries have a slight advantage over Germany. As a large country, Germany remains interested in promoting its own language abroad. The Scandinavians have already adopted English as their primary foreign language, and English has also unquestionably become for the Balts the first foreign language of choice.

Principal Questions in the Foreign Policies of the Baltic States

European Orientation and Minimizing Links with the CIS

The primary focus of Baltic foreign policy has been to underscore the European orientation of the three countries and to build up their Western ties. They have sought in every way possible to minimize identification and interaction with the CIS. Stressing their peculiar status within the USSR as occupied lands, they have been extremely sensitive to being included indiscriminately among the former Soviet republics in any and all international dealings and projects.

The downplaying of relations with the CIS was especially pronounced in Lithuania under Vytautas Landsbergis. Until very recently, the Lithuanians markedly maintained only a chargé d'affaires rather than an ambassador in Moscow. The appointee, Egidijus Bičkauskas, however, was a member of parliament, and is currently one of the deputy chairmen of the new parliament. The current ambassador, Romualdas Kozyrovičius, a former minister of material resources, clearly indicates that the post is considered important primarily for economic relations. Vilnius was also the last Baltic capital to receive a Russian ambassador. At present a Russian embassy there is still in the process of being set up.

Balts are particularly sensitive to any formulation that maintains or hints at a special relationship with Russia or the CIS. They have been particularly sensitive over Russian formulation of the concept "near abroad," which is viewed as an unabashed unwillingness to forsake hegemony and an effort to secure international sanction for intervention in the domestic affairs of the Baltic states. Landsbergis, then chairman of the Supreme Council of Lithuania, observed in his speech to the UN General Assembly on 28 September 1992 that phrases such as "near abroad" and "conflict" only indicate that old thinking is still very much alive in official Russian circles. He continued that there were no "conflicts" in the Baltic states, and that even the very use of the term merely helped to mask aggression in practice.

In view of their desire to distance themselves from the CIS as much as possible, the focus of the foreign policy activity of the Baltic states has concentrated on seeking as wide and as rapid an integration as possible into the formal structure of the international community. In this respect, they have had an advantage over the rest of the newly independent states of the former USSR. The long-standing nonrecognition de jure of their incorporation into the USSR by most Western countries and the remnants of the old diplomatic and consular services provided a rudimentary entree. Lithuania was in the forefront in this respect. In part it had a slight advantage over the other two in the greater number of surviving diplomatic and consular offices.[1] Lithuania, however, remains considerably behind the other two in utilizing émigré personnel in its diplomatic service and government bureaucracy. At present three ministers in the Estonian cabinet are also citizens of a Western country. The current Latvian ambassador in the United States gave up his U.S. citizenship in order to assume the post. The Latvian ambassador in Germany and Switzerland is an émigré who left Latvia in the 1970s. The Estonian ambassador-designate to the United States is likewise an American citizen willing to give up his citizenship.

Also, Landsbergis made it a personal point to travel widely, not only to Europe and North America but also to such places as Rio de Janeiro and Tokyo, and became especially noted for his frequent appearances at international functions. The underlying rationale for such activity was undoubtedly an effort to anchor a consciousness of Baltic independence in as wide a foreign circle as possible in a situation where future developments in Russia were instinctively viewed as potentially problematic. One Lithuanian politician told me personally that he expected a total breakdown in the east. Therefore the primary task of Lithuania, and by extension the other two Baltic lands, was to sever as many links as possible so as not to be dragged into the maelstrom. A similar point of view was expressed by Estonian Prime Minister Mart Laar in a press conference on 24 March 1993. A victory by Yeltsin's chief rival, Khasbulatov, in the power struggle then under way in Moscow could, Laar felt, have precipitated civil war that would easily have spread to the Baltic states as well. The final outcome of the political struggle in Russia remains unsettled.

Baltic efforts at integration into Europe are continuing. On 2 June 1993, the three heads of state met at Jurmala in Latvia and issued a communiqué that they were sending a request to the European Community for admission as associate members.[2] Disassociation in every possible way from the CIS is also being implemented in practical matters as rapidly as possible. The three Baltic countries were the first former Soviet states to take control over their borders and to replace the old Soviet passports of their citizens. All three have set up extensive systems of border control. Estonia was in the forefront of such developments. It was the first to introduce a visa requirement for CIS citizens. Latvia has followed suit. At the present, only Lithuania still admits CIS travelers and holders of old Soviet passports without a visa. Apparently the principal reason is the practical difficulty in sealing the extensive land border with Belarus. The policy of the new Lithuanian government for maintenance of established trade ties with the East also no doubt will influence this question. At present, visas from each of the three Baltic countries are valid for entry into all three. However, in view of the differing policies on citizens and residents of CIS countries, Estonia announced on 18 March 1993 a suspension of honoring Lithuanian and Latvian visas for passport holders of some countries. These appear to be CIS and Third World countries. One primary refugee and smuggling route from Asia to Germany and the Scandinavian countries runs through the CIS and the Baltic states. On 11 April 1993, over fifty Kurds were reported to have been detained by Lithuanian border guards. They arrived by train from Minsk.[3]

The physical contrast at the Baltic borders with the situation on the other side is marked. While Russia has established credible though somewhat makeshift border controls with Estonia and Latvia, the checkpoints between Lithuania and the Kaliningrad Oblast remain somewhat perfunctory. The Lithuanian side of the border on the principal road between Vilnius and Minsk is a sizable functioning operation. On the Belarus side, as of fall 1992, there was not even a checkpoint at entry. Two militiamen checked trunks of cars leaving Belarus for export of large quantities of subsidized products and did not even bother to check passports. Russian border guards control rail traffic into Estonia and Latvia. However, as late as fall 1992, there was no Belarusian control of trains between Vilnius and Moscow. Only the Lithuanians have set up border control points at the Vilnius station, and it remained possible to travel from Vilnius to Moscow without a visa from any CIS state. Likewise, flights from the Baltic to Kiev land at the domestic rather than the international airport, and passengers on them are not subjected to any Ukrainian immigration or customs control.

Another move underscoring separate identities from the CIS is the introduction of distinct international telephone country codes by each of the three Baltic countries, which now enjoy direct communications with the outside world that are no longer routed through Russia.

Although most former Soviet republics have or are in the process of introducing distinctive currencies, most of such money consists merely of locally printed surrogates for a rapidly depreciating ruble. Estonia was the first to introduce a genuine convertible currency, the kroon, tied to the deutsche mark. Defying all expectations, the value of the Estonian kroon has remained stable. Latvia followed suit in mid-1992, making its coupons, the Latvian ruble, sole legal tender in the country. In March 1993, it began to introduce its own currency, the lat, at a rate of two hundred Latvian rubles to one lat. The Latvian lat has actually appreciated in value against other currencies. The Lithuanian coupons became sole legal tender on 1 October 1992; however, unlike its northern neighbors, Lithuania, especially under its new Lithuanian Democratic Labor Party (LDLP) government, continued to extend credit and to print money. The resulting inflation, although considerably lower than that in Russia or Ukraine, delayed the introduction of its own currency. In May 1993, the Lithuanian government announced its intention to curb inflation through limits on credit emission. The following month, the new national currency, the litas, was introduced at the rate of one hundred coupons to one litas.

In spite of continuing efforts at disassociation, the economic ties established over half a century will undoubtedly continue to tie the three Baltic states to the former USSR. It is an economic necessity rather than an option. Although over time this might change, at present most of the goods produced in the Baltic are marketable primarily within the CIS. Likewise, the bulk of raw materials can only be imported from there. It is unlikely that these trade patterns can change rapidly. Such considerations underlie the pragmatic approach of the new Lithuanian government of maintaining and fostering old commercial ties within the CIS. Of the three, Estonia is making the most considerable strides to reorient its trade, especially to Finland and Sweden. Indeed, Finland has already overtaken the CIS as Estonia's principal trade partner. Estonian exports to the West already surpass those to the CIS. However, that may to a large extent be the result of the drop in production by many factories whose production had been oriented to the military sector.

At the moment, most everyday necessities of life remain subsidized in varying degrees, least in Estonia and most in Lithuania. The subsidies necessitate export controls, but the unevenness with which subsidies are lifted creates imbalances. In the spring of 1993, an effort had to be made to prevent Lithuanian bread from flowing into Latvia to be used as animal fodder. The problem apparently was resolved during a meeting of the Lithuanian and Latvian prime ministers in Riga on 17 April 1993, which concluded with a trade agreement between the two countries. Nevertheless, long delays at border crossings between the two countries continue to be reported.

Several items are now at or close to world prices. Most notable is gasoline. Lithuania's refinery at Mažeikiai has sufficient capacity for supplying the region. Once the planned new pipeline from the coast and a platform oil terminal are completed, Lithuanian dependence on the CIS for oil will cease. Estonia is already importing a significant portion of its fuel from outside the CIS. On 22 March 1993, the first part of the Muuga complex, with storage facilities for 4,000 cubic meters of fuel, became operational.[4]

All three Baltic countries remain entirely dependent on gas supplies from the CIS. And Lithuania needs to import fuel rods for its atomic facility at Ignalina. There is no alternative, in that rods of that particular design are not produced anywhere else.

Military Withdrawal

Closely interrelated with the perceived need to entrench independence, the evacuation of the former Soviet military as rapidly as possible has since the fall of 1991 unquestionably emerged as the primary task of foreign policy in all three countries. The Baltic position on the question has highlighted a legal anomaly. Since the USSR itself has acknowledged in September 1991 that the Baltic states had been occupied, the Soviet military units stationed on their territory had no legal basis for being there. Therefore, the Balts argue, they should be withdrawn immediately. Unlike the agreements with Poland and the GDR, the Soviet troops had invaded the Baltic lands. It could be argued that the Baltic states had, in the fall of 1939, agreed to limited Soviet military contingents on their territories. The response invariably has been yes, but even that was done under duress and, moreover, the ultimatums of mid-June 1940 voided those earlier agreements. In the course of negotiations over the practical implementation of withdrawal, Baltic negotiators have consistently refused to endorse any agreement that could in any way serve to provide a legal basis for the presence of the military of a foreign power on their soil. Publicly, leaders in all three countries have been adamant in this respect. Even the head of the former independent Lithuanian Communist Party, Algirdas Brazauskas, reiterated such a position in the aftermath of the unexpected victory of his party in the elections of fall 1992.

Although the Baltic demands for military withdrawal are based on the principle of international law, their primary rationales, expressed unofficially, are practical. First is the basic mistrust of long-term Russian intentions. As has already been noted, Balts generally tend to consider most Russians incorrigible imperialists who would if circumstances once again proved favorable, as in 1939–40, move to reincorporate their countries into a greater Russia. The military is perceived as being particularly saturated with individuals of such ilk. A second fear is over the possible practical spillover effects from turbulence in Russia, which would leave the units in effect independent. Local commanders could try to take control of the Baltic governments under a whole series of possible pretexts. Historical analogies appear in the activities of German units and the Baltic Germans in Latvia in 1919. The worst-case scenario envisages a total breakdown of military discipline and military gangs looting for survival.

Balts have proved extremely sensitive to various snags in the withdrawal process. They frequently consider the stated causes mere subterfuge to delay the process. There is also an ever-present tendency to impute Russian deception in trying to slip in extraneous matters. On 9 April 1993, during a visit to the Lithuanian parliament by Sergei Stepashin, head of the Russian parliament's Defense Committee,

Landsbergis protested a small detail in a Russian law that provided for hardship pay for officers serving in troubled areas. The Baltic states were included in the phrasing. Stepashin reportedly stated that the intent had been to raise the pay of Russian officers still stationed in the Baltics because of high prices there, not because of its being a troubled area, and promised to rectify the wording.

Although Balts in general have had very little sympathy for the material plight of Russian officers stationed in their countries, all three have expressed a pragmatic willingness to help in the construction of living quarters in Russia (including the Kaliningrad Oblast) if that were to speed withdrawal. On 29 March 1993, Russian Minister of Defense Pavel Grachev announced another suspension due to the insufficiency of housing for returnees. However, this announcement may have been more for internal consumption than as a statement of intent. In response, Estonian Minister of Defense Hain Rebas and his Lithuanian counterpart Audrius Butkevičius issued a joint statement of protest. Rebas offered help in building the necessary housing.[5]

Financing problems, however, have complicated such offers. On 2 June, Col. Valerii Nikitin, head of the construction department of the Baltic fleet, came to Tallinn with projects for construction in St. Petersburg, Narva, Pskov, Ostrog, and Ust' Luga. He was told by Estonian officials that the plans would have to postponed until sufficient funds could be found.[6]

Russia has only reached agreement with Lithuania on a specific timetable for withdrawal. On 8 September 1992, Butkevičius and his Russian counterpart Pavel Grachev signed an agreement according to which all Russian troops are to be gone by 31 August 1993. In general, Butkevičius has observed that the withdrawal is proceeding smoothly. Col. Stasys Knezys, the Lithuanian Commissioner for Withdrawal of the Russian Army, announced that as of 1 March 1993 only 12,000 Russian troops remained in Lithuania, down from the 22,000 that had been there at the time of the signing of the withdrawal timetable.[7]

It can be expected that the newly appointed Lithuanian delegation will be less confrontational and that the process will proceed smoothly.

Problems are greater in Latvia and Estonia, where timetables have yet to be set. It is evident that Russia is holding out in these two countries. The stated reason is the question of the Russian minorities (see below). Yeltsin is on record that Russia has no complaints over Lithuania's treatment of its Russian-speaking population. On the other hand, he has referred to Estonian and Latvian discrimination against their Russian minorities.[8]

The minority issue may only be a pretext. High-ranking Russian military officials have stated that they would like to retain some bases in those two countries indefinitely. It is very unlikely that any Baltic government will agree to any Russian military presence whatsoever on its territory. Moreover, there is doubtless pressure, especially in the case of Latvia, from the large number of retired military and KGB officers resident there. Of the currently remaining 40,000 military personnel in all three countries (8,000 in Estonia, 20,000 in Latvia, and 12,000 in Lithuania) about 15,000 are officers. Many are with families and they would like to stay. In part, that is because they have virtually nowhere to go. They are also attracted by the higher standard of living in the Baltic lands. Some have expressed a willingness to be naturalized and learn the local languages.[9]

Both the Estonian and Latvian governments are resisting all pressures to grant permanent residence permits to military personnel and their dependents. The situation was dramatized in April over a Latvian legislative proposal to limit temporary residence permits to one year. Such legislation affected the dependents of Russian military stationed in the country. About two hundred demonstrators at the Latvian parliament protested the measure as it was being discussed. Russian presidential advisor Sergei Stankevich predicted dire consequences should the measure be passed, and Yeltsin himself denounced the draft legislation as nothing less than a prelude to ethnic cleansing. In the end, the Latvians adopted a compromise law that applied only to dependents of Russian military who had come to Latvia or retired there after 4 May 1990, requiring them to apply for one-year residence permits.[10]

Morale problems abound in the units that remain in the Baltic lands. A Russian parliamentary delegation visiting Latvia in February 1993 found discontent and corruption at all levels.[11] Pay is low and, in the final analysis, the withdrawal may be dictated by economics. Prices in Estonia and Latvia are considerably higher than those in Russia, making the maintenance of these troops an increasingly costly operation.

In spite of the public politicization of the issue, the withdrawals from Estonia and Latvia are likewise proceeding. Although at the conclusion of the twelfth Estonian-Russian negotiation session on 8 June 1993, no formal timetable had been set, an Estonian delegate expressed his confidence that most of the Russian troops remaining in his country would be gone by the end of 1993. The negotiations with Latvia, broken off in April over the residence permit issue, were resumed on 31 May. The principal Russian argument for time is logistics and lack of infrastructure in Russia to absorb the returnees. The chief Russian negotiator with Latvia, Sergei Zotov, characterized the Latvian demand for total withdrawal by the end of 1993 as an ultimatum that was impossible to meet.[12]

The Russian Baltic fleet has announced its intention to withdraw from Latvia completely by the end of 1994. The Russian coast guard stated that its withdrawal would be completed by the end of 1993.

Problems are frequent in the actual process of withdrawal as well. In some respects, they stem from carelessness or simply from pilfering by the withdrawing effectives. The facilities at the large military airport near Šiauliai, Lithuania, were looted extensively by departing Soviet air force troops. In Estonia, withdrawing naval personnel carted off 750 navigational lights and twenty tons of equipment in direct violation of an agreement reached on 17 December 1992.[13] At times the removal process is potentially harmful to the environment. There is fear in Estonia of possible leaks of nitric acid and amine from the large quantity of rocket fuel to be removed from the naval base at Paldiski outside of Tallinn. Some 1,500 Russian military remain at the base. On 12 March, Estonian police and border guards raided the complex looking for arms traders. Some weapons were confiscated and several individuals arrested.[14]

Balts regard the frequent violation by Soviet military of procedures in securing permission to cross borders as deliberate disregard of their sovereignty by Russian officers who have no sympathy for such a status. The Latvian Defense Ministry reported 222 unsanctioned Russian flights and three naval incursions in January and February of 1993. By 23 May, the number of airspace violations had reached 314.[15] In addition, seventy-two Russian recruits sent as unauthorized replacements were detained by Latvian border guards. On 22 February a Russian troopship, the *Shuia*, is reported to have steamed into Paldiski harbor without securing the requisite permission.[16] According to one report, a four-day maneuver was begun in Estonia on 22 April without any notification to the Estonian authorities. It is said to have involved a practice takeover of strategic positions in the country.[17] On 12 May, Latvia sent a formal note of protest over planned maneuvers by the Russian fleet involving the firing of missiles and other weapons. These would disrupt commercial activities in Latvia's western ports, and Latvia had not been consulted when these had been planned.[18] While such incidents are rather frequent, none so far has been major. Whether they stem, as Balts tend to believe, from deliberate action within the Russian military establishment or whether they result from the chaotic conditions that are beginning to manifest themselves in the Russian military establishment is difficult to ascertain.

Citizenship and Minority Rights

The question of the immigrant populations has emerged as one of the thorniest problems in the relations of the Baltic states with Russia. It has also bedeviled their quest for acceptance by the international community as responsible, bona fide democratic states. To a large degree, however, the issue has been muddled with unsubstantiated propaganda by extremists from all sides. The root of the problem lies in differing perceptions over citizenship, human rights, and democracy. It has become acute in Estonia and threatens to become that in Latvia as well. Lithuania, which for a series of reasons has a different demographic composition, has not been faced with its full magnitude and has opted for a pragmatic solution that appears to be working.

The indigenous arguments are based on a legal argument that, as the occupation was illegal, all acts perpetrated by the occupant are likewise illegal. Introduction of large numbers of industrial workers with the purpose of diluting the indigenous ethnic composition of these societies was perceived as tantamount to a form of cultural genocide, especially since these newcomers saw little need to learn the local language and to integrate with the local populations. Latvians have become especially sensitive at being reduced to a bare majority in their own country. It is important to stress that Baltic perceptions are predicated on the premise that such policies had resulted from deliberate efforts by Russian chauvinists in the Moscow bureaucracy. It is frequently overlooked that most of the immigrants over the postwar period had been transient workers in search of the quick ruble. Many came and went. Those settled there presently represent the accretion over many years of those who stayed.

The population losses of the Baltic peoples, especially Estonians and Latvians, resulting from World War II, estimated at around 20 percent of the prewar populations, stand among the highest in Europe.

Table 5.1

Population Increase in Estonia (in thousands)

	Natural	Immigration
1950–54	5.6	6.6
1955–59	6.8	3.6
1960–64	6.8	8.3
1965–69	5.3	9.0
1970–74	6.3	8.0
1975–79	4.4	4.9

Table 5.2

Population Increase in Latvia (in thousands)

	Natural	Immigration
1950–54	9.3	3.9
1955–59	12.7	7.9
1960–64	12.5	15.6
1965–69	7.8	14.2
1970–74	7.4	12.8
1975–79	3.7	9.1

Significant immigration into Estonia and Latvia began in the immediate postwar period and continued into the 1980s. It consisted largely of workers in search of better incomes. It was possible to rebuild most of the prewar industrial plants in Estonia and Latvia with less investment than creation of a new industrial base would have required. Moreover, the indigenous populations in both Estonia and Latvia had low birthrates throughout the postwar period. Figures are not available for the immediate postwar period; however, it has been estimated that the discrepancy between natural and immigration population increase was highest during the late 1960s and the 1970s.[19] The figures for Estonia are in Table 5.1.

The discrepancy was more dramatic in Latvia (see Table 5.2).

The picture is considerably different in Lithuania. Prewar Lithuania remained an overwhelmingly agrarian country. Industrialization, begun in the late 1950s, occurred under particular political circumstances— the relative autonomy of Khrushchev's *sovnarkhoz* system, which al-

Table 5.3

Population Increase in Lithuania (in thousands)

	Natural	Immigration
1950–54	28.3	–20.6
1955–59	34.5	–6.0
1960–64	36.8	2.8
1965–69	29.1	5.8
1970–74	25.4	7.9
1975–79	18.8	6.2

lowed local decision making on capital investment. The Lithuanian Communist Party leadership, largely indigenous and lacking the marked presence of an immigrant element as in Estonia and Latvia, was able to plan industrialization utilizing the demographic resources of the country. Lithuania, a largely Roman Catholic country, continued to have an indigenous birthrate above the Soviet average until the 1980s. As a result, Lithuania experienced considerably less immigration than the other Baltic countries, and the ethnic Lithuanian population remained steady at around 80 percent of the total over the last three decades. The estimates for population increase in Lithuania, analogous to those in Estonia and Latvia, are in Table 5.3.

The principal Russian complaint is over the citizenship legislation in Estonia and Latvia. The premise of the Estonian law is that residence is not the primary criterion for citizenship but only for naturalization. All those, irrespective of nationality, who had been citizens of the Republic of Estonia on 16 June 1940 and their descendants are automatically citizens. A subsequent amendment clarified the law to read that at least one of the parents had to have been a citizen. A two-year residence starting 30 March 1990 is required for an application for naturalization. A one-year waiting period is necessary for the processing of applications. A minimal knowledge of the Estonian language must be demonstrated. In practice, this means about 1,500 words. Those who had worked for the KGB, who are currently serving in the military of another state, or who have been convicted of violent crimes are barred. As the law was passed in 1990, most permanent residents without citizenship can already apply for naturalization. A mere 13,000 have done so. In an effort to force stateless permanent residents to make a decision, Estonia passed legislation on 25 June 1993 giving residents who were not citizens two years to apply for permanent residence permits. Former KGB personnel as well as military and their dependents were specifically excluded from eligibility. The move elicited a strong Russian protest accompanied by a cut-off of gas supplies.[20] While the timing was unmistakably political, the cut-off could also have been prompted by unresolved debt questions, as cutbacks to Lithuania had been implemented on 23 May and a cut-off of supplies to Belarus had been threatened.

In 1992, only 17,000 residents without Estonian citizenship applied for Russian citizenship, suggesting widescale apathy over the issue of citizenship among resident aliens. Likewise, the turnout among the Russian population in Narva for the Russian referendum on 25 April was reported very light.[21]

Such lack of interest may appear puzzling. However, it appears analogous to the situation of other mass immigrant resident populations in other industrialized countries, where immigrant populations seek neither local citizenship nor identification with or protection from the consular officials of their countries of origin. In addition to such immigrants, significant blocs of indigenous citizens in developed countries simply opt out of codified civic practice, such as registration for and participation in elections. It has been observed that, in view of the scale of such developments, the very term "citizen" may be obsolescent.[22]

A final Latvian citizenship law remains to be passed by the parliament elected in June 1993. The 1991 guidelines on citizenship in effect until that time specify that citizens of the prewar republic and their offspring are citizens of Latvia. All others need to be naturalized. All those resident in Latvia during the preceding sixteen years are eligible to apply. Applicants for naturalization need to have a knowledge of spoken Latvian, prove that they do not hold any other citizenship, and demonstrate a knowledge of the constitution. They are also required to swear allegiance to Latvia. The most objectionable conditions, from the Russian point of view, are the language requirement and the need to give up Russian citizenship.

One of the most frequently used complaints against the Latvian guidelines is that it violates human rights by disfranchising all non-Latvians. Evgenii Ambartsumov, chairman of the Russian parliament's Committee on Foreign Affairs, observed that it was "a violation of elementary norms when one-half of a population has no rights to vote in elections. It is one thing if these people were "guest workers," but some of them have been living there for half a century."[23]

Latvian legislators point out that citizenship is separate from permanent residence. Long-term residents need only apply. In Estonia, moreover, permanent residents, irrespective of their citizenship, are allowed to vote in local and district elections, which is considerably more liberal than in most West European and North American countries. The Council of Europe has agreed with the Latvian and Estonian viewpoint and observed that while denial of voting rights to a large part of the population is in itself a flaw from the democratic point of view, it can be justified if such "noncitizens" are in effect immigrant workers from other countries. An agreement was signed on 15 February 1993 according to which a CSCE mission on minority questions began a six-month study in Estonia.[24]

Another frequent argument of human rights violations concerns alleged pressures on the Russian population to move. On 27 February 1993 Foreign Minister Kozyrev, speaking in Copenhagen, accused the Estonian government of supporting small organizations involved in helping Russians move out of the country.[25]

It has been stressed by Baltic leaders that no proposal has ever been made to force permanent residents to move. On 8 February, Estonian Foreign Minister Trivimi Velliste expressed his country's readiness to integrate immigrants, but not at the dictates of the Russian government.[26]

Likewise, Balts like to point out that citizenship is not inexorably tied to access to social benefits, which remain available to all residents. In the traditional Soviet view of things, particularly elaborated in the Brezhnev constitution, subsistence maintenance was considered a human right. In practice, the term "human rights" in the context of the Russian minorities in Estonia and Latvia has become a code word for "standard of living." In this sense, the human rights of Russian residents are being violated in cases of bankruptcy of rust industries. The counterargument has been that for economic reasons, it has been or will become necessary to close large and unprofitable enterprises. Such plants are precisely those that employ large numbers of the immigrant workers. Many of them, such as the uranium processing plant at Sillimae in Estonia are part of the Soviet military-industrial complex. The Baltic governments make no efforts to subsidize them. Moreover, the strength of the Estonian and Latvian currencies and the refusal of the governments of these countries to print money make the production of these plants too expensive in CIS markets. Unfortunately, the imminent collapse of analogous industries in Russia leaves the sizable number of immigrant workers in Estonia and Latvia nowhere to go. Estonian and Latvian sensitivities have been particularly irked by Russian pronouncements, by none other than Yeltsin himself (see above), of linkage between Russian troop withdrawal and the question of minority rights. Estonians have on occasion countered by pointing out the dismal Russian records on the human rights of Finno-Ugric peoples in the Russian Federation.[27]

The Russian declarations appear to be aimed primarily at Russian critics internally. As has been noted, in practice the process of military withdrawal does not seem to have been affected. The depth of Baltic sensitivity to such Russian attitudes has most clearly been demonstrated by Estonian President Lennart Meri, who accused President Clinton of collusion in the slow pace of Russian withdrawal from the Baltic states. At the press conference on 4 April 1993 after the summit in Vancouver, Yeltsin reiterated the position that the pace of the withdrawal would be predicated on the ending of the "persecution" by those countries of their Russian minorities. Meri stated: "I was deeply disappointed that there was no reaction from President Clinton to President Yeltsin's remark. You know as well as I do that President Yeltsin was lying." He was concerned about the passage in the joint communiqué over protection of Russian minorities in the former USSR. "The claims about the oppression of the Russian-speaking population in Estonia are founded on thin air. Not a single delegation from the CSCE or the UN has in any way established that violations are occurring."[28] Latvian head of state Anatolijs Gorbunovs likewise expressed regret that Yeltsin was ignoring an "evident truth" and that the "army was being used to exert political pressure."

Another facet of the problem that frequently upsets Baltic leaders and that is generally overlooked by outsiders is the Russian presumption of representing all minorities in the Baltic lands. While the Russian minority is the largest, there are also considerable numbers of Ukrainians and Belarusians. Neither Ukraine nor Belarus has voiced complaints analogous to those of Russia. In his speech to the General Assembly of the United Nations on 25 September 1992, Landsbergis ironically observed that the Lithuanian minority is equally affected by the Estonian law on citizenship, but that Lithuania did not consider any need to protest.

An often overlooked matter in the question of citizenship is its confusion with nationality. Citizenship is not necessarily tied to ethnicity. In both Latvia and Estonia, all prewar citizens and their descendants are citizens. It has been estimated that of all non-Estonians, numbering some 600,000, one-sixth are adult citizens eligible to vote in national elections. The proportion of old Russians in Latvia is most likely even higher. Therefore, statements that Latvia is disfranchising about half its population are inaccurate. Exact figures are unavailable. The Latvian Department of Citizenship and Emigration has estimated that about 64 percent of the current residents of Latvia are automatically citizens and that a significant proportion of the remainder, not all of whom are Russians, is eligible for naturalization.[29]

The situation in Lithuania is different. A citizenship law was adopted there in 1989 by the old Supreme Soviet, which allowed all permanent residents to opt for Lithuanian citizenship during a two-year transition period. Moreover, as much as half of Lithuania's Russians, who make up about 10 percent of the total population, are old Russians who have been assimilated. The Polish minority, which accounts for another 7 percent of the total, is indigenous. The same can be said for the bulk of the Belarusian and other minorities.

In practice, it appears that the immigrant Russian population is slowly leaving Lithuania. The privatization of apartments has been nearly completed. Many are taking the opportunity to enrich themselves through the sale for hard currency of properties acquired at nominal cost and move to Russia, where prices are considerably lower.

Even the Brazauskas leadership, which seeks good relations with Russia, appears reticent to endorse the Russian position on human rights. During his visit with Brazauskas in late March 1993, Russian Foreign Minister Kozyrev sought approval for the Russian proposal to appoint a neutral human rights commissioner, perhaps a Finn, for the Baltic states. That would help the Russian government in its relations with hardliners at home. Brazauskas appeared cool to the idea, noting that any such move would have to be coordinated with the Baltic Council. Kozyrev is reported to have repeated this request to a closed meeting on 16 March of the foreign ministers of the Council of Baltic Sea States. He supposedly likened the plight of the Russian minorities in the Baltic states to minorities in the former Yugoslavia.[30] The Estonian and Latvian foreign ministers opposed the appointment of any such commissioner.

The Russian efforts, including a personal message from Kozyrev, to delay Baltic membership in the Council of Europe over the status of the Russian minorities did not prove successful. In May 1993, Estonia and Lithuania were accepted as full members. Latvia is likely to join them, since democratic elections were held in June.

Boundary Questions

One little-noted question in the relations of the Baltic states with their neighbors is that of boundaries. In general, the tendency among all governments appears to be to consider the present boundaries fixed, except for minor delineation adjustments. While some in Belarus consider a good portion of eastern Lithuania—including Vilnius—as properly Belarusian, that view has never been espoused by the Belarusian government per se. The statement by Belarusian Foreign Minister Pyotr Krauchanka to a visiting EC delegation in Minsk on 24 February 1992 that Belarus claimed some Lithuanian territory[31] appears to have been a personal opinion. The gaffe was quickly disavowed by the Belarusian government. Likewise, Poland considers the boundary with Lithuania to be settled. It is the same as the prewar frontier. The Polish minority in Lithuania is not contiguous to the border, but separated from Poland by Belarus.

Two exceptions to this general acquiescence exist. Both Estonia and Latvia lost territory to the RSFSR in 1945. Estonia lost a sliver of land across the river by Narva and the Petseri (Pechora) area in the southeast, near Pskov. At the same time, Latvia lost an area in the northeast, Abrene, also to the RSFSR. The issues have been raised publicly in both countries. Estonia has even reached an agreement with Russia over a joint investigation of the human rights of the Estonian minority in the region. In view of the consistent focus by Baltic politicians on the illegality of the Soviet occupation, there is great likelihood that these boundary questions will be raised in the future. On 22 February, 1993, Estonian Foreign Minister Velliste outlined a plan by Estonia to request CSCE mediation of the claim.[32]

Estonia recently passed a law extending its territorial waters twelve miles in most cases, and provided for the possibility of limiting it in some places to allow for international navigation in the Gulf of Finland through negotiation with neighbors. The hard-line point of view that the Soviet twelve-mile limit be kept and that questions of subsequent negotiation with Russia about navigation, especially of warships, be made a trump card for concessions in other matters was narrowly defeated.

The future of Kaliningrad Oblast is another territorial issue that is bound to surface. The enclave of the Russian Federation is a leftover consequence of the territorial readjustments in the aftermath of World War II. The bulk of former East Prussia was given to Poland. Its northern third, including the principal city, Königsberg, was placed under Soviet administration. Although the Russian position that it is eternally Russian land has been voiced on numerous occasions, contrary claims can also be made. The Allied powers placed it within the Soviet zone of occupation at Potsdam in 1945 along with a promise to support Soviet claims on the area at a future peace conference. The following year, the USSR unilaterally integrated the region into the RSFSR. Elements in Lithuania have voiced opinions that it is historic Lithuanian land. The indigenous population, the Prussians, were a Baltic tribe that was overrun by the crusading Teutonic Knights in the thirteenth century and that had died out by the eighteenth century. The regions contiguous to Lithuania had a significant Lithuanian population as late as World War I. It played a pivotal role in the Lithuanian national renaissance of the nineteenth century. During the late 1950s, a significant number of former Lithuanian deportees who had been released from the Gulag but not allowed to return to Lithuania chose to settle in this oblast of the RSFSR, particularly in the areas adjoining Lithuania. At present the Lithuanian population of the oblast has been estimated at around 40,000.[33] Polish circles have voiced opinions that it would be beneficial to join it to the Polish portion of the former East Prussia, which would form a natural unit. And German circles have expressed public interest in the area. The appearance of a German commercial presence in Kaliningrad is clearly evident, and Germans are restoring the ruins of the massive medieval cathedral, which had been left in the center of the city.

Suggestions appeared in the late 1980s of settling Russian Germans, who had been deported en masse by Stalin from the Volga region to Central Asia during the war, in the enclave. Some such resettlement has taken place, but it has not developed extensively. For obvious reasons, Volga Germans prefer to go to Germany. Landsbergis opposed the idea, considering such settlement as potentially provoking unrest in the area.[34]

The question of the future of Kaliningrad is made particularly sensitive by the fact of the overwhelming Russian military presence in the enclave. It is estimated that up to 200,000 of the region's 900,000 residents consist of military personnel and their families. Although supply by sea from St. Petersburg is feasible, the area is, in practice, virtually dependent on Lithuania for transit as well as for its electricity and gas. Some elements in the enclave have protested the Estonian and especially the Latvian decision to require transit visas for CIS citizens crossing by rail or auto, which have to be paid in hard currency, as part of an effort to cut off Kaliningrad from Russia. And it probably remains only a matter of time before Lithuania will also introduce an analogous visa requirement. The matter has already emerged as a bargaining point in Lithuanian negotiations with Russia. During his recent visit with Brazauskas in Vilnius, Kozyrev complained about Lithuanian refusals to permit troop transits to the oblast. Brazauskas threatened to introduce transit fees in general in the event Russia raised energy prices.[35]

Conclusion

The process of post-Soviet reorientation remains ongoing in the three Baltic countries. They exhibit a clear potential for emerging, in a relatively brief period of time, as democratic societies and full-fledged members of the European community of states. Their internal problems do not appear insoluble. And they still need to determine what profile in the international political and economic systems of the region best suits their needs.

In many respects they are considerably more fortunate than the other former Soviet republics. They possess modern nation-state identities established in pre-Soviet times. Their period of Soviet existence was shorter, and their Western cultural traditions mitigated the brunt of imposition of Soviet ways. Although the intense nationalism of their indigenous populations, exacerbated under Soviet conditions, could in a period of economic hardship (which has already arrived and is bound to grow) foster authoritarianism in a search for order and stability, such a development remains unlikely. Their self-perception as Europeans and their strong desire for integration into Europe, for acceptance as

Western societies, provides a strong impetus for development along democratic lines. Democracy has become a precondition for acceptance by the West. That was not the case in prewar times. Several fundamental interrelated questions of foreign and economic policy confront the three states. First and foremost, they need to come to terms with geopolitical and economic reality. In practical terms, that implies mitigation of their overriding desire for disassociation insofar as possible from the rest of the former USSR. Russia, in whatever form or in how many units it emerges from the current period of instability, will continue to occupy a position as the preeminent neighbor in terms of political and economic significance for the three countries. Geographically, they are well suited to serve and to prosper as transit points between Western Europe and the vast hinterland of the CIS. The historic role of Tallinn and the three Latvian ports in Riga, Ventspils, and Liepāja is well known. Lithuanians like to point out that their port at Klaipeda is the only major ice-free port along the eastern Baltic. There is even talk of a role in air transportation between Europe and the Far East. Recently a South Korean concern expressed interest in the former Red Air Force center in western Lithuania around Šiauliai and Panevežys, a giant complex of several bases including some six kilometers of reinforced runways and massive storage bunkers. It had been designed as a reserve area for support of a potential battlefront in Germany. The consideration was over the possibility of using the bases as a Shannon-type refueling and storage area for cargo flights between Europe and the Far East.

It is quite likely that once the current initial period of reemergence is over, the three states will realize the benefits their geographical location imparts. While it is unlikely that they would in the foreseeable future ever voluntarily join any political confederation with Russia or its possible successor states, economic logic dictates the maintenance of close ties to that hinterland. Their size inevitably necessitates accommodation to developments among their large neighbors to the east, with little possibility of influencing such developments. But accommodation to large neighbors has always been imperative for small states.

Notes

1. For a survey of the Baltic diplomatic and consular establishments during the postwar period, see Romuald J. Misiunas, "Sovereignty Without Government: Baltic Diplomatic and Consular Representation, 1940–1990," in *Governments-in-Exile in Contemporary World Politics*, ed. Yossi Shain (New York: Routledge, 1991).

2. *RFE/RL News Briefs,* 2 June 1993.
3. *RFE/RL News Briefs,* 15 April 1993.
4. *RFE/RL News Briefs,* 23 March 1993.
5. *RFE/RL News Briefs,* 30 March 1993.
6. *RFE/RL News Briefs,* 2 June 1993.
7. *Baltic Observer* (Tallinn), 12 March 1993.
8. John Lough, "The Place of the 'Near Abroad' in Russian Foreign Policy," *RFE/RL Research Report,* vol. 2, no. 11 (12 March 1993), p. 28.
9. Michael Tarm, "Russian Officers Want Good Life of Estonia and the Baltics," *American Baltic News* (Kalamazoo, MI), July 1993
10. *RFE/RL News Briefs,* 23 April 1993.
11. *RFE/RL News Briefs,* 22 February 1993.
12. *RFE/RL News Briefs,* 14 May 1993.
13. *Baltic Observer* (Riga), 2 April 1993.
14. *RFE/RL News Briefs,* 15 March 1993.
15. *RFE/RL News Briefs,* 29 May 1993.
16. *RFE/RL News Briefs,* 24 February 1993.
17. *RFE/RL News Briefs,* 23 April 1993.
18. *RFE/RL News Briefs,* 12 May 1993.
19. The three tables that follow are from Rein Taagepera, "Baltic Population Changes, 1950–1980," *Journal of Baltic Studies,* vol. 22, no. 1 (spring 1981).
20. *New York Times,* 24 June 1993.
21. *CSCE Report on the April 25, 1993 Referendum in Russia* (Washington), 12 May 1993, p. 10.
22. Giorgio Agambem, "Au-dela des Droits de L'Homme," *Liberation* (Paris), 9–10 June 1993.
23. *New York Times,* 10 August 1992.
24. *RFE/RL News Briefs,* 16 February 1993.
25. *RFE/RL News Briefs,* 1 March 1993.
26. *RFE/RL News Briefs,* 9 February 1993.
27. *RFE/RL News Briefs,* 14 April 1993.
28. *Baltic Independent* (Tallinn), 9 April 1993.
29. Dzintra Bungs, Saulius Girnius, and Riina Kionka, "Citizenship Legislation in the Baltic States," *RFE/RL Research Report,* vol. 1, no. 50 (18 December 1992), pp. 38–39.
30. *RFE/RL News Briefs,* 16 March 1993.
31. Kathleen Mihailisko, "The Outlook for Independent Belarus," *RFE/RL Research Report,* vol. 1, no. 24 (12 June 1992), p. 10.
32. *RFE/RL News Briefs,* 23 February 1993.
33. *Literatura ir menas* (Vilnius), 1 January 1989. According to the 1979 census, 19,677 Lithuanians resided in the oblast. However, many, including Iurii Ivanov, head of the Kaliningrad Culture Fund, considered those figures too low and considered 40,000 a minimum.
34. For a survey history of postwar and contemporary developments in the region, see "The Kaliningrad Oblast: A New Baltic Land?" postscript in Romuald J. Misiunas and Rein Taagepera, *The Baltic States: The Years of Dependence, 1940–1990* (London: Hurst, 1993).
35. *Baltic Observer* (Riga), 19 May 1993.

6

History as a Battleground

Russian-Ukrainian Relations and Historical Consciousness in Contemporary Ukraine

Zenon E. Kohut

With headlines focusing on tensions over the future of the Common-wealth of Independent States, economic integration, nuclear disarm-ament, the fate of the Black Sea fleet, and border disputes, it may seem strange to address such a seemingly esoteric problem in Ukrainian-Russian relations as the perception of history. Yet it is my contention that the current disputes are symptomatic of a much more fundamental set of problems. Foremost among them is the question of "deimperial-ization"—the adjustment of structures and intellectual concepts to the dissolution of an empire. In the case of Russian-Ukrainian relations the problem is even deeper than what Ukraine's president Leonid Kravchuk has labeled "Russia's imperial disease" or "imperial think-ing." After all, even some staunch Russian nationalists, for example, Aleksandr Solzhenitsyn, are willing to let go of most of the former Soviet Union for a reconstituted Russia. Their "Russia," however, also includes Ukraine.[1] Ukrainian independence, therefore, raises not only the problem of deconstructing an empire but also such fundamental questions as, What is Russia? What is Ukraine? And what is the historical relationship between them? It raises the question of the shaping and reshaping of identities, and the perception of history has been and continues to be a chief battleground in the struggle over identity.

For most of modern history, the Russian point of view had been that

Ukraine is a part of Russia, historically, linguistically, culturally, and even spiritually. While the origins of this view may be traced to Muscovite scribes, its modern foundation was laid by the classic Russian historians from the late eighteenth through early twentieth centuries: Nikolai Karamzin, S.M. Solov´ev, and V.O. Kliuchevskii, who viewed the Kievan Rus´ state, which emerged in the tenth century in central Ukraine, as the first Russian state and its East Slavic inhabitants as Russians. In the thirteenth century Kievan Rus´ was partially destroyed and subjugated by the Mongols. According to the Russian imperial view, this state, despite the "Mongol yoke," survived in the northeast—centered first in Vladimir-Suzdal, then in Moscow, and finally in St. Petersburg—as the Russian Empire. Thus in a series of territorial shifts the Russian state continued from Kievan Rus´ to the nineteenth-century Russian Empire, although the southwestern parts of Rus´ (Ukraine and Belarus) were lost to foreigners, first to Lithuania and then Poland. From the Russian imperial view, therefore, it follows that the ancient unity of the Russian state should be reconstituted by the gathering of all "Russian" lands, including Ukraine and Belarus.[2]

In placing the original Russian state in Ukraine, the traditional imperial scheme had difficulty accounting for the existence of Ukrainians. In 1856, Mikhail Pogodin advanced a thesis that ancient Kiev had been inhabited by Russians, but the Mongol invasion resulted in a massive out-migration to the territories in Russia. New tribes from the Carpathians settled in Ukraine during the fourteenth and fifteenth centuries, forming the ethnic basis for the Ukrainians.[3] Although Pogodin's theory enjoyed some popularity, the occurrence of such a population exchange could not be substantiated. Most Russian historians explained the substantial differences between Russians and Ukrainians in speech, custom, and outlook as corruption of the basically Russian ethos by Polish influences.

The traditional or Russian imperial scheme of history was not just the musings of a few academicians. Disseminated through the educational system and the press, it was the dominant concept in the Russian Empire until the 1917–21 revolutions. Russian émigré historians brought it to Europe and North America, where it enjoys virtual canonicity.[4] This historical scheme was utilized in policy formulations: the justification for the partitions of Poland or for the Russian war aim in World War I of annexing Galicia to the empire. It was the backdrop to banning all public use of the Ukrainian language (1863 and 1876) and the formulation of a policy and attitude expressed so succinctly by the Russian Minister of Interior, Count Peter Valuev, on 8 June 1863, that "there never was any separate Little Russian [Ukrainian] language, there is not one now, and there cannot be one."[5] By combining dynastic, imperial, and Russian national history, the Russian imperial scheme was able to provide a justification for the Russian Empire, equating it with a virtually unbroken thousand-year history of "Russia" and the "Russian people." The scheme left very little room for the history of Ukrainians and Belarusians, except as wayward branches of the Russian national family. As Ukrainians began to achieve a measure of national consciousness and organize a national movement, they could no longer accept the thesis that their history was merely an adjunct to Russian national history. The Russian imperial government, ironically, encouraged the study of Ukrainian history in order to prove that the lands annexed from Poland were from time immemorial genuinely "Russian." Nineteenth-century historians were able to produce many major studies in Ukrainian history, particularly of the Cossack period. Under the influence of Romanticism, the populist historians did not focus so much on state structures as on the "folk" or "common people." In the process, they accumulated more and more evidence that Ukrainians were distinct not only from Poles but also from Russians. Without replacing the Russian imperial scheme, populist Ukrainian historiography demonstrated that in various time frames Ukraine had followed its own separate historical process.[6]

A conceptual breakthrough was made by Ukraine's most outstanding historian, Mykhailo Hrushevs'kyi. In his ten-volume *Istoriia Ukrainy-Rusy,* other monographs, and hundreds of source publications and articles, he refuted the traditional imperial Russian scheme and offered an alternate view. Hrushevs'kyi succinctly summarized his concept in 1904 in "The Traditional Scheme of 'Russian' History and the Problem of a Rational Organization of the History of the Eastern Slavs." In this article, Hrushevs'kyi pointed out that the Russian imperial scheme was illogical in equating the history of dynastic relations with the Russian state and even the Russian nation. He vehemently rejected the concept of the transfer of geographic centers and the mechanical linking of various historical time frames in order to trace a straight linear development of the Russian nation from Kievan Rus'. According to Hrushevs'kyi, the imperial Russian scheme not only left out Ukrainians and Belarusians, but it was also incapable of explaining the origins of the Russian nation.[7]

In discrediting the imperial Russian scheme, Hrushevs'kyi presented his own thesis that Ukrainians, Belarusians, and Russians have separate and distinct histories. He asserted that rather than moving to the northeast, the Kievan Rus' state continued in the Ukrainian territories through the Galician-Volhynian state and subsequently Lithuanian-Rus'. While some legal, governmental, and religious structures were transplanted to the Russian territory, Russia developed *sui generis* and was not organically tied to Kievan Rus'. Thus the history of the Russian nation began with the northeastern territories, while that of Ukrainians began with Kievan Rus'. Subsequently, each nation evolved separately, although at times their fates intertwined.[8]

From the Ukrainian perspective Hrushevs'kyi's impact was immense. By utilizing scholarly critiques, he was able to challenge the prevailing imperial mythology and set up a new historical structure. Hrushevs'kyi replaced a paradigm in which Ukrainians played virtually no role in history—even on their own territory—with one in which they had an ancient past. He provided the intellectual space within which Ukrainian historical studies could develop. As a result, most Ukrainian historians whose works were not under Russian-Soviet control accepted Hrushevs'kyi's views, while most Russian historians did not. This is an indication of the extent to which the work of the historian (with or without his intention) in Eastern Europe has been utilized to legitimize national myths, and why history itself is a battleground in the struggle of competing identities.

At the beginning of the twentieth century, under the impact of the national movement and Ukraine's brief period of independence, the populist approach was abandoned for a new "statist" orientation. The state school historians looked into the past and saw periods when Ukraine was virtually an independent state. They concentrated on such indicators of statehood as foreign relations, internal administration, and judicial procedures. They viewed Kievan Rus', the Galician-Volhynian princedom, and even the Grand Duchy of Lithuania as embodiments of Ukrainian statehood. Like the populists, the state school historians paid particular attention to the various Ukrainian semi-independent Cossack formations and viewed them not as mere instruments of social struggle but rather as representatives of political and national struggle.[9]

Despite the failed attempt at Ukrainian statehood in 1917–21, the state school became dominant in Soviet Ukraine, in western Ukraine under Poland, and in the emigration. In Soviet Ukraine, it was soon challenged by Marxist historians, but this developing clash of interpretations was soon overshadowed by the imposition in the 1930s of an official Soviet scheme. Although proscribed in the Soviet Union, the state school continued in western Ukraine (until its incorporation into the Soviet Union in 1945) and also in emigration.

The official Soviet scheme was in essence a reworking of the Russian imperial one, with added Marxist elements and terminology. It also posited the unity of the East Slavs in the period of Kievan Rus'. The East Slavs were referred to as the "old Rus' people" or, as translated by some, the "old Russian people" composed of proto-Russians, Ukrainians, and Belarusians. As in the imperial scheme, the Soviets also claimed that the unity of "the old Russian people" was shattered by the Mongol invasion, allowing the subsequent development of a separate Ukrainian and Belarusian people. Although Ukrainians were considered to be a part of the "old Rus' nation," some Soviet scholars frequently equated "the old Rus' nation" simply with Russians. The primacy of Russians was further elaborated in the doctrine of the "elder brother," which presupposes that Russians were more ancient and more accomplished than their younger brothers, the Ukrainians.[10]

While recognizing the existence from the fourteenth and fifteenth centuries of a separate Ukrainian people, Soviet scholarship claimed that the Ukrainians wanted nothing more than to be "reunified" with their Russian brethren. Thus, the theme of unity with Russia extended to all times—even when Ukrainians were outside Russian political structures. In this scheme the Pereiaslav Agreement of 1654, when the Ukrainian hetman Bohdan Khmel'nyts'kyi conditionally recognized the suzerainty of the Muscovite tsar, was treated as the pivotal event that symbolized the "reunification" of the two lands and peoples for all times. This thesis was sanctified by a decree of the Central Committee of the Communist Party in 1954 and remained obligatory until the collapse of the Soviet Union.[11]

The Soviet scheme also assumed complete Russian-Ukrainian solidarity and communality of interests. Ukrainians were not to be concerned with the status of their own nation but to rejoice and glorify in Russian accomplishments. At no point in history could Ukrainians have any legitimate interests that would not coincide with Russian ones. Nor did Ukrainians have any future as a separate nation, since

Soviet nationality policy called for their merger into a wider Soviet people. Ukrainians, therefore, emerged in the fifteenth century in order to reunify with Russians and then ultimately to disappear into the Soviet people.[12]

Within this narrow conceptual straitjacket, Soviet Ukrainian historians attempted to study various aspects of Ukrainian history and culture. The accepted dogma required either expunging a good part of the historical record or manipulating it to fit the myth. Yet some good work could be done within the narrow official parameters, and through the Soviet period historians attempted to test the official boundaries.[13] Nevertheless, only with the policy of glasnost could historians really move beyond the proscribed dogmas in any significant way.

When beginning in 1990 the rigid boundaries suddenly evaporated, it was hardly surprising that the first great debate over history in the era of glasnost was over the work and figure of Mykhailo Hrushevs'kyi. The Soviet regime had proscribed him on two accounts: (1) as a historian Hrushevs'kyi had developed a scheme that negated both the Russian imperial and Soviet schemes; (2) as a politician he had headed the Central Rada government of an independent Ukraine and had opposed the Bolsheviks. In early 1988 some scholars attempted to reintroduce his scholarship—a move fiercely attacked by the Soviet Ukrainian scholarly establishment.[14] Nevertheless, by 1989 several Ukrainian journals began to serialize some of Hrushevs'kyi's works, and a number of articles attempted to portray his political activity in a positive manner. The attempt at rehabilitation gained further credibility when the leading Ukrainian specialist on Kievan Rus', Petro Tolochko, endorsed the Hrushevs'kyi scheme of history.[15]

As Ukraine was moving toward greater sovereignty and finally independence, the opposition to Hrushevs'kyi began to dissipate. In August 1991 an International Congress on Hrushevs'kyi held in Lviv, presented a plethora of papers, many of which presumed the correctness of his historical scheme.[16] In the same year, volume 1 of his classic *History of Ukraine Rus'* was reprinted jointly by the Archeographic Commission of the Ukrainian Academy of Sciences, the Harvard Ukrainian Research Institute, and the Canadian Institute of Ukrainian Studies.[17] Even Ukraine's declaration of independence referred to the "thousand-year-old tradition of state creation in Ukraine"—an indirect acceptance of Hrushevs'kyi's periodization of history.[18] In 1992 a collection of Hrushevs'kyi's political articles was reprinted with a foreword by President Leonid Kravchuk.[19] It is clear that Hrushevs'kyi's scheme will be the basis for a newly defined Ukrainian national history and will be utilized as historical justification in the promotion of Ukrainian statehood.

The struggle against the Russian imperial scheme of history became particularly evident in Ukraine's religious and ecclesiastical life. History proved again to be the principal battleground driving church politics and religious ferment.[20] The traditional Russian imperial view was, and to a large extent still is, represented by the Russian Orthodox Church. The Church traced its origins to the 988 Christianization of Rus' in Kiev, lamented the subsequent division of the Church into Ukrainian and Russian branches, and celebrated the "reunion" of the two when, in 1686, the Kiev metropolitan was subordinated to the Moscow patriarchate. Adopting the imperial historical scheme, the Russian Orthodox Church has been a firm supporter of the concept of unity of the East Slavs in some larger "Russian" entity in which it was the only legitimate Orthodox Church.[21] The Church de facto approved and cooperated in the proscription of such rivals as the independent Ukrainian Orthodox churches and the Ukrainian Catholic (Uniate) Church.[22]

The Ukrainian Orthodox and Catholic churches had a very different historical vision. They, too, traced their origins to the Christianization of Rus' in 988, but they viewed this event as primarily a Ukrainian one.[23] They considered Russia's Christianization to have occurred much later, by Ukrainian missionaries.[24] In contrast to the Russian Orthodox Church's emphasis on early and later East Slavic unity, both Ukrainian Orthodox and Catholics focused on Ukraine, particularly the Ukrainian Church's struggle to preserve its Eastern and Orthodox character under pressure from Roman Catholic Poland.[25] The Ukrainian Catholic solution was the Brest Union (1596), by which a portion of the Church recognized the primacy of the Pope but retained Orthodox rituals.[26] The Ukrainian Orthodox viewed this union as a betrayal rather than a solution. They emphasized the flourishing of a revitalized Ukrainian Orthodox Church in the seventeenth century and condemned its subsequent incorporation into Russian Orthodoxy.[27]

Within the Russian Empire neither the Ukrainian Orthodox nor the Ukrainian Catholic churches survived but were merged into the Russian Orthodox Church. The Ukrainian Catholic Church had survived in Galicia, which was first under Austrian and then, after World War I, under Polish control. During Ukraine's brief period of independence, an independent Ukrainian Autocephalous Orthodox Church was established in Ukraine, but in the 1930s it was merged into the Russian Orthodox Church, as was the Ukrainian Catholic Church when Galicia was incorporated into the Ukrainian SSR (1946).[28] Thus, alternative views to the Russian Orthodox Church could be expressed only in emigration or by the Ukrainian Catholic Church, which went underground.

The different historical perspectives were clearly evident in 1988 with the celebrations of the millennium of Christianity in Rus'. After some hesitation, the officially atheistic Soviet government launched elaborate celebrations of what was popularly labeled the millennium of "Russian" Christianity and the millennium of the "Russian Orthodox Church." Although the original site of the baptism was Kiev, most of the celebrations occurred in Moscow, a city that did not exist in 988. From the perspectives of both the Soviet government and the Russian Orthodox Church, the celebrations were an opportunity to bolster the concept of the ancient unity of Russians, Ukrainians, and Belarusians. Yet by making the celebrations primarily a "Russian" event, the official ceremonies also underscored the prominence of Russia and Russian history, language, and culture.[29]

Ukrainians in the diaspora also celebrated the millennium of Christianity. Major commemorative events were staged in Rome; Washington, DC; South Bound Brook, New Jersey; and Toronto. Scholarly and commemorative books were published, and the Harvard Ukrainian Research Institute launched a major series of publications of premodern Ukrainian literature.[30] Through such activities, the Ukrainian diaspora attempted to counter the claim that it was the millennium of the Russian Orthodox Church and "Holy Russia," and emphasized the continuity of Ukrainian Christianity and culture from the time of the 988 baptism. At the same time, the Ukrainian diaspora raised questions as to the incorporation of the Ukrainian Orthodox Church into the Russian Orthodox Church and the banning and persecution of the underground Ukrainian Catholic Church.[31]

The abatement of religious persecution in the USSR in the late 1980s led to the emergence of the Ukrainian Autocephalous Orthodox Church and the Ukrainian Catholic Church. In a fierce three-way struggle over parishes and faithful, the two churches virtually eliminated the Russian Orthodox Church from the most nationally conscious and traditionally Catholic areas of western Ukraine.[32] In eastern Ukraine, however, the Russian Orthodox Church was able to hold its dominant position. By 1990 the Russian Orthodox Church in Ukraine was sufficiently challenged by the Ukrainian Autocephalous Orthodox Church to announce its autonomy from Moscow and rename itself the Ukrainian Orthodox Church.[33] After Ukraine's declaration of independence, the Ukrainian Orthodox Church asked for its autocephaly, or independence, from the Moscow patriarch—a request denied by Moscow. In response, a part of the Ukrainian Orthodox Church joined with the Ukrainian Autocephalous Orthodox Church.[34] Although at this time the institutional relationships are not all clear, the trend toward autocephaly—now also favored by the Ukrainian government—has clearly been established.[35]

While it is complicated by politics, personal ambitions, various scandals, and questions of canon law, the current situation in Ukraine has been and continues to be defined by the fundamentally different historical visions of the various churches. Both the Ukrainian Orthodox and Catholic traditions see Ukraine as having developed since the 988 baptism a distinct and rich tradition of spirituality, which needs to be reestablished. For the Ukrainian Orthodox this can be accomplished through establishment of an independent or autocephalous church; for Catholics, through a Ukrainian particular church in union with Rome. Another historical vision is that of a common East Slavic spirituality and heritage embellished in a Russian-dominated Orthodoxy. These clashing historical outlooks continue to shape the religious struggle within Ukraine and contribute to tensions between Russia and Ukraine.

Sovereignty and independence also brought new historical themes to the foreground: the development of the Ukrainian nation, statehood, and a plethora of previously forbidden topics. Yet Ukrainian historians and journalists were ill-prepared to present new histories, new interpretations, and new research. For the most part, they turned to the already available material from the past, particularly the work of historians who had been neglected or partially or wholly proscribed. Works were published or republished on or by Dmytro Bahalii, D.I. Iavonyts'kyi, Mykola Kostomarov, and particularly Volodymyr Antonovych, the precursor to Hrushevs'kyi.[36] These historians were favored because they had been nationally conscious and promoted Ukrainian history in spite of tsarist or Soviet restrictions. Scholarly and popular journals began reprinting articles that had been published in the nineteenth century or abroad.[37]

The gap in historical knowledge was also partially filled by Western scholars. A recent textbook on Ukrainian history by Orest Subtelny published in Toronto was quickly translated into Ukrainian and published in massive quantities in Ukraine. Sections of the book were serialized in *Ukrains'kyi istorychnyi zhurnal*, and the textbook became part of the officer training of the Ukrainian military.[38] Other Western scholars published in Ukraine included Omeljan Pritsak, Roman Szporluk, Taras Hunczak, and Thomas Prymak.[39]

A central theme in the revival of a distinct Ukrainian historical consciousness has been the Cossack experience. In this connection, it is interesting to note that there is also a Cossack revival in Russia. However, the two revivals are working in diametrically opposite directions: the Russian one is fueled by the desire to defend the integrity of the Russian Empire,[40] while the Ukrainian Cossack revival celebrates Ukrainian national consciousness and defends the territorial integrity of Ukraine.

The Cossack experience is capable of rallying Ukrainian public opinion because it strikes a chord in virtually all areas of Ukraine, even in heavily Russified eastern and southern Ukraine, where few Ukrainian traditions remained. Thus, when Rukh, the popular movement for a Ukrainian rebirth, wanted to penetrate and partially de-Russify these regions in 1990, it settled on a series of celebrations commemorating the five hundredth anniversary of the Zaporozhian Cossacks. Through such celebrations, Rukh attempted to demonstrate that the area and its population have a link to the Ukrainian Cossacks and Ukraine. This is in opposition to the Russian imperial vision of southeastern Ukraine being associated with the colonization efforts of Catherine II and the Russian Empire.[41]

Since in the past various Cossack formations were indeed independent or semi-independent, the Cossacks are also seen as precursors of Ukrainian statehood. At the time of the 1991 elections, the then chairman of the Supreme Rada, Leonid Kravchuk, and his principal opponent for the Ukrainian presidency, Viacheslav Chornovil, were photographed holding the mace, the symbol of office of an independent Ukrainian hetman. A similar symbolic reference to Ukraine's Cossack past was Viacheslav Chornovil's elaborate ceremony abrogating the Pereiaslav Agreement of 1654—that is, renouncing what only recently had been referred to as the "reunion" of Ukraine and Russia.[42] In Ukraine today, there is hardly a folk festival, rock concert, or major public event without a number of individuals dressed in colorful Cossack garb. As it is intoned in the recently rehabilitated Ukrainian national anthem, Ukrainians indeed consider themselves descendants of the Cossacks. The widespread Cossackophilia is very much evident in both popular and scholarly publications. Cossacks are presented as models for democracy and as having drafted a constitution in 1710, "the first in Europe."[43] Military newspapers and the journal *Army of Ukraine* feature Cossack military campaigns and suggest that the Cossack heritage has something to offer in developing a Ukrainian military doctrine.[44] In a more scholarly vein, a leading specialist on the Cossacks has suggested making the study of Cossacks a special discipline within Ukrainian history, with its own research institute.[45] Numerous articles on Cossacks and Cossack hetmans extol those who had struggled for "the sovereignty and statehood of Ukraine." In this context, hetman Ivan Mazepa, who fought against Russia in 1709 and was characterized as a "renegade" and "enemy of the people" in Russian imperial and Soviet historiography, is now considered a hero.[46]

A second historical theme with virtually universal appeal has been the exposition of Stalinist crimes. For western Ukraine, these included executions, mass arrests, and deportations in the 1940s and 1950s. For eastern Ukraine, attention has been focused on the man-made famine of 1932–33, in which five to seven million people died. Although the topic had been completely taboo until the era of glasnost, many Ukrainians had some knowledge of relatives' having died in the famine. A film about the famine shown on television on the eve of the December 1991 referendum is credited with influencing the over 90 percent pro-independence vote.[47] Much material on the famine had been revealed in the three years prior to independence.[48] The fact of the famine has been accepted by virtually everyone, but there are still differences in interpretation, with more and more Ukrainians becoming convinced that the famine was not simply the result of forced collectivization but an act of purposeful genocide against the Ukrainian people.[49]

Another historical topic that is just coming to the foreground is Ukrainian statehood in 1918–21, particularly the Ukrainian People's Republic (UNR). Only four years ago these formations were viewed as the epitome of evil and reaction, while today they are considered honorable examples of twentieth-century Ukrainian state building. A plethora of articles has focused on the politics, foreign relations, military policy, policy toward minorities, and other activities of the independent Ukrainian governments.[50] On a symbolic level, independent Ukraine has underscored its link to the UNR by adopting the same national emblems, the trident and the blue and yellow flag. Awareness of the UNR and other independent Ukrainian formations of 1917–21 is now beginning to penetrate the consciousness of the wider Ukrainian public.

Other historical issues are regionally based and have the potential for being divisive rather than creating a unifying vision. One of the most controversial has been the rehabilitation of the Organization of Ukrainian Nationalists (OUN) and the Ukrainian Insurgent Army (UPA). The UPA fought partially against the Germans but primarily against Soviet rule in western Ukraine until 1952.[51] The popular press has carried many articles about the heroic struggle of the UPA against Soviet occupation. Even the Ukrainian military paper and journal had extensive favorable press coverage about the activities of the UPA.[52] However, other articles object to the veneration of the UPA, arguing that it had cooperated with the Germans and committed atrocities against the Ukrainian and Polish populations.[53] The picture is further complicated by newly released archival materials showing that special detachments of the NKVD posed as UPA and destroyed entire villages in order to discredit the UPA. Opposition to the full rehabilitation of the UPA—whose few remaining members are demanding veterans' pensions—is particularly strong from Red Army veterans who had fought the UPA. It is very difficult to reconcile images of the heroic Red Army defenders against the Nazis and the UPA into a common historical consciousness. Yet this is exactly what the official organ of Ukraine's Defense Ministry attempted to accomplish, with only limited success.[54]

In an effort to determine the extent of the struggle over these historical interpretations and the possible emergence of a new or renewed Ukrainian historical consciousness, I have examined the daily *Pravda Ukrainy* from 1990 to early 1993. This newspaper was chosen because it is a Russian-language paper that until the banning of the Communist Party was the official organ of the Central Committee of the Communist Party of Ukraine. It had represented conservative, communist, pro-union forces. Even after its transformation into a general civic newspaper—one week after the attempted coup—*Pravda Ukrainy* retained much of its conservative and anti-Ukrainian nationalist character. Thus I believe *Pravda Ukrainy* can serve as a barometer of the extent to which certain historical views have gone beyond the narrow stream of nationalist intelligentsia and are beginning to penetrate the Communist and, since independence, ex-Communist political mainstream.

As a daily newspaper, *Pravda Ukrainy* was not primarily interested in historical issues. Yet in its struggle against the Ukrainian movement and particularly Rukh, the newspaper devoted much space to Ukrainian history. For example, when Rukh was preparing to commemorate the 500th anniversary of the Zaporozhian Cossacks in the summer of 1990, *Pravda Ukrainy* attacked these preparations.[55] In this article and a subsequent one, *Pravda Ukrainy* objected to Rukh's attempt to present the Cossacks as a unique Ukrainian phenomenon without reference to Russia and the common Ukrainian-Russian struggle against Polish control over Ukraine.[56] Abruptly, on 31 July 1990, *Pravda Ukrainy* published an article on the Cossacks that treated them as primarily a Ukrainian experience and a bastion of freedom and democracy. The about-face occurred fifteen days after Ukraine's declaration of sovereignty and on the eve of the Cossack commemorative events in early August. The Communists decided to co-opt the Cossack issue, and from late summer 1990 *Pravda Ukrainy* has consistently presented the Cossack experience as forming the core of Ukrainian history and culture. At the same time, the paper continued to oppose the glorification of any anti-Russian aspects of Cossack history. In December 1990, *Pravda Ukrainy* denounced Rukh's commemoration of Hetman Mazepa's stance against Russia at the Battle of Poltava (1709).[57] By January 1992 a more balanced picture of Mazepa emerged, but the hetman was still referred to as an egotist and political adventurer, indicating *Pravda Ukrainy*'s reluctance to accept fully the nationalist pantheon of heroes.[58]

A somewhat similar about-face occurred on the question of Ukrainian independence of 1917–21. *Pravda Ukrainy*'s extensive coverage of this issue was also sparked by the activities of Rukh. On 22 January 1990, on the anniversary of the declaration of independence in 1918 and the union of the West Ukrainian People's Republic in 1919, Rukh sponsored a human chain that linked Lviv and Kiev. The mobilization in the dead of winter of several hundred thousand people to commemorate "bourgeois nationalist" independence and the union of eastern and western Ukraine in one state presented a serious challenge to the

Soviet Communist scheme. *Pravda Ukrainy* repeatedly attacked the event and any revision of the official view that the UNR was a bourgeois nationalist entity, opposed to the workers and peasants, and was in the service of Germany, Austria, and Poland. It particularly lambasted the figure of Symon Petliura, the military chief of the Directory of the UNR, as an epitome of evil, responsible for pogroms and a general bloodbath in Ukraine. The paper reiterated that all aspirations of the Ukrainian people were fulfilled through the Bolshevik Revolution and the formation of the Ukrainian SSR within the Soviet Union.[59]

By November 1990, after the sovereignty declaration, the position of the paper toward the UNR softened, with some positive comments about Volodymyr Vynnychenko and Mykhailo Hrushevs'kyi.[60] In 1992 *Pravda Ukrainy* published several positive articles about the Central Rada,[61] the UNR government, and even a reprint of a factual, neutral report on Petliura's assassination.[62] It had finally accepted the UNR as a legitimate example of Ukrainian independence and statehood.

Kievan Rus' was represented in *Pravda Ukrainy* as an example of ancient Russian-Ukrainian unity, now threatened by both Russian and Ukrainian nationalism.[63] On the eve of Ukrainian independence but prior to the attempted putsch of August 1991, *Pravda Ukrainy* featured an extensive interview with Petro Tolochko, a leading specialist who linked Kievan Rus' firmly with Ukrainian history.[64] The full rehabilitation of Mykhailo Hrushevs'kyi as a historian placed the paper even more firmly behind the Ukrainian historical view on the origins of the East Slavs.

On the famine of 1933, *Pravda Ukrainy* was silent until June 1991, when it interviewed Serhii Diachenko, who had produced a film on the topic. Since then, the famine has been touched upon and represented as genocide against the Ukrainian people, for which Stalin was responsible.[65]

No historical theme received so much space in 1990 and 1991 as did the OUN-UPA. In 1990 sixteen issues had materials on the subject; in 1991 there were at least twenty-five.[66] All of these articles were in essence attacks on Rukh and Ukrainian separatists. In fact, the movement for Ukrainian independence was represented as either a front for or as leading to an OUN type of "fascism." *Pravda Ukrainy* was particularly shrill in trying to dispel the notion advocated by some that the UPA was the backbone of armed resistance to Stalinism. For *Pravda Ukrainy* the OUN-UPA was and probably remains the incarnation of evil beyond any rehabilitation. The virtually continuous exposé of OUN leaders and activities ceased suddenly with the declaration of independence. During all of 1992 there appeared only one factual note on the UPA.[67] Most likely the newspaper, unsure of its own status in a postcommunist independent Ukraine, decided not to take up such a sensitive issue. But an editorial in early 1993 that railed against a planned reunion in Lviv of surviving members of the SS Galicia division also deplored the attempted rehabilitation of the UPA as an equal insult and profanity.[68] *Pravda Ukrainy,* it seems, is not ready to accept OUN-UPA as part of a new Ukrainian historical consciousness.

It is clear that history has been a battleground first and foremost in Ukraine. With independence, historical views that had been underground in Ukraine and more fully developed in the emigration have come to the foreground. A new historical vision is emerging, in part spontaneously and in part by deliberate promotion on the part of historians, journalists, and publicists.

At this stage, Ukrainians are still groping for a shared vision of the past. Some themes, such as the Cossack experience, the Ukrainian view of Kievan Rus', Ukrainian Church traditions, the 1917–21 struggle for independence, and the horrors of Stalinism, particularly the 1933 famine, seem acceptable components of such a vision. Other themes involving World War II, OUN, and UPA have a more narrow political or regional appeal, continue to be divisive, and at this time cannot be incorporated into a broader Ukrainian historical identity.

Although debates over historical interpretations have been normal components of nation building, the Ukrainian case does have some peculiar characteristics. Thus far, the emerging Ukrainian historical consciousness has avoided anti-Russian or anti-Polish rhetoric, despite the fact that some of the historical themes could readily be used for such purposes. The process is largely one of differentiation from, but not rejection of, Russia. It is a search for one's own historical symbols rather than shared ones.

The measured approach toward establishing a historical identity is due to Ukraine's need to simultaneously build a state and a nation. There seems to be a consensus for most Ukrainians that nothing should jeopardize independence, not even nation building. Avoidance of conflict is paramount, not only vis-à-vis Ukraine's minorities but also with former Communists. For example, the exposition of Stalinist crimes is a frequent historical theme, yet no reference is ever made to living perpetrators of such crimes.

The formation of a new Ukrainian historical consciousness is still in a rudimentary stage, limited to the more nationally conscious elements of the population. A rapid and widespread introduction of a Ukrainian view of history is difficult, because imperial Russian and Soviet rule has resulted in the common acceptance of the dominant interpretations, even among many Ukrainians. Moreover, there is consensus on only some themes and interpretations. At least a preliminary codification of a Ukrainian view will occur with the adoption of new curricula and the publication of new textbooks. Adoption in school curricula would also make the Ukrainian historical view more prevalent among the wider public.

What impact will the emergence of the new Ukrainian historical consciousness have on Ukrainian-Russian relations? Much will depend on further developments in Ukraine. Increased political and economic tensions with Russia have the potential for an anti-Russian historical orientation. Of equal importance is how the Ukrainian historical view is received in Russia and the type of historical outlook that will emerge in post-Soviet Russia.

In Russia, the collapse of communism and the breakup of the Soviet Union have given new urgency to the debates about the "Russian question" and Russian identity. As Russians also are searching for their historical roots, they have attempted to cleanse their history of Marxist ideology and internationalism. The academician Dmitrii S. Likhachev has been in the forefront of the attempt to restore to Russia the essence of its history and culture. According to Likhachev, the Russian nation emerged in the tenth century in Kievan Rus', and even after the split "into two entities, Russia and Ukraine formed not only a political but also a culturally dualistic unity: Russian culture is meaningless without Ukrainian, as Ukrainian is without Russian."[69] The most noted Russian author in exile, Aleksandr Solzhenitsyn, has echoed very similar views.

The Russian unity myth has been and continues to be so embedded in the Russian psyche that it is very difficult for Russians—from conservative nationalists to liberal democrats—to acknowledge the right of Ukrainians to their own history and national identity. In a round-table discussion, the editor of *Moscow News*, Lev Korpinskii, insisted that Kiev was "the mother of Russian cities" and that "millions of

Russians are convinced that, without Ukraine, it is impossible to speak not only of a great Russia but of any kind of Russia at all."[70] The liberal thinker Aleksandr Tsipko came to the conclusion that "without today's Ukraine, there can be no Russia in the old, real sense of the word."[71] Viktor Aksiuchits, the leader of the Russian Christian Democratic Movement, argued that "despite what we are told now, I am absolutely sure that Belarusians, Ukrainians, and Russians even today continue to belong to one great Russian nation, formed during our joint history on the basis of the Orthodox faith."[72] The emphasis on unity takes on shrill dimensions in the right-wing Russian popular press. Such journals as *Molodaia gvardiia, Iunost'*, the newspaper *Literaturnaia Rossiia*, and, in their own specialized fields, *Voenno-istoricheskii zhurnal* and *Zhurnal Moskovskoi patriarkhii* have been advocating[73] a "one and indivisible Russia" that includes Ukraine both in the past and for the future. This position has been most systematically elaborated in *Molodaia gvardiia*, with the claims that Russia has a thousand-year-old history, that only within this Russian state can Ukraine exist, and that only a reconstituted Russia can provide stability for Europe and the world.[74]

While the more liberal Russian press does not advocate a "recovery" of Ukraine, it has not challenged the intellectual underpinnings for the "Russian idea." So far there has been hardly any attempt to differentiate between the history of Russia and that of the Russian Empire, or to view Russian history as primarily the experience of the Russians. Thus the Russian historical outlook still stresses unity and still presupposes that much of the history and culture of Ukraine is part and parcel of the Russian experience. Such a view is in direct opposition to the emerging Ukrainian historical consciousness, which stresses an autochthonous historical process and differentiation from Russia.

What impact does the emergence of a Ukrainian historical consciousness and the persistence of the Russian unity myth have on foreign policy? While historical considerations have not been the primary factors in the conduct of foreign policy of either Russia or Ukraine, they do color the attitudes of each side toward the other. The Russian government, even under the relatively "liberal" foreign policy of Andrei Kozyrev, treats Ukraine more as a wayward child than as an equal partner. Ukraine sees in virtually every action of Russia hegemonic and imperialistic intentions. Moreover, some Russian leaders seem willing to act out the old Russian imperial myth and bring the

Ukrainians and Belarusians into a "Great Russian nation." Any such attempt would run against the growing Ukrainian national and historical consciousness and could result in bloodshed, chaos, and a Yugoslavia-type tragedy. One way to avert such a tragedy would be for Russian historians to focus their attention on historical events that occurred on the territory of contemporary Russia and not seek to legitimate Russian statehood beyond Russian borders. Politicians, moreover, should be careful to act on the basis of genuine national interests of Russia and Ukraine rather than to pursue nineteenth-century national myths.

Notes

1. See his article, "Kak nam obustroit' Rossiiu," in *Komsomol'skaia pravda*, 18 September 1990. This also appeared in *Literaturnaia gazeta* on the same day and was reprinted in the Russian émigré periodical *Russkaia mysl'* (Paris) on 21 September. Here, in a section titled "Slovo k ukraintsam i belorusam," Solzhenitsyn adopts a traditional, but still popular, Russian scheme of history when he states that "our people split into three branches only because of the menacing misfortune of the Mongolian invasion and Polish colonization." A full English translation of his "Word to Ukrainians and Belorussians" can be found in *Ukrainian Weekly*, no. 42 (1990). Subsequently the entire work was published in English as *Rebuilding Russia: Reflections and Tentative Proposals* (New York: Farrar, Straus and Giroux, 1991). See also the commentary piece by Roman Solchanyk in *Ukrainian Weekly*, no. 11 (1993), for Solzhenitsyn's recent proclamations regarding Ukraine.

2. N.M. Karamzin's *Istoriia gosudarstva rossiiskogo* was published in twelve volumes in St. Petersburg between 1816 and 1829. It was here that he outlined the so-called official scheme of Russian history, which later Russian or Russophile historians have embraced to this day. For a wider discussion of this scheme and how it conflicts with the Ukrainian scheme, see the study by Lubomyr R. Wynar, *Mykhailo Hrushevsky: Ukrainian-Russian Confrontation in Historiography* (New York: Ukranian Historical Association, 1988).

3. On Pogodin's views, see vol. 7 of his work, *Issledovaniia, zamechaniia i lektsii o russkoi istorii* (Moscow, 1856), especially pp. 425–28.

4. Most North American textbooks follow the Russian imperial scheme. See Nicholas V. Riazanovsky, *A History of Russia*, 4th ed. (New York: Oxford University Press, 1984); Michael T. Florinsky, *Russia: A Short History* (New York, 1964); G. Vernadsky and M. Karpovich, *A History of Russia*, 4 vols. (New Haven: Yale University Press, 1946–59); John M. Thompson, *Russia and the Soviet Union: An Historical Introduction* (New York: Scribner, 1986), among others.

5. Quote from Michael Hrushevsky, *A History of Ukraine* (New Haven, 1970), p. 496. For the background to the formulation of Russian imperial language policies in 1863 and 1876, see Ivan L. Rudnytsky, *Essays in Modern*

Ukrainian History (Cambridge: Harvard University Press, 1987), pp. 131–32; and Fedir Savchenko, *The Suppression of the Ukrainian Activities in 1876* (Munich, 1970).

6. On populist historiography, see Dmytro Doroshenko, "A Survey of Ukrainian Historiography," in a special issue of *Annals of the Ukrainian Academy of Arts and Sciences in the United States* (New York), vols. 6–7, no. 4 (1957), pp. 116–87.

7. M. Hrushevs'kyi, "Zvychaina skhema Russkoi istorii i sprava ratsional'-noho ukladu skhidnoho slov'ianstva," *Sbornik statei po slavianovedeniiu* (St. Petersburg, 1904), pp. 298–304; the English translation appeared in *Annals of the Ukrainian Academy of Arts and Sciences in the United States*, vol. 2, no. 4 (1952), pp. 355–64, and has been reprinted several times.

8. Ibid. See also his ten-volume *Istoriia Ukrainy-Rusy* (New York, 1954–58).

9. A sample of works by representatives of the "state school," which touch specifically on this topic, include Nataliia Polons'ka-Vasylenko, *Two Conceptions of the History of Ukraine and Russia* (London, 1968); and Nicholas D. Chubaty, "The Meaning of 'Russia' and 'Ukraine,' " in *Readings in Russian History*, ed. Sidney Harcave (New York: Cromwell, 1962). See also Doroshenko, "Survey of Ukrainian Historiography"; and Olexander Ohloblyn, "Ukrainian Historiography, 1917–1956," *Annals of the Ukrainian Academy of Arts and Sciences in the United States*, special issue, vols. 6–7, no. 4 (1957), pp. 300–303; 307–435.

10. See Lowell Tillet, *The Great Friendship: Soviet Historians and the Non-Russian Nationalities* (Chapel Hill, 1969); and the chapter "Soviet Interpretation of Ukrainian History" in Yaroslav Bilinsky, *The Second Soviet Republic: The Ukraine after World War II* (New Brunswick: Rutgers University Press, 1964), pp. 203–25. For a more recent assessment of this topic, see Roman Szporluk, "The Ukraine and Russia," in *The Last Empire: Nationality and the Soviet Empire*, ed. Robert Conquest (Stanford: Hoover Institution Press, 1986), pp. 151–82.

11. For a discussion of the Soviet official view of the Treaty of Pereiaslav, see the work by John Basarab, *Pereiaslav 1654: A Historiographical Study* (Edmonton: University of Alberta, 1982). The theses alluded to have been published as *Tezy pro 300-richchia vozz'iednannia Ukrainy z Rosiieiu (1648–1654 rr), skhvaleni Tsentral'nym Komitetom Komunistychnoi Partii Radians'koho Soiuza* (Kiev, 1954). The Soviet interpretation was challenged by the dissident Mykhailo Braichevs'kyi in his work *Pryiednannia chy vozz'iednannia* (Toronto, 1972).

12. This is discussed in Roman Solchanyk, "Molding 'the Soviet People': The Role of Ukraine and Belorussia," *Journal of Ukrainian Studies*, vol. 8, no. 1 (summer 1983), pp. 3–18; see also his study of Soviet language policies, "Russian Language and Soviet Politics," *Soviet Studies*, vol. 34, no. 1 (January 1982), pp. 23–42. The Ukrainian dissident Iurii Badz'o protested to the Communist Party of Ukraine against the Soviet historical scheme and the lack of any possibility for Ukrainians to develop their own identity: see his *Vidkrytyi lyst do Prezydii Verkhovnoi Rady Soiuzu RSR ta Tsentral'noho Komitetu KPRS* (New York, 1981).

13. Examples of this include D.K. Kasymenko, "Novi osiahy ukrains'kykh istorykiv," *Ukrains'kyi istorychnyi zhurnal*, vol. 3 (1963); F.P. Shevchenko, "Chomu M. Hrushevs'kyi povernuvsia na Radians'ku Ukrainu," *Ukrain'skyi istorychnyi zhurnal*, vol. 11 (1966), pp. 13–30; O. Apanovych, *Zbroini syly Ukrainy pershoi polovyny XVIII st.* (Kiev, 1960).

14. For a discussion of the official Soviet attitudes to Mykhailo Hrushevs'kyi and the debate sparked by glasnost, see Bohdan W. Klid's, "The Struggle over Mykhailo Hrushevs'kyi: Recent Soviet Polemics," *Canadian Slavonic Papers*, vol. 33, no. 1 (March 1991), pp. 32–45.

15. P. Tolochko, "Istoriia Ukrainy-nove vysvitlennia," *Ukraina*, no. 41 (1989), pp. 4–6.

16. *Mykhailo Hrushevs'kyi* . . . izhnarodna iuvileina konferentsiia prysviachena 125-i richnytsi vid dnia narodzhenni (Lviv, 1991).

17. M. Hrushevs'kyi, *Istoriia Ukrainy–Rusy*, vol. 1 (Kiev, 1991).

18. The text of the act of independence can be found in *Robitnycha hazeta*, 9 March 1991, p. 1. For an English-language translation, see *Ukrainian Weekly*, no. 35 (1991), p. 1.

19. *Velykyi ukrainets'* (Kiev, 1992).

20. The few paragraphs on church politics are intended only as a vivid example of how history was and continues to be a battleground in Ukraine. The topic will be treated separately and certainly more comprehensively in a forthcoming volume in this series.

21. The basic view of the Russian Orthodox Church has been consistent; for the classic nineteenth-century exposition see Makarii (Bulgakov), *Istoriia russkoi tserkvi*, vols. 1–12 (St. Petersburg, 1882–84); for a contemporary assessment see *The Russian Orthodox Church, 10th to 20th Centuries* (Moscow, 1988); and Archbishop Makary, *The Eastern Orthodox Church in Ukraine* (Kiev, 1980).

22. Bohdan Bociurkiw, "The Uniate Church in the Soviet Ukraine: A Case Study in Soviet Church Policy," *Canadian Slavonic Papers*, vol. 7 (1965), pp. 89–113; Frank Sysyn, *The Ukrainian Orthodox Question in the USSR* (Cambridge, MA, 1987), pp. 9–20.

23. For a summary of the Ukrainian view on Christianity, see M. Chubatyi, *Istoriia khrystiianstva na Rusy-Ukrainy*, 2 vols. (Rome–New York, 1965–76); I. Vlasovs'kyi, *Narys istorii Ukrains'koi pravoslavnoi tserkvy*, 4 vols. (South Bound Brook, NJ, 1955–66); O. Lotot'skyi, *Avtokefaliia*, 2 vols. (Warsaw 1935–38).

24. See, for example, Ihor Kutash, "The Soviet Union Celebrates 1000 Years of Christianity," *Christian History*, vol. 7, no. 2 (1988), pp. 12–13.

25. Vasyl' Ivanyshyn, "Ukrains'ka tserkva i protses natsional'noho vidrodzhennia," *Ukrains'ke vidrodzhennia i natsional'na tserkva* (Kiev, 1990), pp. 30–31.

26. Ibid., pp. 34–35.

27. See the article by Frank Sysyn, "The Russian Sobor and the Rejection of Ukrainian Orthodox Autocephaly," *Ukrainian Weekly*, no. 30 (1990), pp. 8–9; see also "Tretie vidrodzhennia UAPTs," *Ukrains'ki visti* (Detroit), 7 October 1991.

28. Sysyn, *Ukrainian Orthodox Question in the USSR*, pp. 12–13; Bohdan Bociurkiw, "The Rise of the Ukrainian Autocephalous Orthodox Church, 1919–22," in *Church, Nation and State in Russia and Ukraine*, ed. Geoffrey A. Mosking (New York: St. Martin's Press, 1990), pp. 228–49; and his "Uniate Church in Soviet Ukraine," pp. 89–113.

29. "The Russian Orthodox Church: Its Role in History and the Modern World," *Commission of the Ukrainian SSR for UNESCO Bulletin*, vol. 1 (1988), pp. 1–5.

30. For more information on these publications, the reader is referred to the

catalogue *Harvard Ukrainian Research Institute Publications* (Cambridge, MA, 1992).

31. For example, see Kutash, "Soviet Union Celebrates 1000 Years of Christianity," pp. 14–15; and the pamphlet *The Millennium of Christianity in Rus'–Ukraine: The Harvard Project (988–1988)* (Cambridge, MA, n.d. [c. 1988]).

32. "1991: A Look Back," *Ukrainian Weekly*, no. 52 (1991), p. 7.

33. Metropolitan Philaret [Filaret], "Slovo Mytropolyta Kyivs'koho i vsiiei Ukrainy Filareta na vidkrytti Soboru Ukrains'koi pravoslavnoi tserkvy," *Sobor Ukrains'koi pravoslavnoi tserkvy* (Kiev, 1992), p. 5.

34. "Zvernennia Soboru Ukrains'koi pravoslavnoi tserkvy do sviatiishoho Patriarkha Moskovs'koho i vsiiei Rusi Aleksiia II i iepyskopatu Rus'koi pravoslavnoi tserkvy," *Sobor Ukrains'koi pravoslavnoi tserkvy*, pp. 32–33; Sysyn, "Russian Sobor," pp. 8–9; see also Serhii Plokhy, "Ukrainian Autocephaly and Metropolitan Filaret," *Ukrainian Weekly*, no. 31 (1992), pp. 5 and 12.

35. For the most recent assessment of developments with the churches in Ukraine, see the article by Khristina Lew, "Church Split Continues to Plague Orthodox Faithful in Ukraine," *Ukrainian Weekly*, no. 12 (1993), p. 3.

36. On Dmytro Bahalii, see "Dmytro Bahalii: Avtobiohrafiia," *Kyivs'ka starovyna*, no. 4 (July–August 1992), pp. 81–95; on Volodymyr Antonovych, see Oleksandra Kyiana, "Kafedral'ne 'viruiu' Volodymyra Antonovycha: Z neopublikovanoi spadshchyny," *Kyivs'ka starovyna*, no. 3 (May–June 1992), pp. 63–69. Recent works on Mykola Kostomarov include the book by Iu.A. Pinchuk, *Mykola Ivanovych Kostomarov* (Kiev, 1992); and the article by Petro Tolochko, "Vydatnyi istoryk Ukrainy i Rosii," *Kyivs'ka starovyna*, no. 5 (September–October 1992), pp. 7–14. Examples of the recent interest in D. Iavornyts'kyi include the memoirs of a specialist on this historian, Ivan Shapoval, published in *Kyivs'ka starovyna*, no. 3 (1992), pp. 94–100.

37. Journals such as *Kyivs'ka starovyna* in particular and, to a lesser extent, the popular weekly *Ukraina* have been making this a regular practice.

38. His well-received *Ukraine: A History* (Toronto: University of Toronto Press, 1988) was translated and republished as *Ukraina: Istoriia* (Kiev, 1991), and serialized in nos. 4, 6, 7, 8, 9, 11, and 12 (1991) of *Ukrains'kyi istorychnyi zhurnal*.

39. Examples include O. Pritsak, "Ahatanhel Kryms'kyi," *Kyivs'ka starovyna*, no. 1 (January–February 1992), pp. 11–26. Taras Hunczak and Thomas Prymak are both published in *Ukrains'kyi istorychnyi zhurnal* (nos. 10 and 1 [1991], respectively), while Roman Szporluk has had works published in a variety of forums, ranging from *Ukraina, Nauka i kul'tura* in Kiev (1991) to *Geneza* in Lviv (1992).

40. On such tendencies among the Cossack movements in Russia, see Andrew Wilson and Nina Bachkatov in *The World Today* (London), vol. 49, no. 1 (January 1993), pp. 2–4.

41. An elaboration on these points and an assessment of how Cossack history has been treated can be found in Frank Sysyn's "The Reemergence of the Ukrainian Nation and Cossack Mythology," *Social Research*, vol. 58, no. 4 (winter 1991), pp. 845–64.

42. *News From Ukraine* (Kiev), nos. 36–37 (1992) features a picture on its front page of President Leonid Kravchuk holding a mace on the first anniversary

of Ukrainian Independence Day. In a book devoted to interviews with and speeches by him, Kravchuk is again shown holding a Cossack mace; see Leonid Kravchuk, *Ie taka derzhava—Ukraina* (Kiev, 1992). Viacheslav Chornovil was elected leader of Ukraine's burgeoning Cossack Brotherhood, in the process of which he characteristically held a gold and silver *bulava*, or mace. It was during this event, on 21 June 1992, that the Cossack Brotherhood revoked the Treaty of Pereiaslav. See *Ukrainian Weekly,* no. 27 (1992), pp. 8–13.

43. Volodymyr Zamlyns'kyi, "Het'many u borot'bi za suverenitet i derzhavnist' Ukrainy," *Kyivs'ka starovyna,* no. 4 (July–August 1992), pp. 2–6.

44. Ivan Storozhenko, "Kozaky pro doktrynu ne chuly, ale ii znaly," *Viis'ko Ukrainy,* nos. 2–3 (1993), pp. 16–18; and the interview with General Volodymyr Muliava in *Ukraina,* no. 1 (1993), pp. 14–15.

45. Iurii Mytsyk proposed this in his article "Istoriia ukrains'koho kozatstva: Aktual'ni problemy doslidzhen'," *Kyivs'ka starovyna,* no. 3 (May–June 1992), pp. 2–6.

46. For recent assessments of Mazepa, see the foreword to the translation of Alfred Jensen's work, *Mazepa* (Kiev, 1992), by Bohdan Iakymovych, pp. 5–21.

47. On Saturday, 30 November 1991, Channel 1 of Ukrainian TV premiered the film *Holod–'33* (Famine '33) at 1430 hours. An interview followed with the producers of the film.

48. *Holod 1932–1933 rokiv na Ukraini: ochyma istorykiv, movoiu dokumentiv* (Kiev, 1990); and Mezhdunarodnaia komissiia po rassledovaniiu goloda na Ukraine 1932–1933 godov, *Itogovyi otchet 1990 god* (Kiev, 1992).

49. Vasyl' Marochko, "Bodai te lykho ne vertalos'. . ." *Suchasnist',* no. 2 (1993), p. 92.

50. A number of articles have appeared in *Ukrains'kyi istorychnyi zhurnal,* nos. 5–9 (1991). The organ of the Ukrainian parliament, *Holos Ukrainy,* on the seventy-fifth anniversary of the declaration of Ukrainian independence, has also sympathetically reviewed the UNR past, in nos. 12, 13, and 17 (1993). See also *Molod' Ukrainy,* 19 January 1993 and 21 January 1993.

51. There is a vast literature on the history of the OUN and UPA, some of which is partisan, or otherwise hostile. A useful study that deals with the OUN is John Armstrong, *Ukrainian Nationalism,* 3rd ed. (Englewood, CO: Ukranian Academic Press, 1990); and chapters 1–4 of Bilinsky, *Second Soviet Republic.*

52. Favorable articles on OUN-UPA appeared in *Narodna armiia,* 14 October 1992; 16 October 1992; 28 October 1992; 2 February 1993; 4 February 1993; 23 February 1993; and 24 February 1993. The journal of Ukraine's National Guard, *Viis'ko Ukrainy,* devotes a whole section to the heroic UPA: see no. 1 (1992), pp. 52–80. A very spirited defense of OUN-UPA appeared in *Ukraina,* no. 1 (1993), pp. 18–19.

53. See, for instance, Volodymyr Poniza, "Ne vsim spivaimo slavu!" *Holos Ukrainy,* no. 9 (1993), p. 13.

54. The call for reconciliation between World War II and UPA veterans was published in *Narodna armiia,* 28 October 1992; 4 February 1993; and 24 February 1993. However, several World War II veterans' groups continue to oppose the rehabilitation of the UPA; see *Narodna armiia,* 14 January 1993; 23 February 1993.

55. *Pravda Ukrainy,* 6 June 1990.

56. *Pravda Ukrainy*, 25 July 1990.
57. *Pravda Ukrainy*, 12 July 1990.
58. *Pravda Ukrainy*, 21 January 1992.
59. *Pravda Ukrainy*, 23 January 1990; 24 January 1990; and 26 July 1990.
60. *Pravda Ukrainy*, 22 November 1990.
61. *Pravda Ukrainy*, 17 March 1992.
62. *Pravda Ukrainy*, 29 April 1992.
63. *Pravda Ukrainy*, 23 March 1990; 28 December 1990.
64. *Pravda Ukrainy*, 7 August 1991.
65. *Pravda Ukrainy*, 13 June 1991.
66. *Pravda Ukrainy*, 1990: 11 February, 11 April, 19 August, 13 September, 14 October, 1 November, 30 November, 14 December, 16 December, 19 December, 21 December, 22 December, 23 December, 25 December, 26 December, 29 December; 1991: 9 January, 27 February, 28 February, 28 May, 8 June, 14 June, 18 June, 20 June, 21 June, 25 June, 26 June, 27 June, 28 June, 3 July, 5 July, 6 July, 9 July, 10 July, 12 July, 13 July, 18 July, 19 July, 22 August, 23 August, 24 August.
67. *Pravda Ukrainy*, 29 April 1992.
68. *Pravda Ukrainy*, 2 March 1993.
69. Dmitrii S. Likhachev, *Reflections on Russia* (Boulder, CO: Westview Press, 1991), p. 74.
70. *Moskovskie novosti*, no. 51 (1991).
71. *Komsomol'skaia pravda*, 14 January 1992.
72. Radio Rossii, 7 January 1993, as cited in Vera Tolz, "The Burden of Imperial Legacy in Russia," *RFE/RL Research Report*, 22 March 1993.
73. To gain some idea of current Russian views, I have perused the following Russian periodicals and newspapers: *Voprosy istorii*, nos. 1, 2–3, 4–5, 8–9 (1992); *Otechestvennaia istoriia*, nos. 2, 3, 4, 5, 6 (1992); *Molodaia gvardiia*, nos. 1–2, 3–4, 5–6, 7 (1992); nos. 1, 2 (1993); *Voenno-istoricheskii zhurnal*, nos. 1, 2, 3, 6–7, 9 (1992); *Grani*, no. 165 (1992); *Kentavr*, October–December 1992, May–June 1992; *Moskva*, nos. 1, 2–4 (1992); *Posev*, nos. 1, 2, 3, 4, 5, 6 (1992); *Iunost'*, nos. 1, 2, 3 (1992); *Oktiabr'*, nos. 9, 10, 11, 12 (1992); *Zhurnal Moskovskoi patriarkhii*, nos. 7, 10, 11, 12 (1991); nos. 1, 2, 3, 4, 5 (1992); *Literaturnaia Rossiia*, nos. 1, 2, 3, 4, 5, 6, 7, 8, 9, 10, 11 (1993).
74. *Molodaia gvardiia*, no. 3 (1992); no. 1 (1993); no. 2 (1993); and no. 7 (1993).

7

Historical Debates and Territorial Claims

Cossack Mythology in the Russian-Ukrainian Border Dispute

Serhii M. Plokhy

Introduction: The Russian Challenge

The dissolution of the USSR—the last world empire—brought to the fore the whole range of problems that usually accompanies the dissolution of empires. The disintegration of the Ottoman, Habsburg, and, to some extent, French empires took place in the midst of war. Despite the fact that Britain and later Portugal withdrew from their colonial territories almost peacefully, the national, tribal, and religious conflicts that commenced after the departure of colonial administrations eventually resulted in bloody conflicts and wars.

Among the many problems that have followed from the dissolution of the USSR is the border question. Although the border disputes in the former USSR have not been as sharp as they are in the former Yugoslavia, they do constitute a serious threat to peaceful relations between the former Soviet republics. It was hardly accidental that the first major manifestation of national unrest in the USSR came with the events in Nagorno-Karabakh, a region claimed by two former Soviet republics, Armenia and Azerbaijan. The five-year war between Armenia and Azerbaijan for control over Nagorno-Karabakh demonstrates how dangerous the border conflicts in the former USSR can be. The transformation of administrative borders into state borders is proving to be a very complicated and uneasy process.[1]

With the disintegration of the USSR, the border question has raised to the level of special importance the relations between two other republics of the former Soviet Union—Russia and Ukraine. The problem came to light in late August 1991, after the proclamation of Ukrainian independence. On 29 August the spokesman for the Russian president, Pavel Voshchanov, announced that if Ukraine seceded from the USSR, Russia would reserve the right to revise its borders with Ukraine.[2] In fact, the new Russian authorities claimed Russia's right to the eastern and southern oblasts of Ukraine, areas that underwent a high degree of Russification under the Communist regime, and to the Crimean Peninsula, a region transferred from Russia to Ukraine in 1954.

Since the results of the Ukrainian referendum (held in December 1991) demonstrated overwhelming support for the idea of Ukrainian independence (more than 90 percent of the voters that took part in the referendum voted for independence), the nationalistic faction in the Russian leadership was forced to abandon previous Russian claims to the eastern Ukrainian oblasts and concentrate specifically on the issue of Crimea, the only region in Ukraine where ethnic Russians constitute the majority of the population and where the vote for independence was the lowest in Ukraine (54 percent in favor). As the "all-Union resort" and home of the Black Sea fleet, Crimea is viewed by many Russian politicians as an "ancient Russian territory." Leaders of the parliamentary nationalistic factions have been using every single opportunity to publicize their opinion that the transition of Crimea to Ukraine in 1954 was conducted in violation of the Russian constitution and that there are more than enough legal arguments in place to demand the transfer of Crimea back to Russia.[3]

In April 1992, when the confrontation over Crimea had reached its peak, Russian Vice President Aleksandr Rutskoi on his visit to Crimea made a direct claim to that territory, justifying this claim on the basis of historical arguments. Rutskoi rejected one part of Crimean history—the transfer of the peninsula to Ukraine in 1954—and emphasized another—the annexation of Crimea by the Russian Empire and its military presence there:

> If one turns to history, then again history is not on the side of those who are trying to appropriate this land. If in 1954, perhaps under the influ-

ence of a hangover or maybe of sunstroke, the appropriate documents were signed according to which the Crimea was transferred to the jurisdiction of Ukraine, I am sorry, such a document does not cancel out the history of Crimea.[4]

In another remark made by Rutskoi during his April 1992 visit to Crimea, he asserted that the Black Sea fleet was and would remain Russian.[5] This same position was shared by the commander of the fleet, Admiral Igor Kasatonov, who in December 1992 stressed in an interview with the Russian nationalist newspaper *Literaturnaia Rossiia* that Russia in any form cannot be imagined without its glorious Black Sea fleet. According to Kasatonov, the Ukrainian takeover of the Black Sea fleet and its naval bases in Crimea and the Black Sea region would throw Russia back three centuries, to the times before the rule of Peter I.[6]

For Rutskoi, Kasatonov, and other nationalistically oriented Russian leaders, the history of the Russian presence in Crimea is closely connected to the history of the fleet and hence to the history of its main base in Crimea—Sevastopol. The myth of Sevastopol as a "city of Russian glory" has been used often as a cornerstone in the historical justification for all current Russian territorial claims to Crimea.[7] This myth is based on the events of the Crimean War of 1853–56 and presents the heroism of the multinational imperial army at the siege exclusively as the heroism of the Russian soldiers. It was used to justify and protect the imperial aggrandizements of the Russian Empire in the eighteenth and nineteenth centuries and received its second life under the Stalinist regime, especially during World War II and later in the circumstances of the Cold War.[8] With the disintegration of the USSR and rebirth of the Russian imperial ideology, this myth, like other imperial myths that survive from the Soviet period, was once again invoked to preserve Russian interests beyond the state territory of the Russian Federation. It was in the tradition of Sevastopol mythology that Admiral Kasatonov was really proud to say in his interview with *Literaturnaia Rossiia* that during his tenure as a commander of the fleet, the tomb of Admirals Lazarev, Nakhimov, Kornilov, and Istomin, who were killed during the Sevastopol siege of 1854–55, was restored in the St. Volodymyr Cathedral of Sevastopol.[9]

The exploitation of the Sevastopol myth by leading Russian politicians and military commanders in their territorial claims to Ukraine pressed the Ukrainian side to fight back with the same weapon—historical arguments and justifications. Ukrainian president Leonid Kravchuk in his interview with Sevastopol TV in January 1993 proposed to solve the Sevastopol question peacefully, by not questioning whose glory is symbolized by the city of Sevastopol, "because otherwise," he said, "it would be possible to return to the times of Alexander of Macedonia and Julius Caesar." And he continued, "Why do we limit ourselves to the hundred-year period. Could we not take under consideration a thousand years? Really, there are no limits. One person might like to start with the 1920s, and another with the 1940s."[10] Thus he tried to question not the history of the Russian presence in the region, but first of all the legitimacy of the claims made on the basis of a relatively short period in the history of the peninsula, when in fact its history is much longer and includes the years of Greek colonization. To counter the Russian position, Ukrainian historians and politicians chose to base their policy of preserving their country's territorial integrity on the basis of a highly elaborate Cossack mythology.

One of the main differences between East and West European nationalism is often viewed in their attitudes toward the past. As Hans Kohn put it:

> Nationalism in the West arose in an effort to build a nation in the political reality and the struggles of the present without too much sentimental regard for the past; nationalists in Central and Eastern Europe created often, out of the myths of the past and the dreams of the future, an ideal fatherland, closely linked with the past, devoid of any immediate connection with the present, and expected to become sometime a political reality.[11]

From the historiographical point of view, Ukrainian nationalists in the nineteenth and early twentieth centuries based the idea of an independent Ukrainian state on two main myths: that of Ukraine as the direct and only successor to medieval Kievan Rus', and the myth of the Ukrainian Cossacks. Mykhailo Hrushevs'kyi, the first president of the Ukrainian People's Republic in 1918 and, like many other leaders of the national awakening in Eastern Europe, a prominent historian, contributed much to the development of both myths. It was his initiative to adopt the trident—the symbol of power of the medieval Kievan princes—as the national coat of arms. It was also Hrushevs'kyi who could be considered the most prominent twentieth-century student of the Cossack era.[12]

This chapter takes as its point of departure John A. Armstrong's definition of the myth as *the integrating phenomenon through which symbols of national identity acquire a coherent meaning.*[13] The author also shares his approach to the study of the myths, based on Claude Levi-Strauss's method. "I am utterly incompetent to judge whether the version of Kiev and its successors that Hrushevsky presented is 'truer' than other versions," argued Armstrong in his discussion of Ukrainian historical mythology. "The basic insight provided by the anthropological approach is that such questions are irrelevant for identity except insofar as they affect a constitutive myth."[14]

Thus the main goal of this chapter is not to define whether the Cossack myth is "true" or "false," but to determine how the myth was created and how it has been transformed in order to meet the challenges of the current Russian-Ukrainian border dispute. In the conclusion I will also attempt to provide an answer to the question of the possible consequences of foreign-policy decisions that are based on the grounds of historical mythology.

Cossack Mythology I: Ukrainian Cossacks and the History of the Russian Imperial Border

Cossack mythology, which was based on the accounts of the most glorious pages of Cossack history and the Cossack struggle against Poland, Turkey, the Tatars, and Russia, became an important part of the ideology of Ukrainian national awakening in the nineteenth century. The leaders of the movement were searching for examples of their glorious national past, and for the periods of independent or semi-independent existence of their nation. It was hardly a surprise that the history of Cossack uprisings and the polity created by Hetman Khmel'nyts'kyi in the middle of the seventeenth century were chosen by them as a basis for a new national mythology.[15]

It is generally accepted that the Cossack period covers the sixteenth to eighteenth centuries in Ukrainian history. In fact, the first accounts of the activity of the Ukrainian Cossacks come from the last decade of the fifteenth century, but only a century later could the Cossacks emerge as a significant military and to some extent political force. As a social group the Cossacks came into existence following a colonization wave of the local Ukrainian population eastward to the steppe territories of southern Ukraine. The majority of them were fugitive peasants looking for new lands to cultivate and trying to avoid the serfdom imposed on them by the Polish and local Ukrainian nobility. Relatively soon the Cossacks found themselves in a position strong enough to oppose the politics of the Polish state in the frontier area. A series of Cossack uprisings against Polish rule started at the end of the sixteenth century and culminated in 1648 with the Cossack revolt led by Hetman Bohdan Khmel'nyts'kyi. The latter managed to create a separate Cossack polity—the hetmanate. For a short time this polity enjoyed an independent status, but in 1654, unable to resist a Polish offensive on its own, Khmel'nyts'ky recognized the suzerainty of the Muscovite tsar.[16] The hetmanate became an autonomous part of the Muscovite state, and its eastern borders, based on the eastern borders of the Kiev and Chernihiv palatinates of the Polish-Lithuanian Commonwealth, were at that time transformed into the first Russian-Ukrainian boundary. The origin of this boundary goes back to the turn of the sixteenth century. In 1503, during a war between Muscovy and Lithuania, the Chernihiv princes shifted their loyalty from Lithuania to Muscovy, and the Chernihiv territory was incorporated into the Muscovite state. It was lost by Muscovy to the Polish-Lithuanian Commonwealth in the first two decades of the seventeenth century. Owing to the Deulino peace of 1618, the Chernihiv area was transferred to Poland.[17]

In the 1620s and 1630s, after a range of unsuccessful uprisings against Polish rule, the Ukrainian Cossacks started emigrating to the territory belonging to Muscovy. They were allowed by the tsar to settle in the unpopulated areas of the Donets River basin and there established block settlements in what later would be called Sloboda Ukraine, an area that today constitutes one of the Russian-Ukrainian borderlands.[18]

Muscovy's drive to the west and its incorporation of the Ukrainian territories began on a large scale after the conclusion of the Pereiaslav treaty in 1654. The years of the Russo-Ukrainian-Polish war that followed the Pereiaslav Agreement established a new international order in Eastern Europe. Due to the Andrusovo 1667 peace treaty, Ukrainian territories were now divided between Russia and Poland. The Dnieper river was chosen as the major delimitation line. Left-bank Ukraine came under the tsar's rule, and the existence of an autonomous Cossack polity—the hetmanate—was allowed there. Right-bank and western Ukraine remained under Polish control. In the Polish zone, the autonomous rights of the Cossack formations were significantly diminished at first and then completely abolished. The same process was under way in Russian Ukraine. The Cossack uprising, led by Hetman Ivan Mazepa in 1708, tried to stop the process of the hetmanate's decay with the help of Sweden. Mazepa and his ally Charles XII of Sweden were defeated by the Russian tsar, Peter I, in the battle of Poltava in 1709, which resulted in a further limitation of the hetmanate's autonomous rights. The Russian-Polish border along the Dnieper continued to exist for more than a century, and remnants of this border may be seen in some parts of the contemporary Ukrainian-Belarusian border in the Chernihiv area.[19]

The second half of the eighteenth century witnessed the extension of Russian imperial territory further to the west and south. The victorious wars of the empire with Turkey resulted in the annexation of the vast areas along the coast of the Azov and Black seas and finally in the annexation of Crimea in 1783.[20] Three subsequent partitions of Poland in 1772–95 brought under the tsar's rule the majority of Ukrainian ethnic territories: right-bank Ukraine, Volhynia, Podillia, the Kholm region, and Pidliassia.[21]

The Ukrainian Cossacks played an important role in the acquisition of the new territories, especially those areas that were annexed as a result of the Russo-Turkish wars. The Ukrainian elite, who collaborated with the imperial government, demonstrated their special support for Russian actions against their traditional enemies: the Tatars, Turks, and Poles. A principal architect of Russian foreign policy in the last quarter of the eighteenth century was Prince Oleksandr Bezborod'ko, a descendant of the well-known Ukrainian family and initially a Cossack officer himself, who was especially anxious to annex to the Russian Empire the new territories in western and southern Ukraine that once belonged to Poland and Turkey.[22]

The Russo-Turkish wars of the second half of the eighteenth century resulted not only in the expansion of Ukrainian territory under the rule of the Russian Tsars but also in the abolition of autonomous Cossack bodies in Ukraine. By the 1770s both the hetmanate and the Zaporozhian Sich, the Cossack Host in the lower Dnieper region, ceased to exist as a result of actions taken by Empress Catherine II. The Zaporozhian Cossacks were resettled partly in the territories along the coast of the Azov and Black seas, the territories that they had helped attach to the empire, and partly in the Kuban region (now a territory in the Russian Federation) and the trans-Danube territory (now part of Romania). The new territorial acquisitions of the empire opened the way for Ukrainian peasants to emigrate from densely populated areas of left- and right-bank Ukraine to southern and eastern Ukraine, and to the Voronezh, Don, Kuban, and Stavropol regions now in Russia. This resettlement of the Ukrainian population, which started in the seventeenth century, lasted until the beginning of the twentieth and defined the boundaries of Ukrainian ethnic territory in the east.[23]

Cossack Mythology II: Formation of the Myth

Despite the initial spread of Cossack formations over the vast territories of left-bank and right-bank Ukraine, Volhynia, and Podillia, the origin of the Cossack mythology has been linked to the relatively small part of Ukrainian territory once controlled by the Cossacks—the territory of the hetmanate. It was the only Cossack area that enjoyed the elements of autonomy for a relatively long period of time and where maintaining the historical memory of the Cossacks was essential for the survival of the ruling elite.

There is enough evidence in place to state that the process of the creation of certain elements of the Cossack mythology began as early as the first decades of the seventeenth century. Nevertheless, till the turn of the eighteenth century there was a lack of "bearers of the high culture" closely associated with Cossacks to create any sort of elaborated mythology. The process began on a large scale only in the first decades of the eighteenth century. This period witnessed the emergence in the hetmanate of the new social strata composed of a mixture of Cossack officers and old nobility, defined by Zenon Kohut as the Ukrainian gentry.[24] This gentry strived for the preservation of the autonomous rights for its political entity and attempted to build the concept of the hetmanate's legitimacy on the legacy of Cossack treaties with the tsars, creating in that way one of the first stages in the development of Cossack mythology. In fact, the myth was shaped in such a way to support the power of the emerging gentry. The gentry needed the Cossack myth to secure not only the political rights of the hetmanate, but also its own economic rights based on the Cossack-Muscovite treaties of the second half of the seventeenth century.[25]

The defeat of Hetman Ivan Mazepa in the battle of Poltava in 1709 constituted in many ways the turning point in the development of Cossack mythology. Threatened by Peter I, the gentry mobilized in defense of the rights of the Cossack *starshyna* gained from the tsar by Hetman Bohdan Khmel'nyts'kyi. It was in the atmosphere of the Poltava defeat that the Cossack chronicles of Hryhorii Hrabianka and Samiilo Velychko were written and the cult of Bohdan Khmel'nyts'kyi reemerged and gained its new characteristics, which developed later into one of the main cults of Ukrainian national ideology.[26]

The next wave of commemorating and recalling the Cossack heroic past came in the second half of the eighteenth century. This was the period when the gentry undertook its last attempt to avoid the abolition of the hetmanate and found itself involved more than ever in a struggle for official recognition of its noble rights by the imperial authorities. In both cases the historical arguments were considered extremely important, and a range of historical works recalling the glorious Cossack past were written at this time, beginning with the book of Petro Symonovs'ky and ending with the anonymous *Istoriia Rusov*.[27]

It was the gentry of the hetmanate—the ruling elite of a comparatively small part of contemporary Ukrainian territory—who created the Cossack myth as a reflection of their own political necessity and historical belief, and it was necessary for a new generation of Ukrainian patriots to come into the political arena in order to transfer the Cossack myth from the rank of local historical mythology to the rank of nationwide ideology that would bring together the most remote parts of Ukrainian ethnic territory. This work was done by the nationalists of the nineteenth century.

The most prominent role in the development and popularization of Cossack mythology belongs to the apostle of the nineteenth century Ukrainian national revival, the poet and artist Taras Shevchenko (1814–1861).[28] His views on the Cossack past were based primarily on two main sources: Cossack mythology elaborated by the hetmanate elite and popularized by the early nineteenth-century political work *Istoriia Rusov*, and, in addition, popular memory. The outstanding event in Cossack history that was remembered by the simple peasants in right-bank Ukraine—Shevchenko's homeland—was the *Koliivshchyna*, the popular uprising against Polish rule in 1768–69, led by the Cossack officers Ivan Honta and Maksym Zalizniak. This revolt was launched under the slogan of the protection of Orthodoxy against a Uniate offensive. Shevchenko also brought into his poems the popular memory of the Zaporozhian Cossack Host in the lower Dnieper, generally viewed without any heroization by the authors of the hetmanate, and popularized by Nikolai Gogol in his novel *Taras Bulba*. Despite the fact that Shevchenko challenged the Bohdan Khmel'nyts'kyi myth on the grounds of the hetman's pro-Russian policy, he managed to combine in his poems the historical experience and views on the Cossack past of two generally hostile social strata—landlords and peasantry—and presented this unified vision in his historical verses and poems first published in the 1841 edition of the *Kobzar*, the bible of the Ukrainian national revival.

There is no doubt that for this new type of Cossack mythology, created and popularized by Shevchenko's poetry, it was much easier to win the hearts of readers in the central and southern regions of Ukraine, where popular memory of the Cossacks was still alive, than to find its way to the western regions of Ukraine, where the Cossack experience was but a short-lived phenomenon of the seventeenth century. At the same time, Shevchenko's poetry was a much better vehicle for propagating the new Cossack mythology than the writings of the hetmanate elite. Unlike *Istoriia Rusov*, which was written in the highly Russified, bookish language of the late eighteenth–early nineteenth century, read and understood only in Russian Ukraine, Shevchenko's poems were written in vernacular Ukrainian. This opened the way for the spread of his writings, and with them Cossack mythology, to the ethnic Ukrainian territories under Austro-Hungarian rule.

Especially important for the fate of the Ukrainian national movement was the case of Galicia in the Austro-Hungarian Empire.[29] The path of Cossack mythology to Galicia was not easy, due to a combination of different political, confessional, and historical reasons. There was never any Cossack organization in Galicia, despite the fact that many of its natives, such as the seventeenth-century Hetman Petro Konashevych-Sahaidachnyi, took part in the Cossack movement in Dnieper Ukraine. Presenting Galicians as active participants of the Cossack movement was the only possible approach that could provide a logical link between the Galician national revival and the Cossack past. Special sub-myths and family legends were created in Galicia to bring the Cossack past closer to its population—a theory of the migration of people from Galicia to Dnieper Ukraine and then from the lower Dnieper region back to Galicia was developed and popularized among the Galician intelligentsia.

This situation was complicated not only by the fact that the Cossack system never existed in Galicia but also by the pro-Orthodox and very often anti-Uniate character of the Cossack mythology. To accept Cossack mythology in its full shape with all its anti-Uniate pathos was not an easy task for the Ukrainian movement in Uniate Galicia. So the myth was modified, reshaped, and adapted to local circumstances. In a very short time, due to the spread of Shevchenko's cult and the activity of the *narodovtsi* (populists), Galician Ukrainians became more zealous adherents of the Cossack mythology than their eastern Ukrainian counterparts.

The triumph of Cossack mythology as the unifying factor of the Ukrainian national revival came with the events of the Ukrainian revolution of 1917–20. The "Sich riflemen" detachments, named after the tradition of the Host of the Zaporozhian Cossacks (Sich), were formed in Galicia during World War I and later played an important role in the struggle for Ukrainian independence both in western and eastern Ukraine. In 1918 eastern Ukraine, occupied by German forces after the Brest-Litovsk treaty, witnessed the rule of Hetman Pavlo Skoropad'skyi, imposed under the slogan of the restoration of the hetmanate traditions. The armed forces of the Directory, the next Ukrainian government, which took over from Skoropad'skyi after the withdrawal of German troops, were also built according to the preservation of Cossack tradition. Even the Bolshevik army that fought for the control of Ukrainian territory with Ukrainian forces claimed to be the successor to the Cossack tradition—special units of "Red Cossacks" were formed as an integral part of the Red Army.[30]

When the Bolsheviks took over eastern and central Ukraine, they initially tolerated the Ukrainian national and cultural revival, but then crushed it in the first half of the 1930s. The Cossack mythology was restructured by Soviet historians to meet the demands of vulgar Marxism and growing Russian nationalism. Only those Ukrainian hetmans who served Russia were tolerated in the new textbooks of Ukrainian history. Cossacks were replaced as the main heroes of the seventeenth and eighteenth centuries by peasants, who were not connected to the tradition of Ukrainian nation building and therefore did not present any threat to the communist rulers.[31]

"Independent" Cossack mythology survived only in western Ukraine—in Galicia and Volhynia—the two regions that were under Polish occupation from 1920 to 1939. When in 1943–44 Soviet troops entered western Ukraine to fight the German army, official Soviet propaganda was forced to take into account the national aspirations of the local Ukrainian population. The Ukrainian government started to present itself as an independent one, groups of Soviet armed forces (fronts) that fought in Ukraine were renamed "Ukrainian fronts," and finally a special military award, named after the Cossack hetman Bohdan Khmel'nyts'kyi, was introduced in the autumn of 1943 by the Soviet authorities.[32] It was only a temporary suspension of official Soviet ideology. After the war most expressions of Ukrainian national ideology that were tolerated during the war were officially banned.

Cossack mythology, revived in Ukraine after Stalin's death, reached its highest point in the 1960s but was banned again in 1972. At that time, Petro Shelest, the first secretary of the Communist Party of Ukraine, was accused of the "idealization of the past" and replaced by his rival Volodymyr Shcherbyts'kyi. The purge of "Cossackophiles" had begun in the institutes of the Ukrainian Academy of Sciences and the universities, and many of the academics who specialized in Ukrainian history and the literature of the Cossack era were removed from their positions or forced to shift to the study of other topics unconnected with the officially condemned Cossack past.[33] Despite the persecution of Cossack studies, Cossack mythology appeared to be deeply rooted in the historical consciousness of western Ukraine, which was "sovietized" only in the late 1940s, and reemerged there with the beginning of perestroika and glasnost.

Cossack Mythology III: Territorial Integrity and Territorial Claims

In the spring of 1990 in the southeastern Ukrainian city of Nikopil, in an area where the majority of Zaporozhian Hosts were established, the local branch of the Ukrainian Republican Party—one of the most anti-Communist organizations at that time—endorsed the idea of a local student of Cossack history, Pavlo Bohush, to celebrate the five hundredth anniversary of the Ukrainian Cossacks. The initiative for this extensive ideological campaign, named "March to the East," came from the Dnieper region, but was actively supported and realized by the national democratic organizations of Galicia that came to power after the first relatively free elections in the USSR. They considered the Cossack myth their main weapon in the political fight for eastern

Ukraine. Thousands of people from all parts of Ukraine, but especially from Galicia, travelled in summer 1990 to the lower Dnieper region to take part in these festivities.[34] One of the ironies of history was the fact that Galicians, people that had no direct links to the Cossack past, were bringing the Cossack myth back to eastern Ukraine, the homeland of the Ukrainian Cossacks. The CPSU functionaries in eastern Ukraine tried to fight back, challenging the Galicians' right to the Cossack heritage and exploiting the anti-Uniate motives of nineteenth-century Cossack mythology. For example, in Dnipropetrovs'k oblast they did not want to allow Greek-Catholic (Uniate) priests to serve a liturgy on the grave of the Cossack ataman Ivan Sirko.[35] But all these attempts to split the movement and to isolate the Galician participants of the march from the local population had little, if any, effect. The government officials were pressed to join the 1990 Cossack festivities, and in 1991, in order to take control of the Cossackophile movement, they organized conferences and festivities of their own to mark the Cossack anniversary. The official celebrations took place in the lower Dnieper region: Dnipropetrovs'k, Zaporizhzhia, Nikopil; and in Volhynia—near Berestechko, on the site of the 1651 Cossack battle with the Poles.[36]

The rise of Ukrainian national aspirations in 1990–91 and the massive offensive of national democratic forces from Galicia to the east provoked some Russian separatist initiatives on the part of the Communist elite of the eastern and southern oblasts of Ukraine. These separatist moves were also based on historical arguments. They attempted to prove that eastern and southern Ukraine were never a part of ethnic Ukrainian territory but were colonized and settled by Russians. Similar ideas were expressed around the same time by Aleksandr Solzhenitsyn, who, in a highly publicized article in the former USSR titled, "How Shall We Reconstitute Russia," claimed that New Russia, Crimea, and Donbass "were never part of old Ukraine."[37] The term "New Russia" once referred to the territory of the southern Ukrainian oblasts and was introduced for the first time in the second half of the eighteenth century. Despite the fact that the term used for the territory included the lands of Zaporozhian Cossacks, colonized by them long before the first appearance of the imperial authorities in this region, the idea of establishing New Russia as a Russian polity in southern Ukraine was put forward by some scholars and historians, including the Odessa professor A. Surilov. Around the same time the idea of restoring the Donets'k-Kryvyi Rih and Crimea republics, once proclaimed by the Bolsheviks in 1918 to stop the German seizure of the territory after the conclusion of the Brest-Litovsk treaty, was put forward in some eastern and southern Ukrainian newspapers.[38] These attempts were a direct challenge to the Cossack mythology, used by the national democrats to accelerate the process of Ukrainian national awakening in this region.

The adherents of Cossack mythology accepted the challenge, and a dozen articles appeared in the national and local press trying to adjust Cossack mythology to the new political demands. Since the territory of Zaporozhian Sich even at its apogee did not cover the whole territory of Ukraine's eastern and southern oblasts, the Cossack myth had to be modified. To provide historical justification for Ukraine's right to these territories, Cossack mythology was forced to challenge Russian imperial mythology on one hand and its own anti-Tatar character on the other.

New emphasis was placed by Ukrainian historians on the role of Cossack detachments in the history of the Russo-Turkish wars of the second half of the eighteenth century. It was emphasized in numerous publications of 1990–91 that it was not so much the imperial army as the Ukrainian Cossacks who conquered and colonized Ukrainian territories during the Russo-Turkish wars. This was true in part, especially in the case of colonization, because otherwise Ukrainians would never have constituted the majority of the region's population, but in the case of military history it was an exaggeration of the Cossack role in these military actions and a diminishing of the role played by the well-trained Russian imperial army. Ukrainian authors wrote about the participation of Cossack detachments in Russian attacks on the Turkish fortresses of Ochakiv, Izmail, and Akkerman and their takeover of other forts—Berezan and Khajibei. On the site of the latter, the Cossacks and their families were the first inhabitants of the newly founded city of Odessa.[39] Some articles attempted to challenge even the "cornerstone" of the Russian imperial ideology—the Sevastopol myth. The historian of the Ukrainian navy, V. Kravtsevych, citing an eighteenth-century description of Sevastopol, claimed that the "city of Russian glory" was built by Cossacks and local Ukrainian peasants and that in the first decades of its existence Sevastopol looked like a typical Ukrainian settlement.[40]

Another modification of Cossack mythology was connected with the reexamination of the history of Cossack-Tatar relations. The Cossack was usually viewed by the creators of Ukrainian national mythology as a defender of his homeland—Ukraine—from Turkish and Tatar attacks. Accordingly, Tatars were treated in this context as the worst enemies of Ukraine. During the 1950s and 1960s, in official Soviet historiography, Tatars were usually portrayed as the main adversaries of the Ukrainian Cossacks. It was almost prohibited at that time to study the Cossack conflicts with Russia or to pay special attention to Cossack-Polish conflicts. Socialist Poland was a close ally of the USSR, and one could hardly find any remarks about Cossack-Polish conflicts or Ukrainian-Polish wars. Instead the formula of "peasant-Cossack uprisings against the *shliakhta* and magnates" was used by official Soviet historiography. At the same time the official historians did speak about "Tatar attacks" on Ukrainian lands.[41]

This new approach to the Tatar problem was introduced in the 1960s by the representatives of the Ukrainian democratic movement. The role of General Petro Hryhorenko (Petr Grigorenko) in the defense of the rights of the Crimean Tatars is well known in the West, but Hryhorenko was not alone in his attempts to "rehabilitate" the Tatars. In 1968 the well-known Ukrainian writer Roman Ivanychuk published a novel titled *Mal'vy* (*Mallow*), in which he attempted to reexamine the history of the decline of the empires and the role of the national traitors—the janisaries. Actually, he also presented a new approach to the dramatic history of Ukrainian-Tatar relations in the sixteenth to seventeenth centuries. The novel was severely criticized, banned, and confiscated from bookstores and libraries.[42]

Ukrainian historians renewed their attempts to reexamine the history of Cossack-Tatar relations with the beginning of glasnost. This initiative was launched by publications of scholars from Dnipropetrovs'k University in southern Ukraine—the only center of Cossack studies in Ukraine that survived the period of persecution of Ukrainian historiography in the 1970s and 1980s. In his articles on the history of the Cossack army, the Dnipropetrovs'k historian Ivan Storozhenko pictured the Tatar troops of *Murza* Tuhaj Bej, the ally of Bohdan Khmel'nyts'kyi, in predominantly positive terms, and Storozhenko's colleague, Iurii Mytsyk, whose main works have also been devoted to Cossack history, published a series of articles on Tatar history in a Crimean Tatar newspaper.[43] In some other Ukrainian publications of this period the history of Cossack-Tatar collaboration in the struggle against Russia and Turkey received special attention.[44] It has also been stressed that in the seventeenth century the majority of Crimea's population was not Tatar but Ukrainian people, captured by the Tatars during their attacks on Ukrainian territories. Contemporary data stated that there were 920,000 Cossacks (Ukrainians) and 180,000 Tatars in Crimea in the middle of the seventeenth century. This information was drawn from the memoirs of a Turkish traveler, Evlia Chelebi, who visited Crimea in 1666.[45]

These and other attempts to reexamine the history of Cossack-Tatar relations to a certain extent present an effort to modify Cossack mythology in such a way as to meet the new demands for the creation of a Ukrainian-Tatar political union in the fight against Russian claims to the peninsula. For this reason, the Cossack myth has been dropping its original anti-imperialist character and giving up some features of its ethnic exclusivity to meet the goal of building a multinational civic society and preserving Ukraine's territorial integrity.

In Ukraine, the Cossack legacy is also viewed as an important instrument in the legitimization of the Ukrainian claims to the USSR Black Sea fleet. Proponents of Ukrainian national ideology usually begin the history of the Ukrainian navy with the period of the Kievan princes Askold, Dir, Oleh, and Ihor, who on a number of occasions in the ninth and tenth centuries attacked Constantinople from the sea, but most attention is usually devoted to the history of Cossack activity in the Black Sea region. Contemporary organizations of the Ukrainian Cossacks have established close links with the newly born Ukrainian navy and its commander, Admiral Borys Kozhyn. He has promised that the first anniversary of the Ukrainian Black Sea fleet will be celebrated on the Dnieper island of Khortytsia—the legendary homeland of the Zaporozhian Cossacks.[46]

Ironically, Cossack mythology has had fewer problems claiming some Ukrainian territories beyond the country's state borders than securing the territorial integrity of the Ukrainian state. Among the territories settled by the Cossacks in the seventeenth and eighteenth centuries are the Kuban peninsula and the southern regions of the Kursk and Voronezh oblasts of the Russian Federation, and some trans-Dniester and trans-Danube areas, now parts of Moldova and Romania. The Kuban region is separated from Crimea by the Kerch Strait and initially was settled by the former Zaporozhian Cossacks in the 1790s. Later, more Cossacks and Ukrainian peasants, together with Don Cossacks and Russian peasantry, moved into the area. During the years of the revolution there was a strong pro-Ukrainian movement in Kuban, and the local government negotiated with Hetman Pavlo Skoropads'kyi on the conditions of a Ukrainian-Kuban federative treaty. After the revolution, Kuban was included in the Russian Federation. In 1926, 47.1 percent of the region's population considered themselves Ukrainian and 41 percent Russian. Ukrainian national schools, newspapers, and even a Ukrainian department in the local university existed for a short period, but a policy of Russification of the Ukrainian population was launched by the Communist authorities in the 1930s, and with the introduction of a passport system, all residents of Kuban were declared to be Russian.[47]

The Kuban Cossack organizations like those of the Don and Stavropol regions were reestablished in 1990 with some support from the local authorities, who wanted to use Cossacks to counter the growing political activity of non-Slavic peoples in the Northern Caucasus and to fight crime. With the proclamation of Ukrainian independence there emerged a strong pro-Ukrainian sentiment among the Cossack leadership of the Kuban region—a development that was not welcomed by the local authorities. Unlike their Don colleagues, the Kuban Cossacks developed close links with Cossack organizations in Ukraine. It is quite characteristic that when in March 1993 one of the leaders of the Kuban Cossacks, Ievhen Nahai, was arrested by local authorities in Kuban on the charges of preparing a Cossack coup, the other high-ranking officer of the Kuban Cossacks, *Koshovyi Otaman* Pylypenko, made a statement that in the case of further violation of the civil rights of his colleague the Cossacks would call for support from their historical homeland—Ukraine—and from the Ukrainian diaspora in the United States and Canada and would even defend themselves with arms. A special committee for the "Return of the Kuban to Ukraine," led by General Siverov, was established in the Kuban region.[48]

Ukrainian Cossack organizations from the very beginning declared Kuban to be a sphere of their special interests. There in 1992 they implemented tactics similar to those used by Galician Ukrainian organizations in eastern and southern Ukraine in 1990: a Cossack march to the area was organized to mark the bicentennial of Cossack resettlement to Kuban. The idea was supported by the hetman of the Ukrainian Cossacks—the head of the social-psychological directorate of the Ukrainian army and its chief ideologist, General Volodymyr Muliava.

In August 1992, forty-four men, representing not western but eastern and southern Ukrainian oblasts, including the Donbass and Zaporizhzhia regions, took part in a horse march to the Kuban. The march was reportedly met with enthusiasm on the part of the local population.[49]

There is no doubt that Ukrainian Cossack mythology is spreading to the former Cossack territories beyond the state borders of Ukraine. The Cossack past of these regions, which include also parts of the Voronezh Oblast in Russia and Trans-Dniestria in Moldova, is viewed by proponents of Ukrainian nationalism as an important instrument in the rekindling of Ukrainian national identity among the six million-plus Ukrainian diaspora in the former Soviet Union. With the development of Cossack movements in Russian Cossack regions of the Don and the North Caucasus, Ukrainian Cossack movements in those areas are gaining some sort of legitimacy for their presence in the Russian Federation. Despite the fact that the Russian Cossacks are generally viewed as partisans of the restoration of the Russian Empire, their demands for the self-government of the Cossack regions, including the Don area, are accelerating the disintegration tendencies in the Russian Federation.

On a number of occasions Ukrainian officials have rejected any claims made by proponents of Ukrainian nationalism to territories beyond the Ukrainian border, but the further development of the Russo-Ukrainian border conflict sooner or later could put forward Ukrainian territorial claims based on the principle of "historical justice," and a highly developed Cossack mythology could be used not only as an instrument for preserving Ukrainian territorial integrity but also as an argument for Ukraine's own territorial claims.

Conclusion

It is difficult if not impossible to overestimate the significance of the idea of national territory to the system of beliefs of every modern nation. Of no less importance for this system is the complex of historical myths that provides a nation with its own view of its past and tries to explain and justify a nation's territorial possessions or territorial claims against its neighbors. With the collapse and disintegration of world empires, the problem of the division of the territories between "old" imperial and "young" stateless nations has arisen. Historical ar-

guments and historical myths are of special importance for the justification of conflicting territorial claims of different nations.

The legitimacy of Ukrainian borders has been challenged often by
Russian politicians on the grounds of historical legitimacy. The majority of them are rooted in the highly developed former Soviet Sevastopol
mythology. In the case of Ukraine, as in other cases of territorial
claims against other former Soviet republics, Russian politicians take
as a point of departure the borders of the Russian Empire of the late
eighteenth to early twentieth centuries, the period when the empire had
reached its maximum territorial expansion. There is nothing new in
this approach. For instance, Romanians usually claim the territory once
united under the leadership of Michael the Brave at the beginning of
the seventeenth century, while Poles claim the territory that belonged
to their state in the sixteenth and seventeenth centuries.[50] On this issue
a student of Russian foreign policy, N. Narochnitskaia, has posed a
rhetorical question: "Why in the case of Crimea do we follow the
borders of 1954, in the case of the Baltic region those of 1939 and in
the case of the Kuril Islands those of 1855?"[51]

From the Ukrainian perspective, Cossack mythology is used to protect the national integrity of Ukraine. The myth emerged locally in
Dnieper Ukraine in the early eighteenth century, and then with the help
of the nineteenth-century nationalists, including the celebrated poet
Taras Shevchenko, it was spread all over the Ukrainian ethnic territory.
It was preserved best of all in a historically non-Cossack territory,
Galicia, and with the beginning of glasnost made its successful return
to the Cossack historical lands—the eastern territories of Ukraine on
its current borderland with Russia. Cossack colonization during the
seventeenth and eighteenth centuries of the majority of these territories
helped Ukrainian historians in their justification that these territories
were a part of the Ukrainian state. Another argument used was Cossack participation in the imperial army, which, in the second half of the
eighteenth century, helped to annex the vast territories of southern
Ukraine to the empire and open them to Ukrainian colonization. In
view of the current Russian-Ukrainian dispute over Crimea, the traditionally anti-Tatar character of Cossack mythology has dramatically
changed. To foster cooperation between the Ukrainian and Tatar national movements, episodes of such cooperation in the past have been
revived, thus transforming traditional Cossack mythology into the
realm of countermyths. Being by its nature national and anti-imperialist,

66 SERHII M. PLOKHY

the Cossack myth at the same time gives an opportunity to Ukrainian nationalistic circles to put forward claims to territories that were colonized by the Cossacks in the seventeenth and eighteenth centuries but in the twentieth century were included into the Russian Federation. Russian-Ukrainian territorial disputes are based on conflicting historical arguments and historical mythology. The periods of maximum territorial expansion of the Russian imperial state and the Cossack autonomous polities have been taken as a point of departure in the process of making territorial claims. Russian-Ukrainian conflict over the future of Crimea, Sevastopol, and the Black Sea fleet has developed in an atmosphere of the further deterioration of the economic situation and living standards of the Russian and Ukrainian populations and the activization of nationalistic and pro-communist forces. Both of these potentially dangerous processes are under way and threaten to bring current territorial disputes between Russia and Ukraine to the brink of military conflict. Conflicting territorial claims based on Russian imperial mythology and Ukrainian national myth could have dangerous consequences if one of the two sides were to try to realize its "historic right" by force. Historical arguments that have received so much attention and have become so important in the current Russian-Ukrainian dispute have to make way for the arguments of international law.

Notes

1. On the problem of imperial disintegration, national self-determination, and border conflicts, see Alfred Cobban, *The Nation State and National Self-Determination* (London: Collins/Fontana, 1969), pp. 295–99; J.R.V. Prescott, *The Geography of Frontiers and Boundaries* (Chicago: Aldine, 1965), pp. 109–78; John Coakley, "National Territories and Cultural Frontiers: Conflicts of Principle in the Formation of States in Europe," in *Frontier Regions in Western Europe,* ed. Malcolm Anderson (London: F. Cass, 1983), pp. 34–49.
2. See the statement by P. Voshchanov, *Izvestiia,* 29 August 1991.
3. See quotations from the internal memorandum on Crimea, prepared by V. Lukin, then chairman of the Commitee on International Affairs of the Russian parliament and currently Russian ambassador to the United States (*Komsomol'-skaia pravda,* 22 January 1991); interview with S. Baburin and N. Pavlov, members of the Russian parliamentarian group that visited Crimea in December 1991 (*Literaturnaia Rossiia,* 31 January 1992); and Ukrainian protests on the creation and activities of the Russian Supreme Soviet ad hoc committee on Sevastopol's status, called into existence at the Seventh Congress of People's Deputies of Russia in December 1992 (*Uriadovyi kur'ier,* 11 December 1992; *Pravda Ukrainy,* 23 January 1993; *UKRAINFORM Reports,* 20 February 1993).

4. See *Pravda Ukrainy*, 7 April 1992. Quoted by Roman Solchanyk, "Ukraine and Russia: The Politics of Independence," *RFE/RL Daily Report*, 14 May 1992, p. 3.

5. Ibid.

6. See *Literaturnaia Rossiia*, 8 January 1993. Compare to similar statements made by N. Narochnitskaia, *Literaturnaia Rossiia*, 21 August 1992.

7. One of the best expressions of the Sevastopol myth is found in a verse by Aleksandr Nikolaev, published by *Literaturnaia Rossiia* on 8 January 1993:

> Na oskolkakh nashei Sverkhderzhavy
> Velichaishii paradoks istorii:
> Sevastopol'—gorod russkoi slavy,
> No . . . ne na Rossiiskoi territorii?

8. The Sevastopol siege of 1854–55 was the topic of "The Sevastopol Sketches" by Leo Tolstoy, which was approved by the Soviet authorities and included in the school curriculum on Russian literature. Soviet works on the Crimean War and the Sevastopol siege started to appear on the eve of World War II. See E.A. Berkov, *Krymskaia kampaniia* (Moscow, 1939); A.N. Lagovskii, *Oborona Sevastopolia: Krymskaia voina 1854–1855 gg.* (Moscow, 1939). The topic was very popular during the "Great Patriotic War of the Soviet people of 1941–45" and then during the Cold War. The majority of works that dealt with the topic treated the heroism of the imperial army at the Sevastopol siege as the heroism of the Russian people. This approach to Crimean War history was most profoundly expressed in a book by Evgenii Tarle, published by the publishing house of the USSR Ministry of Defense in 1954: *Gorod russkoi slavy: Sevastopol v 1854–1855*. The definition of Sevastopol as a city of Russian glory had become from that time a symbolic one and was widely used in tourist guide books and propagandistic literature.

9. *Literaturnaia Rossiia*, 8 January 1993.

10. *Robitnycha hazeta*, 23 January 1993.

11. Hans Kohn, *The Idea of Nationalism: A Study in Its Origins and Background* (New York: MacMillan, 1944), p. 330.

12. There is significant literature on Mykhailo Hrushevs'kyi and his writings. One of the latest publications on Hrushevs'kyi is T. Prymak's *Mykhailo Hrushevsky: The Politics of National Culture* (Toronto: University of Toronto Press, 1987).

13. John A. Armstrong, "Myth and History in the Evolution of Ukrainian Consciousness," in *Ukraine and Russia in Their Historical Encounter*, ed. Peter J. Potichnyj et al. (Edmonton, 1992), p. 133.

14. Ibid., p. 128.

15. On the development of Cossack mythology, see Frank E. Sysyn, "The Reemergence of the Ukrainian Nation and Cossack Mythology," *Social Research*, vol. 58, no. 4 (Winter 1991), pp. 845–64; O.W. Gerus, "Manifestations of the Cossack Idea in Modern History: The Cossack Legacy and Its Impact," *Ukrains'kyi istoryk*, no. 1–2 (1986), pp. 22–39.

16. For an outline of the Cossack period in Ukrainian history, see Orest Subtelny, *Ukraine: A History* (Toronto: University of Toronto Press in association

with the Canadian Institute of Ukrainian Studies, 1988), pp. 105–98; and O. Subtelny and I. Vytanovych, "Cossacks," in *Encyclopedia of Ukraine* (Toronto: University of Toronto Press in association with the Canadian Institute of Ukrainian Studies, 1984), vol. 1, pp. 593–95.

17. On the history of the Chernihiv region, see O. Backus, *The Motives of the West Russian Nobles in Deserting Lithuania for Moscow, 1377–1514* (Lawrence: University of Kansas Press, 1957); O.I. Derykolenko, M.T. Iatsura, "Chernihivs'ka oblast'," *Radians'ka Entsyklopediia istorii Ukrainy* (Kiev, 1972), vol. 4, p. 480; M.T. Iatsura, "Chernihivs'ka oblast'," *Istoriia mist i sil Ukrains'koi RSR: Chernihivs'ka oblast'* (Kiev, 1972), pp. 15–17.

18. On the history of Ukrainian settlement in Sloboda Ukraine see D. Bagalei (Dmytro Bahalii), *Ocherki po istorii kolonizatsii stepnoi okrainy moskovskogo gosudarstva* (Moscow, 1887); A.G. Sliusarskii, *Sotsial'no-ekonomicheskoe razvitie slobozhanshchiny* (Kharkiv, 1964); L.N. Chizhykova, *Russko-Ukrainskoe pogranich'e. Istoriia i sud'by traditsionno-bytovoi kul'tury (19–20 veka)* (Moscow, 1988), pp. 14–69.

19. For an account of the events, see Subtelny, *Ukraine: A History,* pp. 143–73.

20. See Elena Druzhinina, *Kiuchuk-Kainardzhiiskii mir 1774 goda (ego podgotovka i zakliuchenie)* (Moscow, 1955); idem, *Severnoe Prichernomor'e v 1775–1800 gg.* (Moscow, 1959). The history of the imperial absorption of Crimea is presented by Alan W. Fisher in *The Russian Annexation of the Crimea* (Cambridge: Cambridge University Press, 1970) and in *The Crimean Tatars* (Stanford: Hoover Institution Press, 1978).

21. On the partitions of Poland see Oskar Halecki, *Borderlands of Western Civilization: A History of East Central Europe* (New York: Ronald Press Co., 1952), pp. 258–75.

22. For Bezborod'ko's views on the main goals of Russian foreign policy, see Zenon E. Kohut, *Russian Centralism and Ukrainian Autonomy: Imperial Absorption of the Hetmanate, 1760s–1830s* (Cambridge, MA: Harvard University Press, 1988), pp. 261–62.

23. On Ukrainian settlement of the new territories in the eighteenth and nineteenth centuries, see Nataliia Polons'ka-Vasylenko, *The Settlement of Southern Ukraine (1750–1775), Annals of the Ukrainian Academy of Arts and Sciences in the USA,* special issue, no. 4 (1955); V. Golobutskii (Volodymyr Holobuts'kyi), *Chernomorskoe kazachestvo* (Kiev, 1956); idem, *Zaporozhskoe kazachestvo* (Kiev, 1957), idem, *Zaporiz'ka Sich v ostanni chasy svoho isnuvannia 1734–1775* (Kiev, 1961); V.M. Kabuzan, *Zaselenie Novorosii (Ekaterinoslavskoi i Khersonskoi gubernii) v 18–pervoi polvine 19 veka (1719–1859)* (Moscow, 1976); S.I. Bruk, V.M. Kabuzan, "Migratsii naseleniia v Rossii v 18–nachale 19 veka (chislennost', struktura, geografiia)," *Istoriia SSSR,* no. 4 (1984).

24. Kohut, *Russian Centralism and Ukrainian Autonomy,* pp. 7, 29–32.

25. Ibid., pp. 59–63, 258–76.

26. On the reemergence of the Bohdan Khmel'nyts'kyi cult after the Poltava defeat, see Serhii Plokhy,"The Symbol of Little Russia: Study in the Ideology of the Pokrova Icon," *Journal of Ukrainian Studies,* vol. 16, no. 1 (forthcoming).

27. On the gentry's struggle for the recognition of its noble rights, see Kohut, *Russian Centralism and Ukrainian Autonomy,* pp. 248–57. On the Ukrainian historiography' of the period, see Dmytro Doroshenko, *A Survey of Ukrainian*

Historiography, Annals of the Ukrainian Academy of Arts and Sciences in the USA, special issue, vol. 5–6 (1957), pp. 44–115. *Istoriia Rusov* was extensively studied by Oleksander Ohloblyn. See his "The Ethical and Political Principles of *Istoriia Rusov,*" *Annals of the Ukrainian Academy of Arts and Sciences in the USA,* vol. 2, no. 4 (1952), pp. 670–95; *idem,* "Where Was *Istoriia Rusov* Written?" *Annals of the Ukrainian Academy of Arts and Sciences in the USA,* vol. 3, no. 2 (1953), pp. 670–93.

28. There is a great amount of literature that examines Shevchenko's life and writings. On Shevchenko's interpretation of Cossack history, see George Grabowicz, "Three Perspectives on the Cossack Past: Gogol', Ševčenko and Kulis," *Harvard Ukrainian Studies,* no. 5 (1981), pp. 179–94.

29. On the national revival in Galicia, see Jan Kozik, *The Ukrainian National Movement in Galicia, 1819–1849* (Edmonton: University of Alberta, 1986); Ivan L. Rudnytsky, "The Ukrainians in Galicia under Austrian Rule," in *Essays in Modern Ukrainian History,* ed. Peter L. Rudnytsky (Cambridge, MA: Harvard University Press, 1987), pp. 315–52; John-Paul Himka, "Priests and Peasants: The Greek Catholic Pastor and the Ukrainian National Movement in Austria, 1867–1900," *Canadian Slavonic Papers,* vol. 21 (1979), pp. 1–14; *idem,* "The Greek Catholic Church and Nation-Building in Galicia, 1772–1918," *Harvard Ukrainian Studies,* vol. 8 (1984), pp. 426–52.

30. See Subtelny, *Ukraine: A History,* pp. 255–79; *Radians'ka entsyklopediia istorii Ukrainy* (Kiev, 1972), vol. 4, p. 461.

31. A general overview of the Soviet interpretations of Ukrainian and Belarusian history was done by Roman Szporluk in "National History as a Political Battleground: The Case of Ukraine and Belorussia," in *Russian Empire: Some Aspects of Tsarist and Soviet Colonial Practices,* ed. Michael S. Pap (Ohio, 1985), pp. 131–50. On Soviet interpretations of the Cossack past see John Basarab, *Pereiaslav 1654: A Historiographical Study* (Edmonton, 1982).

32. On the national "awakening" among Soviet Ukrainian intelligentsia of the period, see M. Koval', "Pid 'Kovpakom' Beriivskoi Derzhbezpeky," *Ukrains'kyi istorychnyi zhurnal,* nos. 10–11 (1992), pp. 116–18.

33. On the political purge of the 1970s in Ukraine, see Roman Solchanyk, "Politics in Ukraine in the Post-Shelest Period," in *Ukraine Since Shelest,* ed. Bohdan Krawchenko (Edmonton: University of Edmonton Press, 1983), pp. 1–29. On the fate of one of the persecuted, author and high Soviet official in the Zaporizhzhia region Mykola Kytsenko, see Olena Apanovych, "Nam bronzy ne treba!" *Ukrains'ka kul'tura,* no. 1 (1993), pp. 8–9.

34. On the 1990 celebrations of the five hundredth anniversary of the Zaporozhian Cossacks, see Sysyn, "Reemergence of the Ukrainian Nation," pp. 858–59.

35. This information is based on the author's interviews with Communist Party officials in Cherkassy and Dnipropetrovs'k regions (summer 1990–spring 1991).

36. On the participation of CPSU officials in the celebrations of the 340-year anniversary of the Berestechko battle in Volhynia, see the joint statement on the occasion of the L'viv, Volhynia, and Rivno regional committees of the Communist Party, *Radians'ka Ukraina,* 13 February 1991.

37. A. Solzhenitsyn, "Kak nam obustroit' Rossiiu?" *Literaturnaia gazeta,* 18

September 1990. See also Solzhenitsyn's "Appeal on the December 1991 referendum," in which he proposed to calculate the results of the referendum in Ukraine for each region separately: *Christian Democracy*, no. 17 (1992), pp. 9–10.

38. On the separatist tendencies in eastern and southern Ukraine, see M. Khudan, "Daiosh Respubliku Novorossiia," *Literaturna Ukraina*, 22 November 1990; O. Oliinykiv, "Nashchadky Chepihy i Holovatoho," *Kul´tura i Zhyttia*, 5 August 1990; Sysyn, "Reemergence of the Ukrainian Nation," p. 861.

39. See Leonid Zalizniak, "Vid kozats´koi vol´nosti—do Novorosii," *Pamiatky Ukrainy*, no. 2 (1991), p. 21, and Volodymyr Kravtsevych, "Berezan´ i Izmail vziali zaporozhtsy," *Narodna armiia*, 28 October 1992.

40. See V. Kravtsevych, "Kto zhe stroil 'Russkuiu Slavu'?" *Narodna armiia*, 6 November 1992.

41. See the articles on Cossack history in *Radians´ka entsyklopediia istorii Ukrainy*, vols. 1–4 (Kiev, 1969–72).

42. See Roman Ivanychuk's memoirs in *Berezil´*, nos. 11–12 (1992), p. 125. The novel *Mal´vy* (first edition: *Mal´vy: Roman* [Kiev, 1968]) was not mentioned in the bibliographies of Ivanychuk's works until the beginning of glasnost.

43. See I. Storozhenko's essay on the 1648 Zhovti Vody battle in Iu. Mytsyk, I. Storozhenko, S. Plokhy, A. Koval´ov, *Tii slavy kozats´koi povik ne zabudem* (Dnipropetrovs´k, 1989); and list of Iu. Mytsyk's publications in *Bibliohrafiia prats vchenykh Dnipropetrovs´koho universytetu. Istoriia Ukrainy XV-XVIII stolit, 1918–1990* (Dniptopetrovs´k, 1992).

44. See V. Butkevych, "Pravo na Krym," *Narodna armiia*, 8 July 1992. Pointing to the first abolition of the Sich by Peter I in 1709 and the resettlement of the Cossacks to the territories controlled by Crimean Tatars, Butkevych claimed that from 1709 to 1734 Zaporizhzhia and Crimea made up one state body, which gained international recognition according to the Prut Peace Treaty, signed between Russia and Turkey in 1711. He also stressed the special relations between Crimea and Zaporizhzhia on the eve of the imperial abolition of the Zaporozhian Sich in 1775.

45. *Literaturna Ukraina*, 10 January 1991.

46. For a report on the visit of the folk ensemble "Cossacks-Zaporozhians" from the city of Zaporizhzhia to Sevastopol, see *Molod´ Ukrainy*, 14 January 1993.

47. See the article on the history of Ukrainian settlements in Kuban by V. Ivanys, V. Kubijovyc, and M. Miller in *Encyclopedia of Ukraine* (Toronto: University of Toronto Press, 1988), vol. 2, pp. 687–95. For a current interpretation of Kuban history in Ukraine, see Petro Lavriv, "Kubans´ki kozaky," *Narodna hazeta*, no. 8 (1993).

48. *Biuleten´ Ukrains´koi respublikans´koi partii*, no. 10 (1993). On the collaboration of the Ukrainian and Kuban Cossacks, see the statement of Hetman Volodymyr Muliava on the results of the meeting of the delegations of the Ukrainian and Kuban Cossacks in Kiev on 2 March 1993: *Molod´ Ukrainy*, 19 March 1993.

49. See the article on this march in the newspaper of the Ukrainian armed forces, Anatolii Zaborovs´kyi, "Kozaky v kinnomu pokhodi, *Narodna armiia*, 21 October 1992."

50. See Coakley, "National Territories and Cultural Frontiers," p. 41.

51. *Literaturnaia Rossiia*, 21 August 1992.

8

Basic Factors in the Foreign Policy of Ukraine

The Impact of the Soviet Experience

Yaroslav Bilinsky

For many Russians—from the conservative former vice president of the Russian Federation, Aleksandr V. Rutskoi, to President Boris N. Yeltsin's political advisor, the democratic reformer Sergei B. Stankevich—the very existence of Ukraine as an independent state is fundamentally illegitimate.[1] On the other hand, many Ukrainians—beginning with Ukraine's first popularly elected president, Leonid M. Kravchuk—see in their country's independence the only salvation from Soviet-imposed genocide.[2] Despite its thousand-year history, the Ukrainian nation was nearly wiped out under Soviet rule. It is also an unspoken assumption among many Ukrainians that, as a nation, it is the Russians who profited from the genocide of Ukrainians, albeit indirectly. The Ukrainian government bears most of the responsibility for the economic, political, and diplomatic problems that in mid-1993, only two years after the Ukrainian parliament's Act of Independence of 24 August 1991, have brought the country to—or, in the opinion of some, even over—the brink.[3] But Russia's aggressive policy of economic and political destabilization and diplomatic isolation has helped in pushing Ukraine to the brink. As early as mid-January 1992, Vladimir Lukin, then chairman of the Russian parliament's Committee on Foreign Affairs and International Economic Relations, and later Russia's ambassador to the United States, formulated what might be called the Lukin Doctrine. In a letter to Ruslan I. Khasbulatov, then chairman of Russia's parliament, Lukin advocated that Russia exert simultaneous economic and diplomatic pressure on newly independent Ukraine: by immediately cutting off Russian defense contracts to plants located in Ukraine and by raising at one and the same time the issues of the return to Russia of Crimea and of the entire Black Sea fleet, together with adjacent portions of the littoral on the Ukrainian mainland. Significantly, the strong pressure on Ukraine on all fronts was praised as a device to help the citizens of Russia weather the inevitable hardships arising from economic reforms.[4]

From this deeper perspective, this chapter's seemingly unorthodox approach makes sense. It does not cover the background of all the individual diplomatic controversies between Russia and Ukraine in which the United States has become involved, sometimes on the side of Ukraine, but more often—at least, so far—on the side of Russia.[5] I believe that all those individual issues are of secondary importance. They pale in significance next to the basic question: Why should there be an independent Ukraine at all? Why should the Ukrainians not revert back to their old subordinate position in a newly restored Soviet Union (Rutskoi's dream) or in a conservative East Slavic state domi-nated by the Russians, as envisaged in 1990 by Aleksandr I. Solzhenitsyn?[6] These are tough questions. Ultimately, the Ukrainian people and their leaders must answer those questions for themselves. My contribution here will be to elucidate those basic factors in the Soviet experience that have led to the independence of Ukraine in 1991, that still bear on the existence of Ukraine in 1993, and that, in a fundamental sense, underlie Ukraine's foreign policy.

The seventy-odd Soviet years—roughly from December 1920 to December 1991—have been a decidedly mixed blessing for indepen-dent Ukraine. Essentially, they have been positive. Without a defini-tion of the boundaries, particularly the Russo-Ukrainian frontier; without the symbolic state building in the Ukrainian SSR, which, in turn, formally joined four other republics in establishing the Soviet Union on December 30, 1922; without the on-and-off cultural revival (the large Ukrainization in the 1920s and the little Ukrainizations in western Ukraine in 1939–41 and in all of Ukraine under Khrushchev and early Brezhnev, from about 1956 to 1965); without, above all, Stalin's annexation of western Ukraine in 1939, independent Ukrainian statehood in late 1991 would have been impossible. But the eventual progress, which culminated in the splendid referendum on independence and the decisive presidential election of 1 December 1991, was bought at the price of plain genocide in the 1930s, for which, incidentally, the full bill has not yet been presented to the Russians. It was bought by large-scale linguistic and considerable identificational assimilation to the Russians after World War II, which, in turn, is a form of cultural genocide. There have also been numerous deportations of guerrilla fighters and their supporters from Western Ukraine under Stalin, and selected terror against Ukrainian dissidents under Brezhnev, his two interim successors, and even the early Gorbachev. Another political price was the humiliation by Moscow of basically loyal Ukrainian Communist leaders. Economically, Ukraine developed under the Soviets, but not always in the best direction for a rapid transformation to a market economy.

For better or for worse, the overwhelming popular confirmation of the Ukrainian parliament's Act of Independence of 24 August 1991, in the December 1991 referendum, was one of the four miracles of the twentieth century. The other three were the establishment of Israel in 1948 after a hiatus of almost two thousand years; the reestablishment of independent Poland in 1918, after Poland had been partitioned out of existence in the late eighteenth century; and the fall of the Berlin Wall and German reunification in 1989–90. Within a week of the Ukrainian referendum, the Soviet Union was disestablished into the rather amorphous Commonwealth of Independent States (CIS).

From the perspective of 1993, the disappearance of the second global superpower was only seemingly easy: the CIS could still become reunited into a quasi-federal union minus a few old republics, probably including Ukraine among the permanently departed republics. But insofar as Ukraine has been the immediate cause for the transformation of the old and tried USSR into a still amorphous and unpredictable CIS, Ukrainian leaders have predictably incurred the resentment of many Russians, and surprisingly also of some policy makers in Washington who seem to prefer a single big, de facto imperial, negotiating partner in security, economic, and ordinary diplomatic relations to a multiplicity of new and relatively untried—and, therefore, unpredictable—negotiating partners from the recently independent CIS national states. Not only this; to salve their consciences (after all, during the Cold War, the United States did support to a large degree the national aspirations of the three Baltic nations, Ukraine, and

Belarus, not to speak of the even more popular and politically more influential East European states), in early 1993, some influential policy advisors and policy makers in President Clinton's Washington have redefined the concepts: the former non-Russian proponents of national and human rights have been dubbed "ethnics," with the all the pejorative connotations that the word entails, while the formerly dominant Russian minorities in the Baltic states and in Ukraine have been solicitously watched over and analyzed to see whether their human and civil rights may have been violated by the non-Russian successor regimes. This has given the Russian government more than its geopolitical and diplomatic due; its claims to the right to protect its far-flung fellow nationals throughout the former Soviet Union appear to have been swallowed by some persons in Washington hook, line, and sinker, despite the warnings of Henry Kissinger and Zbigniew Brzezinski— even though a perceptive American history professor in New York has rightly termed such claims the "Sudeten syndrome."[7]

To call a spade a spade, in 1993, partly as a result of the near-successful Soviet policies of genocide, linguistic-political assimilation (cultural genocide), and economic-political integration, newly independent Ukraine faces numerous domestic problems. In addition, Ukraine is confronted with expected friction vis-à-vis severely disappointed Russia, which had been the beneficiary of many Soviet policies, and with somewhat unexpected tension with the United States, which, in theory, should be benevolently neutral toward Ukraine, especially since Ukraine has done a yeoman's job in melting down the old Soviet conventional forces.[8] Another legacy of the Soviet period is territorial disputes, not only over Crimea, but also with Romania, over a portion of the Ukrainian Black Sea littoral in the southwest, which stretches to the estuary of the Danube. As a most gratifying surprise, however, the Polish government and the majority of the Polish people appear to have become reconciled to the incorporation into Ukraine of eastern Galicia and Volhynia.

The territorial disputes, in my view, are secondary to two major questions. First, will Ukraine be able to survive as an independent state? Second, will it be able to continue on the road to democracy and interethnic harmony on which it started in 1990–91? Will, in short, the Ukrainian miracle prevail? Will Ukraine, according to an Armenian wit, prove that elephants can fly—or at least run freely—or will Ukraine be later remembered as the butterfly of the 1990s: beautiful

while aloft but soon destined to perish and change into a lowly cater-
pillar; that is, will it more or less resume its assigned subordinate role
from 1917 to 1991 and also throughout most of its history, with the
exception of the glorious Middle Ages (the Kievan Rus' of the ninth–
thirteenth centuries) and the romantic, quasi-independent Cossack
states in the sixteenth–eighteenth centuries. That is the question of
1993 and beyond, and a more systematic analysis of Ukraine's Soviet
past can shed some light on that question.

The democratic nationalists who declared Ukraine's independence
on 22 January 1918 and its union with Galicia a year later, on 22 January
1919, both lost and won. Most obviously, as of late 1920 Ukraine
remained dependent and disunited. The Russian Federation annexed
the lion's—or bear's—share in the east, while Galicia and Volhynia
became Polish. The new Czechoslovak Republic took Transcarpathian
Ruthenia, and Romania incorporated northern Bukovina and Bessarabia. But at the same time, the Ukrainians' prolonged and bitter struggle
for independent statehood was at least symbolically recognized by
Lenin's Russia, after the Bolsheviks failed to take over the nationalist
Ukrainian People's Republic (UNR) in Kiev by a coup d'état in December 1917 and after strong Bolshevik units occupying Ukraine were
forced to leave that republic three times in as many years.[9] After some
flirting with the idea of dismembering Ukraine, Lenin, strongly nudged
by Ukrainian Communist leader Mykola Skrypnyk, his personal representative in Ukraine, recognized the Ukrainian SSR within the boundaries of today's Ukraine, minus the Crimean Peninsula in the south,
Bukovina and Bessarabia in the southwest, and Galicia, Volhynia, and
Transcarpathia in the west.[10] This is important because before World
War I and the struggle for independence (1917–20), the frontiers of
Ukraine vis-à-vis Russia had never been properly defined. With his
superior political tact, Lenin even invited the Soviet Ukrainian government to join the Russian Federation, Belarus, and the Transcaucasian
Federation in forming the Soviet Union of equal "sovereign" republics,
which was accomplished through a treaty on 30 December 1922. (Historians and political scientists pondering what "might have been" in
1917–20 may conclude that, given the inevitable breakup of the Austro-
Hungarian and Romanovs' Russian empires, and given the relative
lack of readiness on the part of the Ukrainian people to win independence by themselves, Ukraine's most realistic chance would have been
in an alliance with newly independent Poland. This was not to be, alas:

the price of that alliance was Galicia and, furthermore, the Polish leadership was divided between the pro-Ukrainian federalist Jósef Pilsudski and the pro-Russian exclusionary nationalist Roman Dmowski. In 1991, however, Lech Walesa and the entire Polish government backed independent Ukraine. Some statesmen learn from history!)

Never mind the paper federalism of the USSR—the Communist Party was, of course, unitary and centralized to a fault, and Stalin did not share Lenin's solicitude for non-Russian susceptibilities. In any case, the USSR itself was regarded by some as a transitional formation on the road to a World Soviet Socialist State, which made Lenin's constitutional concessions seemingly ephemeral. But from the perspective of 1991, it should be emphasized that, whatever his reasons, Lenin did more to advance the idea of Ukrainian statehood than the Russian Whites. Symbolically, Lenin did even more for Ukraine than the Western states, which were then led by France and Great Britain, with the United States first asserting a strong claim for world leadership and then abruptly withdrawing into a cocoon of isolationism. But Lenin's gift had to be paid for: the Ukrainian patriots in the USSR, whether Communist Party members such as Mykola Skrypnyk and Oleksandr Shums'kyi or non-Party intellectual and political leaders such as Professors Mykhailo Hrushevs'kyi and Serhii Iefremov, were all faced with the challenge of filling Lenin's symbolic shell with cultural and political contents.

The Ukrainians in the Soviet republic were at first favored in that the Communist Party, as centralized as it was, decided to "sink roots" in its multinational realm. In Ukraine, with its large peasant population, *korenizatsiia* inevitably meant introducing the Ukrainian language in schools, books, and newspapers, in the Party itself, and in its subordinate Soviet state administration, but with Lenin's incapacitating illness and Stalin becoming general secretary of the Party in early 1922, the initially bright political constellation for the patriotic Ukrainians darkened.

The ethnic or assimilated Russians who were still in charge of the relatively small Communist Party (Bolshevik) of Ukraine (henceforth abbreviated CPU) fought Ukrainization tooth and nail. They even went so far as to expel from the CPU several thousand ethnic Ukrainians, former Social Revolutionaries or Borotbists, who had been expressly accepted into the Party in order to increase its Ukrainian contingent.

The most notorious of the opponents of Ukrainization was Dmitrii Z. Lebed', the organizational or personnel secretary of the CPU's Central Committee. Lebed' developed the theory of the two cultures. In March 1923 he wrote, "The artificial implantation of the Ukrainian language in the Party and the working class, given the present political, economic, and cultural relationships between town and country, would mean taking the position of the *lower* culture of the countryside in preference to the *higher* culture of the city"(emphasis added).[11] Earlier, the very same Lebed', qua organizational secretary, had purged about 3,900 of the 4,000 newly admitted ex-Borotbists.[12] As late as 1922, the CPU was "an urban military-bureaucratic non-Ukrainian apparatus."[13] Despite all those political obstacles, at the end of the 1920s, the Soviet Ukrainians registered considerable gains in building Ukrainian culture. To point out the high benchmarks: in 1930, 2.4 million, or as many as 83.2 percent, of all the schoolchildren attended Ukrainian-language schools; in 1931, over three-quarters (76.9 percent) of all books printed in Ukraine were published in Ukrainian; and in 1929, 92.4 percent of all newspapers came out in Ukrainian.[14] (It must be recalled that, according to the December 1926 population census, Ukrainians formed 80.1 percent of the republic's total population.)

But by 1926 there were unmistakable signs that Stalin would support the opponents of cultural Ukrainization and would keep the leadership of the CPU reserved to non-Ukrainians. In Stalin's memorable words:

> At a time when the proletarians of Western Europe and their Communist Parties are in sympathy with "Moscow," this citadel of the international movement and of Leninism, at a time when the proletarians of Western Europe look with admiration at the flag that flies over Moscow, the Ukrainian Communist Khvilevoy [Mykola Khvyl'ovyi] has nothing better to say in favor of "Moscow" than call on the Ukrainian leaders to get away from "Moscow" "as fast as possible." And that is called internationalism!. . .
> Shumsky is right when he asserts that the top leadership (Party and other) in . . . Ukraine should be Ukrainian. But he is mistaken about the tempo. . . . While his perspective is correct, he disregards the question of tempo. And tempo is now the main thing.[15]

Three years later, in 1929, Stalin embarked on what can only be described as genocide[16] directed against the Ukrainian nation. Two hundred and fifty members of the Ukrainian intelligentsia, not counting ordinary peasants, were arrested in that year.[17] Some of them were shot after secret trials. The most prominent of them, however, forty-five leaders of Ukrainian cultural life, who had been active deputies of the nationalist Ukrainian Central Rada of 1917–18, militant members or leaders of pro-independence Ukrainian political parties (including several ministers of UNR governments), members or associates of the All-Ukrainian Academy of Sciences, and organizers of the Ukrainian Autocephalous Orthodox Church, were all accused of belonging to the Union for the Liberation of Ukraine ("SVU" in Ukrainian) and were publicly tried in Kharkiv, 9 March–19 April 1930. Ostensibly, no death sentences were handed down, only jail terms, some of which were even suspended. But it so happened that, because of later re-arrests, only seven of the forty-five SVU defendants either survived the 1930s or died a presumably natural death, meaning that thirty-eight of them had effectively been sentenced to death.[18] Later, the secret police "uncovered" at least twenty-eight more oppositional groups. At the height of the Great Purge, in 1937, shortly before Khrushchev's assumption of rule over Ukraine, practically the entire CPU Politburo and Council of People's Commissars, that is, the government of the Ukrainian SSR, were taken to Moscow and executed. Panas Liubchenko, a former prosecutor at the SVU trial of 1930 and Ukraine's prime minister in 1937, committed suicide just before his arrest. Earlier, in May 1933, the Ukrainian Communist writer Khvyl'ovyi, the subject of Stalin's 1926 letter, had shot himself; in July 1933 he was followed by Skrypnyk, the old Ukrainian Bolshevik and Lenin's associate, who had been former People's Commissar of Education and de facto leader of the Ukrainization drive.[19] According to President Kravchuk, over two million Ukrainians were killed under Stalin *in addition* to the over five million victims of the terror-famine.[20] The total number of victims from 1 January 1935 to 22 June 1941 has been put at 19,840,000 arrested as "enemies of the people," of whom seven million were shot, with the majority of the remainder perishing in the labor camps.[21] Of those numbers, many were obviously non-Ukrainians. But one is struck by the fact that the purge of the Ukrainian politicians was more comprehensive and intensive than that of regional Russian leaders and, above all, that the purges of the 1930s were accompanied by the braking and reversal of the Ukrainization process, precisely at a time when Stalin began to build up the Russian national heritage in historiography, literature, and other areas.

The attacks on the Ukrainian intelligentsia, state administrators, and Party leaders were also accompanied by the horrible terror-famine of 1932–33, the sixtieth anniversary of which was officially commemorated in Ukraine 5–12 September 1993. Opening a scholarly conference on 9 September, President Kravchuk said, "It was an action planned by the state and by Communist Party authorities. One in five Ukrainians starved to death. This was genocide against one's own people on the basis of instructions *issued from outside*. The dreadful pressure put on Ukraine was based on a striving to uproot the entire Ukrainian soul. . . . Unacceptable living conditions were created to destroy a nation" (emphasis added).[22]

This is not the place to present the details on the cruelties committed by the regime nor to engage in an analysis of the number of victims: President Kravchuk's 1992 figure of over five million dead, which is also found in the major work by Robert Conquest, is a reasonable estimate, on the conservative side.[23] Here it must be emphasized that the terror-famine, which was ostensibly directed against Ukrainian and other peasants who refused to join collective farms, was also considered by Stalin a political weapon against Ukrainians as a group, or genocide, in Raphaël Lemkin's comprehensive original definition. According to a statement by former secret police (OGPU) chief in Ukraine Vsevolod Balitsky (which admittedly passed through several sources before it was published in Ukraine on the eve of independence in 1991), Stalin, with his macabre sense of humor, at a meeting in Moscow in March 1933 told his henchman in Ukraine, the Russian Pavel Postyshev: "Paul, my boy, we have sent you there in the role of Commander in Chief of Famine [*Glavgola*]. . . . With that weapon you will accomplish more than Semen [Budenny] could do with several of his cavalry armies. Little Stas [(Stanislav) Kossior] . . . has become somewhat confused. As to those slugs [(Vlas) Chubar′ and (Hryhoriy) Petrovs′kyi] . . . don't pay any attention to them."[24]

More cautious academics will find incontrovertible proof that Stalin was well aware of the political importance of peasants in the following quotation from Stalin's attack on the Yugoslav Communist Semić in 1925:

> That mistake [to reduce the "national" or nationality question to a constitutional issue—Y.B.] leads him to another, namely his refusal to regard the national question as being, in essence, a peasant question.

Not an agrarian but a peasant question, for these are two different things. It is quite true that the national question must not be identified with the peasant question, for, in addition to peasant questions, the national question includes such questions as national culture, national statehood, etc. That explains the fact that *the peasantry constitutes the main army of the national movement, that there is no powerful national movement without the peasant army, nor can there be.*[25] (Emphasis added)

In 1925, Stalin was, of course, well aware of the peasant question in Ukraine, perhaps more than he was of the peasant question in Yugoslavia, and in 1926 Stalin used his knowledge of Ukrainian cultural and ideological developments to attack the Westernizer Khvyl'ovyi. It stands to reason that in 1932–33, as in 1925, Stalin regarded the peasants as the "main army of the [Ukrainian] national movement" that had to be smashed by "Commander in Chief of Famine" Postyshev, who was regarded as even more powerful than Budenny with his cavalry divisions.

But it was not only the numbers of dead peasants that were shocking, not only the horrible manner of their deaths. There is the sensitive question of the qualitative impact. In the moving language of Lidiia Kovalenko, now deceased:

We must not forget that there is another bitter truth in evaluating the indirect [*viddaleni*] consequences of the terror-famine. It is the best who have gone into the mass-grave [*mohyla*], where seven million and a half Ukrainian peasants were buried. It is the industrious and independent-minded farmer-entrepreneurs [*khozyai*] who have perished: falsely, they were accused of being "*kurkul'* [kulak, or farmer] saboteurs." Disappearing into nothingness were the farmers' artisans and inventors, who had always been well-represented in Ukraine and among whom there were a great many with major natural talents. Into the damp earth were laid the rebellious descendants of the Cossacks who proved unable to knuckle under to the arbitrary violence of the authorities. It is not a coincidence that among the witnesses' testimony there are so many tales about the tragedy of ancient Cossack villages, known [both] for their independence and for their prosperity. Among those who perished there was the village intelligentsia, the carrier of culture and of the national idea. They constituted the object of particular attention and concern for the GPU and NKVD [DPU—NKVS, the Ukrainian acronyms for political police—Y.B.].[26]

Now, what has all this got to do with the foreign policy of Ukraine? For a number of reasons, such as the prominent, if not controlling, position of the Russian minority in central and especially in eastern and southern Ukraine; the necessity of achieving a modus vivendi with part-democratic, part-authoritarian Russia; the proverbial tendency of many Ukrainians to pull their punches; and, last but not least, the confusing fact that ethnic Ukrainians loyal to the center did participate in imposing the collectivization on their fellow nationals and in the Great Purge of Ukrainian politicians and intellectuals—the Ukrainians have not yet presented the full bill for genocide to the Russians, as the Israelis have to the Germans. Nor had such a bill been drawn up at the commemorative ceremonies in September 1993.[27] Nevertheless, numerous Ukrainians, even members of the intelligentsia, many of whom are one or two generations removed from their peasant roots, are acutely aware of having been victims of Stalin's genocide. They also know that many Russians profited from that genocide. This acute awareness pushed at least one ethnic Ukrainian Party leader to advocate independence in 1991. Given a lack of sensitivity on the part of some Russian politicians, that awareness can be a complicating factor in Ukraine's relations with Russia. Furthermore, the acute consciousness of being victims may also lead some Ukrainian politicians to have unrealistic expectations of Western statesmen, who, while universally deploring the Holocaust, have somehow managed to come to terms with genocide perpetrated against Kurds and Shi'a in Iraq and Muslims in Bosnia-Herzegovina.

In a kind of "superdialectic," in the fall of 1939, within two months of the outbreak of World War II, the terrible bloodletting in eastern Ukraine in the 1930s was followed by the incorporation of almost five million Polish Ukrainians. This incorporation, together with the future and less important additions of Bessarabia and northern Bukovina in 1940, with a little over half a million Ukrainians, and of Transcarpathian Ukraine (0.5 million Ukrainians) in 1945, more than any other factor, strengthened the Ukrainian people in an enlarged, modern Ukrainian SSR. Moreover, the growing interaction between western Ukraine and eastern Ukraine in the three decades beginning in the 1960s may be considered one of the foremost causes of Ukraine's declaration of independence in August 1991. The question almost begs for an answer: Why did Stalin enlarge Ukraine?

First, Stalin knew that Ukrainian nationalism in Galicia was red-hot, in reaction to strong Polish nationalism. It had grown primarily as a result of a combination of the Polish ideal of denying the Ukrainians any political and cultural group rights and the practical inability of the nontotalitarian, semidemocratic Polish interwar state to realize that ideal by suppressing Ukrainian aspirations altogether. Second, Stalin also knew that to defend themselves against the Poles, the right wing of the Galician Ukrainians, the so-called integral nationalists, who since 1929 had been organized in the Organization of Ukrainian Nationalists, or OUN, began a political and intelligence relationship with Weimar Germany, which was carried over into Hitler's Third Reich. Insofar as Germany had designs on the Soviet Union, it would have been in Stalin's interest to end that relationship once and for all.

Third, because the Galician Ukrainian Communists found a strong protector in Skrypnyk, who, in turn, was active in the Communist International, the persecution of the Ukrainians—Communists and non-Communists—by the Poles found its way onto the Comintern agenda. The Communist Party of western Ukraine, in turn, interfered in Soviet domestic politics by strongly backing Shums'kyi's drive for early Ukrainization in eastern Ukraine. In 1938, the Communist Party of western Ukraine was formally dissolved, as was its parent body, the Communist Party of Poland. At the very least, from Stalin's point of view, the Galician Ukrainian Communists were a pesky nuisance. Among other things, they kept repeating their demands that Polish Ukraine be united with eastern Ukraine under Soviet auspices.

Fourth, it is difficult to avoid the impression that ultimately, all things considered, Stalin's decision to enlarge Ukraine, which he himself had weakened in the 1930s, could be explained by hubris. Stalin wanted to bring about a "final solution" to the Ukrainian question under Soviet, that is, his own auspices. The Poles had botched up the handling of Ukrainian resistance. For this and also because Stalin hated the Poles as much as he hated Ukrainians, the Poles themselves would get more than a taste of genocide. Between 1939 and 1941 about 1.2 million Polish citizens, mostly ethnic Poles, were deported from the so-called eastern territories (western Ukraine and western Belarus),[28] where the majority of the population was non-Polish. Furthermore, 21,857 carefully selected Polish leaders were executed without any formal trial by the Soviets in 1940, in accordance with Politburo resolution no. 144 of 5 March 1940. The victims included over 14,000 Polish POWs and 7,305 Polish civilians held in NKVD prisons in

Galicia and western Belarus.[29] It stands to reason that the remainder of the civilian prisoners, the eight thousand non-Poles held as "hardened and uncompromising enemies of Soviet authority," who were mentioned in Beria's memorandum to Stalin of 5 March 1940, were also put to death. A later Ukrainian underground publication, *Ukrains'kyi visnyk*, puts the total number of Ukrainians who were killed in Soviet jails in Galicia at forty thousand.[30]

The incorporation of western Ukraine into the Ukrainian SSR, however, like the incorporation of new Poland into Soviet-controlled Eastern Europe, increasingly made Ukraine indigestible to Moscow. Not that Stalin and his successors did not try to pacify Ukraine and assimilate the Ukrainians. In a singular miscalculation, in 1946 Stalin liquidated the Ukrainian, or "Greek," Catholic (Uniate) Church. The Church simply went underground and furnished mass support for Ukrainian political dissent in western Ukraine. Gorbachev had to legalize it by 1990. Western Ukraine played a disproportionate role in the Ukrainian dissent movement of the 1960s and 1970s: even though some of the leaders of that movement (Levko Luk'ianenko, for instance) were eastern Ukrainians, they had occupational and friendship ties with western Ukraine.[31]

Another irony of unintended consequences stems from Stalin's decision in 1944 to change the Soviet constitution, allow the Soviet republics to establish their own Foreign Ministries (then called People's Commissariats of Foreign Affairs), and ultimately insist that the United States and Great Britain admit Ukraine and Belarus, in addition to the USSR as a whole, as charter members of the soon to be founded United Nations. Stalin's insistence on Ukraine and Belarus entering the UN was not simply, as commonly assumed, a device to gain more votes in the UN, about which Stalin cared less than did many Americans. It was partly a stratagem to symbolically reward Ukrainian Communists, who faced the formidable double task of economic reconstruction in all of Ukraine and political pacification in Galicia. More importantly, Stalin wanted to legitimize the forcible incorporation of the three Baltic states in 1940 and also pave the way for a possible future incorporation of other states in Eastern Europe. Significantly, as late as the Yalta Conference in February 1945, Molotov was asking for the admission to the UN of one Baltic state in addition to Ukraine and Belarus.

But Stalin's legitimation ploy failed: in 1945, the United States refused to indirectly recognize the takeover of the Baltic states. Later, Poland and other East European states strenuously objected to formal incorporation of these states into the USSR. (Not only that—if anywhere, it was from Eastern Europe that the unraveling of the Soviet Union began in the late 1980s.) The Soviet Ukrainian delegates to the UN General Assembly and other UN organs and agencies did, of course, vote together with USSR-Russia, even though the Ukrainians used English to announce their votes, not Russian. The small Soviet Ukrainian foreign policy personnel in the UN, UNESCO, and elsewhere acquired limited diplomatic experience and were repeatedly and poignantly reminded of their republic's real subordinate position in the USSR, when compared with those of East European states and the countries of the rapidly emerging Third World. However few professional diplomats Ukraine inherited in 1991, without their apprenticeship in the UN there would have been even fewer.

In 1953, Stalin's successor Khrushchev made a wise decision in allowing an ethnic Ukrainian to take over the leadership (the first secretaryship) of the CPU for the first time ever in that party's history. In general, Khrushchev, a declared Russian who had held that Ukrainian post himself from 1938 until late 1949 and who had been helped in his political career by the local Party organizations of Moscow, Leningrad (today's St. Petersburg), and Ukraine, helped the Ukrainian Party organization to advance in both membership and influence. Khrushchev's economic decentralization (1957–64) was a boon to autonomy-minded Ukrainian state and Party officials. But, with the benefit of hindsight, it appears that both the later, or post-1958, Khrushchev and Brezhnev's close associate Mikhail Suslov made a fundamental mistake in pressing for the abolition of the union republics as a maximum and for linguistic and political identificational assimilation as a minimum. In the Ukrainian case, the latter meant assimilation to the Russians, or cultural genocide.

Successive Soviet population censuses depicted as inexorable an apparent progress of identificational and linguistic assimilation. For instance, the first post-World War II census of 1959 showed that 32.2 million citizens of the Ukrainian SSR, or 76.8 percent of the total, gave Ukrainian as their nationality. In the same year (1959) self-identified Russians in Ukraine numbered 7.1 million, constituting 16.9 percent of the republic's population. In 1989, a generation later, the absolute number of self-declared Ukrainians in Ukraine had increased to 37.4

million, but their relative share in the total population had fallen to 72.7 percent. By 1989 the number of ethnic Russians in Ukraine, however, had increased in both absolute and relative terms, to 11.4 million, or 22.1 percent, almost a quarter of the total population. Moreover, linguistic assimilation among the self-declared Ukrainians appears to have gained. In 1959 only 2.1 million, or 6.5 percent, of the self-declared Ukrainians gave Russian as their "native language" or language of usage. In 1989, 4.6 million self-declared Ukrainians, or 12.2 percent—that is, one-eighth—gave Russian as their "native language."[32]

It is an open question to what degree the identificational and linguistic assimilation was truly voluntary and to what extent the decrease in the relative numbers of Ukrainians was caused by in-migration of ethnic Russians and, above all, by Stalin's, Khrushchev's, and Brezhnev's Russification drive, which latter could also be gleaned from school, book, and newspaper statistics. But as a result of the official Russification drive, a strong reaction set in among the Ukrainian intellectual leaders: the poets, writers, journalists, scholars, even some patriotic jurists. From a distance, they were witnessing the decolonization of Asia and Africa, and they were acutely aware of the nationalist revival in socialist Eastern Europe, which was open for travel (Poland, Hungary, and Czechoslovakia). To them, Moscow's policies in the USSR seemed to be going in the opposite direction, against history.

Wisely, their demands for Ukrainian national rights were increasingly couched in terms of universal human rights, as were the demands of the Poles or of the neighboring Lithuanians. This universalization of the Ukrainian dissent movement reached a peak after Brezhnev's signing of the Helsinki Final Act in August 1975, notably in the creation of a Ukrainian Helsinki Watch group, which functioned parallel to and was also personally linked to Moscow Helsinki Watch. This development in the 1970s and early 1980s had two major consequences for the foreign policy of Ukraine. Most importantly, the Helsinki Watch activists and their eventual successors from the better-known Rukh, or Movement for the Advancement of Restructuring (Perestroika) in Ukraine, developed the habit of cooperation not only with like-minded Lithuanians but also with democratically minded Russians who were sympathetic to, or at least neutral on, the question of Ukrainian independence, as was the late Academician Andrei D. Sakharov, who supported the democratic Ukrainian activist Major-General Petro Hryhorenko (Petr Grigorenko) and even helped the Ukrainian nationalist and prisoner of conscience Valentyn Moroz. This habit of Russian-Ukrainian cooperation, which was established in the 1960s and developed in the 1970s and 1980s, is directly responsible for the enlightened policy on national minorities in Ukraine taken by the Kravchuk government. To some little degree, that policy has undercut Russian claims and pretensions to Ukraine.

Second, by universalizing their own demands and showing much tolerance toward non-Ukrainians, the Ukrainian democratic dissenters established a good channel to American policy makers, notably in the U.S. Congress. Despite the misgivings of the Nixon and Ford administrations, Ukrainian dissidents thus opened a second, public channel to Washington, the human rights channel. Prior to the 1960s, by and large, the Ukrainians' only access to Washington was via the intelligence community, all of whom were interested in what was happening in the Soviet Union and some of whom were also planning to destabilize the archenemy of the United States during the Cold War.

Writers and poets, even jurists, do not a strong political opposition make. In my judgment, Brezhnev and his successors committed the second blunder in publicly humiliating Ukrainian political leaders when they showed their concern for their national culture. Petro Shelest was an orthodox Ukrainian Communist leader, very much in favor of heavy industry and a strong East Germany, with some reservations against the U.S. bombing of North Vietnam and President Nixon's visit to Moscow and Kiev in 1972. In May 1972, however, Shelest was ignominiously removed from his post of First Secretary of the CPU after he insisted on Ukraine's greater political autonomy—not independence!—and showed concern for Ukrainian language rights that were advocated by the intellectual dissenters. His successor Volodymyr Shcherbyts'kyi, a protégé of Brezhnev's, who had spoken Ukrainian before 1972, upon assuming Shelest's post started conducting the official Party business in Russian. Nonetheless, Shcherbyts'kyi, a senior member of the all-union Politburo and a Moscow loyalist, was semi-publicly humiliated when he was requested to sign off on a Politburo decision to invade Afghanistan thirteen days after it had already been taken and two days after special KGB units had already been flown to Kabul.[33] Shcherbyts'kyi was an economic and social conservative, that is, not a leader in Gorbachev's perestroika mode, but he was kept in his post by Gorbachev until September 1989 because he was a Russifier par excellence. Apparently it was not enough to be fundamentally loyal to the policies of Moscow—a leader in Ukraine had also to advance Russification. In the face of the increasingly strong intellectual opposition, first provoked by Brezhnev and then really unleashed under Gorbachev's glasnost and perestroika, this was demanding too much. It was in 1990, when the Party leadership in Ukraine, notably Kravchuk, joined forces with the intellectual-political opposition of Rukh, that independence from Russia became a real possibility. The conservatives' abortive coup d'état of August 1991 proved to be the coup de grace for the already disintegrating Soviet Union.

In conclusion, the foremost basic factor underlying Ukraine's foreign policy is its drive for independence. For Ukraine, independence is not a luxury but the only means for survival in the face of both physical and cultural genocide. The Soviet years have indeed had a tremendous impact on the foreign policy of Ukraine. In 1917–22, the Ukrainians had been courted by Lenin, only to be killed by Stalin in the 1930s by the millions, in a policy of physical genocide. Stalin enlarged Ukraine in 1939–45 and then vainly tried to eliminate the Ukrainian problem altogether. After Stalin's death in 1953, Khrushchev both courted and fought the Ukrainians. The later Khrushchev and, of course, Brezhnev and his successors tried to force the Ukrainians to merge with the Russians. That last assimilationist push—a form of cultural genocide—is ultimately responsible for the independence of Ukraine and the breakup of the Soviet Union.

This complex historical heritage is a major burden on any foreign policy of Ukraine, particularly one toward Russia. Territorial and similar disputes apart, the fundamental question is whether Russia will really recognize Ukraine's independence and agree to a mutually beneficial modus vivendi. Conversely, the question is, will the Ukrainians, who had nearly been wiped off the world's map several times in their history, assert themselves sufficiently to make the real independence of their country permanent?

A strong and democratic Ukraine would, moreover, help both the new Eastern democracies, such as Poland, and the old Western democracies—the United States, England, France—to maintain a strong strategic position in Eastern Europe. Ukraine could help them dominate the northern littoral of the Black Sea, thus making a repetition of the Crimean War of 1854–56 completely unnecessary. In its policy of recognizing and supporting an independent Ukraine and of discreetly sponsoring Ukraine's entry first into the East European security zone and then, eventually, into NATO, Poland may have played the most farsighted role. But even Poland has recently swung to the socialist left in its domestic policies. The old Western democracies, alas, have grown tired of world leadership, and more and more the diplomatic landscape in Europe is coming to resemble that of the 1930s. But if the partition of Bosnia-Herzegovina at Geneva in 1993 reminds one of the partition of Czechoslovakia at the conference at Munich in 1938, can a replay of 1939 be far behind? Effective loss of independence of Ukraine would be a tragedy not only for Ukrainians and genuinely democratic Russians but also for Europe, for the world, and—last but not least—for the United States.

Notes

This article is essentially a by-product of the author's work on a book titled *Ukraine: From Nationality to Nation*, to be published by Westview Press, which has graciously consented to the publication of the article in the present volume. The author is also grateful to the official commentators, Dr. Andrus Park, of the Estonian Academy of Sciences, and Dr. Andrzej Kaminski, of Georgetown University, as well as to the volume editor, Dr. S. Frederick Starr, President of Oberlin College. Any remaining imperfections are the author's sole responsibility.

1. It is well known that Vice President Rutskoi kept a map of the Soviet Union in his office and did not hide his predilection for the restoration of the USSR. Stankevich has told an American scholar, "We will create a representative government, so that the republics [sic] now acting *semi-autonomously* [sic] will feel that they have a decisive voice in Moscow, that their representatives are involved in establishing national [sic] laws, and that they are therefore bound by those laws. We will remain socially responsible, because that is absolutely crucial in this country, but we will take reasonable steps toward economic reform. I think we will accomplish these goals with moderate, conciliatory behavior, to create a *single, strong united Russia* [sic]" (emphasis added). Andrew Solomon, "Young Russia's Defiant Decadence: Some Sex, More Drugs and an Insatiable Lust for Money and Power in the Brave New Post-Communal World," *New York Times Magazine*, 18 July 1993, p. 42.

2. See especially Kravchuk's interview given to the German magazine *Der Spiegel*, on the eve of his first visit to a Western country as president: " 'Habt keine Angst vor uns': Der ukrainische Präsident Leonid Makarowitsch Krawtschuk über seinen neuen Staat" ("You need not fear us": Ukrainian President Leonid Makarovych Kravchuk [talks] about his new state), *Der Spiegel*, 3 February 1992, pp. 160–61.

3. For instance, Steven Erlanger, "Ukraine Questions the Price Tag of Independence," *New York Times*, 8 September 1993, p. A8; "Ukraine over the brink," *Economist*, 4 September 1993, pp. 45–46.

4. I. Sichka, "V vysshikh sferakh SNG: Luchshe otkryt' kingstony, chem

Ukrainskii front" (In the highest spheres of the CIS: Better to open the 'kingstons' [the flood valves, in order to scuttle the Black Sea fleet—Y.B.] than the Ukrainian front), *Komsomol´skaia pravda* (Moscow), 22 January 1992, p. 1. I owe the translation of *kingstony* to Dr. S. Trofimenko, of DuPont Company. Few readers of that notorious critical article remember that Lukin advocated the return to Russia of the Black Sea fleet together with three of its deployment and repair bases, including among the latter Nikolaev [Mykolayiv], which is on the Ukrainian mainland.

5. For a good treatment, see Roman Solchanyk, "Ukraine's Search for Security," *RFE/RL Research Report*, vol. 2, no. 21 (21 May 1993), pp. 1–6.

6. Aleksandr I. Solzhenitsyn, "Kak nam obustroit´ Rossiiu . . ." *Komsomol´-skaia pravda*, 18 September 1990; Francis X. Clines, "Russia Gets Call by Solzhenitsyn for Slavic State," *New York Times*, 19 September 1990, pp. A1, A8, with excerpts from Solzhenitsyn's article. On critique by Gorbachev and protests by Ukrainian deputies to the USSR Supreme Soviet Borys I. Oliynyk [Oleinik] and Iurii I. Shcherbak, see V. Dolganov and A. Stepovoi in *Izvestiia*, 26 September 1990, pp. 1–2; or "Gorbachev Assails Solzhenitsyn Article," *Current Digest of the Soviet Press*, vol. 42, no. 39 (1990), pp. 14–15.

7. Henry R. Huttenbach, "The Sudeten Syndrome: The Emergence of a Post-Soviet Principle for Russian Expansionism," in Association for the Study of Nationalities (Eurasia and Eastern Europe), *Analysis of Current Events*, vol. 4, no. 3 (December 1992). Huttenbach cited the following statement by the Foreign Affairs Committee of the Russian Supreme Soviet: "Russian foreign policy must be based on a doctrine that proclaims the entire geopolitical space of the former Union, a sphere of vital interest . . . Russia must secure . . . the role of political and military guarantor of stability on all the territory of the former USSR."

8. Bohdan Pyskir, "The Silent Coup: The Building of Ukraine's Military," *European Security* (London), vol. 2, no. 1 (spring 1993), pp. 139–60.

9. In the spring of 1918, Soviet troops were pushed out by the Germans, with whom both Ukraine and Communist Russia had concluded the Peace of Brest-Litovsk; in 1919, they left under pressure of a temporary alliance of eastern and western Ukrainian troops and White Russian troops; in 1920, sections of Ukraine were occupied by eastern Ukrainian and Polish units. See also Orest Suhtelny, "The Ukrainian Revolution," chap 19, in *Ukraine: A History* (Toronto: University of Toronto Press, 1988), pp. 355–79; and Y. Bilinsky, "The Communist Takeover of the Ukraine," in *The Ukraine, 1917–1921: A Study in Revolution*, ed. Taras Hunczak (Cambridge, MA: Harvard University Press for the Harvard Ukrainian Research Institute, 1977), pp. 104–27.

10. See, for instance, Jurij Borys, *The Sovietization of Ukraine 1917–1923: The Communist Doctrine and Practice of National Self-Determination* (Edmonton: The Canadian Institute of Ukrainian Studies, 1980; rev. ed.), pp. 188–95, on the creation of the first Soviet government in Ukraine and Lenin's secret support of the "Kharkovians," who wanted to detach the Donets Basin from Ukraine (p. 191). Also, Yaroslav Bilinsky, "Mykola Skrypnyk and Petro Shelest: An Essay on the Persistence and Limits of Ukrainian National Communism," in *Soviet Nationality Policies and Practices*, ed. Jeremy R. Azrael (New York: Praeger Publishers, 1978), pp. 108–9.

11. *Kommunist*, 27 March 1923; as cited in James E. Mace, *Communism and*

the Dilemmas of National Liberation: National Communism in Soviet Ukraine 1918–1933 (Cambridge, MA: Harvard University Press, 1983), p. 88.

12. Bohdan Krawchenko, *Social Change and National Consciousness in Twentieth Century Ukraine* (New York: St. Martin's Press, 1985), pp. 99–100. Original source is Skrypnyk.

13. Krawchenko, *Social Change*, p. 100.

14. For comparative figures and detailed documentation, see Tables V–4, V–8, and V–10 in Yaroslaw Bilinsky, *The Second Soviet Republic: The Ukraine After World War II* (New Brunswick: Rutgers University Press, 1964), pp. 162–64 (for data on schools), 175 (books), 178–79 (newspapers).

15. "To Comrade Kaganovich and the Other Members of the Political Bureau of the Central Committee, Ukrainian CP(B)U," in J.V. Stalin, *Works* (Moscow: Foreign Languages Publishing House, 1954), vol. 8: 1926 (January-November), pp. 161–63.

16. I prefer the original definition of genocide in Raphaël Lemkin, *Axis Rule in Occupied Europe: Laws of Occupation, Analysis of Government, Proposals for Redress* (Washington, DC: Carnegie Endowment for International Peace, 1944), p. 79: "Generally speaking, genocide does not necessarily mean the immediate destruction of a nation, except when accomplished by mass killings of all members of a nation. It is intended rather to signify a coordinated plan of different actions aiming at the destruction of essential foundations of the life of national groups, with the aim of annihilating the groups themselves. The objectives of such a plan would be disintegration of the political and social institutions, of culture, language, national feelings, religion, and the economic existence of national groups, and the destruction of the personal security, liberty, health, dignity, and even the lives of the individuals belonging to such groups. *Genocide is directed against the national group as an entity, and the actions involved are directed against individuals, not in their individual capacity but as members of the national group*" (emphasis added).

17. Heliy [Helii] (Ievhen) Sniehir'ov, *Naboi dlia rozstrilu ta inshi tvory* (New York: Sniehirov Fund and Novi Dni, 1983), p. 140. This is a moving reconstruction of the SVU trial by the late dissident cinematographer, whose mother had allegedly testified for the prosecution at that trial.

18. See Hryhory Kostiuk, *Stalinist Rule in the Ukraine: A Study of the Decade of Mass Terror (1929–1939)* (Munich: Institute for the Study of the USSR, 1960), pp. 88–89; Sniehir'ov, *Naboi*, passim; Iaroslav Bilins'kyi, "Spilky Vyzvolennia Ukrainy (SVU) protses," in *Entsyklopediia ukrainoznavstva*, ed. Volodymyr Kubijovyc (Paris: Shevchenko Scientific Society, 1978), vol. 8, pp. 3005–6; Bilinsky, *Ukraine: From Nationality to Nation.*

19. The best source is still Hryhory Kostiuk, *Stalinist Rule in the Ukraine*, (New York: Praeger, 1961).

20. Kravchuk, " 'Habt keine Angst vor uns,' " p. 160. President Kravchuk did not specify the time period in which those "over two million casualties" of Stalinist terror occurred. For simplicity's sake, I have placed them in the worst period, the 1930s.

21. See the major exposé "Fal'sifikatsiia: vospominaniia veterana partii . . . ," *Argumenty i fakty*, no. 22 (503), 2–8 June 1990, p. 7. This is a report based on the recollections of O. Shatunovskaia, former member of the Committee on Party

FOREIGN POLICY OF UKRAINE 191

Control of the CPSU Central Committee and member of a commission that had
been established in 1960 by the Presidium (Politburo) of the CPSU to investigate
Kirov's assassination and the political trials of the 1930s.

22. As cited in "Famine Observance in Ukraine: Kravchuk Accuses Moscow
of Premeditated Murder," *America* (Philadelphia, PA; English ed.), vol. 82, no.
102 (24 September 1993), p. 1.

23. Kravchuk, " 'Habt keine Angst vor uns,' " p. 160. Also Robert Conquest,
The Harvest of Sorrow: Soviet Collectivization and the Terror-Famine (New
York: Oxford University Press, 1986), p. 306 passim. A major U.S. government
source is Commission on the Ukraine Famine, *Investigation of the Ukrainian
Famine 1932–1933: Report to Congress* (Washington: U.S. Government Printing
Office, 1988). The report was adopted by the Commission 19 April 1988 and
submitted to Congress 22 April 1988.

24. See the memorandum by Pantaleimon K. Vasilevs'kyi in Volodymyr
Maniak, "Povernuty narodovi istoriiu, a istorii—pravdu," in Lidiia Kovalenko
and Volodymyr Maniak, comps., *33-i: Holod: narodna knyha-memorial* (Kiev:
"Radians'kyi pys'mennyk," 1991), p. 580.

25. Stalin, "Concerning the National Question in Yugoslavia: Speech Deliv-
ered in the Yugoslav Commission of the E[xecutive] C[ommittee] C[ommunist]
I[nternational], March 30, 1925," in Stalin, *Works*, vol. 7 (1925), pp. 71–72.

26. Lidiia Kovalenko, "Dukhovna ruïna," in Kovalenko and Maniak, comps.,
33-i: Holod, p. 22.

27. President Kravchuk diplomatically referred to the Communist state as the
planner of the terror-famine. His dignified reference to "instructions issued from
the outside," however, is a transparent reference to Moscow.

28. Louisa Vinton, "The Katyn Documents: Politics and History," *RFE/RL
Research Report*, vol. 2, no. 4 (22 January 1993), p. 21.

29. Ibid., p. 20 passim (the total of executions from Shelepin's 1959 handwrit-
ten report to Khrushchev).

30. Maksym Sahaydak, ed., *Ukrains'kyi visnyk, nos.* 7/8 (spring 1974) (Balti-
more: Smoloskyp, 1975), p. 56.

31. For a detailed analysis, see Jaroslav Bilinsky, "The Incorporation of Western Ukraine and Its Impact on Politics and Society in Soviet Ukraine," *The Influence of East Europe and the Soviet West on the USSR*, ed. Roman Szporluk (New
York: Praeger Publishers, 1976), pp. 180–228.

32. Absolute figures from Tsentral'noe statisticheskoe upravlenie pri Sovete
Ministrov SSSR, *Itogi vsesoiuznoi perepisi naseleniia 1959 goda: Ukrainskaia
SSR* (Moscow: Gosstatizdat TsSU SSSR, 1963), p. 168; and from Gosudar-
stuenhyi komitet SSSR po statistike: Informatsionno-izdatel'skii tsentr, *Natsional'nyi sostav naseleniia SSSR: po dannym vsesoiuznoi perepisi naseleniia 1989
g.* (Moscow: "Finansy i statistika," 1991), p. 78. Latter source courtesy of Dr.
Stephen Rapawy. Percentages calculated by author.

33. See facsimile reproduction of secret Politburo decision in Michael Dobbs,
"Secret Memos Trace Kremlin's March to War," *Washington Post*, 15 November
1992, p. A1. (Shcherbyts'kyi's signature is the last from the left, apparently dated
25.12.79, or possibly even 26.12.79.)

III

The Southern
Newly Independent States

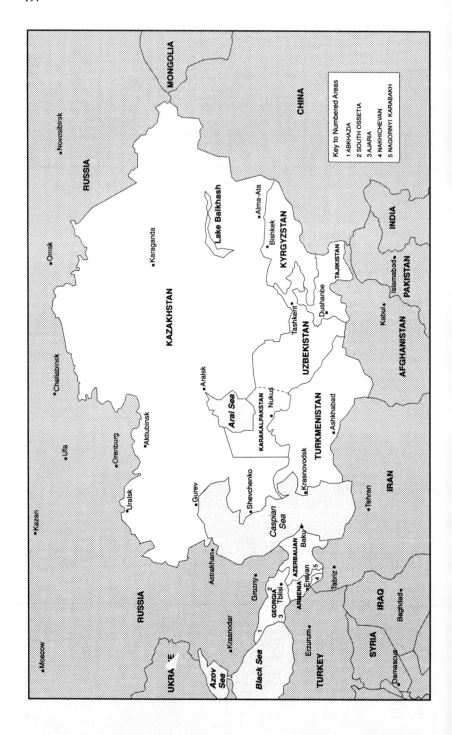

Key to Numbered Areas

1 ABKHAZIA
2 SOUTH OSSETIA
3 AJARIA
4 NAKHICHEVAN
5 NAGORNYI KARABAKH

9

Central Asia's Foreign Relations

A Historical Survey

Firuz Kazemzadeh

With the sudden collapse of the Soviet Union, Central Asia, a land almost forgotten for the last hundred years, has reemerged onto the world stage. Peoples that have long lived in isolation are beginning to develop relations with their neighbors as well as with distant nations with which they have never before had any contact. The foreign relations of the newly independent states of Central Asia are obviously of interest to the rest of the world. To better understand the present, one may briefly look into the past and its uses.

History, that most political of disciplines, has served countless contenders for power in Central Asia. The Achaemenian legacy, the empire of Alexander the Great and his successors, Muslim dominion, descent from Chingiz Khan, ancient legends, and half-forgotten treaties have been invoked over the centuries to justify conquests, usurpations, and rebellions. Today, as in the past, the elites of Central Asian states are constructing mythologies to legitimize their claims to independence, nationhood, or territory. It is therefore important to attempt to study Central Asia's past without succumbing to the influence of partisan mythmakers, whether tsarist, Stalinist, Pan-Turkist, or nationalist.

The area that stretches from the eastern shore of the Caspian into China and from the tree line of Siberia to the mountain fastness of the south has for millennia played a dramatic and important role in the history of humanity and human culture. Sitting astride the land route from the Mediterranean to China, forming at various times part of great empires, this land of mountains, steppes, deserts and oases, climatic contrasts, and ethnic and linguistic diversity has attracted attention since ancient times and yet has remained largely unknown except to its immediate neighbors. Today the names Bactria and Sogdiana mean nothing to the general public and, except for a few students of classical antiquity, no one reads of the campaigns of Alexander the Great in Persia and beyond. Chingiz Khan and Tamerlane have fared no better than their Macedonian predecessor.

The Distant Past

From the days of the Achaemenians, Central Asia formed part of the Iranian cultural realm, although the shahs of that dynasty never ruled the entire region. Under the Greek Seleucid rulers of Iran and under their Parthian successors, Central Asia maintained lively relations with Mediterranean lands as well as with China and India. The Silk Road became one of the world's principal commercial arteries and would continue to be the only link between Europe and East Asia until the Portuguese rounded the Cape of Good Hope.

About the fifth century, Central Asia began to experience the intrusion of numerous Turkic peoples, who would come to dominate the entire area, absorbing its original inhabitants or driving them toward the mountains of the south, where some of them have to this day preserved their ethnic and cultural identity. The struggle between the cultivators of the soil and the nomads, between the civilized and the primitive, and between Iran and Turan, became the subject matter of ballads and epics and left its imprint on the attitudes, values, and culture of the peoples of Central Asia.

The Arab conquest in the seventh century and the subsequent conversion of its population to Islam only briefly made Central Asia a province of the caliphate. A century or two later there arose local dynasties that claimed descent from the Sasanids and strove to preserve or revive the traditions and culture of Iran. The Persian language, enriched by the inclusion of thousands of Arabic words, survived, flourished, and became the vehicle of a Perso-Islamic culture. In fact, the southern rim of Central Asia became the locus of a civilization that blended elements of classical Greece, Judaism, Nestorian Christianity, Buddhism, and Islam.

The balance between the nomads and the settled population, however, remained precarious. Turkic tribes continued to infiltrate the area, inexorably moving west into Iran and beyond. Turkic mercenaries gained control of the Abbasid caliphate in Baghdad, and Turkic dynasties supplanted Iranian dynasties in Khorasan and east. The quality of Mongol armies, the superb generalship of their commanders, the disunity of their opponents, and the presence in the area of large numbers of only partially assimilated Turks made Central Asia easy prey for Chingiz Khan (1162?–1227). The conquest was bloody, and as is usually the case, the sedentary agricultural and urban population suffered the most. Dozens of cities were leveled and their inhabitants massacred. Irrigation systems, indispensable for raising crops in an arid climate, were ruined, forcing the abandonment of cultivation and the reversion of large areas to pasture.

Disastrous though it was in most respects, Mongol rule had a positive side. The largest empire yet known to history made travel fairly safe, permitting Marco Polo to visit China, and goods to move virtually unimpeded from the Atlantic to the Pacific. For a brief time Central Asia was at the center of the world.

And yet decline had already set in. Some of the most fertile and productive regions never recovered from the original Mongolian assault. Chingiz Khan's empire, divided among his sons and grandsons, proved unstable and soon fell apart. Conquerors bloodier than Chingiz Khan fought their unceasing wars. Teymur the Lame (Tamerlane, 1336?–1405) built his pyramids of skulls. While the conqueror was beautifying his capital with the labor of captive architects and tile makers, fresh waves of uncivilized nomads kept flowing in, displacing sedentary populations and plunging the land into anarchy and chaos.

Beginning of Isolation

Two developments helped push Central Asia off the world stage: the voyage of Vasco da Gama to India (1498) and the rise of the Safavid dynasty in Iran (1501). The opening of the sea route from Europe to India and China deprived Central Asia of its historical monopoly of transit trade. As seaborne commerce grew, the number of caravans that crossed the deserts and skirted the mountains on their way from the Middle East to China declined. The day would come when it would be cheaper for Istanbul merchants to buy Chinese goods from Venice than to import them via the Silk Road. Many prosperous towns along that road suffered in consequence. Bazaars were deserted, wells were abandoned, and many inhabitants left.

The rise of the Safavid dynasty was a more immediate disaster for Central Asia. While its population was solidly Sunni, Shah Ismail Safavi, the founder of the dynasty, was a fervent Shi'i whose ancestors had founded and led a Sufi religious order that spread Shi'ism in northern Iran and eastern Anatolia.

The triumph of Shi'ism in Iran more or less coincided with the establishment in Central Asia of a dynasty belonging to a Tatar clan that had left the Golden Horde, overthrown the weakened remnants of the Timurid dynasty, and subdued the Turco-Iranian population. These new invaders called themselves Uzbeks, probably because more than a century earlier the first ruler of the Golden Horde to convert to Islam was Uzbek Khan. It should be noted that one of the defeated Timurids, Zahiru'd Din Babur, fled to Kabul, where he gathered a strong force with which he invaded India and established himself as the first Mogul emperor (1526). Thus once again Central Asia's upheavals had important consequences for the larger world.

Under their powerful leaders, who claimed descent from Chingiz Khan, Abu'l Khayr, and his grandson Muhammad Shaybani Khan, the Uzbeks attempted to unify Central Asia and extend their rule into Afghanistan and Iran. It was in the eastern Iranian province of Khorasan that the veteran warrior Shaybani Khan, a strong Sunni and hater of Shi'a, clashed head on with the boy-king Ismail Safavi at the battle of Marv (1510). The Uzbeks were routed and Muhammad Shaybani Khan himself fell on the battlefield. In consequence the Uzbek power did not extend to Khorasan, and a permanent line was drawn between Sunni Central Asia and Shi'i Iran.

The new frontier proved a strong political and ideological barrier. The Shi'i shahs of Iran, heretics to the majority of Muslims, could no longer appeal to the Sunni peoples of Central Asia as defenders of the faith. Nader Shah Afshar's conquest of much of Central Asia unraveled almost immediately after his death in spite of his attempts to placate the Sunnis and reconcile the two antagonistic sects of Islam. Whatever religious loyalties the peoples of Central Asia had they now vaguely attached to the Ottoman sultan, who strengthened his influence on Sunni Muslims by assuming the title of caliph. Ottoman influence, however, would always remain a minor factor in the affairs of Central Asia. Short of conquering Iran, the Turks would have no access to the lands beyond the Caspian, a sea on the shores of which they never gained a foothold. Conversely, Shaybanids and their successors would never be able to subdue Iran. The division that had once lain along linguistic and cultural lines, between the sedentary speakers of Persian and the Turkic-speaking nomads, was now religious. The Safavids themselves were of Azerbaijani origin, and Azeri Turkish was Shah Ismail's native tongue. His army included Turkmen cavalry as well as Persian-speaking troops. The bond that held Persian and Turk together was Shi'ism.

Another blow befell the Uzbek states of Central Asia when the Tatar khanate of Kazan fell to the Russians in 1552. Four years later the Russians easily conquered the khanate of Astrakhan, thus closing the only remaining land route that led from Central Asia to the Ottoman-protected khanate of Crimea and thence to Istanbul. Fugitive Tatar khans from the Volga may have strengthened the Uzbek element in Central Asia, but Russia's acquisition of the entire course of the Volga was from then on a constant menace.

Separated from the Muslim Middle East, having lost the monopoly of transit trade from the Mediterranean to China, Central Asia entered a period of stagnation. Nomad aristocracies engaged in continuous small-scale wars uncontrolled by their nominal suzerains. Diminished security was particularly damaging to city dwellers, who were the principal payers of taxes and were unmercifully exploited by their nomadic overlords. Throughout the eighteenth and nineteenth centuries old centers of art, science, religious learning, and literature grew progressively more provincial and poorer; the khans more rapacious and cruel; the bureaucracies more corrupt; the ulama, religious leaders; more fanatical; and society in general more conservative and isolationist.

The Three States

The decline seems to have been part of a general decline of Muslim societies, whether Ottoman, Iranian, or Mogul Indian; but in Central Asia it was especially dramatic and deep. By the early nineteenth century, the three independent khanates of Bukhara, Khiva, and Kokand (Khuqand, Qoqan) were backward, misgoverned societies with largely illiterate populations that had retrogressed even in terms of their own recent past.

Each of the three states had ethnically mixed populations that almost defy classification. The northernmost, the khanate of Khiva under the Uzbek Qonghirat dynasty, was inhabited mostly by Uzbeks, Turkmens, Kazakhs, and Karakalpaks (Black Hats, closely related to the Kazakhs). Khiva, the old glorious Khwarazm, had fallen on evil days. It was the poorest, the least civilized, and the weakest of the three states, but it was protected by deserts and by warlike Turkmen, who enjoyed almost total autonomy even when they acknowledged nominal dependence on the khan of Khiva or the shah of Iran.

More prosperous and powerful than Khiva was Kokand, especially after its khan annexed Tashkent, the largest city of Central Asia and an important center of manufacturing and commerce. Here, too, the ruling dynasty was Uzbek, as was a large proportion of the population. Kokand engaged in bitter rivalry with Bukhara and with Russia as the latter consolidated its control of the Kazakh steppe to the north. Kokand's foreign relations were with few exceptions confined to conflicts with Russia.

The third and strongest of the Central Asian states was the emirate of Bukhara, ruled in the nineteenth century by the Uzbek Manghit dynasty. The population of the emirate also included Tajiks, the principal inhabitants of the major cities, Kirghizes, Turkmens, Kazakhs, Jews, and Iranian slaves. The emirs of Bukhara acquired a justified reputation for despotism, greed, cruelty, duplicity, disloyalty, and debauchery. Emir Nasrullah Khan, who reigned for thirty-four years, practiced every imaginable vice and accelerated the ruin of the state, even if he made some attempts to modernize his army and rationalize the administration. His successors may not have been his equals, but they contributed their share of oppression, injustice, and impoverishment to the life of society.

In the nineteenth century the foreign relations of Central Asian states were limited. Contacts with China, Mogul India, and Ottoman Turkey were sporadic. The Chinese were slowly consolidating their hold on Singkiang (Chinese Turkestan), creating occasional inconsequential incidents. The Mogul state of northern India, having never recovered from the sack on Delhi perpetrated by Nader Shah, saw the impotent descendants of Turkic conquerors successively become clients of the warlike Marathas and then of the British, who finally abolished the state after the Indian Mutiny of 1857.

Much more lively and continuous were relations with Afghanistan, which in some senses was a part of Central Asia. The Afghan states—

Herat, Kabul, Qandahar—had large Tajik, Uzbek, and Turkmen populations, although political control was mostly in the hands of Pathan clans of the south. Relations with Afghanistan became significant, however, only in the context of European imperialism in the second half of the nineteenth century. Iran continued to be an enemy. True, there was some trade and occasional exchange of diplomatic missions, but the old hatred of Shi'i heretics did not abate. In the theological colleges of Samarkand and Bukhara mullahs taught, contrary to the generally accepted doctrine of Islam, that it was licit to abduct Shi'i Iranians and sell them into slavery. This provided religious justification for Turkmen slave raids into Khorasan and the sale of Iranians in the markets of Khiva, Bukhara, Samarkand, and Tashkent. Gradually Iranian slaves become an important element in the Central Asian economy.

However, there existed no regular diplomatic relations between Iran and its neighbors to the north and the northeast. While Tehran considered the Turkmens beyond the Atrak River subjects of the shah, they were in effect independent. Neither could the claims of the khans of Khiva to the territories along the eastern shore of the Caspian be enforced. Turkmen depredations against the Iranian provinces of Khorasan and Astarabad continued, and the several campaigns waged by Iran against the tribes ended either inconclusively or in the defeat of Iranian forces. Although the principal buyers of Iranian slaves were Bukharans and Khivans, Iran had insufficient military power to stage a major invasion and impose its will on them. As for Kokand, its relations with Iran were insignificant. Kokand, like Bukhara, bought Iranian slaves, but distance and intervening principalities protected it from any possibility of retaliation.

The Russians

In the sixteenth century, in the reigns of Ivan IV and Fyodor Ivanovich, Russia appeared on the northern horizon of Central Asia. The Tatar khanates of Kazan, Astrakhan, and Crimea had close ties with the ruling clans of Turkestan and Transoxania. The fall of Kazan in 1552 sent shock waves south to Bakhchisaray and Istanbul, east to Sibir, and southeast to Khiva and Bukhara.

For more than two centuries Russia had been the northwestern march of the Golden Horde. Muscovite princes had collaborated with their conquerors, had served the Tatars as military recruiters and tax collectors, and had used the khans in the bloody struggle for supremacy in Rus'. The ties between the princes of Muscovy and the khans even included intermarriages. When the Golden Horde and its khan, Uzbek, embraced Islam, Muscovy acquired a Muslim overlord and was made part of a Muslim empire.[1] Thus the Muscovites came to know the Tatars well. As the power of Muscovy grew, many Tatar nobles who lost the never-ending struggles for the throne at Sarai, the capital of the Golden Horde on the lower Volga, began to move to Moscow and enter the service of the Grand Prince. When Ivan IV conquered Kazan, among his military commanders was Shah Ali, khan of Kasimov (a satellite state of Muscovy), thrice khan of Kazan and faithful servant of the tsar.

The conquest of the khanates of Kazan and Astrakhan made Muscovy their successor and justified Russian claims to the patrimony of Chingiz Khan. In its diplomatic relations with the khanate of Sibir, ruled in the late sixteenth century by members of the same Uzbek tribe that controlled Central Asia and acknowledging the suzerainty of Bukhara, Moscow stressed the fiction that Sibir, like Astrakhan and Kazan, had always been part of the Muscovite domain. No such claims were ever advanced against the Iranians or the Ottomans.

Shortly after Russia conquered the lower Volga region, Bukharans and Khivans began to send representatives to negotiate with the new Caspian power. Contacts were irregular and interrupted by the Time of Troubles, when Russia was deprived of legitimate royal authority, plunged into anarchy, invaded by the Poles and the Swedes, and seemed on the brink of disappearing as a sovereign power. Recovery took time, but even in the most trying circumstances Russia's eastward advance did not slacken. Under the first Romanovs, Cossacks reached the Pacific, and contacts were made with the Chinese in the distant and unmapped wilderness.

In that same century Russia began to absorb the land of the Bashkirs and move into the steppes sparsely inhabited by the nomadic Kazakhs, originally part of the Uzbek horde but on the way to developing a distinct identity. Early in the eighteenth century Peter the Great gave a strong impetus to Russia's expansionism both in the west and in the east. The defeat of Sweden brought Russia to the shores of the Baltic. Poland now fell under Russian influence, which grew until the Commonwealth was partitioned at the end of the century.

Fascinated by India, Peter sent, as early as 1715, a young officer, Artemii Volynskii, to Iran on an extensive spy mission to ascertain whether Iran could serve as a route to India. Volynskii reported that Iran was weak, its government ineffective, and the country ready to fall even to a small Russian military force. Volynskii's analysis was correct. In 1721 Iran was invaded by the Afghans. Taking advantage of the invasion and of the fall of the corrupt and debilitated Safavid dynasty, Peter occupied the Caspian provinces of Iran: Gilan, Mazandaran, and Astarabad. Simultaneously a military expedition under Prince Bekovich-Cherkasskii was sent across the Kazakh steppe toward Khiva. The expedition failed and its members perished, but Peter did not abandon his dreams of establishing trade relations with Bukhara, reaching India, controlling Iran, and renewing the struggle with the Ottoman Empire, the only country at whose hands he had suffered a humiliating defeat.[2]

Through the rest of the eighteenth century Peter's successors continued to absorb the Kazakh steppes and impose their rule on the Kazakh hordes. Their task was relatively easy and cost few Russian lives. Kazakh society was primitive. There existed no state, no common political structure, no unified military command, and no military technology that could compare with that of the post-Petrine Russian army. The leaders of the hordes into which the Kazakhs were divided acted independently of one another. Given proper inducements, heads of clans, batyrs and manaps, often went over to the Russian side. The Muslim clergy were weak and unable to mobilize the people for a jihad against Christian intruders. Thus the takeover of the Kazakh steppes does not quite fall into the same category as the conquest of established states such as Khiva, Kokand, and Bukhara.

In the first half of the nineteenth century Russia concentrated its efforts in the west and the south. Several wars with Turkey and Iran brought Russia Bessarabia and Transcaucasia. Russia achieved a dominant position at the court of the Qajars in Tehran and encouraged their attempts to annex Herat, but did not become directly involved in Iranian campaigns in Afghanistan or Iran's hostilities against the Turkmens. A poorly organized Russian expedition against Khiva in 1839 failed miserably because of climate and supply problems. No significant initiative was shown until Russia's defeat in the Crimean War by a coalition of Britain, France, and Turkey indirectly led to the renewal of Russia's thrust to the east.

During the Crimean War the French, the British, and the Turks made a few weak and ineffective attempts to provoke Central Asian states to hostilities against Russia. None of the allied powers was acquainted with the situation in Central Asia or had any notion of the military potential of its states, which later in the century were regarded by some Western statesmen and diplomats as a buffer between the Russian and the British Indian empires. In retrospect it is difficult to imagine what the Western allies thought Khiva, Kokand, and Bukhara could have possibly achieved against Russia. A few raids on Cossack settlements in the Kazakh steppes, the kidnapping of a handful of Russian peasants and merchants, and a brief disruption of trade that was of no great importance to start with would have been the sum total of damage the three khanates could have inflicted even had they combined their forces. It is instructive that the British, well informed of Iran's weakness, understood its incapacity to render serious aid against Russia and discouraged the Shah's feelers about entering the war on the side of the Western coalition.

The humiliating defeat in Crimea temporarily closed the door on the Russian advance toward Constantinople and the Turkish straits. Central Asia, however, was wide open to Russian expansion, which was made attractive by the necessity of finding employment for the military, the hope of building a strategic base from which to threaten the British in India, and the possibility of improving the flow of commerce frequently disrupted by the irregular behavior of Khivans, Kokandians, and Bukharans. The need, cited by some historians, to ensure a steady supply of cotton to the Russian textile industry, supposedly because of the problems on the world cotton markets caused by the American Civil War, does not seem to be reflected in Russian documents of that era.

Desire for revenge played a role in the enthusiasm with which the Russian military embraced the cause of expansion in Central Asia. England was Russia's chief antagonist, and it was in Asia that England was most vulnerable. As early as 1856 a secret memorandum titled "Thoughts on the Possibility of a Demonstration against English Possessions in India," prepared for high officials, began with an exhortation to Russia to play its historic role in the world. The Russia that saved Europe from Napoleon had been repaid with ingratitude. "But the future of Russia does not lie in Europe. To Asia should she turn her eyes, to Asia where Providence itself calls upon her to carry the torch of Christianity and education."[3] But since the prevailing ethos of nineteenth-century Europe was one of industry and commerce, the author of the memorandum also dwelt on the importance of acquiring Asiatic markets for Russia's manufactured goods. Moreover, he attributed Britain's hostility toward Russia to the fear of Russian commercial competition. Therefore, Russia should find the area where Britain was most vulnerable and find the means to shake British might in India.

The ideological conflict between the proponents of a European orientation of Russian foreign policy and advocates of an Asian direction had not yet developed. It would grow with the spread of anti-Western sentiments later in the century, but would remain a relatively minor factor in determining the actions of the Russian government. Neither the army nor the Asiatic Department of the Ministry of Foreign Affairs, the principal institutions in which the "Asianists" achieved considerable influence, was in a position to impose their will on the autocrat and his ministers.

The Ignat'ev Mission

Between 1856 and 1858 several plans for a military advance through Central Asia toward India were prepared by Russian staff officers. The issue was discussed in the highest spheres and was followed by the tsar himself. The director of the Asiatic Department of the Ministry of Foreign Affairs, E.P. Kovalevskii, advocated the sending of expeditions to study the various routes to India. When N.P. Ignat'ev, a young officer, was assigned in 1858 to head the mission to Bukhara and Khiva, Tsar Alexander II and Grand Duke Konstantin Nikolaevich gave him a farewell audience during which Empress Alexandra blessed him with an icon, made him kneel before her, took his head in her hands and kissed it, and invited him to stay for dinner.[4]

Ignat'ev's mission proved to have been a turning point in relations between the Central Asian khanates and Russia. Whereas in the past there had been a pretense of equality of status, Ignat'ev was determined to demonstrate Russia's superiority and the overwhelming power of the tsar. When on his way to Khiva Ignat'ev ran into a Bukharan envoy who was waiting in Orenburg (an outpost on the edge of the desert) for permission to proceed to St. Petersburg, the envoy expressed the wish that Ignat'ev go to Bukhara before going to Khiva. Otherwise, the envoy hinted, the emir of Bukhara might not receive Ignat'ev. "Obviously, I did not pay any attention to this," Ignat'ev commented.[5] Like most Westernized Russians, he held all Asians in low esteem, particularly the officials. "Khivans," he wrote, "are animals who only know how to lie, suspect, treat everything with mistrust; they are cowardly, base, angry, perfidious, and low."[6]

The movement of Ignat'ev's mission with its imposing armed escort raised fears in Khiva.[7] Rumor had it that the mission was only an advance guard of an army of invasion. The presence on the Amu Darya River of a Russian steamship, whose captain was busy studying the channels and mapping the area, aroused suspicions, especially when news spread that a Persian slave had found refuge on the ship and the Russians had refused to surrender him to Khivan authorities. Slave owners were disturbed, Ignat'ev recorded. "They are threatened with personal property loss, because all their land is cultivated by Persian slaves sold to them by Turkmens." Sayyid Muhammad Khan, the ruler of Khiva, himself insisted that the slave be returned, while the rulers of Kokand and Bukhara demanded that the khan of Khiva not permit the Russians to navigate the Amu.[8]

The negotiations with Sayyid Muhammad Khan were carried out in an atmosphere of mutual suspicion. The khan was reluctant to accept Russian demands, fearing the diminution of his power and the wrath of his neighbors Kokand and Bukhara. Yet he did not have the courage to reject them either. Ignat'ev feared for his life, knowing that in the past Central Asian despots were not above imprisoning and killing envoys. In the name of his sovereign, Ignat'ev demanded that the khan undertake no action inimical to Russia and not incite Turkmens, Kirgiz (the Russian term for Kazakhs), and Karakalpaks who lived close to Khivan territory to hostility toward Russia or toward one another. The khan was to promise never to attack or capture Russian subjects, to assume personal responsibility for the security of every Russian subject in Khivan territory and for every caravan going to or coming from Russia, and to send to Russia the property of any Russian subject who died in Khiva. Moreover, the khan was to permit Russian ships free navigation on the Amu Darya, not impose tariffs of over 2.5 percent *ad valorem* on goods going to or coming from Russia, and permit a Russian commercial agent (*karavan bashi*) to reside permanently in Khiva.[9]

Having concluded an agreement with Khiva, Ignat'ev reluctantly proceeded to Bukhara, whose emir, Nasrullah Khan, was infamous throughout Central Asia. In a letter to the Ministry of Foreign Affairs,

Ignat′ev argued that the emir, farther removed from Russian military power and thinking himself the mightiest sovereign of Central Asia, was unlikely to cooperate. Nasrullah had conquered Shahr-i-Sabz, "cut off the ears of Kokandian envoys, demanded that the khan of Kokand give up his throne" and that the khan of Khiva yield his to Nasrullah's son-in-law. Nasrullah, Ignat′ev wrote, had virtually gone mad from opium and other excesses, and it would be better to wait for him to die and then deal with his successor.[10]

To Ignat′ev's surprise he found Emir Nasrullah Khan a strong, lively, and intelligent individual. The Russians were well received, although there were some points of protocol that had to be resolved first. For instance, Ignat′ev refused to sit on the floor at audiences with the emir and threatened to bring his own folding chair. He also demanded the right to ride his horse in the city where non-Muslims were only permitted to walk. The Bukharans gave in.[11]

Ignat′ev's substantive demands were standard: freeing Russian captives held in Bukhara, cutting in half tariffs charged Russian merchants of Orthodox faith, who traditionally paid four times as much as Muslim Russian subjects; permitting a Russian commercial agent to visit Bukhara from time to time; opening a caravansary for Russian merchants such as Khivan and Indian merchants enjoyed in Bukhara; regularizing the evaluation of Russian goods by Bukharan officials; and permitting Russia free navigation on the Amu for the purpose of transporting goods to and from Bukhara. These were accepted by the emir and embodied in a treaty.[12]

Ignat′ev's mission was not only to conclude agreements with the khans of Khiva and Bukhara but also to counteract supposed British intrigues there and to sow dissension between the two Asiatic states. He quickly discovered that there were no British agents lurking in either, and that enmity between the two needed no encouragement.

In January 1859, having returned to St. Petersburg, Ignat′ev was instructed by Prince A. M. Gorchakov, the minister of foreign affairs, to submit in writing his views on the next steps Russia should take in Central Asia. Unsure of Khiva's compliance with the terms of the recent treaty, Ignat′ev proposed that if Khiva prevented the steamship *Perovskii* from sailing to Bukhara on the Amu, Russia should occupy the delta of that river. Russia should also encourage the "Kirgiz" (read "Kazakhs"), Turkmens, and Karakalpaks to separate themselves from Khiva. Moreover, Russia should consider separating Tashkent and

Turkistan (town) from Kokand and Bukhara "so as to occupy, under favorable circumstances, these two towns and link the Syr-Darya and the Siberian lines, but not before 1861, quietly preparing the means."[13]

While Prince Gorchakov, lover of literature and friend of Pushkin, a man of "European orientation," is usually characterized as an opponent of Russian advances in Asia, he raised objections not so much to the substance but to the form of Russian activity there. He cared not at all about the khanates but was very much concerned about England's reaction to the Russian approach to India. Gorchakov endorsed plans for the linking of the Siberian and Orenburg lines, a move certain to involve Russia deeply with Kokand and Bukhara. The order for the linking was given by the tsar himself on 1 January 1864, opening the final phase of the Russian conquest of Central Asia, a phase that would last less than thirty years and would incorporate Kokand and Khiva in Russia and leave Bukhara only nominally separate as a protectorate. In this final phase the diplomacy of Central Asian states played but a minor role. The contest was now between Russia and Great Britain, with Britain powerless to stop its formidable rival until the Russians had reached the mountain barrier along the borders of Iran and Afghanistan.

Twenty years later, Ignat'ev, then adjutant-general and head of a committee appointed to review Russian administration in Central Asia, wrote "A Historical Sketch of the Spread of Russian Rule in Central Asia." He attributed the 1863 decision to link the Orenburg and Siberian lines and to take possession of Kokand to the position assumed by Great Britain "in the matter of the Polish uprising and the conviction that such possession would give Russia an opportunity to threaten in case of war with England." Thus the fates of Kokand and Tashkent was sealed before the orders for the original advance had been given.

The Russian Conquest

As Russian columns marched from two directions and occupied Aulia-Ata and Turkistan (the town), Kokand, perceiving the immediate threat, concentrated its forces at Chimkent, roughly halfway between the two towns that had fallen. On 2 October 1864, General Cherniaev occupied Chimkent, completing the linking of the Orenburg and Siberian lines. The initial goal of the campaign was now accomplished; but, contrary to the assurances of Russian diplomats, the advance deeper into Central Asia was only beginning.

Diplomacy, never very important in Russia's dealings with local rulers, was pushed to the limit when Turkestan Oblast was formed in February 1865. The government decided that the Ministry of Foreign Affairs "should not conduct useless negotiations with Central Asiatic governments" and entrusted such relations to the governor-general of Orenburg, N.A. Kryzhanovskii.[14] Thus it was the military in command in Central Asia who were given the power on the spot to plan and execute the next moves. Such moves included the separation of the city of Tashkent, the most prosperous and largest in Central Asia, from the khanate of Kokand.

The initial attempt of General Cherniaev in October 1864 to take Tashkent by storm had failed, but Russian determination to detach the city from Kokand did not weaken. It seemed especially important to the Russians to prevent Tashkent from falling into the hands of Muzaffaru'd-Din, the emir of Bukhara, who, taking advantage of Kokand's troubles, tried to extend his power in every direction. The notion of turning Tashkent into a Russian protectorate was abandoned when a pro-Bukharan party began to form in the city. In June 1865 Cherniaev, with fewer than two thousand men at his command, stormed Tashkent, defended by tens of thousands. "The brilliant military action of General Cherniaev in 1864 and 1865," N.P. Ignat'ev rhapsodized twenty years later, "created a firm and unshakable position for Russian rule in Central Asia."[15]

While assuring the British that Cherniaev had exceeded his authority in occupying Tashkent and that Russia had no intention of annexing any more territory in Central Asia, the Russian government celebrated the victory, honored the victor, and sent its troops forward. Emir Muzaffaru'd-Din provided a pretext by placing on the throne of Kokand Khodayar Khan, a man who had reigned there and been overthrown twice before and who was willing to subordinate himself to the Bukharan ruler.

The newly appointed commander of Russian troops, General D.I. Romanovskii, continued Cherniaev's policy. On 20 May 1866 at Irjar, on the road to Samarkand, his detachment of 3,600 men routed the Bukharan army of 40,000. Approximately one thousand Bukharans were killed, the Russians losing one dead and eleven wounded. Romanovskii then turned to Kokand and on 7 June took the fortified city of Khojand by storm, killing 2,500 Kokandians and losing but five Russians. In subsequent battles the ratio of Russian to native losses remained unbelievably low. Thus at Ura-Tiube in October 1866 the Russians under General Kryzhanovskii killed some two thousand natives, while losing only seventeen of their own men. At Jizak, a few days later, six thousand natives were killed, with Russians losing six men. Russian campaigns continued year after year. On 15 May 1868 Samarkand, the fabled capital of Tamerlane, fell to General Konstantin von Kaufmann, recently appointed governor-general of Turkestan. The emir, demoralized and frightened, wanted to abdicate and leave for Mecca, but Russia preferred to keep him as a puppet to fend off British protests.

> Finding it convenient for Russia's interests to have Bukhara headed by a person who had personally [sic] tasted the power of Russia's arms, General Kaufmann in all conflicts of the emir with his subjects supported the rule of the former. In 1868, at the time of the rebellion of the emir's eldest son, . . . Russian troops entered the borders of Bukhara, took Karshi and returned it to the emir. In 1870, during the revolt in Shahr-i-Sabz, our troops took Kitab by storm, then returned it to the emir.[16]

Next came the turn of the khan of Khiva, Muhammad Rahim II, who had anticipated a Russian attack ever since the advance had begun in 1864. The following year he sent an emissary to Constantinople to beg for Ottoman mediation. The Ministry of Foreign Affairs would accept no meditation either by Turkey or by any other power. Its relations with Khiva were to be treated as a domestic matter.[17]

Year after year Muhammad Rahim Khan was accused by the Russians of protecting bandits who raided Russian territories and of fomenting mutinies among the Kazakhs of the Orenburg region.[18] "Thus the dignity of our state authority, the material interests of Russia, and the general perspectives of our policy demanded the subjection of the khanate to our influence."[19] The khanate was simply an inconvenience; there was no place for it in the Russian scheme of things. Contrary to the later assertions of Count Shuvalov in London, the decision to occupy Khiva had been made by the tsar himself, in a meeting attended by Minister of War D.A. Miliutin, Prince Gorchakov, General von Kaufmann, and other high military and civil officials.

Once Khiva was occupied (1873), the world was assured that the occupation was temporary. However, Russian troops never left, the khanate itself was abolished, and even the pretense of its autonomy was abandoned. Neither did Kokand survive as a protectorate. It too was absorbed directly into the empire, leaving only Bukhara with the status of a semi-independent khanate under Russian protection.

Thus only a decade after the launching of the offensive Russia had achieved its principal goals. There was, of course, mopping up to do. The Turkmens of Transcaspia were not "pacified" for another decade, and occasional uprisings called for the use of force. However, Russian rule was not seriously challenged until 1918.

To the khanates of Central Asia diplomacy proved of no avail once the Russian advance had begun. Khiva, Bukhara, and Kokand had no ties to any country that could have offered them assistance or protection. China had only limited interests there and was, in any case, in no position to dispute Russia's intrusion. Iran was both weak and hostile to the Sunni states. Turkey was too distant and struggling for its own survival. The Russians had no fear of Iranian or Turkish intervention and nothing but contempt for the local population. Only Great Britain was a power with which they reckoned. After 1864 serious diplomatic activity in regard to Central Asia took place in London and St. Petersburg.

Following the conquest the peoples of Central Asia continued to be isolated from the rest of the world. While the Russians built railways, established Russian military outposts, brought in officials and their families, and opened schools for Russian children, the native population remained largely undisturbed and uninfluenced by the intruders. Persians, once numerous in Khiva and Bukhara as slaves, now began to settle, mostly in Transcaspia, as merchants, and so did Azerbaijanis and Armenians, but they too constituted separate communities that did not integrate into local society.

Unfortunately, the reaction of the local population to Russian conquest and rule is not very well known. Neither under the tsars nor under the Bolsheviks, except for a brief interlude after the Revolution, did the Russians find it useful to explore or publicize the sentiments of the conquered peoples. Archival and literary sources in Persian and in Turkic languages await serious study.

Soviet Rule

The great change in the life of the Central Asian masses came with the Bolsheviks, who maintained Russian power but brought a radically different attitude toward the native population. As Marxists the Bolsheviks held Western views of nationality and ethnicity. Nationality to them was a transitional stage corresponding to the capitalist stage of economic development. The peoples of Central Asia, they felt, were still in the feudal stage and were only beginning to coalesce into nations. Under the aegis of Moscow they would skip the capitalist stage and achieve socialism while developing into modern nations like the French, the Germans, or the Russians.

Among the obstacles to the development of nations in Central Asia, the Bolsheviks believed, were Islam and Pan-Turkism. Islam claimed universality and called for the union of all believers, transcending race, nationality, and class. To the Marxists its message was false, since Islam was a product of prefeudal society without relevance in the modern world. Moreover, it was a religion and therefore, like all religions, an instrument of traditional exploiting classes. Pan-Turkism was also reactionary in its nature, for it too was an obstacle to the development of modern nationalities. Pan-Turkism also seemed to be an immediate threat to Bolshevik domination of Central Asia. A Pan-Turkic empire stretching from the Urals to Afghanistan and from Istanbul to Sinkiang would be a political threat to Moscow, the capital of world revolution. The appearance in Central Asia, at the head of the anti-Soviet guerrillas, the basmachis, of Enver Pasha, son-in-law of the sultan and commander of the Ottoman armies in the Caucasus in World War I, was a warning of grave danger.

The Commissariat of Nationalities, headed by Stalin, worked out plans for the "national delimitation" of Central Asia. Some of its decisions reflected the interests of central authorities, which, fearing the growth of Pan-Turkic solidarity, strove to divide Central Asia into docile segments. The national terminology chosen by Moscow did not necessarily reflect the real ethnic divisions that existed in Central Asia. The lines drawn between the Kazakhs, the Kirgiz, the Karakalpak, and others were often artificial. Yet the states that emerged took root.

After half a century of existence Uzbekistan, Turkmenistan, Kyrgyzstan, and Kazakhstan acquired a reality that cannot be disputed. However, as members of the Soviet Union or, more correctly, as Russian colonies, they were completely isolated from the outside world. The border with Afghanistan was sealed with the liquidation of the Basmachi movement after 1930. Soviet Uzbeks and Tajiks lost all contact with their ethnic brothers, millions of whom inhabited

Afghanistan and Iran. In the mid-1930s thousands of foreign nationals, mostly Iranians, were either expelled from Soviet Central Asia or sent to concentration camps. Even private contact with the outside world ceased.

To strengthen his diplomatic position at the United Nations at the end of World War II, Stalin instituted foreign ministries in each of the union republics and won UN seats for two (Belorussia and Ukraine). The foreign ministries were pure fiction. There were no diplomatic relations with the outside world, no foreign embassies or even consulates in any of the capitals, and the Belorussian and Ukrainian delegations to the United Nations were in reality part of the Soviet delegation. This situation continued until the USSR began to break down.

The Russian-Soviet impact on Central Asia has been enormous. Russian is today the common language of the newly independent republics. The ruling classes have had a common educational experience and use the same terminology in expressing their political and cultural thought, a terminology made in Moscow decades ago.[20] Land ownership, agriculture, industry, law, the educational system, government structures, the press, all are faithful copies imported from Moscow. While some features of the system will be modified, the basics will remain in place indefinitely.

After the Soviets

The Soviet Union has ceased to exist. In its place have emerged countries that have achieved varying degrees of independence from Russia and have entered into diplomatic and commercial relations with the outside world. The states of Central Asia entered the realm of international relations with a minimum of preparation and with virtually no experience. The domestic needs and conditions that determine the foreign policies of each republic are so different that no easy generalizations are possible. One may expect, however, that certain patterns conditioned by geography, economic need, religion, culture, and history will emerge.

Kazakhstan, with its enormous oil wealth, is nevertheless heavily dependent on Russia. The Kazakhs, a minority in their own country, are outnumbered by Russians and other Slavs who, like any Europeans, tend to unite in the face of threatening "natives. The Slavic majority in Kazakhstan plays the leading role in industry, education, administration, communications, the armed forces, and the police. The Kazakh elite is the most Russified of Central Asian elites and the least attached to the traditional forms of its own culture and to Islam, which came to the Kazakhs late and had a limited impact on them. Thus one may confidently expect that Kazakhstan will continue to move within the Russian orbit and maintain strong ties with the nation to which half of its population belongs.

Turkmenistan, Uzbekistan, and Tajikistan, in spite of great differences in resources, geography, demographics, language, and traditions, can also be expected to maintain strong ties to Russia in the next several decades. In fact Russia will continue to play a dominant role there; Turkey, Iran, Pakistan, and China are in no position to seriously challenge that role. The factors that brought Russia to Central Asia and permitted it to easily establish its rule over the region's peoples continue to exist, albeit in modified form. Economic dependence on Russia will not disappear soon. Russia will continue to be a major, if not the only, market for Central Asian agricultural products, and will continue to control banking, railways, and airlines. Higher education will remain largely in Russian hands, and many members of the native elites will continue to be educated in Russia and to be influenced by Russian culture. Russian political traditions, blending with local practices, will continue to exercise influence even if some republics pro forma adopt constitutions modeled on that of the United States. Russian minorities in each of the republics will exercise strong influence because of their numbers, education, organization, and technological competence.

These factors, then, will establish the framework within which the international relations of Central Asian states will develop.

Notes

1. The original Uzbeks were a Tatar clan of the Golden Horde that made its way into Central Asia, where it became a ruling aristocracy.
2. It has been frequently stated by Western historians that Peter and his successors were motivated in their expansion by the desire to acquire a "warm-water port." Peter indeed won and lost a foothold on the Black Sea at Taganrog but never considered it even remotely comparable in importance to St. Petersburg and the Gulf of Finland, which freezes for several months every year.
3. Central State Archive of the October Revolution (TsGAOR), fond 730, opis. 1, edinitsa khraneniia 273.

4. N.P. Ignat'ev, "Vospominaniia," TsGAOR, f. 730, op. 1, ed. kh. 132.
5. Ibid.
6. Ibid.
7. The mission included 117 members with 178 horses, 20 carts, and 352 camels. Ignat'ev to Kovalevskii, no. 420, 22 May–3 June 1858, TsGAOR, f. 730, op. 1, ed. khr. 136/1.
8. Ibid.
9. The Farman of the Khan of Khiva Concerning the Conclusion of the Treaty with Russia, 1257 A.H., TsGAOR, f. 730, op. 1, ed. khr. 307.
10. TsGAOR, f. 730, op. 1, ed. khr. 132/4.
11. N.P. Ignat'ev, Report to Tsar Alexander II, January 1859, TsGAOR, f. 730, op. 1, ed. khr. 300.
12. Russian translation of the proclamation of Nasrullah Bahadur Khan of the treaty of perpetual peace and close friendship with the Illumined and Potent Russian Empire, TsGAOR, f. 730, op. 1, ed. khr. 308.
13. N.P. Ignat'ev, memorandum, January 1859, TsGAOR, f. 730, op. 1, ed. khr. 136.
14. N.P. Ignat'ev, "A Historical Sketch of the Spread of Russian Rule in Central Asia," TsGAOR, f. 730, op. 1, ed. khr. 1760.
15. Ibid.
16. Ibid.
17. Vsepoddanneishii doklad. St. Petersburg, 2–14 March 1864, Arkhiv vneshnei politiki Rossii, S. Pb., Glavnyi arkhiv, I–1, op. 781, ed. khr. 105, 1865, Ministry of Foreign Affairs, Moscow.
18. Kaufmann to the khan of Khiva, Tashkent, 12–14 August 1869, enclosure in Kaufmann to Miliutin, Tashkent, 25 August–7 September 1869, MSS Division, f. 169, karton 65, ed. khr. 23, Lenin Library.
19. Ignat'ev, "Historical Sketch."
20. A leader of one of the Central Asian republics, addressing a meeting in Washington, DC in Russian, referred frequently to *bratskaia Turtsiia*, "fraternal Turkey."

10

The Rediscovery of Uzbek History and Its Foreign Policy Implications

Kadir Z. Alimov

Now that the old USSR has collapsed as a result of the dramatic developments culminating in the coup of August 1991, important questions arise about the international implications of the tumultuous changes in that former country. What course will the Muslim republics take? How will their evolution affect the Muslim factor in the volatile politics of the southern rim of the Eurasian continent?

What is the potential for instability and conflict inherent in such a large-scale change in sociopolitical realities? What impact will it have on the international balance of power? Finally, what can be done to reduce the potential for conflict and ease the process of change, based on the experiences of other nations in dealing with similar problems?

Working out solutions to nationality issues in the former (and future?) USSR is a major problem, not just for that country but for the entire international community. Unless acceptable and durable solutions are to be found in the near future, dangerous destabilization may follow, with all its grave implications for international security, including the problems of the Middle East. Developments in the newly independent republics of Central Asia (Uzbekistan, Tajikistan, Turkmenistan, Kyrgyzstan), with all their complexity and unpredictability, will necessarily have a considerable impact on the situation in this vitally important region of the world.

Uzbekistan has definitely started to revise its history as it was written during the Russian and Soviet periods. Russian historians during both the Russian and the Soviet eras tried hard to convince Central Asians that Russia's role was necessary in bringing modernization to the nomadic societies of Central Asia. The Russians have usually seen themselves as superior to Central Asians and have always tried to convince the Central Asians that their joining the Russian Empire was done peacefully and according to the desire of the Central Asians themselves. Of course this view should not be taken as it is, or even tolerated, since it reflects only the position of the colonizer and not the colonized. In other words, the views of such "Stalinist historians" serve nothing but the continuation of the negative image of Central Asia.

The Russians are responsible for changing the Uzbek script twice: from Arabic to Latin in 1929 and then from Latin to Cyrillic in 1937. The change of script kept the Uzbek people ignorant of their history and culture and made them rely heavily on what was written in Russian. Contrary to what Russians say, new documents released by the archives of the Uzbek Academy of Sciences' Oriental Institute prove that the Russian expansion into Central Asia was brutal and unmerciful. It was indeed not much different from any other colonialist experience. Yes, the Russians brought some economic development to the urban population in Central Asia, but this development was overwhelmed by their exploitation of the region's natural resources and labor power.

The experience of the Central Asian republics with the Soviet Union was to a great extent different from their experience with the Russian Empire. Through its center, Moscow, the Soviet Union exploited Central Asia not only economically, as the Russian Empire had done, but also ideologically. Muslims were forced to become communists, mosques were demolished, religion was not tolerated, and all Central Asians' efforts to revive their history were condemned as nationalistic and subversive. Moreover, the Soviet period created several problems for Central Asia that today are undermining the region's attempt at recovery. These problems are twofold.

First, the Soviets created artificial administrative units that were transformed later on into sovereign republics. The Soviets had divided homogeneous regions into different states. The Bukhara emirate, for example, was divided between Uzbekistan, Turkmenistan, and Tajikistan, and the Khiva khanate between Uzbekistan, Karakalpakstan, Turkmenistan, and Kazakhstan.

Second, the Soviets unwittingly promoted ethnic tension in Central Asia by ignoring people's memories of their historical native lands. Large groups of Turkmen, Uzbeks, Tajiks, and Kyrgyz, for example, were forced by the Soviet authorities to move from one Central Asian republic to another. The Soviet-made borders have created a map that is full of contradictions and ethno-territorial divisions.

In post-independence Uzbekistan, people are searching for their historical roots, and an energetic process of "Uzbekistanization" is under way. Streets, for instance, are being renamed after the great heroes of Uzbekistan, like Tamerlane and Babur. Here it is worth mentioning that the current debate over history in Uzbekistan allows very limited contribution by historians of Russian origin, because their message is not welcome among the Uzbek population. The Uzbeks seem more willing to hear about *their* ancestors than about anyone else. Furthermore, the influence of hardline Uzbek historians, who happened to share some of the views presented by Russian historians, is declining, and the balance within the community of historians is shifting toward a new generation of historians, who are more committed to their republic's version of history.

The history of Uzbekistan is definitely being revised. The Russian Empire and its Soviet successor have collapsed. Communism is dead. What historical path will Uzbekistan choose: a Western-type liberal society, an Islamic state, or something else?

Francis Fukuyama predicted the end of political history with the victory of liberalism all over the world in his book *The End of History and the Last Man*. Fukuyama's worldview would require alterations in Asia's political process to satisfy this forecast, however. In a recent article Fukuyama notes:

> As we survey the world's ideological horizon after the collapse of communism, it is clear that there is one potential competitor to Western liberal democracy whose strength and legitimacy is growing daily. This alternative is not fundamentalist Islam, but rather the soft authoritarianism said to exist in Japan, Singapore and other of the region's economically vibrant states.[1]

These developments have a bearing on the situation of the Russian population in Uzbekistan. The Russians have evidently lost their status as a majority in the Soviet Union and have become a minority in

Uzbekistan in particular and in Central Asia in general. This change carries significant meaning for Uzbek-Russian relations. On the one hand, Russia is worried about the safety of the Russian population in Uzbekistan and seems ready to protect Russians there even if the situation entails the use of force. On the other hand, Uzbekistan has declared its intention to treat all its population equally regardless of origin or nationality. Although the Russians living in Uzbekistan do not currently represent a challenging threat to Uzbekistan's relations with Russia, they could possibly become a weapon in the future to be wielded by all interested forces.

In academic circles and among the political elite of Uzbekistan, in fact according to public opinion, the Uzbeks regard themselves as a part not of Russian but of Asian history. The Asian mentality, based on collective forms of economic and social life, is different from the Western type, whose base lies in the values of individualism. This distinction does not mean that all Asian nations share a common future, but it will be the main feature of future development of the political process in Asia. These ideological differences between East and West may provoke future conflicts.

The Problem of Ethno-territorial Divisions

Uzbekistan's foreign policy since the collapse of the USSR is being rooted in the context of a unique Uzbek culture, a culture that is to be found in a rediscovery of Uzbek history. Elements of this history, which seek to emphasize a long-suppressed and dormant Uzbek identity, have as a consequence aggravated relations with the numerous ethnic minority communities residing in Uzbekistan, particularly those of Russian and other Central Asian descent. Protestations in support of these communities by their respective governments have in turn prompted Uzbek officials to tighten and further restrict indigenous sociopolitical participation in ways that do not correspond to Western-style democratic models. In sum, therefore, Uzbekistan faces a difficult conundrum: it must simultaneously promote and implement a rediscovered history to the satisfaction of domestic elements, while restraining those elements from pursuing an overzealous application of Uzbek ethnic identity. Whereas such restrictions may alleviate the fears of its various internal ethnic minorities that this phenomenon poses a threat to the insurance of their cultural rights and concurrently removes points of conflict with its powerful neighbors, such impediments to democratic values do little to elicit critically needed economic assistance from the West.

In *Nationalism in Uzbekistan*, the American historian James Critchlow wrote:

> The national delimitation of 1924 was in many ways a giant ethnic oversimplification. Many members of the emergent nationalities had only a tenuous relationship to their national classification. In the case of the "Uzbeks," many were more apt to think of themselves primarily in other terms, as members of tribes with names like Barlas or Loakait, or as inhabitants of localities, such as the Bukharans or Samarkandis.[2]

Whatever the basis, or lack thereof, for the creation of an Uzbek "nationality," there can be little doubt that all the indigenous Muslim inhabitants of the territory now known as Uzbekistan have a strong attachment to their homeland and its Islamic culture.

There are several factors that contribute to the worsening situation in the Asian republics. First, there is the varied ethnic composition of the population in the Fergana Valley, the areas adjoining Lake Ysyk-Köl, Semirech'e (a historical territory located in the southeast of Kazakhstan and north of Kyrgyzstan, named for the seven rivers that flow through its territory), and several other regions.

Second, the current national-administrative division into republics has a short history dating back only to the early years of Soviet power. As mentioned earlier, the new boundaries cut through the formerly monolithic states of Bukhara, Khiva, and Kokand.

Third, several Asian peoples living for centuries in the same territory consider themselves rightful heirs to the cultural traditions of their ancestors. Both present-day Uzbeks and Tajiks, for example, claim to be descendants of Timur and Ulugh Beg and heirs to the great cultural tradition from Al-Biruni to Avicenna and Jami. In 1924–26, when new boundaries were set, some of the Uzbeks were registered as Tajiks, and some Tajiks as Uzbeks.

Fourth, people's memories of their historical native lands are still strong. Large groups of Turkmen, for example, once inhabited the Mangyshlak Peninsula in Kazakhstan; a group of Kyrgyz populated the Karategin country in Tajikistan; and many Uzbeks lived near the city of Chimkent in Kazakhstan. Many of them, like the Karategin

Kyrgyz, were ousted from their historical motherland long before Soviet power was established there. In the 1920s Soviet authorities organized massive migrations from one Central Asian republic to another.

Last, there are demands for administrative and cultural autonomy in different former Soviet republics for the repatriation of peoples that suffered during the Stalinist purges, including Germans, Koreans, Kurds, Crimean Tartars, Assyrian-Aysors, and Meskhetian Turks, thus creating tensions between Uzbekistan and other newly independent states.

Even a cursory glance at the map, however, is enough to see that the majority of conflicts occur around ethno-territorial borders. Drawn up long ago and of practically no importance for a long time, these borders have now turned into battle lines for people of different ethnic origins.

But it would be impossible to put an end to the current interethnic strife by sealing regions within state borders or by changing these borders—practically all of them fail to coincide with actual ethnic distribution. It would be impossible to draw such ethnic boundaries, since no ethnic group is sufficiently compact.

Thus the USSR's ethno-territorial divisions, while only stimulating conflicts, hinder any kind of solution. The disintegration of the USSR along the existing borders between the former union republics cannot do away with the numerous territorial claims.

Cultivation of Bilateral Ties and Diplomatic Relations

A distrust of Russia and misgivings over its true intentions are not new additions to Uzbek history, although they were firmly suppressed during the Soviet era. Indeed, if the collapse of the USSR offered Tashkent its first post-Soviet opportunity to discern between "Russian" and "Soviet," the formation process of the Commonwealth of Independent States (CIS) demonstrated that there was little difference as far as Uzbekistan was concerned. Initially excluded from the CIS by the original founding Slavic states of Russia, Ukraine, and Belarus, Uzbekistan, along with the other Central Asian republics, rejected what it saw as an afterthought invitation to join the organization, and demanded to be admitted as a founding member, a status granted in Alma-Ata on 21 December 1991. Uzbekistan's initial exclusion, however, engendered skepticism among Uzbek leaders about Russian designs for the CIS; within weeks Uzbekistan President Islam Karimov was expressing considerable distrust of Russia and its intent to head the commonwealth military forces. Instead, Karimov proposed that the CIS armed forces follow the North Atlantic Treaty Organization model of command. Even prior to the CIS dispute, in fact, Uzbekistan had demonstrated signs of historical distrust of Russia or of any other state having influence over its external affairs. On 31 August 1991, for example, just after the failed Moscow putsch, Uzbekistan approved a law on independence that asserted its right to establish diplomatic, consular, and trade relations with foreign states and called for the creation of a defense ministry and national guard and control over Soviet troops stationed in the republic. A Ministry of Defense and National Guard Affairs was set up and a defense minister appointed on 10 September. A National Guard of seven hundred personnel is envisaged to serve as an honor and presidential guard. On 13 January 1992, President Karimov issued a decree placing former Soviet troops stationed in Uzbekistan under the Uzbek Republic's jurisdiction.[3]

Continued misgivings about the CIS as an institution as well as Russia's role in it have prompted Uzbekistan to focus instead on cultivating bilateral ties with the other former Soviet republics. To this end, Tashkent has concluded economic and trade treaties with Russia, Ukraine, Azerbaijan, Kyrgyzstan, Moldova, and Kazakhstan. Primarily, however, the process of historical reawakening in Uzbekistan has oriented Tashkent's foreign policy scope and emphasis toward its regional Muslim and Islamic neighbors. On 20 January 1992, for example, President Karimov called for a Central Asian union to surmount the present economic difficulties plaguing the region's five states.[4] Despite a clear recognition of their dire economic straits, however, the other Central Asian countries, with their own impressions of Uzbek historical revisionism, remained fearful of Uzbek dominance and thus responded tepidly to Karimov's proposal.

Uzbekistan has, of course, also sought to broaden its foreign policy beyond the Central Asian steppes. Almost immediately achieving independence following the Soviet collapse, Uzbekistan applied for membership in the United Nations and expressed its intention to sign the Nuclear Nonproliferation Treaty. By the end of January 1992, moreover, Uzbekistan had become a member of the Conference on Security and Cooperation in Europe (CSCE). Professions of praise and admiration for the Turkish secular model of development from top Uzbek officials have doubtless expedited the process of international recognition. Nonetheless, the scope of Uzbekistan's foreign policy has been sharply regionalized to focus on its historical allies and neighbors. Over the past two years Uzbekistan has signed several bilateral treaties and agreements with neighboring states, such as Tajikistan and Turkmenistan in October 1990. Furthermore, Uzbekistan and Kazakhstan have signed accords on mutual assistance in case of natural disasters and have expressed the intention to establish joint conservation projects.

The most important external political event of the second half of 1992 for Uzbekistan was the establishment of diplomatic relations with the countries of Southeast Asia and Pacific Asia, personified by official visits by President Karimov. The diplomatic missions of the Uzbek president to South Korea, Malaysia, and Indonesia were part of his longest trip abroad.[5] During the trip he achieved concrete agreements in the economic sphere: the participation of South Korea in the building of an automobile assembly plant in the Andijon region, the building of a creamery with the assistance of Malaysia, and a $100 million credit from Indonesia.

The visit to South Korea, Malaysia, and Indonesia is important because just prior to departing, Karimov clarified his attitude toward the so-called Turkish model of development. In an interview with the Moscow correspondent for the South Korean newspaper *Ton'a Ilbo*, he said that Uzbekistan would not copy the Turkish or any other model thoughtlessly but would instead look for "its own Uzbek model," borrowing everything valuable from others' experience, including the experiences of Asian countries.[6] Karimov's remarks were prompted by the following factors.

First, Uzbekistan needs to coordinate its internal and external orientation. In this a connection one-sided orientation toward the Turkish model necessarily narrows the horizons of republican development. And what the West calls the Turkish model is understood in Uzbekistan as an openness to the world, a readiness to borrow the positive experiences of different countries, and a willingness to adapt these experiences to local conditions. Turkey, for example, has followed the recommendations of the International Monetary Fund and is active in its relations with the United States and the European community, as well as with other countries.

Second, by geographically widening its relations away from states to which it has been historically linked, such as Russia and Turkey, Uzbekistan can create more freedom in its actions, not binding itself and its future too strictly to this or that country or region. Closeness with South Korea is also prompted by the presence in Uzbekistan of one of the biggest Korean diasporas in the territory of the former USSR (according to the 1989 census, 183,000 thousand persons).

Third, through such diversification of its external political course, Uzbekistan will be taking a demonstrative step toward improving relations with other developed countries of Asia. Stimulating Turkey to greater activity in its promised assistance and credits can be a part of that effort.

Finally, Uzbek leaders have taken into consideration the position of Turkey itself, and they have shown a growing distrust not only of Turkish designs on Uzbekistan and the rest of the Central Asian region but also of the consequences of a close identification with Pan-Turkism. Uzbek officials are well aware that any strong Pan-Turkic sentiment emanating from Tashkent will serve to create tensions in both Russia and the other Central Asian states. For Russia, Pan-Turkism is historically equated with a spread of Turkish influence, and Moscow is opposed to any increase in Ankara's influence in Central Asia, which it sees as detracting directly from its own influence. Doubtless, as commentators have written, recent talks between Turkish President Suleyman Demirel and Russian President Boris Yeltsin focused on the situation in Central Asia, and it is likely the leaders spoke about their spheres of influence and a coordination of their actions in this region.[7]

On the other hand, Pan-Turkism from the perspective of other Central Asian countries has historically been seen as little more than a vehicle for Uzbek dominance. Consequently, attempts by Ankara to increase its influence in Central Asia are resisted by Tashkent on the grounds that such Pan-Turkic sentiments would be viewed with great suspicion as an attempt to impose Uzbek regional control.

Uzbekistan also sees reason to question the motives of any Turkish initiatives. As is seen in an article by the MBI television company correspondent Khakan Aksai, Turkey does not want to lose its chance of becoming an influential member of the international community.[8] Thus, the world is witnessing greater diplomatic and political activity on the part of Turkey as it tries to play three roles at the same time: the role of the elder brother for the Central Asian republics, the role of a peacemaker in the Caucasus region, and the role of the strong rival of Russia in the traditional policies toward Central Asia. The Central Asian leaders who would rather see Turkey as a sincere and open assistant helping the republics out of the crisis than a seeker of its own benefits in Central Asia may be disappointed.[9]

On 30 May 1992, the world witnessed an event that essentially changed its image of the external political priorities of Uzbekistan. If during the previous two months there was an active course of friendship with Turkey, then after the signing of the Agreement on Collective Security by the leaders of CIS states in Tashkent in the middle of May and the adoption (with Russia) of the Agreement on the Basis of Interstate Relations, Friendship and Cooperation on 30 May it became clear that a military-strategic unit of Russia and the Central Asian republics had appeared. The coalition was formed in response to the government's anxiety over Islamic fundamentalism (from Afghanistan), which carries the threat of regional destabilization and Islamic revolution. In neighboring Afghanistan such a revolution is apparent. Thus it is clear why the Agreement on Collective Security and other bilateral agreements (Russia and Kazakhstan, Kyrgyzstan, Turkmenistan, and Uzbekistan) have been signed in such a hurry.

The republics have different versions of the agreements in the military sphere. The bilateral agreement between Russia and Turkmenistan, for example, envisages the transfer of some part of the military forces based in the republic (anti-aircraft defense, air force, frontier guards) to the jurisdiction of Russia.[10] According to the version accepted in Uzbekistan, all military forces of the former Turkestan military district, which was dissolved in July 1992, form the military forces of Uzbekistan.[11] Urgent measures have been undertaken to ensure the social welfare of military people, especially officers (their salary has been doubled, in comparison with a salary increase of 1.8 times in Russia), and an active solution of the problem of poor living conditions. Owing to these steps, the presidential power of Karimov and other Central Asian leaders (excluding Tajikistan's Rakhman Nabiev) was significantly strengthened, and fears of an unstable "bacilli" infiltration from the southeast have been allayed somewhat.

Emergence of Sociopolitical Groups and Movements

The reemergence of history as an element of a growing Uzbek identity has given rise to a number of domestic sociopolitical groups, many of which are somewhat overzealous in their support of Uzbek nationhood. This of course cannot help but affect Uzbekistan's foreign policy, given the country's minority communities and its geographical location. As a consequence, Uzbek authorities have moved to create a special buffer zone to protect the constitutional government, including social and political organizations loyal to it, against ex-Communists. At the moment the zone includes two structures. The first is the party Vatan Tarakkieti (Progress of the Motherland), whose leader, Usmon Azim, is a writer and a counsel to the president. The party is a moderate-reformist force, oriented toward statehood ideology and national patriotism.

The second force is the Movement of Businessmen of Uzbekistan. It is supported by the Uzbekistan branch of AECAK (Association of Exchanges of Central Asia and Kazakhstan). This movement was declared on 2 June 1992 at a meeting of the businessmen of Uzbekistan at the exchange Toshkent. The participants adopted a declaration stressing that the efforts undertaken by the president for the reformation of the economy, democratic development, and civil agreement "need support and help." A view of the created movement as a buffer zone, whose task is to alleviate contradictions between the constitutional government and the opposition, was given by a member of the organization committee, the executive director of Toshkent, Vladimir Ergashbaev.

In the last two to three years free enterprise activity in the republic has become so widespread that some Uzbeks, particularly the exchanges, question Uzbekistan's political representation. The political influence of the exchanges is growing. The chairman of the leading republican exchange Toshkent, Kabul Usmanov, thinks, for example, that "now we can speak not only about the formation of market structures, but also about the revival of the class of businessmen."[12]

What is the reason for creating a buffer zone? Each side, directly (the parties themselves) or indirectly (the president), is interested in this process; each has its own aims. Some of the socially active and patriotic intelligentsia would like to have their say in the political arena, but they do not like any of the present political parties—neither the National Democratic Party of Uzbekistan, because of its Communist past, nor the opposition, because of its uncompromising position. The only party other than the renamed Communists that was allowed to register as such prior to mid-1992 was Erk (Will), which had broken from the Birlik (Unity) mass movement in 1990 over the issue of whether violence should be condemned in all circumstances as a means of pursuing legitimate goals. Erk's membership is less heterogeneous than that of Birlik, consisting primarily of urban intellectuals and minor government officials. As Bess Brown wrote, "At its height Erk's membership was around 5,000, while Birlik claimed up to 500,000 members (in 1989) and several million sympathizers throughout Uzbekistan."[13] But after government oppression of Birlik, its membership dropped to less than several thousand. The Uzbek branch of the Islamic Renaissance, which was established in 1990, was immediately banned, and as a result, Islamic forces went underground, thereby escaping government observation and control.

Businessmen have two goals: to preserve stability (as the condition for normal business activities) and to find some defense from bureaucratic administrative organs, changing, so they think, the president's policy. The president looks for opportunities to spread the social base of his authority. Hence there is a corresponding tactic to supplant uncompromising and oppressed opposition parties (Birlik and more recently Erk) with a "soft" opposition or political structure loyal to the government. Such a policy, however, risks prompting radical elements of the excluded opposition into resorting to underground terrorist activities.

The Question of Russian-Speaking Peoples

The situation is further complicated by the aggravation of the ethnic problem in some regions of the former Soviet Union, especially the problem of the Russian-speaking population in the former union republics. Russian leaders have increasingly stressed that an integral part of Russian foreign policy is the protection of the Russian minority communities outside the borders of the Russian Federation. Attempts by Moscow to ensure the protection of the national, religious, linguistic, and cultural rights of this Russian diaspora have led to growing pressures on the new independent states under the pretext of defending the rights of national minorities. The situation is likely to be further aggravated if the protection of the Russian-speaking minorities' rights in the former republics continues to be a critical card in the fight of various political forces inside Russia itself.

In Central Asia the stumbling block is the language problem. A step-by-step realization of Uzbek law on the state language raises the problem of Russian-speaking peoples staying in Muslim republics. In the given situation there are three possible alternatives for the Russian-speaking population in Uzbekistan. The first is to study the Uzbek language, accept the native citizenship, and integrate into Uzbek society. Not everybody is ready for such a way of life. The second is emigration. Not everybody is ready to emigrate. And Russia is not waiting for repatriates with open arms. The third alternative is a hope that it is possible to coexist without any change in lifestyle. Until recently this hope was nourished by the status quo in language policy during the last two years. The Uzbek language was proclaimed a state language, but that was only a symbolic step in the minds of the Russian-speaking population. Now it seems that the search for a solution to the problem has been put in motion, compelling Russian-speaking peoples to decide one way or another. According to the press, in a meeting of the cabinet of ministers, members of the government Commission on Language expressed their dissatisfaction with the lack of progress in the introduction of the state language into the spheres suggested by the law, and with the direction of planned measures for its implementation.[14] Citizens are only now beginning to see results. Metro station names are identified only in Uzbek. Some organizations have even begun to write their official papers in Uzbek.

Theoretically, there is a fourth alternative to the language problem solution: language monism at the state level, with the use of Russian in science and education (as well as Uzbek). President Askar Akaev of Kyrgyzstan thinks that in all schools there should be two languages that must be studied in addition to the state language: English and Russian.[15] Such an approach holds the opportunity to preserve Russian-speaking cadres, at least in the sphere of intellectual activities.

The Russian-speaking population's hopes are connected mostly with the possibility of using Russian, especially in education, and preserving its cultural self-identification. The establishment of a national association such as the Russian Culture in Uzbekistan is one means to this end. Its officially proclaimed aims and tasks are loyal to the government and apolitical: "preserving and increasing Russian and Slavonic cultural inheritance, harmonization of international relations." As association chairman V. Emel'ianov said in an interview, "We see one of the strategic tasks in the study of the

culture of the people who gave the name to the republic, their traditions, language."[16] However, it is evident that with the creation of such
an association there would be some political structure for defending
the Russian-speaking minority's rights in the republic. Analogous processes are taking place in the republics where the Russian-speaking
population has no great desire to emigrate, as in the Russian communities in Estonia and Latvia.

Among the Central Asian republics, Kazakhstan is especially active
in preserving the Russian-speaking population's cultural identity and
political rights. But the ethnic situation there is different from
Uzbekistan's. *Izvestiia* reported that on 28 May 1992 a new parliamentary group, the Civil Agreement, consisting of fifty-one members of
nonnative nationality, made an open statement against the Kazakhstan
government's policy on the creation of a national state and for the
building of a civil society. Group members felt such a statement was
warranted, given new tendencies in the external political course of
the Russian government and the increasing support of "patriotic"
forces in Russia. Their first task is to achieve a ratification of the
"Declarations of Human Rights" by the Supreme Council and a
change in some formulations of the "Declaration On State Independence of Kazakhstan," the decree on state language, and other legislative acts.[17]

In Uzbekistan, however, such protests are impossible at the moment, because Russians constitute only 8.3 percent of the population
and are not politically active. The consequence has been a steadily
growing emigration. The government is in an awkward situation; it is
trying to combine measures that are difficult to combine. On one side,
under pressure from national-patriotic forces widely represented both
in the administrative structures and in the opposition, the government
must undertake measures to implement the law on language realization and increase quotas for the training of national cadres. On the
other side, it is evident that the government is trying to stop the
outflow of a highly skilled workforce, consisting mainly of Russian-
speaking citizens. Thus, the situation of the Russian-speaking population in the republic became a special subject of the talks between
Presidents Yeltsin and Karimov, who accordingly signed the Agreement on the Basis of Interstate Relations, Friendship and Cooperation between the Russian Federation and the Republic of Uzbekistan
on 30 May 1992.[18]

Controverting Criticism

Nonetheless, Uzbek officials have reacted angrily to outside commentaries, particularly from Russia, on Uzbekistan's commitment to human rights and democratization. The crux of the problem is that outside Central Asia there is little understanding of, or appreciation for, the historical traditions of authority and government within the Central Asian experience. There exists a strong historical tradition of autocratic rule both in Uzbekistan and Central Asia as a whole—a tradition that was only augmented, not imported, during the Soviet era. If the West were to attempt to create or impose a Western-style democratic model in Uzbekistan today, the result would be another Afghanistan or Tajikistan. In the Uzbek example, Samuel Huntington's theory of democratic transition is correct: to pass from totalitarianism to democracy, Uzbekistan must first go through autocracy. Western observers have thus far shown little understanding of the different circumstances of the Uzbek situation. The Western type of mentality in both politics and religion is based on individualism, which allows the West to quickly and fully embrace the concepts of liberal democracy.[19] In Uzbekistan, however, the mentality is based on the collective form of societal and governmental organization; thus, strong authoritarian governments and leaders have traditionally existed in the Uzbek historical experience.

It is noteworthy that while there has been virtually no criticism of the Karimov government from the other Central Asian states, Western and Russian commentators have been sharply critical. There are grounds for criticism. Karimov's treatment of his opposition, especially the repressions from September 1992 to April 1993, has drawn negative comment in the international press.[20] The criticism has prompted the Uzbek government to attack the foreign press for trying to undermine Uzbekistan's reputation abroad and to disrupt internal affairs. One can understand Karimov's quest for stability, but it cannot be a justification for political repression. The victims of that repression fear that it will have the opposite effect of that intended by Karimov, and that the removal of moderate opposition forces will leave a vacuum that Islamic extremists will occupy, creating instability and opening the way for a repetition of the tragic fate of Tajikistan.[21] As the reader can see, both sides—President Karimov and his opposition—use the same events in Tajikistan as rationales for their action.

Karimov told *Komsomol'skaia pravda* that he was no dictator, although he admitted that his methods were authoritarian.[22] His justification remains the same: stability at any price. According to this argument, Uzbekistan urgently needs foreign investment and trade and has no hope of obtaining them if the country is perceived to be unstable by potential investors. It cannot afford the luxury of a political liberalization that might release forces such as raged in the Fergana Valley in the summer of 1989. Birlik's counterargument is as follows: repression is the parent of the very extremism that the Uzbek leadership wants to prevent.

As for the effect of Tajikistan's civil war on political life in Uzbekistan, political commentator Bess Brown wrote:

> As long as a conservative and pro-Uzbek government remains in power in Dushanbe, the immediate danger of a spread of Muslim fundamentalism to Uzbekistan seems to be limited. But foreign visitors to the region report hearing rumors that Islamic forces in the Fergana Valley are in touch with Afghan mujahideen groups. The repression of the democratic Uzbek nationalists may prove to have removed an important moderating force from the political scene, and the country may find its conservative communist leadership facing an Afghan-supported Islamic insurgency that would finish off hopes for rapid integration into the outside world.[23]

Relations between the government of Uzbekistan and the Russian press are not very warm. In fact, press reports are often biased, and are regarded in Uzbekistan as attempts to export a new Russian revolution to a backward Central Asian region. There is even an ideological bias, expressed in the concept of a "common democratic space" throughout the territory of the former USSR. In this connection the Russian press uses any chance to blame the present republican regime for its lack of democracy, for witch hunting, and for other vices.[24] The republican government frowns on such interference in the political stability of the nation, even though the attitudes of the Russian press are hardly supported nowadays.

The same solution to all of Uzbekistan's problems were given by the authors of an article in *Komsomol'skaia pravda* titled "Russians in the Background of Mosques."[25] All the issues brought up in the article reflect real problems of the Russian-speaking population in Uzbekistan but are exaggerated to such an extent that the situation of Russians in the republic seems inescapable. Such reporting, lacking in-depth analysis, only aggravates the discontent of nonnative peoples, making their life even more difficult.

Still, the question is not whether there is or is not democracy in Uzbekistan or in Russia, but instead what criteria are being used to measure democracy. Among the radical Russian intellectuals any talk of democracy seems to be governed by the principle *salus revolutionis, suprema lex* (revolution is above the law) (again!). For them democracy has become the latest weapon with which they are going to burn down the rest of the totalitarian system. But though it might seem strange, the Central Asian leaders tend to follow the other principle—*salus patriae, suprema lex* (the nation is above the law)—being more pragmatic in using the favorite phrase of Mikhail Gorbachev, "Policy is the art of the possible." In the conditions of traditional Central Asian society, not everything that the journalist-"democrats" suppose to be true is possible. First of all, the idea of democracy itself can be compromised by Islamic-style democrats. Those who call the May (1992) revolution in Tajikistan an Islamic one are partially right. Igor Rotar, a columnist with *Nezavisimaia gazeta*, wrote:

> One need only look at the participants of the huge meeting in Shokhidon square in Dushanbe for proof. Bearded "democrats" wearing traditional gowns and caps knew nothing about politics and couldn't even explain the meaning of the word "democracy." When our correspondent asked them who had advised them to attend the meeting, they answered that it was their mullah.[26]

The general scheme of Moscow journalists in reporting the events in Central Asia is short on facts and long on propaganda. In their view, in some republics of Central Asia (they mean, first of all, Turkmenistan, Uzbekistan, and Tajikistan—Kazakhstan is for some reason excluded from this list), pro-communist regimes are in power. From the viewpoint of "revolutionary" Moscow, this is inadmissible. Although at present Tajikistan seems to be leaning toward communism, the premise holding that all other republics are so inclined is just not true. Even in the pre-perestroika epoch, communism in Central Asia was not a sincere conviction but a forced adaptation of the traditional hierarchical structure to the empire order. And the communist phraseology was only a camouflage for the tribal struggle for power during the Soviet period. In this connection it is not strange that the National Democratic Party of Uzbekistan got rid of Marxist-Leninist phraseology without any regret in order to preserve more essential things: the party's structure and most of its property. The truth is that one can give different names to the regime of Uzbekistan—democratic, semidemocratic, or authoritarian— but in any case it is neither a communist nor a totalitarian regime, the main feature of which is the monopoly of one ideology that tries to oppress all social and state life and make people think in only one way.

It should come as no surprise, then, that if the radicals in Moscow believe there is a pro-communist regime in the republic, they would think it necessary to destroy it by helping "comrade-democrats." There is even more misunderstanding of Uzbekistan historical realities in this premise. They do not want to admit that Uzbek society develops according to its own rules, and even seventy years of Soviet power could not destroy it. Rude attempts to force Central Asia onto the path of "progressive development" can only give birth to a second Afghanistan. Uzbekistan is indeed facing a dilemma, but not one of dictatorship by Karimov versus civil war Tajikistan-style. The real dilemma is a democratic and stable society (with Karimov or not) in Uzbekistan versus the explosion of the whole of Central Asia into civil war and Islamic revolution. The process of modernization of the Central Asian countries will take a long time, and it will lead to recognition of the universal role of international law. It is no less important that the basic international standards of democratic political regimes—the rule of law, human rights, political pluralism, and free elections—be recognized and adhered to.

The issue is not that those who call themselves democrats in Uzbekistan may not be democrats in reality (democracy, after all, is only relative, according to one's political culture), but that the triumph of democrats will probably be a Pyrrhic victory, allowing greater forces to control mass consciousness (especially of the native population). The democrats will unwittingly become the weapon of destruction of the secular state. Historically, there is a special model of social relations in the republic, one that has undergone constant evolutionary change, but revolutionary breaks are not inherent to it. The majority of the population of the republic prefers its constant and traditional way of life to the misty values of liberalism. Respect for the government (if the government takes care of the people) is not a sign of oppression but a part of Eastern mentality and culture.

Another aspect of the historical reawakening of the Uzbek identity that is certain to have an impact on foreign policy is the campaign to rehabilitate the former first secretary of the Communist Party of the republic, Sharaf Rashidov. The campaign began long ago, and recently some placenames have been changed to Rashidov. According to experts, the campaign of rehabilitation is necessary to get rid of all inferiority and guilt complexes connected with the "Cotton Affairs";[27] to reform those elite members who were connected with Rashidov in business and in other affairs; and to restore Uzbekistan's former prestige.

There is an evident nostalgia for the days when the Uzbek people were confident of the high prestige of their republic in the world arena (together with the USSR). In recent times Uzbekistan was a "Lighthouse of Socialism in the East," and Tashkent a "City of Friendship." Nowadays, as Uzbekistan tries to play a bigger role in the new geopolitical situation in Asia, it is essential to revive the tradition of the peaceful mission of the republic that was the pride of the Uzbek people before perestroika. A people that suffers from a Third World complex will never get any respect from other peoples. And restoring a high level of state prestige is necessary in order to solve many problems in interstate spheres, including the problem of attracting investments.

However, in many people's minds Rashidov represents the past, one-sided economic development, the spoiled Aral. What is more important is putting aside the semicolonial status of Uzbekistan and stepping out as a viable participant in the global community.

Notes

1. Francis Fukuyama, "Is Happiness More Valuable Than Conformity? The New Asia Will Tell," *Los Angeles Times*, 12 February 1992, p. B11.
2. James Critchlow, *Nationalism in Uzbekistan: A Soviet Republic's Road to Sovereignty* (Boulder, CO: Westview Press, 1991), p. 11.
3. See *Pravda vostoka*, 14 January 1992.
4. *Narodnoe slovo*, 21 January 1992.
5. *Izvestiia*, 18 June 1992.
6. *Narodnoe slovo*, 25 May 1992.
7. *Izvestiia*, 25 May 1992.
8. *Central Asia Review*, July 1992.
9. *Moscow News*, 7 June 1992.
10. *Izvestiia*, 10 June 1992.
11. *Izvestiia*, 18 June 1992.

12. *Birzhevoi vestnik vostoka*, 30 June 1992.

13. Bess Brown, "Tajik Civil War Prompts Crackdown in Uzbekistan," *RFE/RL Research Report*, vol. 2, no. 11 (12 March 1993), p. 3.

14. *Pravda vostoka*, 15 May 1992.

15. *Izvestiia*, 10 May 1992.

16. *Narodnoe slovo*, 28 May 1992.

17. *Izvestiia*, 30 May 1992.

18. *Pravda vostoka*, 1 June 1992.

19. See S.P. Huntington, "Will More Countries Become Democratic?" *Political Science Quarterly*, vol. 99, no. 2 (1989), pp. 12–16; S.P. Huntington, *Political Order in Changing Societies* (New Haven: Yale University Press, 1968).

20. See, for example, *Le Monde*, 30 January 1995; *Neue Zürcher Zeitung* and *Newsweek*, 8 February 1993.

21. This argument was advanced by Shukhzat Ismatullaiv in an interview published in *Izvestiia* on 12 January 1993.

22. *Komsomol'skaia pravda*, 15 February 1993.

23. Brown, "Tajik Civil War," p. 6.

24. *Moscow News*, 28 June 1992.

25. *Komsomol'skaia pravda*, 2 February 1993.

26. *Nezavisimaia gazeta*, vol. 3, nos. 22–23 (April 1993), p. 2.

27. A famous anticorruption campaign led by Moscow against Uzbekistan Communist Party leaders in the mid-1980s. Moscow's practice of referring to this matter as "the Uzbek affair" was perceived as a humiliation by most Uzbeks.

11

Historical Memory and Foreign Relations

The Armenian Perspective

Richard G. Hovannisian

The radical changes in the former Soviet Union should portend well for the peoples of the Russian littoral and the international community in general. The end of the Cold War and moves toward economic reforms hold out the possibility of enhanced personal and collective well-being. No less important is the opportunity for peoples to develop in sovereign states according to their own ways and traditions. At the same time, however, the restoration of independent republics in the Baltics and the Caucasus and the emergence for the first time of independent republics in Central Asia have been accompanied by serious economic dislocation, in some areas approaching total collapse, and by militant nationalism and interethnic bloodshed. These developments in the Russian littoral have broad implications for world security and tranquility. The ongoing warfare between Armenians and Azerbaijanis, the civil and ethnic strife in Georgia, and the scramble for primary influence in the Caucasus and Central Asia by Turkey, Iran, and Russia have all converged to make the first taste of independence unexpectedly violent and bitter.

The Soviet Union, with all its shortcomings, managed to keep interethnic conflict in check. Countless publications and manifestations were aimed at demonstrating the paternalistic, symbiotic relationship between the Great Russians and the other constituent peoples of the USSR and the brotherhood of formerly rival nationalities, such as Armenians, Azerbaijanis, and Georgians. The central organs of government, enlisting the Soviet Academy of Sciences, determined the appropriate themes, approaches, and conclusions. Deputations and troupes of one Soviet republic or autonomous region were welcomed in the others with predictable ostentation. Traditional stereotypes, voiced among the masses and in unguarded moments even by members of the nomenklatura, lurked just beneath the surface, but in official parlance the mandatory mutual salutations and applause were omnipresent.

It has been said that the last cardinal sin of the Soviet empire was its uncharted, precipitous, chaotic disintegration, preventing a gradual disengagement, a careful regulation of political, economic, and military affairs, and a requisite period of apprenticeship for the new political elites. While some parts of the Russian littoral impatiently set out on their roads to independence, others, especially the six Muslim republics, remained cautious and conservative until the abortive putsch of August 1991. The unheralded collapse of the Soviet Union in 1991 mirrored the demise of Imperial Russia in 1917, severing the periphery from the center. A difference, however, is that in 1917–18 the Georgians and especially the Armenians tried to prevent the detachment of the Caucasus from Russia, which was viewed as the only defense against a Turkish invasion and the realization of the Pan-Turkic goals of Enver, Talat, and other members of the Committee of Union and Progress (Young Turks) who had already perpetrated the wholesale deportations and massacres of the Ottoman Armenians. In 1991, by contrast, the Georgians and Armenians gave notice of their intent to regain national sovereignty, whether by unilateral decree, as in the Georgian case, or in accordance with the statutes of the Soviet Union, as in the Armenian case.

Historical memory intensely colors the outlook of the peoples of the Russian littoral. In the Caucasus, memories are especially long, and wounds close very slowly. The current bloodshed will bring in its train years of hatred, distrust, trauma, and enervating sentiments of betrayal and injustice. The convenient, simplified characterization of the Armenian-Azerbaijani conflict as a clash between Christians and Muslims is inaccurate, but it does in fact point up the cultural differences, including religion, of two peoples who have lived intermixed for centuries. In some ways they are very similar, but the strands of commonality have been broken by resurgent nationalism, much as the competition for a place in the sun pitted Armenians and Azerbaijanis against one another from 1918 to 1920. The imposition of Soviet rule in the Caucasus suppressed but did not resolve the sources of antagonism.

This chapter will focus on the impact of historical memory on Armenia's current foreign relations. Even though the present Armenian government is attempting to surmount the long-standing obstacles to the normalization of relations with most of the country's neighbors, the ghost of the past is a major deterrent. The crisis in Mountainous Karabagh immediately conjured up direct associations with the Armenian genocide in the Ottoman Empire, a national calamity that continues to affect Armenia's relations with Turkey, Azerbaijan, and all other neighbors.

The Ghost of the Past

The Armenian genocide began in 1915 with the death marches and massacres of most of the Ottoman Armenian population. The Young Turk dictators used the cover of World War I to solve the Armenian question, that is, the movement for civil rights and local self-government, by eliminating the Armenian people and forcibly accelerating the creation of a homogeneous Turkic Muslim society. The period culminated in 1922 with the flight or expulsion of the Armenian survivors who had returned to parts of Asia Minor and Cilicia in modern-day Turkey after the war.[1]

The Armenians had been violently and irreversibly separated from their lands and cultural-religious foundations of three millennia. For the rest of the twentieth century, the collective energies of the survivors were concentrated on the creation of new social, political, cultural, and religious infrastructures in the host countries of the Middle East and, with less success, in Europe and the Western Hemisphere, where the opportunities for social and economic mobility were counterbalanced by the process of rapid acculturation and assimilation. A source of hope during these trying decades was the existence of Soviet Armenia, the smallest of the constituent republics of the Soviet Union.

While most of the historic Armenian territories had fallen within the Ottoman Empire, the easternmost sector was annexed by the Persian Empire and then in the nineteenth century by the Russian Empire. From this division evolved the terms "Turkish" (western) Armenia and "Russian" (eastern) Armenia. The destruction of Turkish Armenia during World War I imperiled Russian Armenia, which also figured in the designs of the Young Turk rulers of the Ottoman Empire. Amid the turmoil created by the Russian Revolution of 1917 and the Turkish invasion of the Caucasus in 1918, the Russian Armenians tried to salvage whatever possible by declaring the independence of the Republic of Armenia around the city of Erevan. The tiny, isolated state managed to survive until the end of the world war in November 1918.[2]

Armenians throughout the world celebrated the Allied victory over the German and Ottoman empires, believing that the time of reckoning had finally arrived and that the Allied powers would punish the perpetrators of the genocide, repatriate and rehabilitate the survivors, and help to organize a united Armenia encompassing both the western and eastern sectors of the historic homeland. Although the Allied Powers finally created such a state on paper in the Treaty of Sèvres in August 1920, they were unwilling to commit the military force necessary to remove the Turkish armies. On the contrary, the Allies and the United States watched stoically as the revitalized Turkish nationalist armies of Mustafa Kemal even invaded and put an end to the small republic in Russian Armenia. Placed in an inescapable vise formed by the Turkish Nationalists and the Soviet Red Army, the Armenian government had to cede half of Russian Armenia to Turkey and save the rest of the country by relinquishing power and acquiescing in the proclamation of Soviet rule.[3]

From 1921 onward, the only part of historic Armenia that still bore that name was the Soviet republic of about 11,500 square miles. With all its limitations and problems, that state alone provided for the uninterrupted flow of Armenian life. National culture was allowed to develop within limits determined by the Soviet system. Between 1920 and 1990 the population of Soviet Armenia increased from barely one million to three million, while the worldwide Armenian population grew to about six million, at last replenishing itself and surpassing its 1914 pregenocidal level.[4]

In the aftermath of the genocide, the survivors and succeeding generations suffered from the emotional trauma caused by the calamity, world indifference, and Turkish attempts to deny or rationalize the crime. Yet the event had passed, and there did not appear to be any real danger of renewed massacres. However great the oppressive ways of the Soviet system, Armenia was protected by the armies and resources of the mighty Soviet Union, and the people could live without serious fear of Turkish invasion or interethnic violence in Soviet Georgia and Soviet Azerbaijan, each with approximately half a million Armenian inhabitants. Armenians were disgruntled that Mountainous Karabagh, which was adjacent to Soviet Armenia, had been awarded to Azerbaijan, and they repeatedly petitioned for the return of that highland district. These measures did not affect the Soviet control mechanism throughout the Caucasus, and life remained relatively secure and predictable.

The trade-off by which Armenia gave up much of its freedom, including the right to seek redress and world recognition of the Armenian genocide in return for the protection afforded by the Soviet Union, changed abruptly in 1988. In the early part of that year, the Armenians of Mountainous Karabagh (who make up 80 percent of the inhabitants) and of Soviet Armenia took General Secretary Mikhail Gorbachev's programs of glasnost and perestroika seriously, as they did his declarations that the time had come to rectify Stalin's historical errors. For the Armenians the cardinal crime of Stalin (Lenin's own role could not yet be mentioned) was the award of Karabagh to Azerbaijan in 1921.[5] When the population and local governmental organs of the Nagorno-Karabagh Autonomous Oblast petitioned on 20 February 1988 for the right of self-determination and incorporation into Soviet Armenia, hundreds of thousands of people in Erevan took to the streets in support of the Karabagh movement.[6] The massive demonstrations were unprecedented in the Soviet Union and captured headlines in the broadcast and print media worldwide. A wave of optimism swept over the Armenians both inside the Soviet Union and in the diaspora. Dormant Armenian communities in Russia began to stir, and the Armenians abroad rallied to the cause. Spirits were high, even festive, as it seemed that for once in the twentieth century the continuous process of diminution of Armenian living space might be reversed, especially since the proposed shift of boundaries could be affected as an internal Soviet matter.

Armenian optimism was dampened at the end of February by the outbreak of anti-Armenian violence in the Azerbaijani industrial city of Sumgait. The killing, mutilation, and looting sent shock waves into Armenian communities near and far. The terms "massacre," "pogrom," and even "genocide" became current, and immediate, spontaneous associations with 1915 were made everywhere. The Azerbaijanis, related by race, language, and culture to the Turks, became in Armenian minds the same heartless people who had participated in the genocide of 1915, and the victims of Sumgait were simply the most recent martyrs exacted from the nation since antiquity and especially since the Turkic domination of Armenia. Seventy years of Soviet mythology about the resolution and elimination of nationality problems and about the friendship and brotherhood of all Soviet peoples dissolved in a single instant, and the traumatized Armenians came face-to-face with the ghost of the past.[7]

What was most disconcerting in the aftermath of the Sumgait pogrom was the failure of the central authorities to take swift, decisive action to apprehend and punish the perpetrators. Gorbachev may not have wished to jeopardize his image as a reformer who had repudiated the use of force. There were those who accused the central government of resorting to the old imperial formula of divide and rule. It was inconceivable that massacres could occur in the Soviet Union without the complicity or tacit assent of the agencies of control. In any event, the inaction of the center exacerbated Armenian-Azerbaijani tensions, the clashes along the entire frontier between the neighboring republics, and the Azerbaijani blockade of Armenia, which normally received some 80 percent of its food supplies and other goods over the railroads that passed through Azerbaijan. Once again, the forced starvation of hundreds of thousands of Armenians in 1915 became a vivid experience for the besieged people of Mountainous Karabagh and Armenia.[8]

The conflict intensified in the fall of 1988, as the Armenians of Kirovabad (pre-Soviet Ganja; Gandzak to the Armenians) and the surrounding countryside were driven from their homes and forced to seek haven in Armenia, while the intimidated Azerbaijani minority in Armenia fled eastward into Azerbaijan. Still greater violence erupted in Baku in January 1990, catching by surprise the 200,000 Armenians of the cosmopolitan Azerbaijani capital. The ferocity of the riots knew no limits, with the worst forms of excess that often characterize interracial or interreligious conflict. Most of the Armenian minority in Azerbaijan abandoned home and business and, taking virtually nothing with them, scattered to many other parts of the Soviet Union. Even the forces of nature seemed to conspire with the perpetrators, as a massive earthquake in December 1988 devastated a third of Armenia, leaving 500,000 people homeless and claiming more than 25,000 lives.[9] Man and nature, it was said, had again joined to deprive the Armenians of peace, prosperity, and justice. However sincerely the new Armenian leadership may try to strike out on a new course in foreign relations, the ghost of the past is ever present to beckon them back to the parameters formed by the collective historical experience.

Armenia and Azerbaijan

Historical memory intensifies the mutual distrust of Armenians and Azerbaijanis. Sporadic clashes throughout the twentieth century have been significant factors in the shaping of the national self-consciousness of the two peoples. The so-called Armenian-Tatar wars of 1905–7 enveloped the provinces of Baku, Elisavetpol, Tiflis, and Erevan and resulted in mutual plunder and razing, yet especially for the Armenians they also served as an important test of arms.[10]

During the Turkish invasion of the Caucasus in 1918, while the Armenians were falling victim to the advancing armies, the Azerbaijanis regarded the Turks as allies who helped create the Republic of Azerbaijan. After the establishment of Soviet rule in Azerbaijan in 1920, it was necessary for Azerbaijani intellectuals to condemn the Musavat-led government of the former independent republic. There was state-sponsored glorification of the Baku Commune of 1918, headed by Armenian Bolshevik Stepan Shahumian, and of the twenty-six commissars, including Shahumian, who were put to death by counterrevolutionary elements in Transcaspia after the fall of the Commune. Schools and factories, parks and memorials. Also an entire Armenian-populated district adjacent to Mountainous Karabagh was named in memory of Shahumian. Other prominent Armenian Bolsheviks such as former Soviet President Anastas Mikoyan ranked high among the Azerbaijani pantheon of heros and champions. The armed clash between Muslim detachments and the Baku Soviet's armed forces, made up largely of Armenians, in the so-called March Days of 1918 resulted in the loss of many Azerbaijani lives. Yet Soviet Azerbaijani historians were required to portray the anti-Soviet elements, that is, their own people, as reactionaries, just as they had to show the fall of Baku (that is, the liberation of Baku from the Armenian and Russian coalition in September 1918) as a victory of the "dark forces" and Turkish imperialists.[11] In recent years these interpretations have been subject to significant revision, and during the past two years there has been a rapid de-Shahumianization of Azerbaijan, including the de-Armenianization and dissolution of the Shahumian district, lying between Ganja and the Mountainous Karabagh Autonomous Oblast.

If the Republic of Azerbaijan and, in large measure, the Musavat Party have been rehabilitated, no such Azerbaijani reevaluation applies to the Dashnakist-dominated Republic of Armenia. In fact, from Baku's perspective, the current struggle over Nagorno-Karabagh is regarded as Dashnakist in spirit if not also physically. Such views are reinforced by the presence of armed units and a political faction owing allegiance to the Dashnaktsutiun Party, which, while making a poor showing in the presidential elections in Armenia in October 1991, has not relinquished the slogan of "Free, Independent, United Armenia." The hostilities all along the Azerbaijani-Armenian frontier from Kazakh in the north to Meghri in the south are a continuation of the incessant clashes of 1918–20. And if the Armenian militia opened up the "Lachin corridor" in 1992, the same was also true in 1918, when the renowned Armenian military figure Andranik (Ozanian) broke through the Azerbaijani defenses in November and approached Shushi, only to be coerced into drawing back to Zangezur by British and French officers who announced that the world war was over and that without further fighting the Armenians would be done justice by the Paris Peace Conference.[12] Again, in 1920, the revolutionary warrior Dro (Kanayan) advanced to the vicinity of Shushi (Shusha), only to withdraw because of the Sovietization of Azerbaijan, the assurances given by the representatives of Bolshevik leader Sergo Ordzhonikidze regarding a just resolution to the Karabagh dispute, and the unwillingness of the Armenian peasantry to take up arms against the Red Army. The sense of being tricked and betrayed both in 1918 and in 1920 now reinforces Armenian disbelief in any terms or truce that require withdrawal or disarmament prior to the implementation of firm and permanent guarantees.[13]

The Karabagh crisis stems from the confrontation of two underlying principles: territorial integrity and self-determination. The questions arise whether any group of people has the inherent right to secede from an internationally recognized state and at what point do legal, historical, cultural, and ethnic bases for such claims warrant consideration. This issue brings into question the very nature of the state, the limitation of sovereignty, and the right of a group to define its own nationality. Both Armenians and Azerbaijanis pose historical, cultural, economic, demographic, and strategic arguments to demonstrate that Nagorno-Karabagh is an inalienable part of their national patrimony and that the other side is the blatant aggressor.[14]

The political debate and military conflict have their counterparts in the Armenian Academy of Sciences and in the Azerbaijani Academy, which have taken the dispute to the very ethnogenesis of the people of Karabagh. In their self-definition, the Azerbaijanis have tended to emphasize their Turkic character, especially when put in competition with Iranian cultural-religious influences. Yet when the issue involves Mountainous Karabagh, the Azerbaijanis assert that they are also the descendants of the Caucasian Albanians, an ancient people living in the vicinity of Karabagh near the Kur River. The Caucasian Albanians, it is argued, were the victims of Armenian political, cultural, and religious imperialism, and those in the region of Karabagh were forcibly Armenianized. Hence the native Karabagh population was not Armenian at all, and by a somewhat creative interpretation the Karabagh Armenians are actually Azerbaijanis, the primary heirs of the Caucasian Albanians. The Azerbaijani Academy has gone so far as to identify Armenian Christian monuments, such as the delicately etched cross stones (*Khach-kar*), as Turco-Azerbaijani works. The process of active revisionism only strengthens indignation and inflames passions.[15]

For the Armenians the historical lessons are clear: Andranik and Dro were duped. Once Andranik had withdrawn to Zangezur at the end of 1918, the commander of the British force that replaced the Turkish army in Baku assented to the formation of a temporary Azerbaijani governorship in Karabagh pending the decisions of the Paris Peace Conference. General William Thomson insisted that his decision was simply to maintain law and order and that the appointment of Governor General Dr. Khosrov Bek Sultanov would have no bearing on the final disposition of the disputed territory. Such, of course, was not the case. The continued resistance of the Armenians in Karabagh and the repeated demands of successive Karabagh assemblies to be made a part of the Republic of Armenia prompted the Azerbaijani authorities to a series of actions, which were to be employed once again by a subsequent generation beginning in 1988. These included: (1) threats and intimidation; (2) attempts to disarm the population; (3) legislative action dissolving previous administrative bodies and incorporating the region directly into Azerbaijan; (4) the imposition of an economic blockade against both Mountainous Karabagh and the Armenian republic in order to demonstrate their vulnerability and to exact political-territorial concessions in exchange for the lifting of the embargo; (5) military measures to break the defiance of the Karabagh Armenians.

Unable to quell Armenian active and passive resistance, Dr. Sultanov had the mounted forces of his brother, Sultan Bek, make an example of four settlements, burning them and killing as many as 600 Armenians in June 1919. A wave of protest issued from the Armenian government and Allied officials in Baku and Tiflis, resulting in the recall of Dr. Sultanov. Once the crisis had passed, however, he was back at his post in Shushi. The impending British military withdrawal from the Caucasus and the failure of the Paris Peace Conference to settle the Karabagh question left the Armenians feeling isolated and abandoned. Hence, in August 1919, the Seventh Assembly of Karabagh Armenians finally yielded and accepted the temporary, conditional jurisdiction of Azerbaijan pending the ruling of the peace conference. Among the twenty-six conditions accepted by Azerbaijan regarding Mountainous Karabagh (historic Varanda, Khachen, Dizak, and Jraberd) was the formation of a council that would have the right of initiative in matters relating to the administration of the governorgeneralship. Dr. Sultanov was to have an Armenian assistant governor, and the Azerbaijani military garrisons would be confined to Khankend (Stepanakert) and Shushi in peacetime strength. Any and all movements of armed forces required the consent of two-thirds of the administrative council, half of whose members would be Armenian. The population would not be disarmed, and Azerbaijan would guarantee the cultural autonomy of the Armenians and offer immediate moral and material assistance in the rebuilding of the devastated villages. Freedom of assembly, speech, and the press was to be inviolable.[16]

The submission of the Karabagh Armenians offered Azerbaijan the prospect of breaking through Zangezur to Nakhichevan and Turkish Anatolia. Within a few weeks, the Azerbaijani army violated the August agreement by moving across Karabagh and attacking Zangezur. The successful Armenian resistance led to an accord by Prime Ministers Aleksandr Khatisian and Nasib Bek Ussubekov to resolve all disputed questions through arbitration or other peaceful means, but the words of the heads of government had little effect in the disputed territories. Repeated violations of the Karabagh conditional agreement led to an abortive Armenian revolt in March 1920, culminating in the beheading of the Armenian bishop of Shushi, the torching of the Armenian quarters, and the flight of the survivors under the cover of dense fog toward the village of Shosh. Armenian Shushi, after Tiflis (Tbilisi), the most important intellectual and cultural Armenian center in the Caucasus, was reduced to cinders and henceforth became the symbol of Azerbaijani political and military predominance.[17]

The failure of the provisional accord of August 1919 and the subsequent ruin of Shushi affect the demeanor of the Armenians today. In their minds mediation, intercession, and intervention have no meaning if they are predicated on the continued wrongful territorial integrity of Azerbaijan or the laying down of arms and withdrawal of all military contingents in exchange for vague promises of cultural or even political autonomy. The challenge, of course, is to establish such firm guarantees, in the event of a compromise that would leave an autonomous Karabagh within Azerbaijan, so that swift and decisive counteraction could be taken in case of a new round of violations. For the present, the Karabagh Armenians apparently do not even want to think of this alternative. They point instead to the example of Sharur-Nakhichevan, which has been denuded of its Armenian population, and insist that the restoration of Karabagh to Azerbaijani jurisdiction will condemn it to the same fate.

Under Russian imperial rule, the lower Araxes River Valley, made up of the *uezds* of Sharur and Nakhichevan, was a part of the Erevan *guberniia*. During the period of the independent Caucasian republics, the Armenian government was able to extend its jurisdiction to Nakhichevan in 1919, but the local Muslim population, then widely identified by the misnomer Tatar, was able, with Azerbaijani and Turkish support, to expel the Armenian armed forces and reestablish a semiautonomous existence. Most of the Armenian minority in the affected districts were forced to flee toward Erevan or Novo-Bayazit. The loss of Sharur-Nakhichevan was a major blow to the Armenians, because the railroad to Julfa on the Iranian frontier passed through the region, and it held enormous economic and strategic importance for the viability of the Armenian republic. In the summer of 1920, the Armenian army launched an offensive and reached the outskirts of Nakhichevan, but the Sovietization of Azerbaijan and the appearance of Red Army detachments in Sharur-Nakhichevan stayed the Armenian advance.[18]

During Soviet-Armenian negotiations in Moscow for a treaty of friendship in mid-1920, People's Commissar for Foreign Affairs Grigorii Chicherin accepted Armenia's economic arguments and proposed a compromise whereby Zangezur and Sharur-Nakhichevan would be awarded to Armenia, whereas Karabagh would go to Azerbaijan. In a draft treaty subsequently initialed in Erevan in October, Soviet envoy Boris Legran went even further by confirming the

inclusion of Sharur-Nakhichevan and Zangezur in Armenia and desig-
nating Mountainous Karabagh as a disputed territory, whose fate
would be resolved through the will of its people and Soviet mediation.[19] When Armenia was Sovietized in December 1920, Dr.
Nariman Narimanov, the president of Soviet Azerbaijan, in a gesture of frater-
nalism, renounced all Azerbaijani claims to Mountainous Karabagh,
Zangezur, and Nakhichevan, a declaration that was broadcast throughout the world as evidence that only the Soviet order could resolve such
complex national questions.[20]

Despite these proclamations and the appointment by the Soviet Armenian government of officials to bring the districts into Soviet Armenia, the decisions were not implemented. In the case of Sharur-
Nakhichevan, considerations of Soviet-Turkish relations took precedence, and in the Treaty of Moscow in March 1921, Turkey saw to it
that Sharur-Nakhichevan was awarded, not to Armenia but to Soviet
Azerbaijan, although the region was separated from Azerbaijan proper
by the intervening Armenian highland of Zangezur. Mustafa Kemal's
representatives required the inclusion of a clause forbidding the subsequent transfer of Sharur-Nakhichevan to any other party (Armenia)
without the express consent of Turkey.[21] As for Karabagh, Dr. Narimanov soon reneged on his declaration and cautioned the central authorities that the award of the district to Armenia would create strong
anti-Soviet sentiment among the Muslim masses. After some indeci-
sion, the Caucasian Bureau of the Russian Communist Party ruled that,
because of economic considerations and for the sake of the solidarity of
the Soviet peoples, Mountainous Karabagh would be left in Azerbaijan
with broad local autonomy. The formation of the Nagorno-Karabagh Autonomous Oblast in 1923 culminated the process.[22]

The Armenian element in Sharur-Nakhichevan on the eve of World
War I ranged from 35 to 40 percent. During the seven decades of
Soviet rule the Armenian minority felt itself pressured to leave, so that
by 1988 only two Armenian villages remained in the highlands of
eastern Nakhichevan. Even these have now been emptied, and there
are virtually no Armenians left in the fertile lands of the lower Araxes
River Valley. The Armenians of Karabagh, and of Erevan, too, insist
that the restoration of Azerbaijani control in Nagorno-Karabagh will
produce the same scenario as that completed in Sharur-Nakhichevan.
They have long charged the authorities of Soviet Azerbaijan with intentionally neglecting Karabagh to draw away the youth and manipu-

lating the economy to diminish the self-sufficiency of the region and make it entirely dependent on Baku and other Azerbaijani cities. Claiming discrimination and second-class citizenship, the Armenians began to petition Moscow as early as 1962, the number and intensity of those petitions escalating rapidly during the Gorbachev era.[23] The swirl of changes since 1988 brought first the Karabagh Soviet's request to join Soviet Armenia, then rejection of the various irresolute compromises of Gorbachev, the unilateral proclamation of secession from Azerbaijan, and ultimately, in January 1992, the declaration of the independence of the Republic of Mountainous Karabagh. On its part, the Baku government responded to the Armenian menace by dissolving the autonomous oblast and asserting that the region was no different from any other part of Azerbaijan proper. The Armenians, like all other minorities, could enjoy religious and cultural freedom but no longer any political autonomy. The Karabagh crisis helped topple the last Communist head of state, Ayaz Mutalibov, and bring to power Popular Front leader Abulfaz Elchibey, who promised upon his election in June 1992 that Azerbaijan would restore control over Shushi and the rest of Karabagh within two months. The initial Azerbaijani offensive after Elchibey was sworn into office was encouraging, as the entire district of Shahumian and the northern half of Mountainous Karabagh were occupied in a single sweeping operation. Azerbaijani air and artillery superiority seemed to doom Stepanakert and the Armenian defenders, but the Armenians showed surprising resilience; in the spring of 1993 they regained much of the territory in the north and—even more significantly—boldly struck out into the mountainous Kelbajar region that separates the eastern boundary of Armenia from the western boundary of Karabagh.

Measured by its political, economic, and military limitations, the Armenian government, it might seem, should be seeking an accommodation with Azerbaijan, which has three times as much territory, twice as many people, and many times more the resources. Even more critical, Azerbaijan has the open and active support of Armenia's awesomely powerful western neighbor, Turkey. Until the spring of 1993, the Armenian government repeatedly denied active involvement in the Karabagh conflict and insisted that any negotiations for peace should include the Karabagh Armenians as direct participants. Despite strong pressure from Karabagh and from within Armenia itself, the government of Levon Ter-Petrosian consistently refused to recognize the

Mountainous Karabagh Republic, reasoning that such an act would complicate matters, since it was tantamount to rejection of the territorial integrity of another state. Hence the Armenian official position has been that there are no territorial claims against Azerbaijan and that the issues are human rights and self-determination. In the aftermath of the Kelbajar operation and the political slaps by the United States and the United Nations in April 1993, Armenian spokesmen became more assertive in their declarations about the right of the Karabagh Armenians to defend themselves and even about Armenia's direct assistance. The logic behind this development is not clear, but it may be linked to covert Russian aid and the fact that the elements in Karabagh associated with President Ter-Petrosian at last gained ascendancy over those elements associated with the party Dashnaktsutiun. Whatever the case, there is yet no apparent viable compromise between the conflicting principles of territorial integrity and self-determination, and the historical record only serves to harden the position of each side. The impasse may be broken by a long period of mutual attrition or by the active military intervention of an external power on behalf of one of the contending parties. It is clear that the Armenian side cannot realistically hope for direct external support and nervously looks westward toward the frontier with Turkey.

Armenia and Turkey

Armenia's largest, most populous, most powerful, and most problematic neighbor is the Republic of Turkey. With more than 50 million people, an enormous military complex, and well-established diplomatic and economic ties worldwide, Turkey has been able almost at will to be considered a part of Europe, of Asia, of the Islamic world, or of any desired combination. Ironically, it is in a position to release Armenia from economic and political isolation by virtue of the developed transportation and trade routes that reach right up to the Armenian frontier. Turkey's reluctance to establish diplomatic relations with Armenia and its passive methods of hindering the flow of supplies from other countries to Armenia were effectively demonstrated during the winter of 1992–93, as the landlocked state shivered in the dark with only a trickle of natural gas and oil from abroad. The widespread praise of Turkey in the West for offering to transport one hundred thousand tons of grain over its railway system to the Armenian frontier and to sell Armenia electrical energy was followed by many delays in the first instance and nondelivery in the second. The administration of President Ter-Petrosian seemed to do its utmost to normalize relations with Turkey, including the dismissal of a foreign minister in October 1992, ostensibly because of comments made in Istanbul at which the Turkish authorities had taken umbrage. Yet by winter's end, it had become clear that in matters of humanitarian aid to Armenia the Turkish government was adept at avoiding a negative reply without taking affirmative action. Most of the Armenian population saw in the Turkish strategy the logical continuation of the long-term policy to keep Armenia helpless and vulnerable and perhaps, at the convenient moment, to seize upon an excuse to eliminate the little that is left of historic Armenia.

For most Armenians, Turkey remains the genocidal regime par excellence. It eliminated entire ethnic groups and confiscated their personal and collective wealth without any subsequent recompense or acts of contrition. On the contrary, much of Turkey's political and economic energies have gone into a worldwide campaign of denial of the Armenian genocide and of recasting the blame so that it will fall upon the Armenians as adherents of, and participants in, terrorism and the attempted destabilization of the NATO alliance. Even fleeting references to past Armenian suffering in Turkey warrant concerted action in order to expunge the record and to prevent any further mention. Disinformation has furthered the Turkish goal of winning worldwide absolution, except, of course, from Kurds, Cypriots, Armenians, and other aggrieved peoples.[24]

The memory of the Armenian genocide lived on in Soviet Armenia even when it was officially disavowed because of considerations of Soviet-Turkish relations. In recent times, the genocide has been memorialized in monuments, sculpture, and painting; in drama, prose, and poetry; and in the scores of villages, city quarters, and districts named after sites in the lost homeland in western Armenia. The daily sight of Mount Ararat, the captive mountain just beyond the frontier, teases the Armenians, there to see but not to touch. For the Armenians, the Turks have been the scourge of history. They overran the Armenian Plateau, which rises up from the Euphrates River, in the eleventh century and continued to swarm into the area for centuries thereafter, destroying much of the Armenian way of life and casting the Armenian in the role of the despised second-class citizen, the infidel (*gavur*). The pogroms of Sultan Abdul-Hamid in the latter part of the nineteenth century were only the precursor of the much more efficient and sweeping death mechanisms of the Young Turks.[25]

In Armenia's struggle with Azerbaijan, Turkey initially declared its neutrality, although it soon became evident that not only Turkish moral support but also material assistance was reaching Baku and that in the world arena Turkey was shepherding the fledgling Azerbaijani diplomats and effectively advocating the Azerbaijani position. Armenian-Turkish relations in the new period of Armenian independence thus have not gotten off to a good start. In its declaration of intent to achieve eventual state sovereignty, the Armenian parliament in August 1990 adopted a program that included but in many ways skirted the genocide issue. Rather than seeking redress and restoration, the proclamation was limited to attaining international recognition of the genocide. For Armenian nationalists the measured tone of the plank was insufficient and even outrageous, whereas for highly circumspect political observers any mention of the genocide seemed untimely for a small state seeking independence from the Soviet Union, a goal that could be realized only with the nonhostility of its neighbors. If the declaration was worded to avoid direct confrontation with the Turks, it was not successful. The Turkish press and foreign ministry were quick to note that if previously it was the Armenian diaspora, headed by the Dashnakists, that had conducted a hate campaign against Turkey, this deplorable behavior had now become an all-Armenian affair.

In fact, however, as Armenia moved toward independence under the direction of the Armenian Pan-National Movement, there was a clear understanding that a modus vivendi with Turkey was essential. In stressing the need to separate Armenia from Russia, intellectuals associated with the movement insisted that there was nothing to fear from Turkey and that no "third force" existed in the Caucasus. While subsequent events have tempered that view, it is of course true that the factors affecting Armenian-Turkish relations were very different in 1918 and 1991. In the first instance, Turkey was a defeated power, an enemy of the European Allies, who had made many solemn pledges regarding the emancipation of Armenia. No Armenian leader in 1918 could imagine a viable state within the confines of the existing territories. Rather, the Allies would create a united Armenian state with an outlet on the sea. Such prospects, together with the immediacy of the genocide, made the government of the first Republic of Armenia reluctant to enter into any kind of relations with either the sultan's government in Constantinople or the nationalist government in Ankara. Armenian calculations proved to be ill-founded, as Turkish Nationalist armies successfully invaded the existing republic in 1920, bringing about its partition and Sovietization. Three years later, in the Treaty of Lausanne, Turkey gained the recognition by the West of this fait accompli.[26]

The new Armenian leadership lives under no illusions of being able to wrest away any Turkish territory. From the outset, the Ter-Petrosian administration sought to normalize relations with Turkey and, in so doing, let it be known in Ankara that the events of the past would not be raised. Optimistically, Ter-Petrosian even enlisted the services of a prominent Armenian-American entrepreneur to win Turkish endorsement of a joint venture that would develop and upgrade the port of Trabzon (Trebizond) as a primary outlet for the Armenian republic. The initial exploratory exchanges were encouraging, but the Turkish press soon sensationalized the venture and intimidated the key Turkish Jewish partner in the project. Facilitating a lifeline to Armenia at a time that the Armenians were laying claim to a part of Turkic Azerbaijan went beyond the realm of a business venture. The undertaking, which was viewed with skepticism among some elements of the Armenian diaspora, was dumped, whereas a bold stroke of Turkish governmental support might have put Armenian-Turkish relations on a much healthier track.

If the Armenian strategy was to downplay the genocide and let it be known that no preconditions existed for the establishment of diplomatic relations, it was the Turkish side that now insisted on preconditions. Not content with the implicit Armenian silence on the genocide and the historic Armenian territories in Turkey, the Turkish government at the beginning of 1992 flexed its political muscle in an attempt to exact an explicit renunciation from Armenia. At the Prague meeting of foreign ministers of the Conference on Security and Cooperation in Europe in January 1992, for example, it was decided to accept all former Soviet states except Georgia into the CSCE. At the preparatory ambassadorial meeting, however, the Turkish representative warned that his government would veto the admission of Armenia unless that country explicitly recognized the territorial integrity and current boundaries of Turkey, waived all territorial claims, reaffirmed the applicability of the Treaty of Kars (between Turkey and the Soviet Caucasian republics in 1921) acknowledging those boundaries, and agreed to drop the issue of the alleged genocide and to condemn terrorism as a precondition to the establishment of full diplomatic relations.

Despite the pressure of Turkey, supported by the United States, the Armenian delegation refused to accept these conditions, maintaining that Armenia was prepared to discuss with Turkey the questions of the genocide, territorial claims, and the Treaty of Kars on a bilateral basis, but not as a precondition for admission to the CSCE.[27] And if Turkey insisted on an excursion into history to a 1921 treaty, then it should also be prepared to go back six years more to 1915. Under these circumstances and the mediation of several European member states, the Turkish ambassador retreated from his threat, although both the Turkish and Armenian delegations did issue for the record a simultaneous but separate *déclaration d'intérprétation*.

During the meeting of the CSCE's foreign ministers in Helsinki in March 1992, the issue of Nagorno-Karabagh was on the agenda. The Armenian foreign minister warned that if Nagorno-Karabagh was not a party to the negotiations and if Turkey did not maintain neutrality, the CSCE peace process would be jeopardized and would reach a dead end. From the Armenian perspective, Turkey has repeatedly violated its pledge of neutrality, both at the conference table and on the battlefield, and has often taken more extreme positions than Azerbaijan. Increasingly, Armenian politicians are coming to the conclusion that Azerbaijan is merely a front for Turkish maneuvers and designs. Throughout 1992 and especially in 1993, President Turgut Özal repeatedly condemned the Armenians as the perpetrators of genocide, and many Turco-Azerbaijani manifestations of solidarity were made. Each time Azerbaijan was hard pressed by the Armenians of Karabagh, President Abulfaz Elchibey appealed to Turkey for intervention and support. While the official Turkish response was reserved, there were numerous reports, no longer denied from Ankara, of Turkish officers and volunteers in the ranks of the Azerbaijani army, of financial and humanitarian assistance, and of an accord on military cooperation between the two countries.[28] The Armenian offensive against Kelbajar produced a Turkish show of force along the Armenian frontier, intense Turkish diplomatic activity abroad, and threats of unilateral intervention in the conflict. Declarations from the Turkish president, prime minister, foreign minister, and ambassador to the United Nations all point to that possibility.

In the best of circumstances the normalization of Armenian-Turkish relations would be taxing and trying yet the new Armenian administration believed that there was no other way to diminish reliance on Russia and gain entry as an equal into the world community. Successful economic and diplomatic relations might in time engender sufficient trust to encourage the Turks themselves to face their own history and the ugly skeleton of the Armenian genocide. Such calculations have been derailed by the Karabagh conflict. Turkey has taken the lead in efforts to isolate Armenia diplomatically, politically, economically, and militarily. Armenia and, especially, the Karabagh Armenians were deeply resentful of President Özal's threats and of Turkey's partisanship in the tripartite American-Russian-Turkish peace initiative. which entailed the withdrawal of Armenian forces from Kelbajar and other Azerbaijani territories in exchange for a two-month cease-fire, the deployment of CSCE observers, and negotiations for a permanent truce.[29] A large segment of the population of Armenia and Mountainous Karabagh was outraged by President Ter-Petrosian's decision to attend Özal's funeral in Ankara only a few days after the Turkish leader had publicly reminded the Armenians of "the lesson of 1915." The ghost of the past is alive and well in Armenian-Turkish relations and makes all the more critical the attitudes of Armenia's two non-Turkic neighbors, Georgia and Iran.

Armenia and Georgia

Like the Armenians, the Georgians are Christians, and the two neighboring peoples have lived without major conflict down through the centuries. Both of them, unlike the Azerbaijanis, boast a series of national dynasties dating back to the pre-Christian era. When feeling oppressed by Russian or Soviet rule, they often intimated their own superiority by recalling that their civilizations were flourishing at a time when the Slavic peoples were still wanderers in the woods and that their national Christian churches predate the Russian Orthodox Church by seven centuries.

The endless invasions of the Armenian Plateau resulted in the elimination of the Armenian nobility (*nakharar*), the backbone of Armenian defense, by the fourteenth century, with only vestiges of that class remaining in remote highland areas such as Karabagh. The Georgian nobility, on the other hand, stayed intact and continued to exist after the Russian annexation of the several Georgian realms at the beginning of the nineteenth century. Tiflis, now Tbilisi, became the Russian administrative center in the Caucasus and remained so through much of the Soviet period.[30]

Georgia and Turkey have some overlapping claims, but at times of tension with Armenia the Turkish government has assured Georgia that it has no hostile or aggressive designs on that country. Following the collapse of the Soviet Union, Turkey acted swiftly to open the borders with Georgia as part of its general penetration into the Caucasus and Central Asia. Still, the future status of Abkhazia and Ajaria and the Georgian historical memory of Turkic invasions make the Georgians somewhat wary. For the Armenians, the fear of a revived Pan-Turkic movement has raised suggestions of a north-south bloc of non-Turkic Georgia, Armenia, and Iran. Yet the realization of such a seemingly natural alliance faces many obstacles, not the least of which is the recent historical rivalry of the Georgians and Armenians.

During the century of Russian imperial rule, the Armenian element in the Caucasus grew rapidly and included aggressive classes of entrepreneurs and capitalists. While most Armenians remained poor peasants, large numbers of urban Armenians dominated the arts, crafts, trade, and banking of many Caucasian cities. The indebted Georgian nobility was forced to sell out to the Armenian nouveau riche, as Armenian capital spread out from Tiflis into the countryside. Because of the property qualifications for voting, Armenians came to dominate the Tiflis city hall in the nineteenth century. Compared with Armenians and Russians, the Georgians had become a minority in their own historic capital. Armenian educational, cultural, economic, professional, religious, and social institutions prevailed in Tiflis, which boasted a larger Armenian population than any other city of the Russian Empire. It was not by coincidence that Tiflis became the hub of Armenian intellectual and political life.

Georgian resentment of Armenian inroads found an effective avenue of response through the Georgian Menshevik Party, which during the period of Georgian independence, 1918–21, was able to use the mantle of internationalism and social and economic reforms to dispossess the Armenians. Following the Bolshevik revolution in 1917 and the Turkish invasion in 1918, the Georgian leaders took advantage of German protection to dissolve the ineffective Transcaucasian Federative Republic and proclaim the independence of the Republic of Georgia on 26 May 1918.[31] By this act, Georgia abandoned Armenia to its fate against the advancing Turkish armies, a self-saving measure that continues to generate Armenian skepticism regarding the present attitude of the Georgian leaders.

During the period of the Republic of Georgia and continuing into Soviet Georgia, the Armenian governments were annoyed by what they perceived as Georgian manipulative policies to serve as the regional balance of power and to take advantage of Armenian-Azerbaijani differences to perpetuate Georgian ascendancy. Not only was Armenian political and intellectual control of Tiflis eliminated, but the Armenians remaining in Tiflis complained bitterly of discrimination and exclusion from influential positions within the country's administrative, economic, and educational institutions. The continued exodus of Armenians from Tiflis and Georgia in general has kept their numbers constant, at about a half million, while the population of the country more than doubled during the Soviet period. By the 1960s the Georgians had finally become an absolute majority in their capital city, Tbilisi.

In Armenian-Georgian relations there is also a territorial dimension, although not of the scope of the Armenian-Azerbaijani dispute. The southern rim of Georgia along the northern frontier of Armenia is populated largely by Armenians. Most of these people are the descendants of western Armenians from the region of Erzerum who moved into Akhalkalaki and Akhaltskha (Akhaltsikh) after the Russo-Turkish war of 1828–29. During the period of the independent republics, the dispute over these districts strained Armenian-Georgian relations, and in December 1918 the two sides even engaged in a brief military conflict in the adjacent district of Lori.[32] Nonetheless, the Armenian-Georgian territorial dispute was relatively limited in scope, and by 1920 there were strong indications that a compromise solution would soon be reached, especially if Armenia were to expand westward into the Turkish Armenian territories awarded by the Treaty of Sèvres.

The question of an Armenian outlet to the port of Batum (Batumi) was more complicated. The Allied powers wanted Armenia to have a narrow strip of land along the Chorokh River to build a railroad from Kars to Batum, where it would have its own quay and facilities. The Georgians resisted ceding a belt of territory and maintained that the existing railway system from Batum to Tiflis and thence to Erevan was sufficient to meet Armenia's needs. This maneuver was regarded as a strategy to keep the Armenian republic economically vulnerable and dependent. The Georgians were roundly criticized by the European peacemakers, but their adamancy bore results in the end, as the last of the Allied battalions withdrew from Batum in July 1920 and the Georgian army and civil administration took over the province. When a shipment of British arms reached a Georgian port in the summer of 1920, the Georgians exacted 27 percent of the shipment as the price for facilitating the transport of the remainder into Armenia.[33] The economic reliance of Armenia on Georgia continued into the Soviet period, and efforts of Armenian Communist leaders to decrease that factor and to cut significantly the distance between Armenia and Russia by creating a branch railway from Erevan to Akstafa, thereby entirely circumventing Georgian territory, were sufficient to bring about the downfall of the promoters of the scheme, who figured among the first victims of Stalin's henchman in the Caucasus, Lavrenti Beria.[34]

All these factors figure in the tenor of Armenian-Georgian relations today. The first president of the new, independent Georgia, Zviad Gamsakhurdia, was regarded with apprehension by the Armenians of Georgia because of his pronounced nationalistic views. There was resentment over the founding of new Georgian villages in the Armenian-populated regions, rival claims to medieval religious sites, and the arbitrariness of the Georgian security forces. Matters became even more complicated when Gamsakhurdia took refuge in Armenia for a time after being forcibly evicted from power. Armenia was unwillingly being drawn into a Georgian civil war. The return of Eduard Shevardnadze to Georgia seemed to ease Armenian-Georgian tensions, and by and large the relations between the two countries remain satisfactory. Georgia has allowed the passage of supplies and natural gas to Armenia, although the Armenians complain that much of the goods are plundered before entering Armenian territory. Moreover, the frequent disruption of the gas pipeline and railroad as they pass through Marneuli, an Azerbaijani-populated district in southeast Georgia, has raised suspicions that the Tbilisi authorities are intentionally not as diligent as they could be in securing these lines. Once again, there are projects on the table to allow the Armenians to develop port facilities at Batumi or Poti, but no significant progress has yet been made. Georgia itself is highly apprehensive about the Karabagh crisis and is less than enthusiastic about the Armenian initiative, since Armenian success in Karabagh would establish an unmistakable precedent for the rights of the autonomous Ossetian, Abkhazian, and perhaps even Ajarian regions in Georgia.

With all these issues to complicate Armenian-Georgian relations, the Armenians at least are clearly cognizant of the fact that Georgia is currently their only relatively reliable link to the outside world. The Armenians of Abkhazia have suffered greatly at the hands of the Georgian militia, yet the Armenian government is working hard not to anger or alienate the Georgians and has acted to quiet Armenian protests in Akhalkalaki and Akhaltskha. The growing disillusion with the Turkish political orientation raises speculation once again about the possibility of a Georgian-Armenian-Iranian counterbloc to the Turkic bloc advocated by the Republic of Turkey.

Armenia and Iran

Iran is regarded by the Armenians as their most friendly and promising neighbor. This may seem ironic in view of the accentuated Islamic character of the Iranian republic and the ancient historical adversarial relationship between the Sasanian Persian empire and Arsacid and post-Arsacid Armenia. To this day the Armenian Church commemorates the martyrdom of Vardan Mamikonian and the flower of the Armenian nobility in A.D. 451, as they defended faith and nation against Persian attempts to reimpose Zoroastrianism in Armenia. The memory of ancient rivalries, however, has been tempered by awareness that the Armenians and Iranians are kindred peoples, that they share an Indo-European heritage, and that historically many aspects of their language, culture, and social systems have been related. It is true that Iran was Islamicized and partly Turkified, but the underlying Irano-Armenian bond has been demonstrated by the tolerance and even benevolence with which Iranian rulers have treated their Armenian minority for nearly four hundred years, since the time of Shah Abbas. Armenians were allowed to live, by and large, according to their own ecclesiastic laws and customs, and the Armenian princes, or *meliks*, of Karabagh were confirmed in office by the royal edicts of the Safavid shahs. There was great turmoil and insecurity under the subsequent Turkic Qajar dynasty, causing many Armenians to welcome the Russian armies and the annexation of the Persian khanates north of the Araxes River between 1806 and 1828. In the twentieth century, thousands of Armenians continued to live in relative comfort and prosperity in such places as Tabriz, Karadagh, Salmast, Qazvin, Tehran, Isfahan and then Avaz, Abadan, and other oil-producing centers. Dur-

260 RICHARD G. HOVANNISIAN

ing World War I many western Armenian refugees found shelter in Iran, and in the period of the Armenian Republic, Prince Hovsep Argutinskii-Dolgorukii was received with high honors as the Armenian plenipotentiary to the royal court in Tehran.[35] During the decades of Soviet rule, electric barbed-wire fences separated Armenia from Iran, and relations between the Armenian communities of Iran and Soviet Armenia were difficult and strained. The reemergence of an Armenian Republic in 1991–92 brought about immediate manifestations of renewed friendship. Armenian Foreign Minister Raffi K. Hovannisian was received in Tehran by President Hashemi Rafsanjani and Foreign Minister Ali Akbar Velayati, laying the groundwork for an official visit by President Ter-Petrosian in May 1992. For the time that the United States and Iran both temporarily housed their embassies in the Hrazdan Hotel in Erevan, the American and Iranian flags fluttering next to one another created a fascinating, symbolic, and hopeful vision for the Armenians.

In the first months after the restoration of Armenian independence, Iran reacted with clear-cut sympathy while at the same time acknowledging its religious-cultural bonds with Azerbaijan and offering to serve as a mediator in the Karabagh conflict. The Iranian initiative seemed to undermine Turkish influence in the Caucasus and held out the possibility of winning respect for the Islamic Republic from the world community. The Iranian leaders were clearly concerned that the proliferation of the conflict could arouse the ten to fifteen million Iranian Azerbaijanis or, as sometimes referred to, the people of "South Azerbaijan." Thus Iran offered Armenia low-key moral and economic assistance and help in breaking out of its physical isolation by laying a pontoon bridge over the Araxes River from Karadagh to Zangezur.

By the end of 1992, however, Iran's attitude had noticeably cooled. The Armenian capture of Shushi in May and the widely broadcast massacre at Khojaly, the Azerbaijani stronghold that had kept the Karabagh airport under firm Azerbaijani control, created a backlash in Iran, especially as the victims were coreligionist Shi'a. What was more, Ter-Petrosian, by dismissing his foreign minister for alleged anti-Turkish statements, and by directing Armenia's political and economic orientation sharply toward the West through Turkey, offended the Iranian leaders. The weakening of Ter-Petrosian's Turkish initiative has now turned Armenia back to Iran, which continues to respond courteously and offer limited assistance while at the same time showing itself to be much more solicitous of the Azerbaijani position. The Armenian offensive in the Kelbajar district in April 1993 elicited a sharp rebuke from the Iranian government, which made specific reference to the inviolability of Azerbaijan's territorial integrity.[36] Significantly, President Elchibey appealed to both Turkey and Iran for intervention, and the Baku government is actively developing linkages with Iran. The loss of Iranian support would leave Armenia in virtual political and diplomatic isolation. Hence the Armenian government is scrambling to retain Iranian sympathy. On its part, Iran was wary of Elchibey's pronounced pro-Turkish orientation and apparent intent to manipulate the "South Azerbaijan" issue. Fear of Azerbaijani and Turkish designs to stir up Iranian Azerbaijanis and perhaps even attempts to dismantle the Islamic Republic make the Armenian pressure on Azerbaijan and tensions with Turkey not so undesirable to the Tehran government. By the beginning of the summer of 1993, Armenian-Iranian relations were clearly on the mend. There are those who suggest that one of the commodities that Armenia could offer the West is the role of acting as a nonthreatening intermediary to Iran. In view of the fact that Armenia has little to offer the West in the way of raw materials, manufactured goods, or technology, the strategic aspect may receive increasing emphasis.

The Russian Connection

For Armenia, the Russian connection constitutes an enigma. The most pro-Russian of the Caucasian peoples, the Armenians felt let down and even betrayed by Mikhail Gorbachev, their anger for a time extending from his person and position to the Russians at large. This was exacerbated by evidence in 1991 that the Interior Ministry's security forces, the OMON, were actively supporting the Azerbaijani side with rapid-fire arms and armored vehicles in its assault on Getashen (Chaikend) and the surrounding Armenian villages at the dividing point between the Azerbaijani-populated sector of Kirovabad (Ganja, Gandzak) and the Armenian-populated reaches north of Karabagh. In Armenian minds there was no doubt that Gorbachev was punishing the Armenians for their declaration of intent to separate from the Soviet Union and rewarding the Azerbaijanis for the firm loyalty to the center of Ayaz Mutalibov's entrenched Communist regime in Azerbaijan.

The Russian equation may have shifted under the Russian leadership of Boris Yeltsin, who seems to be on cordial personal terms with Armenian President Levon Ter-Petrosian and who may be tilting toward Armenia as a way of countering Turkish influence in the Caucasus and of expressing his dissatisfaction with Azerbaijan's refusal to join the Commonwealth of Independent States. The Armenian military success in Mountainous Karabagh during the winter of 1992–93 and the Kelbajar offensive in the spring of 1993 could have been conducted without arms and equipment from some external source. The consensus seems to be that Russia is engaged in a seesaw action to maintain its importance and presence in the area. The parliamentary opposition to Boris Yeltsin is not, as has been portrayed in the West, simply a matter of conservative antireformers opposed to the bold White giant. Rather, many among the so-called conservatives are resentful of Russia's loss of political and military stature in the world and especially the forfeiture of responsibility in the Russian littoral. If there is to be international mediation of the Karabagh conflict, for example, the partners in such action in the age of superpowers would logically be Russia and the United States without direct reference to Turkey, a surrogate of the United States and a strong supporter of one side in the dispute. The participation of Turkey in the tripartite peace initiative would seem to weigh in favor of Azerbaijan and has led Armenia, with tacit Russian tolerance, to engage in evasive and procrastinating measures while endorsing the plan in principle.

After a period of intense anti-Russian sentiment, both the government and the people of Armenia are again turning northward toward the only protection that seems feasible. The collapse of the Soviet Union deprived Armenia of a common boundary with Russia. Georgia and Azerbaijan control the communication routes between the largest and the smallest of the former republics of the USSR. This separation adds to Armenia's vulnerability and sense of isolation. By and large, however, the Armenians are shifting back to a Russian orientation.

Historically, the Armenians have prospered under Russian rule. Already by the seventeenth century the trade route from Iran to Astrakhan and up the Volga River was referred to as the Armenian road. The bejeweled Almaze throne, now in the Kremlin museum, attests to the early links between the Romanovs and Iranian Armenian merchants, who held a virtual monopoly on the silk trade and that of other lucrative goods. It is not surprising, therefore, that Israel Ori, Joseph Emin, and other seventeenth- and eighteenth-century political adventurers and idealists should have looked to Russia for the emancipation of the Armenian people. Moreover, many Armenians rose up through the imperial military establishment to the rank of general, one of them, M.T. Loris-Melikov, becoming the chief advisor of Tsar Alexander II. After the Russian annexation of the Caucasus in the nineteenth century, the Armenians, like all other indigenous populations, were subjected to sporadic Russification policies. Armenian schools were closed for a time, and in 1903 under the governor general, Prince Grigorii Golitsyn, the Armenian Apostolic Church's properties were confiscated in an attempt to undermine Armenian national sentiment and bring the Armenian Church under state supervision and sponsorship. The Russian Revolution of 1905 forced Tsar Nicholas II to rescind the edict, but tsarist agents were widely believed to have fomented the Armenian-Tatar (Azerbaijani) warfare of 1905–07 in order to divert the attention of the Caucasian peoples from the revolutionary movement and to continue to prevail on the principle of divide and rule. Despite these difficulties the Armenians increased more rapidly than any other element in the nineteenth century, in part because of natural growth and in part because of the continued influx of Armenians from the Ottoman Empire and Iran. While Muslims still formed a plurality in the Caucasus, they came to be outnumbered by Christian Armenians and Georgians combined. The demographic changes in the region were accompanied by major economic shifts, as many Armenian villages controlled by Muslim beks and aghas were able to gain freedom, while at the same time Armenian professionals, merchants, and industrialists spread throughout the cities of the Caucasus.[37]

During World War I the Armenians were duped into believing that Russia would emancipate western (Turkish) Armenia and that a national revival was at hand. They served in large numbers in the Russian armies, and even those not required to enlist organized themselves into volunteer battalions to participate in the liberation of the *erkir* (homeland), that is, western Armenia. Once Tsar Nicholas had adhered in 1916 to the secret Allied plan (Sykes-Picot) to partition the Ottoman Empire, the Armenians were no longer needed, for by then the imperial armies were in occupation of all the Turkish territories marked for eventual annexation. Rather, plans were laid to repopulate the new frontier with Cossacks.[38]

The liberal policies of the Russian Provisional Government, which assumed power after the revolution and the involuntary abdication of Tsar Nicholas in March 1917, inspired renewed hope and optimism among the Armenians, prompting thousands of refugees to return to their homes in western Armenia. Such spirits were cut short by the Bolshevik Revolution in November and the resulting Russian Civil War, which completely isolated Armenia and allowed the Turkish armies to recover all of western Armenia and invade eastern (Russian) Armenia. It was in an act of desperation on 28 May 1918 that Armenian leaders declared the independence of an undefined republic around Erevan. The end of the world war raised hopes that the republic would survive and even expand, but the victory of the Red Army in the civil war and the emergence of a Turkish resistance movement under Mustafa Kemal sealed the fate of that state. In relinquishing power to Soviet Armenia in December 1920, the last independent Armenian government received from Soviet Russia a treaty pledge to remove the Turkish armies from the occupied half of the republic and to reestablish the boundaries as they had existed before the Turkish invasion.[39] Once again, however, Armenian interests were sacrificed to broader Soviet policy considerations, and in the Treaty of Moscow in March 1921, Soviet Russia recognized Turkey's expansion up to the Arpachai/Akhurian and Araxes rivers, the loss of Kars, Ardahan, and Surmalu (with Mount Ararat), and the award of Sharur-Nakhichevan to Soviet Azerbaijan. Soviet Armenia was required to acquiesce in these terms by becoming a party to an almost identical treaty signed at Kars in October of that year. Such historical memories make the Armenians believe that the current limited Russian support may be both conditional and temporary, always subject to sudden change in keeping with Russia's foreign and domestic policy considerations.

Understanding that they were offered up as sacrificial lambs in Soviet-Turkish relations, the Armenians nonetheless made the best of the situation and took advantage of whatever opportunities the Soviet system offered. They figured prominently in the administrative, economic, and intellectual circles of the Soviet Union, and a number of them reached prominence in the diplomatic corps. By the 1970s, the Armenian standard of living ranked significantly higher than the norms for the Soviet Union as a whole, and the increased confidence of the Armenians found expression in their intellectual and cultural creativity and in the reevaluation of their entire history. A period of collective rediscovery was in progress.

Under Mikhail Gorbachev, the Armenians were quickly attracted to the program for reforms. The removal of First Secretary Garen Demirjian, who during the Brezhnev years had formed his own widespread patronage system, was met with mixed reaction, but by and large the concepts of perestroika and glasnost were well received in Armenia. The new openness allowed first for subdued and then for bold demonstrations regarding the environment and ecology, nuclear reactor safety, and toxic industrial emissions. These, in turn, spurred the Karabagh demonstrations and put the Armenians on the road to direct confrontation with Gorbachev and the center. The irresolution and contradictory pronouncements of Gorbachev and his advisors, his slowness to act in response to the Sumgait pogrom, his inability to bring about compromise, and ultimately his outright rejection of any territorial rectification were for the Armenians ample evidence that they were once again to be sacrificed for the larger Turkic interests of the Soviet state. While Azerbaijan remained under the firm hand of Ayaz Mutalibov, the power and prestige of the Armenian Communist Party under Suren Harutiunian were being undermined by the refusal or inability of the center to give any satisfaction to the Armenians.

Matters were made worse by the crushing earthquake of December 1988. Gorbachev was forced to cut short his triumphant American visit and to show his concern at the fallen cities of Leninakan (pre-Soviet Alexandropol, now Kumairi) and Spitak. But rather than the anticipated expressions of appreciation, he was greeted with taunts about Karabagh, even in the midst of the Armenian calamity. Not only did Gorbachev leave Armenia in anger, but he used the disarray of the Armenians to have the leaders of the Karabagh movement, including Levon Ter-Petrosian, arrested. The imprisoned intellectuals became instant heroes and martyrs, and a swell of anti-Russian feeling engulfed the country. The various attempted compromises in Karabagh, including its removal from the jurisdiction of Baku and placement under the separate administration of Moscow-appointed Arkadii Vol'skii, ultimately failed. By the end of 1989, Karabagh had been returned to Azerbaijani jurisdiction, and the Armenians continued in their alienation from Gorbachev and Russia in general.

The Karabagh Committee was released in mid-1989, and Ter-Petrosian soon emerged as a leader with a plan that went far beyond Karabagh to the eventual separation of Armenia from the Soviet Union. Elections to the Armenian parliament in 1990 resulted in a victory for Ter-Petrosian's Pan-Armenian National Movement, and he was able to maneuver effectively to win election as president of parliament over the candidacy of the then Communist First Secretary, Vladimir Movsisian. Ter-Petrosian made it clear that the restoration of national sovereignty was a primary objective, and in the Proclamation (*Hrchakagir*) of August 1990, this and other planks were adopted as the national platform.

Armenia, together with Georgia, Moldova, and the Baltic states, refused to participate in the Gorbachev referendum on the continuation of the Soviet Union. Instead, the parliament gave the required six-month notice that it would organize a separate referendum in September 1991 on the question of secession from the union. Armenians assert that this declaration increased Gorbachev's wrath and increased OMON support for the Azerbaijani armed forces bombarding Armenian centers in and around Mountainous Karabagh.

The attempted putsch in Moscow in August 1991 sealed the fate of the Soviet Union and made a referendum in Armenia superfluous. Nonetheless, the Armenian leaders, singularly in the Soviet Union, insisted on proceeding with the legal steps of disengagement and on 21 September 1991 conducted the national referendum, which gave them an overwhelming mandate for separation, the official declaration coming two days later. The pronounced anti-Gorbachev and even anti-Russian demeanor of Ter-Petrosian was mitigated by the collapse of the Soviet Union, as Armenia immediately approved membership in the Commonwealth of Independent States and thereafter became a party to the collective security pact sponsored by Russia. Moreover, the disappointing results of Ter-Petrosian's initiative relating to Turkey have again turned many Armenian leaders toward Moscow. The relationship is still evolving, but history has shown that Russia, with all its vacillation, remains a vital factor in Armenia's security and future. The present physical absence of Russia from the Caucasus, however, allows for some direct encounters with the West.

The Elusive West

The Armenians have long been the most Western-oriented people of the Caucasus and perhaps of the entire Middle East. Armenia's contacts with Europe date back to the ancient world, and they became particularly intense in the period of the Crusades. During the centuries that the Armenian Plateau was divided between the Ottoman and Persian empires, Armenians were often the pioneers of Western innovations and served as interpreters and intermediaries in diplomatic and commercial relations between East and West. Armenians made up the largest segment of the student bodies of American, French, German, and other Western-sponsored schools in the Ottoman Empire. When they failed to achieve civil rights and equality through the Ottoman reforms of the nineteenth century, the Armenians repeatedly turned to the West for help. As it happened, Western diplomatic support without military intervention only aggravated Armenian suffering. This is a major historical lesson that the present Armenian leaders may or may not heed, in view of the powerful draw of the West.

During World War I, the Allied powers condemned in no uncertain terms the Armenian genocide, and after the war Armenia was sometimes referred to as "the little ally." Armenia went to the Paris Peace Conference with the delusion that it would be rewarded for loyalty to the Allied cause and would be treated preferentially compared with neighboring Caucasian republics, one of which had been created with German assistance and the other, with active Turkish armed force. The Allies, victors over both Germany and Turkey, had made scores of pronouncements regarding a safe and prosperous future for the Armenian people, who, in the words of British Prime Minister David Lloyd-George, would never again be subjected to the "blasting tyranny of the Turk."[40]

Despite such declarations and the Armenian belief that a free, independent, united state was within reach, such illusions were shattered within two years of the end of the war. Inter-Allied rivalries, the American refusal to assume a mandate or protectorate over Armenia, the Turkish resistance movement spearheaded by Mustafa Kemal Pasha, and the absence of lucrative raw materials and markets in Armenia to make the country attractive to international financial and commercial interests were all contributing factors. While the Turkish armies rolled over the small Caucasian Armenian state that had never extended beyond the boundaries of Russian Armenia, the League of Nations and the Allied and associated powers contented themselves with stirring resolutions of sympathy. No help came from the West.[41]

If it seemed to the Armenians at the end of World War I that they held the inside position because of their suffering and fidelity to Western principles, the same seemed to hold true at the demise of the Soviet Union. Sympathy had been generated and humanitarian support extended because of the 1988 earthquake, which thrust Armenia into the consciousness of much of the world. There was general opposition to, and condemnation of, the Azerbaijani economic stranglehold on Armenia and Karabagh, and Armenia was repeatedly singled out in Europe and in the United States as a model of democratic reforms, unlike Georgia, which was in the throes of civil strife, or Azerbaijan, which remained in a tight Communist grip.

The administration of President George Bush, only in part because of the existence of a large Armenian-American community, commended Armenia for its moves toward economic privatization and the legal, democratic procedures adopted on the road to renewed national sovereignty. Foreign Minister Raffi Hovannisian seemed to have established a cordial relationship with Secretary of State James Baker, and President Bush received President Ter-Petrosian and Hovannisian in the White House in November 1991. It was significant that only a little more than a month later, on 25 December, Armenia was the only Caucasian state included in Bush's official recognition of five of the former Soviet republics. The lead of the United States was followed by scores of other countries in short order. Again Armenians were euphoric in the belief that such action also implied at least diplomatic support in Armenia's enervating conflict with Azerbaijan.

These hopes were of short duration, however. The United States had much at stake in the Caucasus and Central Asia. It was far more desirable that Turkey be the channel of American interests in these regions than to create conditions that would open the doors to Iran. The Turkish connection and the strategy to counter the spread of Iranian influence were clearly factors in the swift pace of the catch-up experienced by Azerbaijan. Hence, when Secretary of State Baker visited Erevan in January 1992, he made sure to include a stop in Baku on the same trip. Turkey assisted Azerbaijan in making applications to the United Nations and other international organizations, which welcomed both Armenia and Azerbaijan in common ceremonies. The assumption of power in Tbilisi by Eduard Shevardnadze, a familiar figure to Bush and Baker, was followed by the extension of similar support to, and acceptance of, the Republic of Georgia. What was perceived as a strong Armenian advantage at the end of 1991 had dissolved within a short time. It was true that the United States Congress would deplore the continued Azerbaijani blockade of Armenia and try to pressure Baku by imposing trade and aid restrictions, but the White House and State

Department are adept at circumvention, interpretation, and the discovery of loopholes, such as functioning through agencies funded by, but not officially part of, the government.

Armenia seems concerned that the same political, strategic, economic, and military significance assigned to Turkey by the Pentagon and State Department will be extended to Azerbaijan and that Armenia will become increasingly isolated. The reprimand by the State Department and the United Nations Security Council over the capture of the Kelbajar district only serves to deepen these anxieties. The linkage between politics and economics is well understood by the Armenians, who see massive Western investment in the Azerbaijani petroleum industry as a definitive factor that will militate against Armenia politically. There are numerous examples to draw upon. Each time a resolution commemorating the Armenian genocide has been considered by the United States Congress, the Turkish government has only had to issue warnings about harm to the NATO alliance and to caution that trade and American-placed contracts would be affected in order to initiate a filibuster and defeat such resolutions on procedural motions. Armenia has little to attract Western capital at present, and the flow of that capital to Azerbaijan can only augur ill in any long-term conflict. There are already clear indications of this. When former British Prime Minister Margaret Thatcher visited Baku on behalf of a petroleum consortium, she went out of her way to emphasize the primacy of territorial integrity over minority rights or self-determination. There is also concern about the possible erosion of French support. Previously, Armenian activists in France were able to use their contacts with French and other European socialists to get the Strasbourg European Parliament to adopt a resolution calling on Turkey to acknowledge the Armenian genocide and to take other commensurate actions before being admitted to the European Community. It is feared that the decline of socialist power in France and the substantial increase of French trade with Turkey may have repercussions on the Armenian-Azerbaijani conflict, although President François Mitterrand warmly received President Ter-Petrosian in 1993, and French humanitarian aid continues to reach Armenia in spite of Turkish obstacles.

Finally, there is the question of the relationship between Armenia and the Armenian communities in the West. These communities reached an extraordinary pitch of activity in response to the 1988 earthquake. Yet the Armenian organizational infrastructure was unable to retain most of those who returned temporarily to the fold after years of alienation or assimilation. Nonetheless, the Karabagh demonstrations, the declaration of Armenian independence, the admission of Armenia to the United Nations, and the raising of the Armenian tricolor flag on the UN Plaza were deeply emotional moments for the diaspora Armenians. Thus far, the Armenian government has been able to utilize only a small fraction of the potential of the diaspora. The anticipated groundswell of support has been lacking, in part because of the advanced stage of assimilation of a significant segment of the diaspora and in part because of the failure of the Armenian government to assign representatives abroad who can relate to the communities, know their history, speak their language, understand their concerns, and draw them to united action.

The Armenian diaspora has been successful in gaining critical humanitarian assistance for Armenia and, to a lesser degree, for Karabagh, but it has not been so diligent in efforts to win strong political and diplomatic support. The Armenian lobby was not very effective, for example, in drawing obvious parallels between Sarajevo and Stepanakert during the months that the capital of Mountainous Karabagh was under constant bombardment by Azerbaijani artillery, bombs, and missiles and when civilian casualties were daily occurrences. On the other hand, the Armenian defense imperatives of taking control of the regional airport at Khojaly and the Kelbajar salient between Armenia and Karabagh have been portrayed in the media as "ethnic cleansing," with Turkish and Azerbaijani sources equating Armenia to Serbia. Under these circumstances, an obvious role for the diaspora communities would be to persuade the governments and legislatures of their host countries that security and self-determination have the same or even greater priority than the principle of territorial integrity.

Matters have become complicated by the decision of President Ter-Petrosian to expel Hrair Maroukhian, the preeminent figure of the Dashnaktsutiun, just as the party was preparing to open its world congress in Erevan in June 1992. The forced departure of an Armenian political leader from newly independent Armenia created new, deep rifts in the diaspora communities, which were just beginning to overcome long years of fragmentation over their differing positions toward Soviet Armenia and related issues. The challenge remains for both the Armenian government and the leaders of the Armenian diaspora to reach a modus vivendi. The historical memory of past distrust, rivalry, and even hostility are major barriers that have to be surmounted if Armenia hopes to establish the type of teamwork that is so much envied in the case of Israel and the Jewish diaspora.

Conclusion

From this cursory survey of the impact of historical memory on the foreign policy of the new Armenian Republic, the obvious conclusion may be drawn that history is at work at many levels of popular and official behavior. The attempts of the Armenian government to turn a new page and to seek the normalization of relations with traditionally adversarial neighbors have been generally frustrated as much by the reactions of those neighbors as by the modus operandi of the Armenians themselves. President Ter-Petrosian's bold Turkish initiative has not yet borne the desired results and has only reinforced the deeply ingrained stereotypes and distrust.

Georgia remains the most practical avenue to the sea, yet the civil strife in that country has had strong negative repercussions in Armenia. The vital transportation and communication routes that pass through South Ossetia and Abkhazia have been frequently disrupted, adding to the misery of the Armenian populace. Still, there is a certain community of interest with the Georgians and, despite certain Iranian pronouncements, there are persistent allusions to the desirability of a tripartite Georgian-Armenian-Iranian bloc. In the end, however, the historical record may demonstrate that there is no more viable alternative than a permanent, close association with Russia, even in the absence of a common boundary, and that sooner or later Russia will again emerge as a major world power. The question remains whether such a Russia would view the continued existence of the small, landlocked Armenian state as vital to its own interests in the turbulent meeting grounds of the Slavic and Middle Eastern Christian and Muslim worlds.

Notes

1. There is extensive documentation and literature relating to the Armenian genocide. For contemporary eyewitness accounts compiled by Arnold Toynbee at the time, see Great Britain, Parliament, *The Treatment of the Armenians in the*

Ottoman Empire (London: Sir Joseph Causton & Sons, 1916). Among the most recent works are the following: Robert F. Melson, *Revolution and Genocide: On the Origins of the Armenian Genocide and the Holocaust* (Chicago and London: Chicago University Press, 1992); Donald E. Miller and Lorna T. Miller, *Survivors: An Oral History of the Armenian Genocide* (Berkeley: University of California Press, 1993); Richard G. Hovannisian, ed., *The Armenian Genocide: History, Politics, Ethics* (London: MacMillan; New York: St. Martin's Press, 1992). For annotated bibliographies, see Richard G. Hovannisian, "The Armenian Genocide," in *Genocide: A Critical Bibliographic Review*, vol. 1, ed. Israel W. Charny (London: Mansell Publishing; New York: Facts on File, 1988); Vahakn Dadrian, "Documentation of the Armenian Genocide in Turkish Sources," in vol. 2 of this series, published in 1991; Armenian Assembly of America, *Armenian Genocide Resource Guide* (Washington, DC: Armenian Assembly of America, 1988).

2. See Richard G. Hovannisian, *Armenia on the Road to Independence* (Berkeley and Los Angeles: University of California Press, 1967); idem, *The Republic of Armenia*, vol. 1, *The First Year* (Berkeley: University of California Press, 1971); idem, *The Republic of Armenia*, vol. 2, *From Versailles to London, 1919–1920* (Berkeley: University of California Press, 1982). Volumes 3 and 4 of this series will be published by the University of California Press in 1994.

3. For this period, see Firuz Kazemzadeh, *The Struggle for Transcaucasia (1917–1921)* (New York and Oxford: The Philosophical Library, 1951); S. Vratzian, *Hayastani Hanrapetutiun* (The Republic of Armenia) (Paris: Navarre, 1928); Serge Afanasyan, *L'Arménie, L'Azérbaijan et la Géorgie de l'indépendance à l'instauration du pouvoir soviétique (1917–1923)* (Paris: Editions l'Harmattan, 1981); Richard Pipes, *The Formation of the Soviet Union: Communism and Nationalism, 1917–1923*, rev. ed. (Cambridge, MA: Harvard University Press, 1964), pp. 204–41.

4. For this Soviet period, see Mary Kilbourne Matossian, *The Impact of Soviet Policies in Armenia* (Leiden: E.J. Brill, 1962); Claire Mouradian, *De Staline à Gorbachev: Histoire d'une république soviétique: L'Arménie* (Paris: Editions Ramsay, 1990); Ronald G. Suny, *Armenia in the Twentieth Century* (Chico, CA: Scholars Press, 1983), pp. 35–83.

5. Both Armenia and Azerbaijan have published collections of documents on this issue. See, for example, *K istorii Nagorno-Karabakhskoi oblasti Azerbaidzhanskoi SSR: Dokumenty i materialy* (Baku: Institut istorii partii pri TsK KP Azerbaidzhana, 1989); and Istitut istorii Akademii nauk Armenii, Glavnoe arkhivnoe upravlenie, Erevanskogo gosudarstvennogo universiteta, *Nagornyi Karabakh v 1918–1923 gg.: Sbornik dokumentov i materialov*, ed. V.A. Mikaelian et al. (Erevan: AN Armenii, 1992).

6. *Sovetakan Gharabagh*, 21 February 1988. See also *Nagornyi Karabakh: Istoricheskaia spravka*, G.A. Galoian and K.S. Khudaverdian, eds. (Erevan: Armenian SSR Academy of Sciences, 1988), pp. 88; Grant Episcoposian, *Armenian Problem in the Past and Today* (Moscow: "Revival of Armenia" Public Fund, 1993).

7. See Samvel Shamuratian, *The Sumgait Tragedy: Pogroms Against the Armenians in Soviet Azerbaijan*, intro. by Elena Bonner (New Rochelle, NY: A.D. Caratzas and Zoryan Institute, 1990). Death certificates with pictures of twenty-six of the victims of the Sumgait pogrom are reproduced in the English translation of the work by Galoian and Khudaverdian, under the title *Artsakh (Mountainous)*

Gharabagh: Historical Background (Athens: Armenian Popular Movement, 1988), pp. 89–104. Armenian sources maintain that the death toll was far greater than the official figures released by the Azerbaijani authorities.

8. For materials in Russian and Armenian relating to the blockade, see, for example, *Blokada*, 2 pts., publication of the Armenian SSR Ministry of Culture and the Al. Miasnikian State Library (Erevan: Luis, 1990).

9. On the enormity of the earthquake and its effects, see the worldwide print media for December 1988. See also Yuri Rost, *Armenian Tragedy* (New York: St. Martin's Press, 1990); and Bakur Avanesi Karapetian, *Aghet (vaveragir)* (Tragedy [Document]) (Erevan: Gitelik, 1990). The official death toll of twenty-five thousand is widely regarded as having been intentionally minimized from an actual figure of not less than fifty thousand.

10. See, for example, Luigi Villari, *Fire and Sword in the Caucasus* (London: Allen and Unwin, 1906); A. Giulkhandanian, *Hai-tatrakan entharumnere* (The Armenian-Tatar clashes) (Paris: Typographic Franco-Caucasienne, 1933); Tadeusz Swietochowski, *Russian Azerbaijan, 1905–1920: The Shaping of National Identity in a Muslim Community* (London: Cambridge University Press, 1985), pp. 38–46.

11. On the "March Days" and the Baku Commune, see Ronald G. Suny, *The Baku Commune, 1917–1918: Class and Nationality in the Russian Revolution* (Princeton: Princeton University Press, 1972); Swietochowski, *Russian Azerbaijan*, pp. 112–19; Pipes, *Formation of the Soviet Union*, pp. 199–201.

12. *General Andranik: Haikakan Arandzin Harvadsogh Zoramase* (General Andranik: The Armenian Special Striking Division), transcribed by Eghishe Kadjuni (Boston: Azg, 1921), pp. 121–59; Hovak Stepanian, "Andranike Siuniats erkrum (Andranik in the Land of Siunik), *Hairenik Amsagir*, vol. 4 (March 1936), pp. 52–62; United States National Archives, Record Group 84, Tiflis Consulate, 1919, pt. 4, file 710 and file 801.

13. For revealing details on this subject, see Archives of the Armenian Revolutionary Federation (Dashnaktsutiun), file 1649: H.H.D. Gharabagh, Watertown, MA. See also Arsen Mikayelian, "Gharabaghi verdjin depkere" (The recent events in Karabagh), *Hairenik Amsagir*, vol. 1 (October 1923), pp. 118–27; G.A. Hovhannisian, *Sovetakan ishkhanutian hastatume Lernayin Gharabaghum* (Erevan: Erevan State University, 1971), pp. 149–80.

14. For a résumé of the Armenian and Azerbaijani arguments, see, for example, Richard G. Hovannisian, "Nationalist Ferment in Armenia," *Freedom at Issue*, no. 105 (November/December 1988), pp. 29–35; Igrar Aliyev, *Dagly Garabag: Tarikh, Faktlar, Hadisälär* (Mountainous Karabagh: History, facts, events) (Baku: Azerbaijan SSR Academy of Sciences, 1989); Iu.F. Barsegov, *Pravo na samoopredelenie-osnova demokraticheskogo resheniia mezhnatsional'nykh problem: K probleme Nagornogo Karabakha* (Erevan: Hayastan, 1989).

15. For a detailed study of this controversy, see the forthcoming publication of Stephan S. Astourian, "In Search of Their Forefathers: National Identity and the Historiography and Politics of Armenian and Azerbaijani Ethnogeneses," in *The Disunion of the Soviet Union*, ed. Donald V. Schwartz (Toronto: University of Toronto Center for Russian and East European Studies, 1994). Armenian nationalist writers such as Rafayel Ishkhanian and Levon Miridjanian have challenged previous Armenian scholarship showing that the Indo-European Armenians prob-

ably migrated onto the Armenian Plateau between the second and first millennia B.C. They reject the existence of a pre-Armenian Urartian civilization and put forward the arguments of non-Armenian linguists and archaeologists positing the theory that Asia Minor was the original home of the Indo-European peoples and that therefore the Armenians are indigenous to the region and not migrants, however early. See, for example, Rafayel Ishkhanian, *Hai zhoghovrdi tsagman ev hnaguin patmutian hartser* (Question relating to the origins and ancient history of the Armenian people) (Erevan: Hayastan, 1988). For a response and refutation by leading members of the Armenian Academy of Sciences, see B.N. Arakelian, G.B. Jahukian, and G.Kh. Sargsian, *Urartu-Hayastan* (Urartu-Armenia) (Erevan, Armenian SSR Academy of Sciences, 1988).

16. *Azerbaidzhan* (Baku), 28 August 1919; *Hayastani Hanrapetutiun, 1919 tt.* (Republic of Armenia, 1919), file 9/9, and *H.H. Vrastani Divanagitakan Nerkayutstschutiun ev Vrastani Karavarutiun, 1919–1920: Teghakatu, 1919* (Republic of Armenia Diplomatic Mission in Georgia and the Government of Georgia, 1919–1920: Bulletins, 1919); file 66a/3, Archives of the Republic of Armenia Delegation to the Paris Peace Conference, Watertown, MA. "Provisional Accord Between the Armenians of Karabagh and the Government of Azerbaijan," *Eastern Europe*, vol. 1 (16 October 1919), pp. 158–60.

17. Armenian Revolutionary Federation Archives, file 1649; Mikayelian, "Gharabaghi verdjin depkere," vol. 1 (1923), June, pp. 110–22; July, pp. 117–19; September, pp. 110–19; October, pp. 118–24; Hovhannisian, *Sovetakan ishkhanutian hastatume*, pp. 131–45.

18. Details of these operations are included in Hovannisian, *Republic of Armenia*, vol. 3, chap. 7 (University of California Press, forthcoming).

19. State Historical Archives of Armenia (Erevan), fund 200, list 1, file 628, pp. 3–12, and fund 200, list 2, file 12, pp. 29–34. See also Rem Kazandjian, "K voprosu o tak nazyvaemom mirnom dogovore mezhdu RSFSR i Dashnakskoi Armenii ot 28 oktiabria 1920 g., *Vestnik obshchestvennykh nauk* (November 1982), pp. 38–46.

20. *Pravda* (Moscow), 4 December 1920; *Kommunist* (Baku), 2 and 6 December 1920; *Kommunist* (Erevan), 7 December 1920; G.K. Ordzhonikidze, *Stat'ii rechi* (Moscow: Institut Marksisma-Leninisma pri TsK KPSS, 1956), vol. 1, pp. 140–41.

21. For the terms of the Treaty of Moscow, see Ministerstvo inostrannykh del SSSR, *Dokumenty vneshnei politiki SSSR* (Moscow: Izd. Politicheskoi literatury, 1958), vol. 3, pp. 597–604; Jane Degras, ed., *Soviet Documents on Foreign Policy* (London: Oxford University Press, 1951), vol. 1, pp. 237–42.

22. For documents relevant to this subject, see Gabian and Khudaverdian, eds., *Nagornyi Karabakh*, pp. 609–20, 622–70.

23. English translations of several of the petitions are in *The Karabagh File: Documents and Facts on the Question of Mountainous Karabagh* (Cambridge, MA, and Toronto: Zoryan Institute, 1988), pp. 42–52.

24. For descriptions and analyses of the denial of the Armenian genocide, see, for example, Marjorie Housepian Dobkin, "What Genocide? What Holocaust? News from Turkey, 1915–1923;" Richard G. Hovannisian, "The Armenian Genocide and Patterns of Denial;" and Vigen Guroian, "Collective Responsibility and Official Excuse Making," all in *The Armenian Genocide in Perspective*, ed. Rich-

ard G. Hovannisian (New Brunswick, NJ, and Oxford: Transaction Books, 1986). See also Roger W. Smith, "The Armenian Genocide: Memory, Politics, and the Future;" Clive Foss, "The Turkish View of Armenian History: A Vanishing Nation;" and Vahakn N. Dadrian, "Ottoman Archives and the Denial of the Armenian Genocide," all in Hovannisian, ed., *Armenian Genocide: History, Politics, Ethics*.

25. On the massacres of Armenians in the 1890s, see, for example, Christopher Walker, *Armenia: Survival of a Nation* (New York: St. Martin's Press, 1980), pp. 85–176.

26. On the Treaty of Lausanne and its antecedents, see Levon Marashlian,"The Armenian Question from Sèvres to Lausanne" (Ph.D. diss., University of California, Los Angeles, 1992). Records of the negotiations are in Great Britain, Foreign Office, cmd. 1814, Turkey no. 1, 1923, *Near Eastern Affairs: Records of the Proceedings and Draft Terms of Peace* (London: His Majesty's Stationery Office, 1923).

27. For the text of the Treaty of Kars, see Degras, ed., *Soviet Documents*, vol. 1, pp. 237–42; Ministerstvo ino stranykh del, *Dokumenty vneshnei politiki SSSR*, vol. 3, pp. 597–604.

28. In a report from Ankara on 21 June 1993, correspondent Amberin Zaman wrote, "Turkey has 154 officers in Azerbaijan, to help the Azeri army in its war over Nagorno Karabagh. Ankara has been quietly supplying the Azeris with light weaponry. A further 300 Turkish commandos dispatched by the 'Grey Wolves' and paid by the Turkish intelligence agency MIT are also fighting on the side of the Azeris, Turkish officials confirmed." See *Daily Telegraph*, 21 June 1993, International Section, p. 8. On the Turkish-Azerbaijani pact on military cooperation, see *Krasnaia zvezda* (Moscow), 27 April 1993, p. 3, stating: "Under a recently signed agreement, it [Turkey] has undertaken to supply light and heavy weapons to Azerbaijan and train Azeri servicemen." See Russica Information Inc., *Russian Press Digest*, 27 April 1993. See also British Broadcasting Corporation, *Summary of World Broadcasts*, 23 April 1993, pt. 4, Turkey; *Megapolis-Continent*, no. 16, p. 8; *Russian Press Digest*, 22 April 1993, report of Mekhman Gafarly.

29. On the tripartite agreement and the reactions of the involved parties, see *Christian Science Monitor*, 13 May 1993, The World, p. 1; British Broadcasting Corporation, *Summary of World Broadcasts*, 8, 12, 13 May 1993, pt. 1, The USSR; Reuter Library Report, 12, 14 May 1993; *Armenian Weekly* (Watertown, MA), 29 May, 5, 12, 19, 26 June 1993; *Armenian Mirror-Spectator* (Watertown, MA), 15 May, 5, 12, 26 June 1993; *The Armenian Reporter* (New York), 15, 22, 29 May, 5, 26 June 1993.

30. See David M. Lang, *The Last Years of the Georgian Monarchy, 1658–1832* (New York: Columbia University Press, 1957); idem, *A Modern History of Soviet Georgia* (New York: Grove Press, 1962); W.E.D. Allen, *A History of the Georgian People*, new ed. (New York: Barnes and Noble, 1971); Ronald G. Suny, *The Making of the Georgian Nation* (Bloomington: Indiana University Press; Stanford: Hoover Institution, 1988).

31. Kazemzadeh, *Struggle for Transcaucasia*, pp. 79–127.

32. M. Varandian, *Le conflit arméno-géorgien et la guerre du Caucase* (Paris: M. Flinikowski, 1919); *Dokumenty i materialy po vneshnei politike Zakavkaz'ia i Gruzii* (Tiflis: Tipografiia pravitelstva Gruzinskoi respubliki, 1919), pp. 428–81

passim; Hovannisian, *Republic of Armenia*, vol. 1, pp. 93–125; Kazemzadeh, *Struggle for Transcaucasia*, pp. 174–83.

33. On the question of Batum, see Hovannisian, *Republic of Armenia*, vol. 3, chap. 9.

34. Matossian, *Impact of Soviet Policies*, pp. 117–32.

35. See Archives of the Republic of Armenia Delegation to the Paris Peace Conference, files 79–99.

36. Interfax News Agency, 16 April 1993; *Azg* (Erevan), 13, 15, 19 April 1993.

37. On the Armenian experience under Russian imperial rule, see Vartan Gregorian, "The Impact of Russia on the Armenians and Armenia," in *Russia and Asia*, ed. Wayne S. Vucinich (Stanford: Stanford University Press, 1972), pp. 167–218; Richard G. Hovannisian, "Russian Armenia: A Century of Tsarist Rule," *Jahrbücher für Geschicte Osteuropas*, vol. 19, no. 1 (March 1971), pp. 31–48.

38. Richard G. Hovannisian, "The Allies and Armenia, 1915–18," *Journal of Contemporary History*, vol. 3 (January 1968), pp. 155–66.

39. Pipes, *Formation of the Soviet Union*, p. 233.

40. Great Britain, Parliamentary Debates, House of Commons, 5th series, C (1917), col. 2220. See also Hovannisian, "The Allies and Armenia," p. 148.

41. See André Mandelstam, *La Société des Nations et les Puissances devant le problème arménien* (Paris: A. Pedone, 1925); Akaby Nassibian, *Britain and the Armenian Question, 1915–1923* (London and Sydney: Croom Helm; New York: St. Martin's Press, 1984), pp. 180–206 passim.

12

Azerbaijan

A Borderland at the Crossroads of History

Tadeusz Swietochowski

This chapter deals with the interrelation of the legacies of history and the concerns of present-day foreign policy in a nation emerging from the Soviet Union's downfall, a country that by virtue of its location is a borderland in geographical as well as ethnic and cultural terms.

Azerbaijan is the land populated today by the Azeri Turks, the people who inhabit in a solid mass the region stretching from the northeastern slopes of the Caucasus Mountain range along the Caspian Sea to the Iranian plateau. The borders of Azerbaijan as a political or administrative unit have changed throughout history. Its northern part, on the left bank of the Araxes River, had been known by various names—Caucasian Albania in the pre-Islamic period and, subsequently, Arran.

From the time of ancient Media and the Achaemenian kingdom, Azerbaijan shared its history with Iran. The country maintained its Iranian ethnolinguistic character after the Arab conquest in the mid-seventh century and the subsequent conversion to Islam, when it was a separate province under an early Islamic caliphate. Only in the eleventh century, with the influx of the Oghuz Turkic tribes under the Seljuk dynasty, did Azerbaijan acquire a significant proportion of Turkic-speaking inhabitants. The original population began to be fused with the immigrants, and gradually the Persian language was replaced by a Turkic dialect that evolved into a distinct Azeri Turkish language. As a literary idiom Azeri came to be used as far as Baghdad and parts of Anatolia, reaching the first period of its flourishing in the fifteenth and sixteenth centuries in the works of such outstanding poets as Nasimi, Fizuli, and Khatai.[1]

The process of the Turkification of Azerbaijan was long and complex, sustained by successive waves of incoming nomads from Central Asia. At the end of the fifteenth century, Azerbaijan became the power base of a native dynasty, the Safavids, which through conquests and vigorous policies of centralization built a new Iranian kingdom. Shah Ismail I (Khatai, 1501–25), whose capital was Tabriz, made the Shi'a branch of Islam the official religion in his empire, an act that set the Azeris firmly apart from the Ottoman Turks. Under the early Safavids, Azerbaijan was frequently the battleground in the wars between Iran and Sunni Turkey, and because of the threat of Ottoman incursions, the capital was moved from Tabriz to Qazvin and then to Isfahan. Safavid rule, which gradually lost its Azeri character, lasted for more two centuries, to be followed by a period of generally weak central power in the second half of the eighteenth century. These circumstances made possible the emergence of local centers of power in Azerbaijan in the form of khanates (principalities) that were independent or virtually so, inasmuch as some maintained tenuous links to Iran's weak Zand dynasty. The unfolding period of emancipation from the central authority was marked by political fragmentation and its corollary, internecine conflicts among the khanates, whose number included the following: Karabagh, Sheki, Shirvan, Baku, Ganja, Erevan, Nakhichevan, Derbent, Kuba, and Talysh in the northern part of Azerbaijan and Tabriz, Urumi, Ardabil, Khoi, Maku, Karadagh, and Margin in the south.[2]

Azerbaijan lacked a tradition of unity within an autochthonous statehood, and under the conditions of the period, such a statehood could emerge only through the expansion of one of the khanates at the cost of others. Soviet historians noticed such a possibility in the conquest of the khan of Kuba, Fath'ali, during the 1780s: but whatever his ambitions, they were cut short by the threat coming from the Russian forces deployed in the Caucasus Mountains. Russia's interest in the land beyond the Caucasus range was long-standing, and its roots were diverse. There was the lure of lucrative trade with Iran and Asiatic Turkey; the desire for local raw materials, notably silk, cotton, and copper; and the drive for colonization of the sparsely populated regions. But the overriding attraction was the strategic value of the Transcaucasian isthmus as the corridor for deep penetration into Iran and the flanking position on the eastern frontier of Turkey.

Early in the nineteenth century Russia became the first European power to establish direct rule over a part of the Middle East, Transcaucasia, much ahead of the British occupation of Egypt (1882) and the French mandate over Syria and Lebanon (1920). Typically for a colonial conquest, the frontiers of the territories seized from Iran in the peace settlements of Gulistan (1813) and Turkmanchai (1828) were drawn arbitrarily, with the primary aim to suit the strategic needs of Russia. While all Georgians passed under Russian rule following the Gulistan treaty, the Turkmanchai treaty split the Azeri-speaking Muslim population into two parts, a larger part remaining with Iran. Historians see this treaty as a turning point in the history of the Azeri people, inasmuch as those inhabiting the territory north of the frontier river of Araxes found themselves under the rule of a European power.[3] This division of one people and land planted the seeds for the rise of what would become known as the Azerbaijani question, but during half a century following the conquest, changes were limited mainly to administrative reforms. Here was a case of one preindustrial society conquering another, with little initial impact on the structures of economy and society.

Only with the advent of the industrial age, which centered on oil extraction in Baku and which made the city and its environs one of the world's major oil-producing regions before the end of the century, did northern Azerbaijan enter a path of historical development divergent from the south.[4] Even so, the parting of ways was to an extent offset by the forging of new links, and the ties between the two Azerbaijans now grew stronger than before, with mass migration of laborers from the south to the Baku oil belt, the expansion of trade across the border, and the growth of steamship transportation on the Caspian Sea. The Baku Muslim entrepreneurs, who were losing their positions at home to their Armenian competitors, concentrated on enmeshing the economies of the two Azerbaijans. Their efforts had the blessing of the tsarist regime, whose long-range policy was to put all of northern Iran into the Russian sphere of influence.

The age of revolution, which opened with the year 1905 in Russia, to be followed the next year by the constitutional crisis in Iran, heralded a political awakening in Azerbaijan that produced a new kind of link: cooperation between those who opposed the established order on both sides of the Araxes line. In northern Azerbaijan, the feelings of identification with the Iranian revolution, unfolding in a more congenial environment, were stronger than identification with the Russian revolution. In the south, the Armenian-Muslim violence that broke out in 1905 in Transcaucasia awoke a sense of solidarity with the northern Azeris, the more so that among the victims of the mutual massacres were immigrants from Tabriz province.

Tabriz was a major center of the Iranian revolution, a vibrant commercial city with close ties to Russia and Turkey. Its proximity to the revolutionized Transcaucasia accounted in large measure for the city's role in the Iranian upheaval. Contacts between the two Azerbaijans were extensive, ranging from the supportive posture of the Baku press, to organizing the immigrants politically, to sending armed volunteers to Tabriz after the failure of the Russian revolution.[5] The period of the revolutions on both sides of the Araxes was the high point of the closeness of the divided parts of Azerbaijan. Symbolic of the political cooperation across the borders was Mammad Amin Rasulzada, one of the founders of the social-democratic organization Himmat (Endeavor) in Baku, who subsequently became a prominent figure of the Iranian revolution and ended up the foremost Azeri nationalist leader north of the Araxes and the head of the Musavat (Equality) Party.

While in many ways the two parts of Azerbaijan grew interdependent in the wake of the Russian conquest, in other respects they drifted apart. Among the by-products of Russian rule in the north was a measure of social and cultural change that affected the Azeri community. These changes came with the rise of the intelligentsia, a social force as much as a cultural phenomenon that emerged from the contact between two civilizations, the traditional Islamic and the comparatively modern European, as represented by Russia. In remarkable disproportion to its numbers, the intelligentsia was destined to have an increasingly greater impact on the course of Azerbaijani history. The impact began with the rise of modern communications—the theater and press; the achievements of the founder of modern Azeri literature, Mirza Fathali Akhundzada; and Hasan bay Zarbadi, the publisher of the first Azeri-language newspaper, *Akinchi (Plowman)*. Culturally the thrust of the transformations north of the Araxes marked the process of emancipation from the domination of the Persian literary language and the revival of the native idiom, Turki. The revival was promoted by the populist-minded intelligentsia and welcomed by the Sunni minority, which felt itself closer to Turkey than to Iran, and it met with tolerance by the tsarist authorities inasmuch as it weakened the Azeris' gravita-

tion toward Iran. On the other hand, it had no support from the Ottoman state under Sultan Abdulhamid II (1876–1909), who abhorred any
manifestation of national identities in general and Turkic in particular.[6]
Only with the third revolution in as many years, the 1908 Young
Turk coup in Istanbul, did the Turkic cultural and literary revival turn
to a new political orientation in Azerbaijan. Unlike the Abdulhamidian
regime, the new ruling group on the Bosporus took a strong interest in
the Turkic-speaking peoples across the Ottoman borders. For their
part, the Azeri intellectuals began to flock to Istanbul, and two of their
luminaries, Ahmad Aghaoghlu and Ali Huseynzada, gained positions
of influence in the Young Turk regime. With the spread of such interrelated movements as Turkism, the promotion of Turkic identity; Pan-
Turkism, the call for cooperation and solidarity of Turkic peoples;
Turanism, the vision of one state uniting Turkic peoples; or Oghusianism, a more realistic proposition for the unity of the peoples linguistically closest to the Ottoman Turks—notably the Azeris and
Turkmens—Azerbaijan found itself in the triple configuration of Russia, Turkey, and Iran. Its corollary was the rise of the specifically
Azerbaijani dilemma: historical and religious bonds to Iran and ethnic,
linguistic, intellectual, and increasingly political links with Turkey.
     World War I saw a strong upsurge of sympathies for Turkey in both
parts of Azerbaijan, as the Ottoman forces appeared as the potential
liberators from Russian rule or occupation, but only in the summer of
1918 did the civil war in Russia make possible the Ottoman entry into
Transcaucasia as well as northern Iran. In northern Azerbaijan, where
an independent democratic republic had just been proclaimed, the Ottomans indicated their preference to see this region eventually united
with Turkey, a prospect that the elite of the newly born state did not
relish. In the southern part, the Ottomans gave encouragement to those
who were inclined toward separatism from Iran. On closer examina-
tion, the Ottoman-Azerbaijani policy in these last months of the Great
War appears to reflect the mutually exclusive ideas of Turanism and
Pan-Islamism, a program of unity of all Islamic peoples. It was not a
crystallized policy, nor did the Ottoman presence in the two
Azerbaijans last long enough to leave a profound impact.[7]
     Under the period of full independence that followed the withdrawal
of the Ottoman forces in the fall of 1918, the foreign policy of the
Democratic Republic feverishly searched for security from the threat
of Russia. White and Red. In this quest, the most promising avenue for

the Baku regime seemed to be a rapprochement with Iran, which had raised claims in the Versailles Conference to the territories lost to Russia a century before. For the Democratic Republic, a special stimulus was the desire to slip under the shield of British protection, at that time the dominant power in Iran. An agreement of 1 November 1919 provided for a "political-economic link in the form of confederation, whose principles, form, and the means of implementation will be elaborated and discussed jointly by the Persian and Azerbaijani governments and will be submitted for approval by the parliaments of both countries."[8] The scheme, which promised the additional advantage of bringing Baku closer to Tabriz, failed when the Iranian Majlis (parliament) refused to ratify the August 1919 agreement with Britain that would turn Iran into a virtual dependency. This setback did not stop the growth of contacts between the Democratic Republic and its southern neighbor, leading to the Iranian-Azerbaijani treaty of friendship and commerce of March 1920.

By contrast, the relations with the Turkish nationalist movement, led by Mustafa Kemal and based in central and eastern Anatolia, were uneasy, an indication of the complexity of the links between the two ethnic cousins. In a reversal of the Young Turks' expansionist Turanism, the Kemalists were concerned principally with Anatolian-based Turkey proper, and with regard to Azerbaijan they favored the replacement of the Democratic Republic with a regime friendly to the Bolsheviks that would turn the country into a bridge between Soviet Russia and nationalist Turkey struggling against imperialism. Under the new foreign policy set by Kemal, Turkey absented itself largely, though never fully, from an active involvement in the problems of the Turkic peoples outside its borders.

The ruling elite of the Democratic Republic, having exhausted diplomatic means for salvaging independence, did not give serious consideration to the defense against the approaching Red Army invasion. Rather, this invasion was viewed in Baku as a part of the natural process of ingathering, the inevitable restitution of the Russian-ruled multinational empire after its time of troubles. "Baku is the very life of Soviet Russia," the Azeri Communist leader Nariman Narimanov reminded his compatriots, alluding to the importance of the oil resources.[9]

All the same, the Baku regime was anxious to derive the best deal from what appeared to be a historical inevitability. The deal was part of the unwritten contract by which national consolidation continued after the Soviet military takeover of Azerbaijan in 1920, with such policies as *korenizatsiia* (indigenization) of the civil service, the spread of education in the Azeri language, and the growth of native cultural institutions. These all offered a sharp contrast to the forceful policies of assimilation in southern Azerbaijan under the new Pahlavi dynasty. These policies also led to a curtailment of contacts across the Araxes border.

The native cultural and educational expansion in the north was enhanced by the 1926 Latinization of the alphabet, part of the policy of breaking with the Islamic past, which had its parallel in the secularization process in Kemalist Turkey. The alphabet reform further weakened the ties to the south and was in step with the promotion of a Soviet Azerbaijani national identity distinct from Iran and Turkey. The next decade, in the midst of Stalin's purges, saw the coming of Azerbaijanism, a particularistic, ethnically based, and strictly secular nationalism, hostile to any broader vision such as Pan-Turkism, Pan-Islamism, or the closeness of the two Azerbaijans. Characteristically, among the countless victims of the Stalinist purges in the mid-1930s was an outstanding group guilty of *Narimanovshchina* (derived from Narimanov's name), those who had in the past promoted cooperation between Azerbaijan and the revolutionary and national movements in neighboring Muslim countries, most notably Iran.

In tune with the new spirit of the time, the adjective referring to the country's language and its inhabitants became the rigorously observed term "Azerbaijani" rather than "Turkic" *(Tiurskii)*. Stalinist-imposed Azerbaijanism went hand in hand with the effort at assimilation with Russian language and culture, and as the Latin alphabet made reading Turkish too easy and Russian too difficult, another reform changed the script from Latin to Cyrillic as of 1940.[10]

* * *

As Kemalist Turkey washed its hands of the problem of Azerbaijan, and Pahlavi Iran intensified its Persianization drive, the anti-Soviet émigrés cultivated an alternative vision of the future in the form of Transcaucasian federalism, another political tradition that kept reappearing at various junctures of history. The program of federalism dated back to the period of the 1905 revolution, and it had been put to the test in the abortive experiment of a unified state of Georgians, Armenians, and Azeris, which had existed for barely four weeks in the spring of 1918. Yet, as Transcaucasian federalism had failed at that time because of the Azeri-Armenian animosities, and even more because of Ottoman and German pressures, so in the post-1920 period of the nationalist leaders' exile the idea remained frustrated by the Armenians' refusal to be involved in any political action that would be inherently directed against Russia in any guise. The Armenian émigrés continued to hold this position until 1940.[11] Meanwhile, even the Soviets had given their recognition to the merits of regional cooperation and unity by creating their version of the Transcaucasian Federation (Zakfederatsiia), in existence from 1922 to 1936. The Zakfederatsiia was abolished at the high point of Stalin's rule, when the Soviet republics were banned from having horizontal links among themselves, having instead to substitute them with vertical links to the center.

Soviet Azerbaijani nationalism was intended to be thoroughly isolationist, but the vagaries of history revealed that it possessed also an expansionist edge, when the Soviet forces occupied northern Iran in 1941. The Soviet military presence led to the resurgence of Pan-Azerbaijani sentiments—the desire for unity or closeness of the two parts of the divided country. Under the Soviet occupation, the revival of the native literary language, which had largely been supplanted by Persian, was encouraged with the help of intellectuals brought in from north of the Araxes. Some of them might have now seen a prospect for national unification through the agency of the Red Army, on the pattern of the recent unification of Ukraine and Belarus.[12]

In November 1945, with Soviet backing, the autonomous government of Azerbaijan took office in Tabriz under Sayyid Jafar Pishevari, the leader of the Azerbaijani Democratic Party, a man with a long record of Communist activities. There followed an impressive growth of schools, cultural institutions, and publications in the native language, and speculations were rife about the two Azerbaijans drawing together under the Soviet aegis. As it turned out, the issue of southern Azerbaijan was one of the opening salvos of the Cold War, and largely under the pressure of the Western powers, the Red Army withdrew beyond the Araxes. With the autonomist regime of Pishevari left to fend for itself, the central government of Iran repossessed southern Azerbaijan by the end of 1946.[13] Manifestations of Pan-Azerbaijani feelings north of the Araxes were encouraged until the early 1950s and then banned almost entirely, as Moscow chose not to cause difficulties for the Iranian government in its oil nationalization crisis. For a brief time the episode of autonomous southern Azerbaijan was rediscovered under Khrushchev's thaw, along with other issues of the recent past, but it was again singled out for oblivion. This time the reason was the growing friendship of the two declining empires, Pahlavi Iran and the USSR, one of the hallmarks of the long period of stagnation, as the Brezhnev rule would come to be described.

Stagnation in general continued during the tenure of Brezhnev's successors Yurii Andropov and Konstantin Chernenko, although in Azerbaijan the challenge to the status quo came earlier than in other parts of the USSR, through the reverberations of the 1978–79 Khomeini revolution on the other side of the Araxes. As in the past, a major center of the revolutionary ferment in Iran was Tabriz with its tradition of regional identity.

The Soviet view of this clergy-led revolution was that by its nature it would be a transitory phenomenon, a stepping-stone to further upheavals in Iran, no longer driven by puritanical fervor but rather by the interplay of ethnic, social, and economic grievances. These expectations failed to materialize, and instead tension began to develop between Iran and the Soviet Union, at the root of which were Iran's sense of strategic encirclement with the war in Afghanistan and the aggression from Iraq.

If Tabriz was the symbol of Islam triumphant, Baku wished to remain the symbol of Azerbaijani identity. Reacting to the friction with Iran, the Soviet choice was to play the nationality card. Gaidar Aliev, the head of the Communist Party of Azerbaijan, became the foremost spokesman for these tactics. In his speeches he emphasized that the Soviet regime had promoted the national aspirations of Muslim peoples from its first day. Going a step further, in 1981 he encouraged Azeri writers in "strengthening literary links with southern Azerbaijan, developing broad contacts in all sectors of cultural and intellectual creativity."[14] He repeated the call for a rapprochement between north and south on other occasions, and reportedly even told foreign diplomats of his hope to see the two Azerbaijans reunited.

The two parts of Azerbaijan were now frequently referred to as one fatherland. The frontier dividing one people, an "open wound," was destined to vanish, even though it was never said through what means. The Turkmanchai Treaty acquired an ugly connotation as a monument of historical injustice.

Revived Soviet Pan-Azerbaijani agitation was still kept out of the daily newspapers, especially those in Russian, an indication of the absence of the highest degree of official imprimatur. Moscow was playing an intricate game against Tehran and was not willing to commit itself to any long-term course of action. Meanwhile, in Baku, as if through an unspoken agreement between rulers and ruled, the "one Azerbaijan" campaign served as a substitute for the dissident movements that were germinating in the neighboring republics of Georgia and Armenia. For their part, those who represented the emerging phenomenon of an independent public opinion welcomed this less than full encouragement for a vision of unity across the border. Whatever the permissible measure for this vision, it was expected to be of benefit to Azeri national self-assertion, and the very articulation of the idea of "one Azerbaijan" would be a mutual reinforcement of Azeri identity in the face of both Persianization and Russification.

With Gorbachev's perestroika, Moscow abruptly called off the "one Azerbaijan" campaign as an unnecessary irritant in relations with Iran. As in the past, depending on the state of these relations, the "on" or "off" signals would be flashed with no regard to the sensibilities of the Azeris.

The onset of perestroika did not bring the rapid rise of a national movement in Azerbaijan. Rather, its birth came with the violent outbreak of the Nagorno-Karabagh dispute in February 1988, following demands for the incorporation of this Armenian-populated enclave in Azerbaijan into the Armenian Soviet Republic. "Ethnic conflict or decolonization crisis?" a historian of this dispute put the question.[15]

Azerbaijan, which had lagged behind other parts of the USSR in developing a dissident movement, now experienced a political awakening comparable to that of 1905, with the same process of social mobilization around intercommunal strife. In turn, the strife revealed the weakness of the Communist Party as the spokesman for national interests, and in the new spirit of the time, independent publications, action committees, and political association began to mushroom. With the floodgates of glasnost thrown open, a wide array of subjects until recently unmentionable became topics of discussion in the press, official as well as underground. Still, the catalogue of rediscovered themes in the Azeri media of the period was at first more remarkable for what it omitted than for what it included; the most cautiously handled topic was relations between the two Azerbaijans. "There is not a country about which we know less than the southern part of our fatherland," observed a samizdat publication, alluding to official restraints as well as self-censorship.[16] Along with such themes as idealization of the 1918–20 independent republic and the Musavat Party, presentation of Stalinist crimes in Azerbaijan, reviving memories of the public figures of the past—especially—and the opponents of Communism, the alphabet reforms' harmful effect on the continuity of the national culture, voices were increasingly raised in warning of the special dangers inherent in colonialism—linguistic and cultural assimilation and the depletion of natural resources, particularly oil, which precluded Azerbaijan's joining the ranks of prosperous Middle Eastern nations.

With the Nagorno-Karabagh conflict generating echoes in distant places, a new dimension of the issue began to emerge in Azeri eyes. It was apparent that even though the Armenian side had initiated the confrontation, the outside world for the most part showed an anti-Azeri disposition. This seemingly common front of those with a Christian background included the central government in Moscow and the dissidents in the Soviet republics as well as the Western media, which in the Azeris' view victimized them without giving so much as perfunctory consideration to their standpoint.

As resentment with Christian-European attitudes grew, it reinforced fears of a conservative-Islamic backlash, which a samizdat author described as follows:

> The Azerbaijani nation, humiliated in its national feelings, could turn sharply toward the Muslim religion. . . . This in turn will generate a favorable climate for spreading the ideas of the "Islamic revolution". . . . As a natural reaction, the aspiration of the Azerbaijanis to unite with their brothers living in Armenia, in other republics, and in Iran (Azerbaijan) will be developed and strengthened.[17]

It took almost a year for the main opposition group, the People's Front of Azerbaijan (PFA), to coalesce into the chief political force in the country.[18] Its program, adopted in June 1989, though notable for cautious formulations, offered the most comprehensive statement of Azerbaijani aspirations at the time of communism's downfall. Among other issues, it addressed itself to the relationship with the other Azerbaijan across the border as well as to the cultural-historical legacy of the country.

While recognizing the indisputable nature of the frontier between the USSR and Iran, the People's Front supports the restoration of the ethnic unity of Azerbaijanis living on both sides of the border. The Azerbaijani people should be recognized as a united whole. Economic, cultural, and social ties between our divided nations should be restored. . . . The borders of Azerbaijan should be contact points, not barriers. They should no longer be points of estrangement but of cooperation. Border zones should be abolished. . . . The PFA supports the abolition of all political barriers to the development of cultural links with South Azerbaijan.[19]

Likewise, the program marked an attitude toward Islam as well as the Muslim world that was different not only from Soviet views but also from the tradition of native secularism:

The People's Front of Azerbaijan supports the inalienable observance of one of the most basic human rights—the right to freedom of conscience. It is essential that religious beliefs and traditions that are respected by billions of people throughout the world no longer be subjected to the ignorant attacks of the philistines. The PFA supports decisive steps toward the development of understanding and cooperation with the world of Islam.[20]

Although in the fall of 1989 the Front seemed poised to take power in Azerbaijan, it remained an umbrella association beset by divisions that reflected deeper cleavages within the Azeri community.

The underlying issue was typical for a Muslim society in transition anywhere—the rift between the modern-oriented and the traditionalist-minded elements. In the case of Azerbaijan, there was an age-old and never-overcome split between the intelligentsia, the urban population, and the better-educated on one side and the bulk of the tradition-bound, mainly rural or small-town population, often Shi'ite by background, on the other. The two-nations-within-one syndrome reared its head again at a historical turning point, and the very suggestion of Azerbaijani unity in the future was additionally divisive. While the traditionalist-Islamic elements within the Front showed themselves favorable to a rapprochement with the south as a part of Iran, the secular intelligentsia contemplated with horror the possibility, however remote, of Azerbaijan submerged in Iran and ruled by fanatic mullahs.

The Front in effect split into three wings, described as liberal, national-liberation, and Islamic-fundamentalist. Some activists could not find a place for themselves in any of the wings and left the ranks of the PFA. The Islamic wing also drifted apart, and what remained of the Front was, in the words of a witness to the events, "a part of the liberal wing united with the national-liberation wing on the basis of the national-democratic platform."[21]

Against this background the January crisis of 1990 began with the crowds breaking border installations along the Araxes. The images of joyful people clipping the barbed wire evoked the recent scenes of razing the Berlin Wall. At once differences in the perception of what was taking place at the border surfaced, corresponding to the divisions in the Front and, by extension, to foreign policy orientation.

The radical elements saw the opening of the frontier as an effect of popular upheaval, a step in the direction of Azerbaijani unity. Likewise, a group of academicians felt inspired to send an address to the Politburo and the Presidium of the USSR, in which the division of Azerbaijan was compared to that of Korea or Vietnam in the past. "Azerbaijan was artificially split into two parts after the Russo-Iranian wars of the early nineteenth century, which resulted in the tragic Turkmanchai Treaty of 1828." The address called for the "essential relaxation of the frontier regime between the two parts of Azerbaijan."[22]

As for the moderates among the Front's leaders, they showed little enthusiasm for the border demonstrations, fearing that these might be seen as an attempt to change the frontier of the USSR to the benefit of Iran. There arose among them a special sensitivity about accusations of fundamentalism, which could serve as a device to discredit the Azeri national movement in the eyes of Soviet and Western opinion. To counteract the thrust of such allegations, some of the moderates in the PFA leadership would go as far as to question the survival of Islam in the country: "In the strictest sense, there are no Muslims in Azerbaijan. Most Azeris do not even know what's inside the Quran. Religion has been so profoundly suppressed in our republic that it has been nearly forgotten," wrote the future foreign minister Tofiq Gasymov in a Western press publication.[23]

There were other strains in the unfolding drama, and these were quick to surface. Two weeks after the border demonstrations, on 13 January 1990, came the sudden eruption of ethnic violence in Baku when mobs attacked the residences of local Armenians. The accompanying circumstances were such as to reinforce the suspicions of

Moscow's involvement, which in light of the experience of the past would have been aroused in any case. Yet it was also a measure of the ineffectiveness of the Front that it was unable to prevent the violence. The military intervention ordered by Moscow came after the surviving Armenians had already left Baku, but when the authority of the Soviet regime seemed to have collapsed.[24]

In the West, the name "Azerbaijan" became for a few days a household word. The tone of the media reports that came from Moscow-stationed correspondents or Moscow-supplied information tended to be unfriendly to the Azeris, as to those who were about to begin a new round of Armenian massacres.[25] In its comment on such views of the Azeris, Iranian radio asked: "Is a new age of crusades coming?"

The worldwide echoes of the Baku January Days nowhere resounded more strongly than in Iran and Turkey. There were some striking similarities in both countries' reactions to the Azerbaijani crisis and also remarkable differences in perception of the events. The first instinct of the two governments was to keep a distance from the domestic upheaval of their Soviet neighbor. Turkish President Turgut Özal declared offhand that the Azeris "are Shi'ites, we are Sunnis," therefore more of a concern for Iran than for Turkey. He would insist, subsequently, that his remark had been misinterpreted, but he affirmed that "these are internal affairs of the Soviet Union. It is impossible for us to interfere."[26] Özal's counterpart in Iran, Hashemi Rafsanjani, in the words of a newspaper commentary, "has been remarkably silent on the issue, and it was rare for him to be silent on any issue."[27] The ideological zealots in the Islamic Republic of Iran were more outspoken in their views of the Baku upheaval. Ayatollah Ahmad Jannati announced his intention to send Shi'i clerics to proselytize north of the Araxes, a task to be combined with translation of the works of Khomeini into Azeri, in the Cyrillic script. Another Ayatollah, Ali Khamenei, saw an outburst of Islamic zeal in Azerbaijan and warned that it would be "a big mistake to think that ethnic and national motives were behind this move."[28]

The Turkish reactions, by contrast, emphasized what appeared to be anathema to Iranian officials, the ethnic character of the Azerbaijani crisis. The Ankara and Istanbul press proclaimed its sympathy and moral support for the indestructible ties between Azerbaijan and Turkey rooted in a common race, language, and culture, but the same newspapers generally endorsed the cautious position of the government, indeed elaborated on the government's thinking on Azerbaijan. The possibility of reunification of the two Azerbaijans was fraught with the risk of upsetting the regional balance of power. "Turkey should not allow itself to fall into the trap arising from the situation in the Caucasus."[29] As the developments in the Soviet Union gained momentum amidst signs pointing to the disintegration of the old order, Ankara's caution and reserve appeared out of tune with the spirit of the time. By mid-1990, Özal found it appropriate to send to Baku no less prominent a Turkish representative than his wife, with the task of mending fences with the Azeri public. Her visit also marked the onset of an impressive expansion of economic and cultural exchanges between Azerbaijan and Turkey. The Treaty of Friendship and Cooperation, signed in 1991 and renewed in enlarged scope the next year, became the model for similar arrangements with the Central Asian republics of the former Soviet Union.[30] These treaties expanded the Turkish economic presence through investment credits and joint ventures, among which was the project of a pipeline from the Caspian oil fields to the Mediterranean Sea terminal in Turkey. Likewise, cultural and educational ties were further strengthened. In addition to the influx of Turkish press and books, Azerbaijan began to rebroadcast Turkish television and radio programs on a scale that began to affect colloquial Azeri. In Turkey, universities opened their doors to students from the former USSR. In an attempt to influence the debate on new alphabet reform, large quantities of Latin-character typewriters were shipped to Azerbaijan from Turkey. The Latinized Azeri alphabet, a vastly preferred option over the return to Arabic, went into effect as of January 1993, marking the fourth change of the alphabet in less than a century.

President Özal himself would become the victim of Turkish-Azeri friendliness, dropping dead in spring 1993 of exhaustion from his efforts at whipping up international support for Azerbaijan in response to the Armenian offensive in Kelbajar. By this time Azerbaijan had already become an independent state with the largest degree of Turkish presence in the history of the two countries.

* * *

On 30 August 1991, the Communist regime headed by Ayaz Mutalibov, the man who only a few days earlier had endorsed the Moscow coup, proclaimed the independence of Azerbaijan, following suit with other Soviet republics.

The declaration of independence was followed by the dissolution of the Communist Party, but the presidential election held 8 September seemed to send a business-as-usual signal. Mutalibov ran unopposed and was returned to office almost unanimously, by 98.5 percent of valid votes.[31]

Barely half a year later, by March 1992, he would be voted out of the presidency in disgrace by the parliament for mishandling the Nagorno-Karabagh conflict. Here the situation turned into ethnic cleansing of the local Azeri minority with ineffective opposition on the part of the fledgling Azerbaijani army. Once again, Nagorno-Karabagh proved to be the nemesis for an old-regime politician.

Mutalibov's successor, Abulfaz Elchibey, the head of the People's Front, became the first democratically elected president of the republic in June 1992. A typical representative of the intelligentsia and a former dissident, he was known for his closeness to Turkey, a preoccupation with Azeri compatriots in Iran, a somewhat moderate position on the conflict with Armenia, and a conciliatory attitude toward the former nomenklatura. As for relations with Russia, he wasted no time in withdrawing Azerbaijan from the Commonwealth of Independent States, one of the points of his electoral program.

Of the foreign powers, Turkey was the first to recognize Azerbaijan's independence, while the Tehran government at first objected to this haste on the part of Ankara.[32] Before long, Iran established diplomatic relations with Azerbaijan, not willing to be outdone entirely by Turkey. The two powers officially denied that they were in rivalry with each other for influence in the Muslim republics of the former USSR; they were even willing to cooperate on particular issues and projects. The most notable example of this cooperation was the Economic Cooperation Organization (ECO), a group that originally had included Turkey, Iran, and Pakistan, and in 1992 invited the six Muslim republics—Azerbaijan, Turkmenistan, Kazakhstan, Kyrgyzstan, Uzbekistan, and Tajikistan—to join.

Nonetheless, Iranian-Turkish competition has remained a fact and one of growing significance. It was also clear that of the two, Turkey had an edge not only because of its head start but even more because of the ethnic-sectarian affinities of the Soviet Muslims, among whom the overwhelming majority were Turkic-speaking and, by historic-religious background, of the Sunni branch of Islam rather than Shi'i, with the Azeris being a notable exception. Furthermore, the still-ruling group in the post-Soviet nations, the former nomenklatura, is secular-minded, and the same is true of its chief contender, the intelligentsia. "A good part of the Azerbaijani intelligentsia, answering today to the question: Does Muslim fundamentalism exist in our republic? says no with a hastiness behind which is the fear of exposing something which is indisputably ugly and shameful," commented an underground publication in the early stages of glasnost.[33] From this standpoint secular Turkey appeared incomparably closer to them than to the Islamic Republic of Iran. Among the Muslim countries Turkey has historically enjoyed the image of the most modernized Muslim nation, a bridge between their world and the advanced West, a nation that succeeded in mastering much of what Europe and America had to offer. On the Turkish side, amidst the continuous disclaimers that old-fashioned Pan-Turkism was being revived, politicians and the press spoke of the country's readiness to shoulder the responsibility for the state of affairs in the region stretching from the Adriatic Sea to the borders of China.

For Turkey, Azerbaijan is the closest nation linguistically, the linchpin of the old Oghusianism, the stepping-stone in any commercial and cultural expansion in Central Asia, a country with a solidly pro-Turkish following in the most politically articulate groups in the community. In addition, a strong tie linking the Azeris to Turkey became the expectation of its support in the struggle for Nagorno-Karabagh.

In the eyes of Iran, northern Azerbaijan is a country linked with it by countless ties of history, whose educated class only a few generations ago developed the awareness of not being Iranians. This is also a country with a two-to-one Shi'ite majority, the largest groups of co-sectarians outside of Iran, and it is among them rather than the Azeri Sunni minority that the religious revival has been most noticeable. Most Shi'a are apt to look to Iran as their spiritual homeland. Ever-growing secularism is quite likely no longer the wave of the future after the spiritual ravages of Soviet rule, and in this respect Iran may have more to offer to the Azeri Shi'a than Turkey with its commitment to secularism. But there is the opposite side of the coin, and this, more than anything else, accounts for Iran's hesitation and for the fact of lost ground in competition with Turkey. There are almost seven million comparatively well-educated Azeris north of the Araxes, most of them with a sense of nationality, even if unevenly developed in various groups of the population, with well-established cultural institutions, an active leadership, highly organized political life, and an indigenous bureaucracy—all attributes of a distinct nation. The involvement of Iran in the north would run the risk of bringing the two Azerbaijans closer to each other and thus endangering the long Persianization effort of successive Tehran regimes. Already, the ripples of the Nagorno-Karabagh conflict have produced a divisive impact in Iran by generating in southern Azerbaijan solidarity with the north, sentiments not evenly shared in the Persian part of the ruling establishment of Iran. Out of concern for its hold over Tabriz, Tehran is likely to devote special attention to its relations with Baku, all the more so in view of the continuous backing of Turkey for the northern Azerbaijani government.

For its part, Baku's relations with Tehran are likely to remain tainted by the condition of southern Azerbaijan. Concern for the identity of the southern Azeris is no longer the vehicle of Soviet expansionism, and here lies the new dimension of the issue. "As an independent state rises in the north of Azerbaijan, it will make it easier for freedom to grow in the south," stated Abulfaz Elchibey in his capacity as the People's Front leader in the closing weeks of the Soviet regime.[34] He then called for the opening of native-language schools in the south. As the head of state succeeding the discredited Mutalibov, he continued his criticism of Iranian assimilationist policies, dropping hints for the hope of drawing together the two Azerbaijans. At the same time he emphasized the special relationship with Turkey, which would extend to Azerbaijan's foreign policy.

Elchibey's most formidable challenger became Gaidar Aliev, now the head of the Nakhichevan Autonomous Republic's legislature, the virtual ruler of this Azerbaijani enclave surrounded by Armenia, Iran, and a short stretch of the border with Turkey. Aliev conducted his own foreign policy, if anything going even further in the rapprochement with Ankara, and was accused of economically enmeshing his province with Turkey. Yet in an act of careful balancing he also cultivated cordial relations with Iran. Unlike Elchibey, he came to be regarded in Tehran as an Azeri leader with whom the Islamic Republic could deal. On his visits to Iran, Aliev claimed the credit for some two hundred mosques erected recently in Nakhichevan and flaunted his new dedication to Islam, including a pilgrimage to the tomb of Imam Reza in

Mashhad.[35] The Tehran regime did not conceal its satisfaction at the multiplying signs of Aliev's political comeback, which in the end would bring him to power again in Baku. Exactly a year after his election, President Elchibey came to face the same situation that had led to the downfall of his predecessor, Mutalibov. With the fighting around Nagorno-Karabagh turning inexorably to the Armenian advantage, the blame fell on the regime in Baku. A military rebellion against Elchibey, who came to be seen as soft on the Armenians, was launched early in June 1993 in Ganja by Colonel Suret Guseinov. The president, who found himself lacking sufficient popular support, took refuge in his native village in the Nakhichevan region while Aliev was in Baku taking over the reigns of power. The coup appeared in step with the wider pattern of return to power by former Soviet leaders in most of the republics of the defunct USSR. It was also perceived as restoring some of Russia's influence, together with the power of the native nomenklatura. Even more, it was seen as a major blow to Turkey, which showed itself unable to control the causes of the coup, to prevent it from happening, and to contest the undermining of its position in Azerbaijan. In historical perspective, the coup appeared as another failed test for Pan-Turkish aspirations. By contrast with Ankara, the new turn of events was welcomed in Tehran, not only because it alleviated concerns about the pressures on southern Azerbaijan but also because it improved the prospects for a greater Iranian presence north of the Araxes.

By extension, the weakening of Turkey in Azerbaijan was also understood as a setback for Western interests. These have been centered on the exploration of oil fields under the Caspian Sea that held promise for a renaissance of the oldest national industry, sorely in need of investment capital. Multibillion-dollar agreements had already been worked out with a consortium of American, British, and Turkish companies, but significantly, one of the first steps of the post-Elchibey regime was to postpone the signing and order a review of these oil deals.

As in 1920, oil reemerged as a factor in the politics of Azerbaijan independence. Again Azerbaijan may see itself as a small country endowed with an important natural resource and bordering large powers, among which Russia casts the longest shadow. The timing of the June 1993 coup reinforced suspicions of Moscow's behind-the-scenes involvement.

* * *

Will the coup, carried out in the typical fashion of Middle Eastern politics, interrupt the process by which Azerbaijan, historically a part of the Middle East, has begun its homecoming after two centuries of Russian rule?

With the collapse of the Soviet empire, a power vacuum arose in Azerbaijan that was bound to be filled one way or another. Inasmuch as there is no prospect for the revival of the Transcaucasian Federation on the pattern of 1918—at least not until the regional ethnic conflicts run their course—the obvious candidates for filling the vacuum have been Azerbaijan's special relationship neighbors, Turkey and Iran. Both indicated their initial caution, even reluctance, and both came around to being involved in Azerbaijan.

Azerbaijan has resumed its role as an arena of rivalry between Iran and Turan, the centuries-old contests evoking poetic images from the Persian national epic *Shahnameh*. Iran and Turkey, the two chief regional powers in the Middle East, had until recently lived in the shadow of the Russian/Soviet threat, and it was again the perceived assertion of Russian influence in 1993 that momentarily put a damper on their rivalry in Azerbaijan. But even as the postcolonial resurgence of Russia's power in Baku is a possibility, the Azeris will continue to face the fundamental problem of their history, the Siyavush syndrome. A legendary figure of the *Shahnameh*, in whose veins flowed both Turkish and Iranian blood, Siyavush was a hero with a suggestion of split personality whom Rasulzada saw as a symbol for twentieth-century Azerbaijan.[36]

Or will the Siyavush syndrome, instead of perpetuating divisiveness, help the Azeris revive another historical role of their country, the land where the Iranian and Turkish civilizations have for centuries blended in creative harmony?

Whatever the future developments, the Azeris are likely to take guidance from their time-honored political traditions in dealing with the challenges of the outside world—moderation and the ability to compromise. These qualities stem from the realities of the geography and history of Azerbaijan, quintessentially a borderland many times over—between Europe and Asia, Islam and Christianity, Sunni and Shi'i Islam, Russia and the Middle East, Turkey and Iran. In such a configuration, avoidance of any extremism is the most viable proposition for the politics of national survival.

Notes

1. On the formation of the Azeri literary language and classical literature, see S. Berengian, *Azeri and Persian Literary Works in Twentieth-Century Iranian Azerbaijan* (Berlin: K. Schwartz, 1988), pp. 17–18.

2. On Azerbaijan before the eighteenth century, see *Istoriia Azerbaidzhana*, vol. 1 (Baku: Akademiia nauk Azerb. SSR, 1958); also consult V. Bartol'd, *Mesto prikaspiiskikh oblastei v istorii musul'manskogo mira* (Baku, 1925); P.B. Golden, "The Turkic Peoples and Caucasia," in *Transcaucasia, Nationalism and Social Change*, ed. Ronald Suny (Ann Arbor: University of Michigan Press, 1983), pp. 45–68.

3. On the Russian expansion into the Caucasus and the wars with Iran, see Firuz Kazemzadeh, "Russian Penetration of the Caucasus," in *Russian Imperialism from Ivan the Great to the Revolution*, ed. Taras Hunczak (New Brunswick: Rutgers University Press, 1974), pp. 239–63; Muriel Atkin, *Russia and Iran, 1780–1828* (Minneapolis: University of Minnesota Press, 1980). For a current Azeri view of the Russo-Iranian treaties, see M. Aleskerov, "Mezhdunarodnaia protivopravnost' giulistanskogo i tiurkmanchaiskogo dogovorov," *Khazar*, no. 1 (1990), pp. 133–34.

4. On Azerbaijan in the nineteenth century, see Audrey Altstadt, *The Azerbaijani Turks: Power and Identity Under Russian Rule* (Stanford: Hoover Institution Press, 1992), pp. 15–50; Ronald Suny, *The Baku Commune, 1917–1918: Class and Nationality in the Russian Revolution* (Princeton: Princeton University Press, 1972).

5. For a recent discussion of the Iranian Revolution and its links to Transcaucasia, see M. Bayat, *Iran's First Revolution: Shi'ism and the Constitutional Revolution of 1905–1909* (New York: Oxford University Press, 1991), pp. 76–106; see also C. Chaqueiri, "The Role and Impact of Armenian Intellectuals in Iranian Politics, 1905–1911," *Armenian Review*, vol. 42, no. 2 (1988), pp. 1–51.

6. On the rise of the intelligentsia, see Tadeusz Swietochowski, *Russian Azerbaijan, 1905–1920: The Shaping of National Identity in a Muslim Community* (Cambridge: Cambridge University Press, 1985), pp. 23–36.

7. On Pan-Turkism, see J.M. Landau, *Pan-Turkism in Turkey: A Study of Irredentism* (Hamden, CT: Archon Books, 1981); on the 1918 Ottoman occupation of northern Azerbaijan, see A. Balaev, *Azerbaidzhanskoe natsional'noe dvizhenie, 1917–1920 gg.* (Baku, 1990); for a contemporary account of the Ottoman policy in southern Azerbaijan, see *Der Neue Orient*, vol. 3 (1918), p. 378.

8. Great Britain, Foreign Office, 371.1527 43, 13 November 1919. On the Azerbaijani-Iranian negotiations in Versailles, see also A. Raevskii, *Musavatskoe pravitel'stvo na versal'skoi konferentsii: Doneseniia predsedatelia azerbaidzhanskoi musavatskoi delegatsii* (Baku, 1930), p. 50.

9. N. Narimanov, *Stat'ii pis'ma* (Moscow, 1925), p. 20. For a discussion of the independent Azerbaijani Republic and its foreign policy see Swietochowski, *Russian Azerbaijan, 1905–1920*, pp. 129–94; see also G. Jaschke, "Neues zur russisch-turkischen Freundschaft von 1919–1939," *Welt des Islams*, new series, vol. 6 (1961), pp. 205–6.

10. On Soviet policies in Azerbaijan in the 1920s and 1930s, see Altstadt, *Azerbaijani Turks*, pp. 108–50.

11. On émigré federalism, see M.E. Resulzade, *O pantiurkizme v sviazi s kavkazskoi problemoi* (Paris, 1930).

12. For a discussion of Soviet cultural policies in southern Azerbaijan, see David Nissman, *The Soviet Union and Iranian Azerbaijan: The Use of Nationalism for Political Penetration* (Boulder: Westview Press, 1987), pp. 28–37.

13. For a recent monograph on southern Azerbaijan during World War II, see Louise L'Estrange-Fawcett, *Iran and the Cold War: The Azerbaijani Crisis of 1946* (Cambridge: Cambridge University Press, 1992); P. Homayounpour, *L'affaire d'Azerbaidjan* (Lausanne, 1967); E. Abrahamian, "Communism and Communalism in Iran: The Tudah and the Firqah-i Dimuqrat," *International Journal of Middle East Studies*, vol. 1, no. 4 (1970), pp. 96–131.

14. On the "One Azerbaijan" campaign, see Nissman, *Soviet Union and Iranian Azerbaijan*, pp. 73–78.

15. C. Mouradian, "The Mountainous Karabagh Question: An Interethnic Conflict or Decolonization Crisis?" *Armenian Review*, vol. 43, nos. 2–3 (1990), pp. 1–34. For an Azeri view of the Nagorno-Karabagh conflict, see "About the Events in Nagorno-Karabagh Adventure of the Armenian Nationalists," *Central Asia and Caucasus Chronicle*, vol. 7 (1989), pp. 3–4.

16. "Azerbaidzhan: Takie my segodnia," samizdat publication (Baku, 1989).

17. "About the Events in Nagorno-Karabagh," p. 4.

18. For the rise of the PFA, see A. Balaev, *Aperçue historique du Front Populaire d'Azerbaidjan*, no date; on the rise of political associations, see L. Iunusova, "Pestraia palistra, neformal'nykh dvizhenii v Azerbaidzhane," *Russkaia mysl'*, vol. 9, no. 22 (1989).

19. L. Iunusova, "Program of the People's Front of Azerbaijan" (English translation), *Russkaia mysl'*, vol. 8, no. 6 (1989), p. 8.

20. Ibid., p. 9.

21. Balaev, *Aperçue historique*, p. 12.

22. *Azerbaijan* (Baku), no. 2 (11 January 1990).

23. T. Gasymov, "The War Against the Azeri Popular Front," *Uncaptive Minds*, vol. 3, no. 5 (1991), p. 13. See also E. Namazov, "Antiislamskii fundamentalizm," *Elm*, vol. 1, no. 9 (1990).

24. For an official account of the Baku January Days, see Azerbaidzhanskaia SSR, Verkhovnyi sovet, *Zaiavleniie Komissii po issledovaniiu sobytii imevshikh mesto v gorode Baku 19–20 ianvaria 1990 goda* (Baku, 1990); see also *Chernyi ianvar': Dokumenty i materialy* (Baku, 1990).

25. On Western reactions to the Baku days, see "L'Occident regrette mais comprend," *Le monde diplomatique* (March 1990).

26. Foreign Broadcast Information Service, *Daily Report: Western Europe* (FBIS-WEU-90–014), 22 January 1990.

27. *Iran Times*, 2 February 1990.

28. Foreign Broadcast Information Service, *Daily Report: Near East and South Asia* (FBIS-NES) for January–February 1990. See also "Une frontière glaciale dilue l'identite des Azeris," *Journal de Geneve*, vol. 2, no. 3 (June 1990).

29. "Le drame azeri divise la Turquie," *Le monde diplomatique* (March 1990), p. 10.

30. For the full text of the Treaty of Friendship, Cooperation and Good Neighborly Relations between Azerbaijan and Turkey, see *Bakinskii rabochii*, 29 January 1992.

31. E. Fuller, "The Azerbaijani Presidential Elections: A One Horse Race," RFE/RL Research Institute, *Report on the USSR*, vol. 3, no. 37 (13 September 1991), pp. 12–14; see also *New York Times*, 4 September 1991.

32. J. Reissner, "Iran: Regionale Grossmacht?" Stiftung Wissenschaft und Politik, *Mittelasien zwischen neuen Fronten*, Ebenhausen, SWP-AP 2745 (1992), p. 40.

33. F. Agamal'ev, "Mezhdu polumesiatsem i krestom," samizdat publication (no date).

34. *Azadliq*, 19 July 1991, p. 9.

35. *Iran Times*, 15 June 1993.

36. See M.A. Rasulzada, *Asrimizin Siyavushu* (Baku, 1991); for a Russian translation, see *Khazar*, no. 1 (1990), pp. 37–64.

Appendix: Project Participants

List of Workshop Attendees, May 3, 1993
Influence of History on Russian Foreign Policy

Kadir Alimov, University of World Economy and Diplomacy
The Honorable Oleh Bilorus, Ambassador of Ukraine
Jeffrey Brooks, The Johns Hopkins University
Jeffrey Checkel, University of Pittsburgh
Peter Clement, Central Intelligence Agency
John Danylyk, Department of State
Dieter Dettke, The Friedrich Ebert Stiftung
Charles Fairbanks, School of Advanced International Studies
Clifford Foust, University of Maryland
Marcus Franda, University of Maryland
Raymond Garthoff, The Brookings Institution
David Goldfrank, Georgetown University
Thomas Graham, Department of State
Steve Guenther, School of Advanced International Studies
Griffin Hathaway, University of Maryland
Peter Hauslohner, formerly Department of State
Petr Lunak, School of Advanced International Studies
Kendall Myers, Foreign Service Institute
Tom Navratil, Department of State
Susan Nelson, Department of State
Ilya Prizel, School of Advanced International Studies
George Quester, University of Maryland

Vladimir Rakhmanin, Embassy of Russia
Peter Reddaway, The George Washington University
John Sontag, Department of State
David Speedie, The Carnegie Corporation
Angela Stent, Georgetown University
Vladimir Tismaneanu, University of Maryland
Aleksei Voskressensky, Institute of Far Eastern Studies, Moscow
Vladislav Zubok, Institute of USA and Canada Studies, Moscow

List of Workshop Attendees, May 10, 1993
Influence of History on Southern NIS Foreign Policies

Ibrahim Arafat, Cairo University
Stephen Blank, U.S. Army War College
Patricia Carley, Helsinki Commission
Kenneth Currie, National Intelligence Council
Khadisa Dairova, Embassy of Kazakhstan
Adeed Dawisha, George Mason University
Ron Davis, Department of State
Dorothy Delahanty, Department of State
Ulughbek Eshankhojayov, Embassy of Uzbekistan
Marcus Franda, University of Maryland
Philip Gillette, Old Dominion University
Nubar Goudsouzian, School of Advanced International Studies
Thomas Graham, Department of State
Mark Katz, George Mason University
Edy Kaufman, University of Maryland
Catherine Kelleher, The Brookings Institution
Andrew Kuchins, The MacArthur Foundation
Erjan Kurbanov, Moscow State University
Petr Lunak, School of Advanced International Studies
George Majeska, University of Maryland
Sharif Mardin, The American University
Sergo Mikoyan, Institute of Peace, Moscow
George Mirsky, Institute of Oriental Studies, Moscow
Jayhun Molla-zade, Embassy of Azerbaijan
Susan Nelson, Department of State
Nurbek Omuraliev, Institute of Philosophy, Bishkek
Vasilii Pospelov, Embassy of Russia

George Quester, University of Maryland
George Reardon-Anderson, Georgetown University
Sergei Romanenko, Institute of Slavonic and Balkan Studies, Moscow
Cevdet Seyhan, Voice of America
Rouben Shugarian, Embassy of Armenia
Nadia Tangour, Department of State
Lowry Taylor, Department of State
Vadim Udalov, Embassy of Russia
Madeline Zilfi, University of Maryland

List of Workshop Attendees, May 17, 1993
Influence of History on Western NIS Foreign Policies

Kadir Alimov, University of World Economy and Diplomacy, Tashkent
Stephen Blank, U.S. Army War College
Abraham Brumberg
John Danylyk, Department of State
Nadia Diuk, National Endowment for the Humanities
Marcus Franda, University of Maryland
David Goldfrank, Georgetown University
Olexander Gorin, Kiev University
Eerik Gross, Embassy of Estonia
The Honorable Ojars Kalnins, Ambassador of Latvia
Jutta Klapisch, Friedrich Ebert Stiftung
Israel Kleiner, Voice of America
Andrew Kuchins, The MacArthur Foundation
George Liska, School of Advanced International Studies
The Honorable Stasys Lozoraitis, Ambassador of Lithuania
Petr Lunak, School of Advanced International Studies
The Honorable Sergei Martynov, Charge d'Affaires, Embassy of Belarus
Sergo Mikoyan, Institute of Peace, Moscow
Steven Muller, School of Advanced International Studies
Natalia Novgrodskaya, Institute of Far Eastern Studies
Vasilii Pospelov, Embassy of Russia
Ilya Prizel, School of Advanced International Studies
George Quester, University of Maryland
Bohdan Radejko, The Washington Group

Marion Recktenwald, University of Maryland
Darius Szwarcewicz, School of International Advanced Studies
Nadia Tangour, Department of State
Vladimir Tismaneanu, University of Maryland
Michael Turner, University of Maryland
Aleksei Voskressensky, Institute of Far Eastern Studies
Martin Walker, The Guardian
Susan Woodward, The Brookings Institution
Tom Zamostny, Department of State
Jan Zaprudnik, Belarusan Institute of Science and Arts

Index